Mining for Development in the Third World

Pergamon Titles of Related Interest

Barney	THE GLOBAL 2000 REPORT TO THE PRESIDENT OF THE U.S. Volume II
Carman/Varon	OBSTACLES TO MINERAL DEVELOPMENT
Diwan/Livingston	ALTERNATIVE DEVELOPMENT STRATEGIES AND APPROPRIATE TECHNOLOGY
Menon	BRIDGES ACROSS THE SOUTH
Standke	SCIENCE, TECHNOLOGY AND SOCIETY

Related Journals*

INTERNATIONAL JOURNAL OF ROCK MECHANICS, MINING
   SCIENCES AND GEOMECHANIC ABSTRACTS
MATERIALS AND SOCIETY
WORLD DEVELOPMENT

*Free specimen copies available upon request.

PERGAMON POLICY STUDIES ON INTERNATIONAL DEVELOPMENT

Mining for Development in the Third World

Multinational Corporations, State Enterprises and the International Economy

Edited by
S. Sideri
S. Johns

Published in cooperation with
The Institute of Social Studies at The Hague

Pergamon Press

NEW YORK • OXFORD • TORONTO • SYDNEY • PARIS • FRANKFURT

Pergamon Press Offices:

U.S.A.   Pergamon Press Inc., Maxwell House, Fairview Park, Elmsford, New York 10523, U.S.A.

U.K.   Pergamon Press Ltd., Headington Hill Hall, Oxford OX3 0BW, England

CANADA   Pergamon of Canada, Ltd., Suite 104, 150 Consumers Road, Willowdale, Ontario M2J 1P9, Canada

AUSTRALIA   Pergamon Press (Aust.) Pty. Ltd., P.O. Box 544, Potts Point, NSW 2011, Australia

FRANCE   Pergamon Press SARL, 24 rue des Ecoles, 75240 Paris, Cedex 05, France

FEDERAL REPUBLIC OF GERMANY   Pergamon Press GmbH, Hammerweg 6, Postfach 1305, 6242 Kronberg/Taunus, Federal Republic of Germany

Copyright © 1980 Pergamon Press Inc.

Library of Congress Cataloging in Publication Data

Main entry under title:

Mining for development in the Third World.

(Pergamon policy studies on international development)
"Published in cooperation with the Institute of Social Studies at The Hague."
Based on a workshop organized by the Institute of Social Studies at The Hague, in 1979.
Includes index.
1. Underdeveloped areas—Mineral industries—Congresses. 2. Mineral industries—Congresses. 3. Underdeveloped areas—Government business enterprises—Congresses. 4. Underdeveloped areas—International business enterprises—Congresses. I. Sideri, S., 1934- II. Johns, Sheridan, 1935- III. Hague. Institute of Social Studies. IV. Series.
HD9506.A2M544   1980   338.2'09172'4   80-20930
ISBN 0-08-026308-9

Printed in the United States of America

CONTENTS

PREFACE

In the summer of 1979, as part of an ongoing program which brings together key people who are concerned with, and responsible for, specific problem areas in less developed countries, the Institute of Social Studies at The Hague organized a seven-week policy workshop on 'The State Sector and the International Economy'. The focus of this workshop was on the mining component of the state sector. Seven minerals were selected as the subject of case studies: bauxite, copper, iron ore, nickel, phosphate, tin and uranium. An even geographical distribution was aimed at and participants were therefore invited from Jamaica, Guyana and Guinea for bauxite; Chile, Peru, the Philippines and Zambia for copper; Liberia, India, Brazil and Venezuela for iron ore; Cuba, Indonesia and New Caledonia for nickel; Morocco and Tunisia for phosphate rocks; Bolivia and Malaysia for tin; and Niger, Gabon and Namibia for uranium. Unfortunately it was impossible to obtain participants from all these countries. Those who attended the workshop were high level professionals, mainly from state-owned mining companies but also from private firms to enable meaningful comparisons, and from pertinent ministries, planning offices, and universities.

Authoritative knowledge on a variety of subjects germane to the theme of the policy workshop was provided by a number of outside experts who lectured to the participants, and who were closely familiar with particular aspects of the mineral industry, gained either through operational responsibilities within mining companies or international organizations, or through study or policy-oriented analysis in academic institutions. A spectrum of viewpoints, ranging from advocacy of direct foreign investment to vigorous opposition, was explicitly sought. The lectures were viewed as a means:

(i)   to facilitate comparison of the problems faced by the various mineral industries;

(ii) to supplement and enrich the analysis presented by each participant; and,

(iii) to bring into focus the relationship between mineral production and the overall development process, a relationship that is not always central to the interests of mineral specialists.

The desire to explore this latter aspect, which is not very common in development literature but is an interesting one for an institution such as the Institute of Social Studies, made it necessary to invite academics from Europe and from North America, as well as analysts from various United Nations agencies and other international organizations.

The structure and the detailed program of the policy workshop followed logically from the intention to ensure a comparative analysis of the various policies pursued by state-owned mining companies in LDCs, within the framework established by a world economic system which is increasingly shaped by the interests of multinational corporations. The policy workshop assessed, in particular:

(i)   present and alternative mining policies of the public and private sectors, with respect to given national objectives such as maximization of revenue, contribution to employment, technological choice and relative international transfer, encouragement of industrialization, increase in the rate of economic growth, etc.;

(ii)   the type and relevance of constraints imposed by the international economic system on utilization of the state sector for a faster and possibly independent development of the mineral-producing countries.

Analyses were conducted along the following lines for each of the selected minerals:

(a)   the actual and the potential role of the state in the development process, and the international economic dimensions of its domestic policies, e.g. the utilization of alternative fiscal policies;

(b)   the emergence of the state sector, i.e. how mining production has come to be controlled by the state;

(c)   the management of the state, namely, the various economic policies utilized, together with investment strategies, choice of techniques, planning and labor relations;

(d)   the international economy, i.e. the behavior of export markets for the minerals in question; the problems caused by the import of the required technology; the role of the MNCs which frequently provide the operative structure for all these combined functions; international agreements – not only among producers – as complementary measures to alternative domestic policies.

The link that connected these four blocks was the analysis of the advantages and limitations of a state-owned mineral industry, whether voluntarily or involuntarily integrated into the international economy. The fact that mining is only the initial stage of a complex processing system which is often geographically dispersed over the entire world economy, implies that control over mining in itself is not necessarily a powerful instrument for the state. Extension of that control makes it necessary to enter into agreements with other producers and/or users, and more often than not these are the multinationals.

State control over mining is interwoven with such agreements, whose characteristics and conditions were therefore carefully analyzed. They were assessed as to whether or not they contribute substantially to achieving the domestic objectives laid down by the government of each mineral-producing country, regardless of its political orientation.

This present volume is a direct outcome of the policy workshop. Contributions made by some of the lecturers were selected and revised and sometimes rewritten for this purpose, the selection being determined largely by the logic of the framework adopted at the workshop and followed in shaping the outline of this volume. The concern of the editors has been to present analyses from diverse viewpoints which, taken together, address the central issues of mining for national development in LDCs.

The Institute of Social Studies has provided all the necessary funds, facilities and support for this project, which was undertaken with the cooperation of the Department of Political Science and of the Research Council of Duke University.

Finally, we wish to express our appreciation of the organizational and sec-retarial work of Inèz Zwager and of the editorial and proof-reading expertise of Jean Sanders, both staff members of the Institute of Social Studies, and of the typesetting skills of Netty Born.

The Hague - Durham, N.C.   Sandro Sideri and Sheridan Johns
May 1980

ABBREVIATIONS

ACP	African, Caribbean and Pacific Countries
ADB	Asian Development Bank
AfDB	African Development Bank
AIEC	Association of Iron Ore Exporting Countries
CIPEC	Conseil Intergouvernemental des Pays Exportateurs de Cuivre (Intergovernmental Council of Copper Exporting Countries)
COMECON	Council for Mutual Economic Assistance
CPE	centrally planned economy
DC	developed/industrial country
DCF	internal rate of return
EAU	European Accounting Unit
EDF	European Development Fund
EEC	European Economic Community
EIB	European Investment Bank
GNP	gross national product
IADB/IDB	Inter-American Development Bank
IBA	International Bauxite Association
IBRD	International Bank for Reconstruction and Development, an affiliate of the World Bank
ICA	International Commodity Agreement
ICC	International Chamber of Commerce
ICSID	International Center for Settlement of Investment Disputes of the World Bank
IDA	International Development Association of the World Bank
IFC	International Finance Corporation, also World Bank
ILO	International Labor Organization
IMIT	International Minerals Investment Trust
IRB	International Resources Bank, proposed by Kissinger at UNCTAD IV, Nairobi (1976)
ITC	International Tin Council
LDC	less developed country
LME	London Metal Exchange

MEC	market economy country
MNC	multinational corporation
NIEO	New International Economic Order
NIC	newly industrializing country
OAS	Organization of American States
ODA	Official Development Assistance
OECD	Organization for Economic Cooperation and Development
OPEC	Organization of Petroleum Exporting Countries
OPIC	Overseas Private Investment Corporation of the USA
SDR	Special Drawing Right
UN	United Nations
UNDP	United Nations Development Program
UNEP	United Nations Environmental Program

INTRODUCTION

S. Sideri and S. Johns

The role of the state sector in the development process has been amply re-
searched, but less emphasis has been placed on the relationship between that
sector and the international economic system which determines some of the
essential conditions for its operations. The importance of this relationship could
not be clearer than in the mining sector. It is usually the oldest and largest area
of state intervention and also the sector generally most closely connected to,
and shaped by, the world economy. The relevance of the mining sector for the
development process has often been discussed in terms of price stabilization and
revenue maximization. Yet the mining sector is more than a source of foreign
exchange; its potential central role in the overall development process has long
been recognized. It is also clear that any contribution by this sector to the development of the countries concerned is largely determined by its nature and organization — more than by its ownership — and by its links to the world economy.
This means that the development role of the mining sector of any LDC, whether
fully state-owned or fully privately-owned or under mixed ownership, must be
considered with reference to its actual or possible relationship with those MNCs
which dominate the global production, processing and marketing of most minerals even though some of their subsidiaries have been nationalized in specific
LDCs.

MNCs AND THE WORLD MINING INDUSTRY

There is no doubt that 'the main change in the world mining industry this century has been [the] increasing dominance of the multi-national corporation,
coupled with rising demand for a whole range of new minerals.'[1] Building upon
capital-intensive production techniques and organizational patterns fashioned
in the course of American and European industrial development, mining companies based in North America and Western Europe undertook mining production in a wide variety of mineral-rich sites in both colonial Asia and Africa
and politically independent Latin America. Granted favorable conditions under
long-term concessions, the foreign mining corporations expanded operations

Notes to this chapter may be found on page 19.

within LDCs for the sole purpose of providing supplies to the ever more demanding industrial sectors of North America and Europe. Both by integrating backward to obtain ore supplies and by integrating forward to processing or fabrication of a particular mineral, established mining companies extended the scope and range of their activities, in the process coming to dominate, if not control, not only production, but also the major marketing institutions by which minerals mined in LDCs were sold to users in developed countries (DCs).

Already prior to World War II the outlines of the vertically integrated international mining corporations, headquartered in the United States or Western Europe, with operations in a number of countries, both LDCs and DCs, were visible in certain mineral industries. Immediately after World War II the large international mining corporations continued their ascendency, becoming full-fledged MNCs with direct control of mining, refining, marketing, and often fabricating operations, stretching over several continents and comprising a significant share of the production of a specific mineral. Their profitability, the continued strength of their links with DCs (the source of managerial and technical personnel, as well as machinery and consumer goods), and their steadily expanding role as producers of mineral output, made the mining MNCs early targets for increasingly nationalist governments which emerged not only in the course of decolonization in Asia and Africa, but also in Latin America.

In the 1950s and then at an accelerating rate in the 1960s and early 1970s, LDC governments challenged and changed the terms upon which mining MNCs had been permitted to operate. Nationalization of existing mines occurred in many LDCs, either in the form of 100% takeovers or alternative arrangements in which foreign operators were permitted to retain up to 49% of ownership. Even where majority ownership was not sought, LDC governments gained greater benefits from both existing and new mining operations in their territories by taking minority ownership and/or raising taxes and royalties, in tandem with additional regulations designed to channel mining activities more in line with indigenously determined priorities. Ownership of operating mines in the LDCs, particularly in the phosphate, tin, and copper industries, but also in the bauxite and iron ore industries, has increasingly shifted from American and West European MNCs to LDC-owned state enterprises. Most LDC governments no longer accept the type of long-term concessions under which foreign mining companies entered the LDCs in the first half of the twentieth century. Unquestionably, the complete dominance of foreign capital in the mineral sectors of LDCs has been curbed somewhat, yet it is equally certain that the MNCs continue to exert great influence upon the nature and direction of mining activity in the LDCs.

The extension of the LDC state into an increasingly direct role in mineral production within its borders has heightened the salience of the global marketing and distribution systems through which any LDC mineral producer must dispose of its output. The peculiar structure of international mineral markets not only affects their price formation mechanisms but makes their control by the state of the producing country a more complex and often difficult task than it is assumed to be in other sectors. Mineral production and marketing are largely characterized by many oligopolistic elements, large and increasing size of operations, concentration of deposits and often of the processing facilities. The oligopolistic forces of these markets relate not only to the dimension of the firms operating in this sector but also to the conditions which tend to limit the access of new firms to such production. This difficulty of entering the mineral sector is also a function of the 'natural' characteristics of minerals, namely their non-renewability and their locally concentrated availability. International trade is then crucial to their production, which in turn explains the dominant role played by MNCs in the marketing of minerals and in their final utilization.

Under these conditions, price becomes a very doubtful concept and quotations referred to as mineral prices do not accurately reflect the value and amounts of the actual mineral transactions taking place in the world economy. In addition, prices include a rent element due mainly to the non-renewability of minerals, a rent that the state has attempted to capture in the mining countries via a series of instruments from taxation to nationalization. Differential extraction and transportation costs also contribute to the impossibility of establishing a unique and comprehensive price. Thus, any mining LDC striving for a further shift of benefits toward itself is often stymied by the nature of the price and market structures which confront it in the mineral industry of which its mines are a part.

Another frustrating reality for many LDC governments which have asserted greater control over their mining sectors is the continuing preeminence of the DCs (and most often MNCs within the DCs) in the processing of minerals. Mining MNCs, perhaps particularly those which have experienced total, or even partial, takeover of their extraction subsidiaries in LDCs, are anxious to maintain existing smelting and refining subsidiaries, generally located in DCs. Accordingly, the MNCs discourage attempts by LDCs to raise the level of processing within their countries in order to further the forward integration of their respective mineral sectors within the national economy. By virtue of their size, access to financial resources, and technological capabilities the MNCs remain well placed to constrain large-scale increases in processing capabilities by most LDCs (with the exception of relatively affluent newly industrializing countries, e.g. Brazil, Mexico, and India).

In analogous fashion, the MNCs also continue to play a central role in the transporting of most ores from the LDCs to overseas purchasers, either through direct or indirect control of the efficient large-scale ore transport fleets which have become increasingly common in recent decades. For any LDC, or group of LDCs, attempting to gain additional revenue through greater direct participation in the transportation of mineral ores, the barriers to entry in this segment of the industry also remain high.

The need to harmonize differential mining costs, to develop and maintain an efficient distribution network, and finally, to transform raw materials into metal inputs, often to particular users' specifications, combine to explain the creation of a transnational system centered around MNCs which is able to handle these different but highly complementary tasks. It is a system that not only is rather difficult to replace, but which cannot easily accommodate the national interests of some producing countries. The integrated nature of this system and the features of the structures upon which it is based also makes difficult the creation of effective cartels by LDC mineral producers.

Even though the world economy will no longer experience the 'tremendous growth in the world consumption of minerals between 1970 and 2000' forecast by Leontieff, it does nevertheless seem certain that 'these resources will most probably become more expensive to extract as the century moves towards its conclusion.'[2] The higher mineral prices implied in such a forecast could contribute to a possible lessening of the tension between LDC national producers and the MNCs engaged in marketing their minerals. Yet, it may also be accompanied by a deterioration of the economic position of all LDCs dependent upon imports. The ultimate price effect for the producers of minerals is conditioned by the movement of their terms of trade and by the fluctuations in the exchange rates of major currencies. The present floating system of exchange rates and the continuing deterioration of the dollar – a most important currency for mineral transactions – could sharply curtail mining LDCs' ability to expand the financing of their imports even if facing a sustained raise of mineral prices. The need is for a more stable international monetary system based on the special drawing right (SDR) as its principal reserve asset. The increasing difficulties encountered by oil-importing LDCs in their balance of payments – and their resulting growing indebtedness – must also be considered adequately if mining LDCs are to avoid losing most of what they could gain through higher prices for their products.

There is a broad consensus that future mining investment, in LDCs or elsewhere, faces considerable obstacles. As modern mining is a highly capital-intensive industry, the cost of establishing new mines has soared, compounded by the necessity to look further afield and deeper for economically viable projects. The scale of operation has therefore increased, as have capital requirements for mining operations and infrastructure construction. Exploration activities, geological and other research requirements are all necessary, even before production starts. The mastering of complex new technologies, and their application on the scale required in modern mining, usually exceed the capability and the resources of small national companies, while the position of the largest MNCs is further enhanced by their technological leadership. Yet, both small and large enterprises operate in a highly cyclical market and at present the prospect of a rapid growth in demand for minerals does not seem very bright. Any recovery in demand is almost certainly linked to a substantial increase of the Western economies' rate of growth, a development which most analysts do not expect in the near future. A limited alternative market for some of the output of the mines of LDCs might be found within the LDCs, especially in the rapidly industrializing countries, e.g. Brazil, Mexico, and India.

Higher risks, lower returns, larger operations and investment, longer lead periods, have combined to encourage the following developments in world mining:

(i) a search for greater security in exploitation conditions and fiscal arrangements has furthered the concentration of new mining investment in areas like North America, South Africa and Australia;

(ii) a concentration of production only in those areas characterized by a greater mining potential; and

(iii) a consolidation of the position of MNCs, not only in actual mining, but also in processing and distributing the minerals in the LDC markets, even where the latter are going to absorb most of the new production.

On the whole all three developments have accelerated the capital concentration process, a rather crucial characteristic of contemporary mining activities. It is a process which is intertwined with the MNCs' continued interest in vertical integration of mining and basic metal industries. In addition, seabed mining is increasingly attracting the interest — and the necessary research efforts — of the largest MNCs. Very soon seabed exploitation of cobalt, manganese, copper, nickel, etc. could threaten the position of some established LDC producers. The generally soaring costs of developing new mining capacity, fueled as well by inflation, are bringing mining companies together into consortia with banks; and even more significantly the largest oil companies, eager to find investment outlets in which to utilize their swelling cash balances, are entering directly into mining activity.

Paralleling these developments in Western mining, in which large MNCs play probably a greater role than ever, are developments in the mining sectors of LDC states which have strengthened the range and extent of state intervention. Not only have LDC states continued to seek greater financial returns and broader national developmental benefits from their mining sectors, but increasingly they have established themselves directly in the mining sector through state mining corporations. Alone or in cooperation with MNCs, the new state mining corporations are becoming a major vehicle for articulating the interests of LDC states. It is clear that there is a continuing process of redefinition of the terms under which MNCs and LDC states will participate in all stages of the mining industry. MNCs are showing willingness to relinquish full ownership for joint ventures, or even to rely upon service and management contracts; state mining corporations, while determined to advance national interests, continue to turn to established MNCs for assistance in the exploitation of the mineral resources under their control. It is essential that all dimensions of this process be analyzed carefully in order that all interested parties, even if not at present directly involved, be aware of possible areas of common interest between LDC producers, mining MNCs with their great technological, capital, and highly skilled manpower resources, and consumers in both DCs and LDCs.

MINING AND DEVELOPMENT

The crucial significance of mineral exports to particular LDC countries, however, lies in the fact that for many mineral-exporting LDCs a single mineral comprises a substantial, if not predominant, percentage of the country's total exports. Of course, the importance of mineral production varies from country to country and only for about a dozen LDCs do mineral exports amount to more than 50% of total exports. Yet, both in countries where mineral production is the primary export industry as well as in those countries where it is less crucial, the impact of the mining sector upon the country's development is great. The importance of mineral production on GNP, however, is often underestimated. On the one hand, 'available statistics stop showing the contribution of minerals once the resources move from the mining sector to the manufacturing sector.'[3] On the other hand, the enclave nature of the mining sector (i.e. its greater integration into the world economy rather than into the economy of the producing country) has important consequences. The absence of substantial backward linkages, the location of mining activities often in remote, out-of-the-way regions within the producing country, their limited labor absorption and the consequent possibility to concede high wage levels, their dependence on foreign markets and on the availability of the ores, make the producing regions potentially unstable and a source of political and economic dislocation within the country.

In considering the impact of the mineral sector on the economic development of producing countries, it is possible to distinguish positive and negative effects. On the positive side, the mineral sector:

(i)   provides foreign exchange earnings;
(ii) generates additional government revenue through taxes and royalties;
(iii) provides some employment and creates a skilled labor force;
(iv) fosters the emergence of technical and managerial skills.

On the negative side, the mining sector:

(i)   is mostly an enclave industry with all problems related to such a situation, namely:
  (a) utilization of a very high capital-intensive technology, mostly imported;
  (b) consequent relatively limited absorption of indigenous labor;
  (c) importation of a large share of required inputs, material and services, to which the mining MNC may have non-market access through subsidiaries or associated companies;
(ii) has little backward integration with the economy of the producing country;
(iii) experiences wide fluctuations in both foreign exchange earnings and in government revenues;
(iv) tends to create environmental damage and is often operated under poor working and living conditions;
(v)   involves the exploitation of non-renewable resources; once the ore bodies are mined out, or the market disappears, there is nothing left;
(vi) creates powerful labor elites which 'can form a constraint upon a government's policies, while constituting a group whose interests do not necessarily coincide with those of the "nation"',[4] and whose pattern of consumption tends to be higher and different — especially in terms of foreign products — than that of most of the rest of the population;
(vii) has been characterized since the beginning of this century by a highly

monopolistic structure, the rent of which has tended to be appropriated largely by international capital, or the foreign users, who have traditionally controlled the sector. The problem of the distribution of such a monopolistic rent has increasingly become the dominant issue for both foreign investors and LDC governments. The issue is further complicated by the difficulties of determining the size of the rent and of measuring its appropriation, not least because of possible transfer pricing practices which tend to hide real profit levels and minimize the relative tax burden;
(viii) competes often with agriculture for the utilization of fertile soil and scarce water resources.

The nature of the characteristics of the mining sector complicates the usual conflict of interests between producers and users, and to this must be added the conflict between investors — not only foreign ones — and governments in the producing countries. Furthermore, the economic importance usually placed on this sector has to be balanced with the risk of perpetuating an international division of labor which is increasingly objected to by many, both inside and outside governments.

Thus the contribution of the exported-oriented mining sector can best be evaluated in the context of the overall development strategy and institutional arrangements of the LDC concerned. According to Mikesell, 'the appropriate materials policy will differ depending upon the source of the capital for investment (i.e. whether domestic or foreign), the alternative uses of the factors supplied by the producing country, and the nature of the market for the resource commodity which is produced.'[5] Given the diverse impacts that the resource export industry has had on the development of the various producing countries, and given the paramount importance that external and changing factors have on this relationship, it becomes clear that for any LDC a resource policy must be part and parcel of an overall development strategy which not only has to be based on fairly realistic assessments of domestic possibilities and external constraints, but also has to explicitly consider all costs, and not merely economic ones, related to alternative resource policies. The likely cost of an unrealistic policy is lack of development and possibly even little economic growth.

THE ROLE OF THE LDC STATE

Since World War II the role of the state in development has expanded everywhere. Prior to World War II state power in most colonial and post-colonial regimes had been utilized primarily to set the parameters for economic activity in certain sectors (especially in the legal and fiscal spheres, but also in many colonial regimes in the construction of vital infrastructure). It was only in certain Latin American countries that the state had begun to intervene to encourage import-substitution investment and to engage itself directly in production, albeit generally on a limited scale. In the decades immediately after World War II the emergent Latin American pattern became increasingly common, both in newly-independent Asian states and in the remaining colonial regimes in Africa. It was broadly accepted that the state had responsibility for shaping the direction of economic development, including planning, expanded construction of infrastructure, and direct intervention in the economy, particularly if private enterprise failed to initiate activities in sectors deemed crucial by the state. In a climate of rising economic nationalism, most manifest in politically independent states in Asia and Latin America, the economic role of the state was further asserted, often against foreign enterprises, and particularly involving the state directly in production enterprises. In the 1960s and 1970s it was accepted by almost all LDC governments that the state bears first responsibility for economic development, either in cooperation with private interests (domestic or foreign) or within a more explicitly socialist framework in which the role of private enterprise is carefully circumscribed or even eliminated. It is against this backdrop that the relationship between the LDC state and the mining sector must be considered.

State intervention in the mining sector of LDC countries is not a recent phenomenon; only its form and extent have changed dramatically. Initially, state intervention was limited to determination of the conditions under which foreign investors would be allowed to undertake mining activity; it was then generally assumed that further development of some sort would follow as a consequence of the activities of the foreign mining concessionaire, with only marginal intervention by the state. In the postwar period, as governments of very diverse political persuasions have assigned a more direct role to the state in planning and participation in national development, state power has increasingly been utilized, both to secure a greater financial return for governments from foreign-owned mining enterprises and to integrate mining activity within overall national development. Renegotiation of the terms of the concessions increased government revenues through higher royalties, taxes, and exchange control regulations. In parallel policies many governments sought increasingly to dilute the enclave nature of the operations of the foreign firms (by measures to encourage forward and backward linkages, broader geographical development of mineral resources, new enterprises in processing, refining, and fabrication), although the efforts brought uneven and only marginal success. Since the 1960s state intervention in the mining sector has increasingly assumed an even more direct form − the establishment of state mining corporations to undertake new mining activities or to take over established foreign mining enterprises. The expanding role of the state in the mining sector has been animated both by changing assumptions about the appropriate role of the state in development and by growing nationalism which has demanded the limitation of foreign economic power in the interests of national independence. Yet, the problems of the linkages of LDC mining sectors with economic forces beyond the country's borders and of their integration within the national economy remain; the state mining corporations are now increasingly becoming the focal point for the contending interests inside and outside the country which seek to shape state mining policies.

Most state mining corporations in LDCs (in contrast notably to such Latin American state petroleum corporations as PEMEX and PETROBRAS) are new entities, established in the 1960s or early 1970s. In most cases they were created quite suddenly to realize the nationalization of foreign mining firms whose activities were centered on the extraction of a particular mineral for export to Europe, Japan, or North America. Unlike many public enterprises in agriculture and industry state mining corporations had neither devolved slowly from governmental ministries nor did they represent the expansion of institutions established by the colonial administration. Thus, they had neither a national cadre trained within the state sector, nor did they possess accumulated experience as established state institutions. Instead, they generally represented an amalgamation of a large ongoing production enterprise created by a foreign company, generally a subsidiary of a large MNC, and a small group of national directors and managers, drawn from whatever sources were available at the time of nationalization, who were grafted onto the existing enterprise. In many instances, the terms of nationalization left the previous owners with a management contract, if not a minority equity share in the existing mining enterprise. At least in the initial stages of operation such state mining corporations continued with the structure established by the previous foreign owners, in addition to remaining dependent upon them for key technical and management personnel, particularly where company or colonial policy (as in most African countries) had not encouraged the training of indigenous personnel for such positions. At the same time, however, the indigenous labor force in the enterprise generally received wages and benefits higher than those paid to workers in other sectors as well as those paid to other employees of government or public enterprises. This often reflected the success of militant trade unions which had organized the mineworkers successfully against the foreign firm; the same unions might be expected to struggle to maintain their relatively 'privileged' position and to resist any reorientation of policy by the state mining corporation which it perceived as a threat to their position.

By the very nature of the world mineral industry, the state mining sector in most LDCs remains highly dependent in the short run, if not the long run, upon the international economy. Except in the case of selected minerals in a few rapidly industrializing developing countries (e.g. iron ore in Brazil and India) there is limited domestic demand for the output of the state mining sector; it must be exported, as previously, to industrial consumers in Europe, Japan, North America and, increasingly, to the LDCs whose markets are still mostly dominated by large mining MNCs or large buyers' consortia based in DCs. To a large degree, mining MNCs are still the major source of expertise and technology required for the extraction and processing of most mineral resources (for selected minerals it might be possible to draw upon the resources of state mining enterprises in centrally planned economies (CPEs); these are also foreign, however, and might not necessarily fully share the interests of a state mining corporation in an LDC). While capital requirements for reinvestment and expansion could be met through the internally generated resources of the state mining corporation, the large sums required in most types of mining activities will require that substantial sums still be obtained from foreign sources, of which large mining MNCs or large foreign banks are the most readily accessible. Joint ventures, service contracts, and the selected provision of technology in return for a share of output are increasingly acceptable to large mining MNCs (and banking consortia) in lieu of full ownership.

Unlike most large mining MNCs and foreign banking consortia, the state mining corporation has a very limited ability to spread its risks; the consequences of failure are great, not only for the state mining corporation but also for the domestic economy and development projects dependent upon the mining sector for funding or for inputs and outputs. Most state mining corporations would seem to have a limited potential for maneuver, even if they should wish to disengage themselves from their existing foreign linkages. Yet if a state mining corporation is to be responsive to the hopes of the national government that ownership will result in greater returns and contributions to overall national development, it is incumbent upon the state corporation to develop a capability to assess *on its own* the components of the international mineral economy within which it must operate, and then to calculate carefully either on its own, or perhaps in cooperation with other interested LDC institutions, what steps it can take to increase its bargaining power and to reorient its activities in line with domestic, rather than foreign, priorities.

THE APPROACHES SUMMARIZED

The diverse dimensions of the environment within which any LDC state mining corporation must operate are analyzed in the papers which follow in this volume. Rather than focussing upon the state mining sector *per se*, the papers assess from various, and sometimes divergent, perspectives the central features of the international and domestic setting within which LDC mining activity will take place in the last decades of this century.

In the first of the three parts which follow, the overall role of mining for, and within, LDCs is scrutinized, both in the context of an analysis of the nature and importance of mining for LDCs as a group and with respect to the distinctive features of particular mineral industries. In their presentation, Gluschke, Iwase and Zorn highlight the uneven and distinctive role of mining for LDCs by comparing the relative contribution of mining to both LDCs and DCs and by pinpointing the specific LDCs for which mining is crucial to the economy and to any developmental efforts. Their analysis makes it clear that in the postwar period LDCs have come to play a greater role in the global production and processing of minerals (matching that of the CPEs) but that their relative contribution is still overshadowed by that of the DCs, within whose ranks Australia, Canada, and South Africa have increased their weight, noticeably in the last decade. Yet for those LDCs where exploited mineral resources are concentrated, mining is often central in the generation of gross domestic product, export earnings, and of value added, as well as providing the keystone for development planning. The broad dimensions of the contribution of the mining sector in

individual LDCs is outlined, and the impact of the mining sector upon employment, training, and health is discussed. At the same time, Gluschke, Iwase and
Zorn consider both the present nature of markets and prices, and the prospects
of lower future growth rates of mining as a consequence of the slower growth
rates which are anticipated in the DCs, and of the rising cost of mining investment due to inflation, technological demands, and uncertainty. Considering the
possible implications of technological change (which will continue to be generated primarily in the DCs) and the prospects for exploitation of ocean bed resources, the analysis underlines the changing nature of potential challenges to
LDC mining at a stage when its potential importance and contribution is greater
than ever to those LDC countries which are exploiting, or wish to exploit, the
mineral resources that provide perhaps the sole basis for their ongoing development.

Whereas Gluschke, Iwase and Zorn consider the mining industry as a whole
for LDCs, the following analyses of Davis, Mikesell, Rogers, Gluschke and Fox
disaggregate and focus upon the world aluminium, copper, iron, nickel and tin
industries respectively. Although the presentations are not made within a common structure, their analyses complement each other and also that of Gluschke,
Iwase and Zorn in their identification and dissection of the distinctive features
of particular industries, while simultaneously indicating, both implicitly and
explicitly, the elements of each world mineral industry which are common or
analogous to those of the other world mineral industries. In each of the industries, ore production in LDCs has become a progressively greater percentage
of total world production (ranging from the overwhelming LDC concentration
of production in the tin industry, to the intermediate position of copper, and
the smaller but growing LDC production in iron ore, nickel and aluminium),
yet final consumption remains only slightly less concentrated in the DCs than
was the case in the immediate postwar period. In none of the mineral industries
does it appear that a major shift towards sharply increasing final consumption
in the LDCs is about to occur.

The analyses of the structure and markets of the different industries show
clearly that the DCs will continue to play a preeminent role. Yet in the world tin
industry which, in Fox's delineation, is striking by the degree of concentration
of its production in the LDCs and the relative weakness of vertically integrated
MNCs headquartered in the DCs, it would seem that the crucial weight of the
DCs derives from their position as final consumers of the metal. The copper industry, as characterized by Mikesell, would seem to display some similarities to
the tin industry, although the LDCs contribute a far smaller share of total
copper production. Nevertheless, the great strength of the smaller number of
processors and fabricators, and the structure of the market, has permitted
vertically integrated MNCs to continue to maintain a salient role within the
world copper industry. In both the iron and nickel industries, whose features
are presented by Rogers and Gluschke respectively, DC preeminence is sustained
not only by their preponderance as final consumers, but also by the power of a
relatively few large integrated firms which decisively shape the parameters of

both marketing and processing, as well as control iron ore and nickel manufacturing in the DCs. In both industries the relative contribution of LDC mines to
total global production has increased considerably in the postwar period, probably facilitating the entry of new firms into the industry, but MNCs continue to
play decisive roles in the world nickel and iron industries. In the case of the
aluminium industry, presented by Davis, the ownership structure appears to be
dominated by six major MNCs which own more than half the capacity of all
bauxite mines, alumina plants and aluminium smelters, and which exercise great
control over the relevant technologies. Smelters and alumina plants are also concentrated in the DCs; and attempts by bauxite-producing LDCs to gain a more
equitable participation have resulted in frustration, compounded by the escalation of energy prices. It is against the backdrop of the very distinctive global
features of particular mineral industries as well as of the common problems
faced by all LDC mining countries, that further analyses of the role of mining in
LDC development must take place.

In the second part of this volume analysis shifts from consideration of the
global features of the mining industry and specific mineral industries to assessment of the changing relationships between LDC producers and the major actors
in the DCs, including MNCs, governments, and international agencies. The structures and shifts in the pattern of linkages are examined in the context of mineral
markets, financing for mining activities, agreements between LDC governments
and MNCs, prospects for further processing in LDCs, mechanisms for the regulation of markets, and technological innovations.

Almost all analysts point to the centrality of markets in the determination of
the relationship between LDC producers, MNCs and DC consumers. Radetzki
assesses the role of markets in determining bargaining strength and the division
of benefits between suppliers and purchasers. After analyzing from five perspectives (price theory, theory of industrial organization, bargaining theory, experimental economics, and what he calls 'a simple practical approach') of bauxite,
copper and iron markets (each of which he characterizes as a variation of an
oligopoly-oligopsony situation), Radetzki concludes that there are no clearcut
indications whether the prevailing market structures of these industries provide
more benefits to exporters; he suggests that very possibly market structures are
not primarily determinants of bargaining strength and of the sharing of benefits
derived from LDC mineral production.

In two assessments focussing upon markets in specific industries, Rogers and
Jarleborg consider aspects of the iron ore and nickel industries respectively.
Rogers's scrutiny of the increasing importance of long-term procurement contracts in the iron ore industry not only delineates in more detail shifting features
of the distinctive and differentiated global iron ore market structure, but also
throws into relief the mechanism of such contracts as a device which might be
useful for LDC producers in other mineral industries to enhance market stability, assist with the provision of finance, and improve access to markets. In
Rogers's view the long-term procurement contract has shown its utility in the
iron ore industry as a modality for improving stability in the segment of the

market where it predominates, albeit at the expense of greater instability in other segments of the world market. He suggests that it should be considered for greater adoption in other mineral markets, but with adaptations appropriate to the differing institutional features. While this argument is from the perspective of an outside academic analyst evaluating an unusually prominent feature of the iron ore market, Jarleborg's contribution is from the perspective of an insider. As an operating official of a major mining MNC, he explains significant trends within the global nickel market which have led to the increasing importance of new categories of nickel products and the entry of new producers (including his own company) into an industry hitherto dominated by one major Canadian company. It was in this setting that nickel prices softened in the mid-1970s; Jarleborg articulates the necessity from a MNC point of view for restoring 'equilibrium' to a global market in which his firm has a small, but growing, share.

If markets are central for those already engaged in production, the financing of new projects and additions to existing projects is the preeminent concern of any LDC anxious to undertake or expand mining operations. Equity financing by private foreign capital, predominant in the past, has been replaced largely by 'project finance', involving a mixture of equity contributions from MNCs, export credits, and syndicated bank loans. Radetzki and Zorn contend that the initial forms of the project finance mechanism, evolved only in the late 1960s and 1970s, will no longer prove adequate to the funding of all potential economically viable LDC mining projects. They analyze 'project finance' and pinpoint why even more complex financial arrangements involving greater participation by international lending agencies, as well as possibly oil companies and countries, insurance companies, and equipment leasers, must be considered if sufficient financing is to be found for additional mining projects in LDCs.

Perhaps of even more concern to LDC governments are the terms of actual agreements which they have negotiated with MNCs. Mikesell and Zorn offer separate and diverging assessments of the changing terms of such agreements. In his paper, Mikesell sets out the ideal conditions sought by both MNCs and LDC governments, and then through analysis of five agreements of the mid-1970s, brings to the fore what he regards as their innovative features, suggesting the possibility of a new accommodation of interests which could provide the foundations for a new era of cooperation between MNCs and LDCs. Zorn, in his evaluation of developments in the 1970s, including some of the agreements treated by Mikesell, does not deny the trend toward an apparent new accommodation but does not consider that the LDCs have necessarily secured a markedly greater share of the benefits from mining. By carefully disaggregating the goals of LDC governments and assessing their components in turn, Zorn shows how particular strategies have brought incremental gains and how preoccupations with shibboleths such as ownership *per se* may not always secure maximum gains for an LDC negotiator who is determined to achieve effective national sovereignty over the use of natural resources. In his estimation significant problems remain in negotiations between MNCs and LDCs; their solution lies not so much in more skillful bargaining, but in the creation of new instrumentalities within the LDCs which will make them less heavily dependent on MNCs.

Radetzki's subsequent analysis of the arguments by LDCs for additional processing facilities and of the MNC counter-arguments for maintaining the *status quo*, complements the assessments of Mikesell and Zorn. Radetzki meticulously weighs the arguments of both MNCs and LDCs; with care, he delineates the concerns which animate both parties and seeks to identify the areas in which accommodation is possible without great loss to either party. His analysis underscores the difference in outlook and objectives which must be appreciated accurately in any analysis of the interaction between MNCs and LDCs.

Two quite different arenas for shaping the relationship between MNCs and LDCs are assessed by Cuddy and Penrose. Cuddy analyzes the sources of potential benefit for both producers and consumers of minerals under the proposed Integrated Program for Commodities launched by UNCTAD in 1976. After identifying both the price and non-price benefits qualitatively, he then presents a precise calculation of the quantitative benefits which would result from the Integrated Program. He concludes that its application to minerals would result in a positive economic pay-off for the international community. Edith Penrose's analysis is not of a program involving both producers and consumers, but of the most successful producers' association, OPEC. Surveying the history of the organization from 1960 to date, she highlights the changing relationships between the petroleum MNCs and the LDC producers in which the latter have been in control since 1973. Penrose's analysis shows the mutual advantages which the MNCs and OPEC have derived from the relationships which have evolved, albeit relationships to which MNCs acquiesced in recognition of the higher costs of confrontation. She concludes that OPEC does not provide a model for any other would-be successful mineral producers' association; in particular, she singles out the unique contribution of Saudi Arabia to the cartel's success by its willingness to serve as a 'swing' producer, absorbing vacillations in the market through variations in its own output and revenues.

Unlike oil producers, most LDC mineral producers operate in a situation in which potential substitutes are available for the minerals in which they specialize; in addition, there are generally also possibilities for recycling which could limit demand for new production. Iwase describes the major features of the recycling industry and considers the potentials for substitution for a range of minerals. It is clear that this dimension of the mineral industry must be taken into account by LDC producers who wish to calculate as accurately as possible the prospects for the mineral which they are producing, or plan to produce, as an integral element of a national development program.

The nature of such a development program and the most appropriate policies with which to achieve it, constitute the center of discussion in the papers included in the third and final part of this volume. For all the contributors, the relationship between the MNCs and the LDCs is a central issue in assessing the possibilities for development in the latter. That the MNCs will continue to play a major role is foreseen by all — yet there is considerable disagreement upon the utility of this participation for development in producer LDCs.

In the opening paper of this final part, Radetzki surveys the feasible policy choices for LDC producers who are heavily dependent upon mineral production for export. He outlines two strategies to be pursued by governments which seek to lessen dependence and to achieve greater freedom of action — one would concentrate upon collaboration with foreign partners but with a view to steadily increasing the national role, while the other would focus upon coercion and discouragement of foreign partners, with an earlier emphasis upon exclusively national efforts. Without advocating either strategy, Radetzki's analysis dissects the elements of both policies and tries to show the implications which follow from pursuit of each one. In his conclusion he underlines the necessity for any LDC producer, anxious to assert its independence by whatever strategy, to develop a national competence in the mineral field.

Neither Mikesell nor Seidman take 'neutral' positions in their assessments of priority measures. Starting from a consideration of the vast sums that will be necessary to open mines in LDCs in order to provide needed mineral supplies for DCs, Mikesell argues vigorously that MNCs will have to provide the bulk of the investment funds. Their reluctance to invest in LDCs entails that the latter must devise means for reassuring them; otherwise, the MNCs will concentrate their mineral investments in DCs. Mikesell then focusses his attention upon a variety of bilateral and multilateral arrangements which he believes would facilitate continued MNC investment in LDCs. In contrast, Seidman's concern is not the propitiation of MNCs (of whose role she is explicitly critical), but rather the strategy that is most appropriate for any mineral exporting country desirous of broad-based development in addressing the basic needs of the majority of the population. Drawing particularly upon the experience of African countries, Seidman depicts a past pattern in mineral-based LDCs of a dualistic economy oriented to the needs of foreign investors and an emerging 'managerial/bureaucratic bourgeoisie'; the result, in her view, has been increased dependence and further neglect of the needs and demands of the masses. To reverse this process and to end underdevelopment, she argues that it is necessary to restructure the economy by changes in key institutions, incorporating both a vastly expanded role for the state in the 'commanding heights' of the economy and the participation of the majority of working people in the process. In her estimation only such a radical reorientation of government policy can save the majority of the populations of mining LDCs from lives of poverty.

An examination of a development strategy for a particular mineral-rich LDC, i.e. Namibia, is undertaken by Thomas. He is also concerned that the country's resources should be utilized for the satisfaction of the basic needs of the population while the long-run growth potential of the country is simultaneously realized. Thomas presents a quite specific strategy for Namibia, concentrating upon the role which uranium mining could play in a development program sharply different from that presently pursued by the South African administration of the territory. The prescription which Thomas offers differs from that advocated by Seidman in its support for a mixed-economy in which foreign investment would play a still important role along with the state. While his proposals are couched with reference to the specific situation of Namibia, he provides a model which might be attractive for planners in other mining LDCs.

Armstrong's contribution is neither specific to a particular country nor does it present an over-arching development strategy. Instead, it is narrowly focussed upon the ways in which training and localization policies in the context of a variety of differing development strategies can be utilized to further general developmental goals. Armstrong contends that carefully planned training and localization programs can make modest, but substantive, contributions to national development.

It is left to Fortin in the concluding paper of this volume to offer a hypothesis about the most significant contemporary trends in the international political economy of mineral exploitation. His analysis commences with a description of the withdrawal of MNCs from LDC mining in the 1960s and 1970s and delineates the main features of the new relationship which evolved, centered around joint ventures, service contracts, and long-term procurement contracts. He then considers whether the changes can best be satisfactorily understood within analytical frameworks which focus either upon the rise of LDC nationalism, or shifts in bargaining power, or structural trends that affect advanced capitalist countries. Ultimately he opts for the latter framework, arguing that the recent interest shown by MNCs in direct investment in LDCs is best comprehended as a consequence of structural features of world capitalism in conjunction with factors associated with the oil crisis that started in 1973-74. From this perspective, Fortin speaks about a 'second coming' of the MNCs into renewed direct investment in LDC mining, paralleling continued interest in joint ventures, service contracts, and long-term procurement arrangements. In Fortin's view this very probably reflects the concerns of a capitalism in crisis, anxious to preserve both rates of profits and maximum flexibility to deal with systemic stress.

Fortin's provocative hypothesis, and all the arguments presented in the papers of this volume which precede it, should be seen as providing a richly textured backdrop for further discussion and analysis of the evolving role of the state mining sector as one of the central vehicles for the assertion and achievement of national development in mineral-exporting LDCs. Probing analyses of the experiences of particular LDCs are in order.

Any analysis of the role which the state component of the mining sector might be expected to play in a particular country's national development must include close scrutiny of the state mining corporation itself — its origins, its relationship to the government and the public sector, and its relationship to the international economy. Equally, there must be careful assessment of the nature and structure of the international mineral industry of which the state mining corporation is part — including the technological requirements for extraction of the particular mineral, the role of large MNCs in the industry, and the type of export market for the commodity. Attention must also be given to the domestic environment in which the state mining corporation must operate, with particular consideration of the nature of the government, its development strategy, and the level of national manpower and technological capabilities.

Crucial to any assessment of the potential for further assertion of state control over a state mining corporation is an evaluation of the general policies of the government with regard to the role of public enterprises. Such an evaluation should encompass an examination of the policy of the government in the sphere of labor relations generally and within public enterprises in particular; an examination not only of programs for the training and allocation of skilled managerial and technical manpower, but also the specific manner in which newly-trained personnel are to be incorporated into the state mining corporation; and an examination of government policies to integrate the activities of public enterprises generally into national development planning. In the latter area a central concern is the nature of the autonomy given to the public enterprises: is the state mining corporation, in view of its distinctive origin as a public enterprise and its major economic significance, to be treated as a special case? If so, are the special measures designed for it based upon the assumption that it can best contribute to national development by operating largely as it did before nationalization, continuing primarily as a foreign exchange earner and a major source of tax and royalty revenues for government, or is it to be assumed that the mode of operation of the state mining corporation is to be radically reoriented, either in its activity within the country or in its interactions with foreign economic actors, or in both spheres?

The possibilities for any envisaged change are determined almost certainly by the nature of the government and its overall strategy for development. While it is essential to consider the policy of the government towards public enterprise generally, it is also mandatory to consider the broader thrust of government development policy, both as articulated in policy pronouncements and national plans, and as practiced upon a year-to-year basis. To what extent does the government see the establishment of a state mining sector as part of a plan to reorient the national economy away from what it regards as excessive dependence upon foreign MNCs and the uncertainties of world markets for minerals? If so, is the nature of existing economic activity and short-term and medium prospects such that the state mining corporation can be expected to undertake further processing, refining and fabrication or to supply a rapidly increasing proportion of its outputs to domestic industrial consumers, or would reorientation be a much longer-term process, in which case perhaps in the short-term the immediate goals would be a diversification of dependence and the maintenance of the state mining sector as a primary source of finance for development in the industrial and agricultural sectors? Yet even if the government appears determined to utilize the state mining corporation as an instrument in its overall strategy for reorientation of its economy, even to the point of considering major structural changes, what would seem to be its capabilities for doing so? In the mining sector, in particular, does it have the institutions and manpower (either indigenous or foreign) to sustain the shift in the mode of operation envisaged for the state mining corporation; if not, does it appear to have a considered and realizable plan for gaining necessary capabilities in this field? More broadly, does the past performance of the government machinery in the formulation and implementation of national development planning offer an appropriate model and resources for the mining sector?

No matter what the nature of the government or its development strategy, a state mining corporation in the short run almost unquestionably will be mandated to maintain, if not expand, production. But whereas efficiency and increased production within the mining sector and the generation of capital for maintenance and expansion of production were formerly the prime responsibility of a foreign firm, it is now the state mining corporation which has first responsibility. At the same time, it will be expected to continue to be an important direct contributor to national economic activity, a crucial source of government revenue, and a major source of foreign exchange. The state mining corporation will be relied upon more than ever to sustain and accelerate national development, although 'structural dependence, rather than being reduced, has in an important sense been intensified by the partial incorporation of the industry into the national economy *via* the public sector.'[6]

Beyond direct involvement in production processing and distribution, attempts have been made by LDC governments to cooperate among themselves, primarily through producer organizations, in order jointly to control price and volume of their raw material exports. As these endeavors increase the number of parties involved, the possibility of conflicts of interests also rise, together with the scope of maneuvering left to MNCs and/or DCs. To deal with these new difficulties, more careful and precise analysis is necessary of the interests involved, along with new and more imaginative agreements among the producers themselves. International organizations, including exclusively LDC bodies, should be able to contribute to the analysis as well as to the form of the agreements if they would move more boldly in such a direction.

DCs should be willing to accept, and even foster, attempts to arrive at a more equitable international income distribution if they can obtain safe and secure access to mineral supplies. Furthermore, it is mostly up to DC governments to make sure that the rules of the game are respected also by the MNCs, as it is up to them to make everybody realize that mineral resources constitute 'a common heritage of mankind', as agreed in Resolution 2749 XXV of the UN General Assembly of 1970. As the RIO Report rightly notes, however, this concept implies 'a system of world taxation to replace national mining taxation',[7] and eventually the replacement of territorial sovereignty by functional sovereignty in both LDCs and DCs.

It is, in fact, mainly through increasing consciousness of the need to preserve a common heritage that the various conflicting interests of LDCs, DCs, and MNs might somehow be reconciled within a superior order. It is to furtherance of the discussion as to how this goal might be achieved that the following analyses are directed.

NOTES

1. M.H. Govett, 'Geographic Concentration of World Mineral Supplies, Production, and Consumption', in G.S.J. Govett and M.H. Govett (eds), *World Mineral Supplies — Assessment and Perspective* (Amsterdam: Elsevier, 1976), 120.
2. W. Leontieff et al., *The Nature of The World Economy* (New York: Oxford University Press, 1977), 5-6.
3. R. Bosson and B. Varon, *The Mining Industry and the Developing Countries* (New York: Oxford University Press, 1977), 7.
4. W. Page, 'Mining and Development', *Resources Policy*, 2, 4 (December 1976), 241.
5. R. Mikesell, *Foreign Investment in the Petroleum and Mineral Industries* (Baltimore: Johns Hopkins Press, 1971), 18.
6. N. Girvan, 'Multinational Corporations and Dependent Underdevelopment in Mineral-Export Economies', *Social and Economic Studies*, 16, 4 (December 1970), 523.
7. RIO Report, J. Tinbergen (Coordinator), *Reshaping the International Order* (New York: E.P. Dutton, 1976), 148.

PART I

THE MINING INDUSTRY IN GLOBAL PERSPECTIVE

1

MINERAL RESOURCES AND
THE IMPACT OF MINING ON LDCs

W. Gluschke, N. Iwase and S. Zorn

Mining is a relatively small part of total economic activity on a global scale — accounting for about one per cent of worldwide gross product; it is obvious, however, that mining has an impact that is much greater than such figures would suggest. Furthermore, in the presently troubled world economy, the situation of many mineral-producing countries remains uncertain. The market outlook for such important non-fuel minerals as iron ore, copper, bauxite and phosphate rock is still unclear; the real earnings of producers have in many cases declined, and the amount of finance available for the exploration and exploitation of mineral deposits in LDCs is clearly less than satisfactory, either from the point of view of assuring long-term supplies of minerals for the world's economy or from the point of view of enabling the LDCs to proceed with their development plans. In addition, important questions arise from the desire of LDCs to increase the extent to which minerals are processed before export.

ECONOMIC IMPACT OF MINING PROJECTS

Measured by traditional statistical data, the contribution of the non-fuel mineral sector to the world economy is relatively small. This sector accounts for less than one per cent of gross national product in the DCs, approximately one per cent of GNP in the centrally planned economies and between one and two per cent of GNP in the LDCs. But the real contribution of the non-fuel mineral sector is far greater than these figures suggest, for three reasons. First, for many individual LDCs mining is a very significant, and often the single most important, sector of the economy. Secondly, the usual statistics include only mining, smelting and refining in calculating the value of non-fuel minerals; fabricating, semi-manufacturing and manufacturing, using metals and minerals, are not included in cal-

This chapter is a revised and abridged version of material contained in UN Committee on Natural Resources, *Mineral Resources: Trends and Salient Issues* (E/C.7/96) and UN Committee on Natural Resources, *The Economic, Social and Environmental Impact of Mining Projects* (E/C.7/97). The views expressed here are those of the authors and do not necessarily reflect those of the organizations by which they are employed.

Notes to this chapter may be found on page 50.

culations of mineral value, although the value of output at these later stages is much greater than the value of refined metal or processed minerals. For example, copper wire and cable has a value seven to nine times greater, per unit of copper, than the copper ore at the mine; pig iron has three times the value of iron ore; steel pipes and tubes 18 times the value of ore; and steel wire products 30 times the value of ore.[1] Finally, most industry is built on the basis of metals and minerals; if mining products were not available, there could be few industries. These qualifications should be kept in mind in relation to the discussion of the economic impact of mining projects.

The Value of Non-Fuel Mineral Production

The precise value of non-fuel mineral production is difficult to estimate accurately, because many transactions are carried out between units of integrated firms and because prices are not always reported even for arm's-length transactions. According to the comprehensive surveys undertaken by the journal *Annales des mines*, the total value of world mineral production (prior to smelting, refining or other processing) was $57.03 billion in 1976, compared to $49.94 billion in 1973 and $36.55 billion in 1968 (all expressed in 1976 constant dollars). The total value of production, divided among DCs, LDCs and CPEs, is shown in Table 1.1.

The shares of individual metals and minerals in the total value of production are shown in Table 1.2. By far the most important in value are iron ore and copper, each accounting for about 20 per cent of the total value. Gold accounts for about ten per cent of total value and zinc, lead, nickel, silver, salt and potash for between two and five per cent each. Despite the importance of aluminium in world industry, the mine value of bauxite is low; on average, the cost of bauxite is less than ten per cent of the value of aluminium ingot.

The distribution of the value of mineral production among groups of countries shifted markedly in the period 1950-1968, reflecting the emergence of the CPEs as increasingly important mineral producers. Since 1968, however, there has been only a small change, indicating a slowly growing role for LDC producers. Very roughly, the DCs currently account for about half the value of world mineral production and the CPEs and LDCs for about one-quarter each. When the value of production is compared to total land area in the three categories of countries (see Table 1.1), the DCs are found to produce twice as much as the CPEs per unit area, and more than three times as much as the LDCs. While the superior mineral endowments of some DCs and CPEs (notably the USA, Canada, the USSR, Australia and South Africa) may have given these countries some advantages during their industrialization and hence increased their own further requirements for minerals, it is still true that the known resources of the LDCs are relatively under-utilized.

The value of mineral production is also unevenly distributed among individual countries. Five nations, the USSR, the USA, Canada, South Africa and Australia, account for nearly 58 per cent of the total value of production and 25 countries

Table 1.1. *Value of world non-fuel mineral production*[a] *(Billion $)*

	1950 $	1976 $	%	1968 $	1976 $	%	1973 $	1976 $	%	1976 $	1976 %	1976 $ per sq km
DCs	3.75	8.41	56.8	9.95	17.76	48.6	18.06	24.57	49.2	26.91	47.2	804
LDCs	1.67	3.75	25.4	5.47	9.76	26.7	9.50	12.94	25.9	15.91	27.9	234
CPEs[b]	.95	2.13	14.5	5.06	9.03	24.7	9.13	12.43	24.9	14.20	24.9	404
Not specified	.22	.49	3.3	-	-	-	-	-	-	-	-	-
World	6.59	14.78	100	20.48	36.55	100	36.71	49.94	100	57.03	100	418

Source: Calculated from data in F. Callot, 'Production et consommation mondiale des minerals en 1973', *Annales des mines* (December 1975); 'Valeur de la production minière mondiale', *Annales des mines* (September-October 1978); estimates of geographical distribution of 1976 production by the authors.

a Bauxite, copper, lead, zinc, tin, antimony, mercy, iron ore, manganese ore, nickkel, chromite, tungsten, molybdenum, cobalt, titanium, potash, phosphate rock, salt, sulphur, diamonds, asbestos and other metallic and industrial minerals.
b Including China.

Table 1.2. *Value of metal and mineral production, 1973 and 1976*
      (1976 constant $)

	1973 Billion $	1973 %	1976 Billion $	1976 %
Metallic minerals				
Copper	13.60	27.2	9.66	17.0
Iron ore	9.66	19.3	13.33	23.4
Gold	5.71	11.4	5.30	9.3
Zinc	2.04	4.1	2.58	4.5
Nickel	1.77	3.5	2.58	4.5
Tin	1.24	2.5	1.50	2.6
Lead	1.63	3.3	1.36	2.4
Silver	1.06	2.1	1.36	2.4
Bauxite	.76	1.5	.95	1.7
Platinum	.79	1.6	.76	1.3
Other metallic minerals	2.18	4.4	2.72	4.8
Total Metallic Minerals	40.44	80.9	42.10	73.9
Non-metallic minerals				
Phosphate rock	1.18	2.4	2.86	5.0
Potash	1.50	3.0	2.31	4.1
Salt	1.63	3.3	2.04	3.6
Asbestos	.79	1.6	1.63	2.9
Sulphur	.65	1.3	1.36	2.4
Diamonds	1.50	3.0	1.07	1.9
Other non-metallics	2.31	4.6	3.54	6.2
Total Non-Metallic Minerals	9.56	19.1	14.81	26.1
Total Value	49.94[a]	100	57.03[a]	100

Source: Calculated from data in 'Valeur de la production minière mondiale', 179.

a   Totals may not match sum of individual items because of rounding.

account for more than 85 per cent of the total (see Table 1.3). The five most significant mineral producers, however, possess only 37 per cent of total land area and this includes large regions, especially in the USSR, Canada and Australia, which are barely accessible. Among the 25 leading producers, 15 are LDCs.

Because the five leading mineral producers are all DCs, mining accounts for a relatively small proportion of total economic activity in these nations. In the LDCs, however, mining projects are likely to be far more important in relation to gross domestic product, export earnings or value added than in the DCs. In addition, mining is likely to be far more significant as a basis for development planning in countries in which there are few other bases for industrialization.

The Contribution of Mining to GNP

Despite the apparently low contribution of the mining sector to world-wide economic activity, the impact of mining on GNP can be very great for individual countries. Mining and quarrying represent as much as 20 per cent (sometimes even more) of GNP in the copper, iron ore, tin and bauxite exporting LDCs (see Table 1.4), although the precise impact will vary with the price of minerals on world markets. For another five to ten countries, the share of mining in GNP may vary between ten and 20 per cent. On the other hand, mining represents only a small share of GNP in such traditional mining countries as Mexico, Brazil, Malaysia and India, reflecting the diversification of these nations' economies.

The figures in Table 1.4 include the value of mineral processing (smelting and refining or equivalent processes) as well as the mine-head value. In many LDCs the contribution of mining to GNP would be even greater if additional processing were carried out locally. For example, Papua New Guinea and the Philippines export large amounts of copper in concentrates but have no local smelting and refining. Similarly, most of the bauxite-producing LDCs process only a small proportion of the ore locally.

Value Added in Mining

Value added by mining and mineral processing can be defined as the total value of gross output, less the sum of (1) materials and supplies, (2) fuels, (3) services supplied by others, (4) repair and maintenance work performed by others and (5) purchased electricity. In general, reliable data on value added in the mineral sector are not readily available for many countries because of measurement difficulties and other problems. Table 1.5 indicates representative figures for the most important LDC mineral producers and major DCs (comparable information for the USSR and other CPEs is not readily available but value added for the USSR is roughly comparable to that for the USA).

As Table 1.5 indicates, the range of value added *per capita* is from less than $2 in India to more than $400 in Canada. The difference is attributable both to the greater degree of mineral processing in the DCs and to the greater extent to which inputs for the mining and processing industries can be supplied locally in those countries.

The Contribution of Mining to Export Earnings

The five most important non-fuel mineral export commodities are copper, iron ore, bauxite, tin and phosphate rock. Together, these five account for approximately 80 per cent of the total value of LDC mineral exports. Another four minerals — zinc, nickel, lead and manganese ore — account for an additional ten per cent of total LDC mineral exports. The total value of exports of these nine commodities from LDCs in 1974-76 averaged $10.6 billion per annum (see Table 1.6). A roughly comparable value can be inferred for 1977 and 1978, since prices for copper, iron ore, nickel, phosphate rock and manganese ore have generally been weaker while those for tin have been higher, with little change in the remaining commodities.

Table 1.3. Value of non-fuel mineral production in selected countries, 1973[a] (Mine value in constant 1976 US $)

Country	Area (sq km)	Estimated 1976 population (millions)	Value of non-fuel mineral production			
			million $	%	$ per capita	$ per sq km
USSR	22,402	256.7	9,230	18.5	35.9	412
USA	9,373	215.1	6,920	13.9	32.2	738
Canada	9,976	23.1	5,176	10.4	224.1	519
South Africa	1,221	26.1	5,170	10.4	198.1	4,234
Australia	7,687	13.9	2,300	4.6	165.4	299
Chile	757	10.5	1,618	3.2	154.1	2,137
China	9,561	852.1	1,586	3.2	1.9	166
Zambia	753	5.1	1,391	2.8	272.7	1,847
Zaire	2,345	25.6	1,176	2.4	45.9	501
Peru	1,285	16.1	933	1.9	58.0	725
Brazil	8,512	109.2	876	1.8	8.0	103
Mexico	1,972	62.3	824	1.7	13.2	418
France	547	52.9	672	1.3	12.7	1,228
India	3,268	610.1	578	1.2	.9	177
Philippines	300	43.8	551	1.1	12.6	1,837

Germany, Federal Republic of	248	61.5	540	1.1	8.8	2,177
Sweden	450	8.2	530	1.1	64.6	1,179
Poland	312	34.4	529	1.1	15.4	1,696
Japan	370	112.8	517	1.0	4.6	1,397
Mongolia	1,565	1.5	431	.9	287.3	307
Namibia	824	.9	376	.8	417.8	457
Morocco	447	17.8	355	.7	19.9	793
Liberia	111	1.8	313	.6	173.9	2,811
Venezuela	912	12.4	292	.6	23.5	258
Bolivia	1,099	5.8	275	.6	47.4	518
First five countries	50,659 (37.3%)	534.9 (13.2%)	28,796	57.7	53.8	568
First 25 countries	86,297 (63.5%)	2,580.0 (63.8%)	41,496	86.5	16.1	481
World	135,830	4,044.0	49,940	100.0	12.3	368

Sources: Calculated from data in F. Callot, 'Production et consommation mondiale des minerals en 1973', and *Statistical Yearbook 1977* (UN, E/F. 78. XVII.1).

a   Countries with mineral production over $260 million.

Table 1.4. *Contribution of mining and quarrying to GNP in selected countries*

Country and year	Share of GNP (percentage)		Major products
	Mining and quarrying	Manufacturing	
LDCs			
Chile (1974)	9.5	23.3	Copper, iron ore
(1976)	7.7	21.1	,, ,, ,,
Papua New Guina (1973)	25.5	6.0	Copper, gold
(1974)	13.4	7.5	,, ,,
Peru (1976)	6.3	28.5	Copper, iron ore, lead
Zaire (1974)	22.1	8.2	Copper, tin, cobalt
(1975)	10.4	10.8	,, ,, ,,
Zambia (1976)	17.5	15.9	Copper
(1977)	12.6	17.9	,,
Philippines (1975)	1.5	19.4	Copper, chromite
Guyana (1976)	13.0	12.0	Bauxite
Suriname (1975)	20.0	5.0	,,
Jamaica (1976)	8.7	19.5	,,
Jordan (1975)	4.3	11.6	Phosphate rock
Bolivia (1975)	11.0	13.2	Tin, copper
Malaysia (1974)	5.6	16.9	Tin
Mauritania (1973)	32.9	4.8	Iron ore, copper
Liberia (1976)	19.9	3.9	Iron ore
Brazil (1975)	1.1	25.0	Iron ore
India (1976)	1.3	15.0	Iron ore, chromite
Mexico (1976)	4.2	24.5	Silver, copper, lead
DCs			
Australia (1975)	3.6	19.0	These countries produce
Canada (1976)	3.6	18.8	several minerals and metals;
South Africa (1976)	12.1	23.7	gold dominates in South
USA (1976)	2.5	23.9	Africa

Source: Calculated from data in UN, *Monthly Bulletin of Statistics* (ST/ESA/STAT/SER. Q/70)

Note: Figures are given for two different years for Chile, Papua New Guinea, Zaire and Zambia to show the effect of changes in the market price of copper.

Table 1.5. *Mining and processing: gross value of output and value added for selected countries*[a]

Country	Year[b]	Estimated 1976 population (millions)	Value added[c] Million $	$ per capita	Value of gross output[c] (million $)
LDCs					
Zambia	1973	5.1	960.7	188.4	1,334.9
Jamaica	1974	2.1	327.8	156.1	672.5
Peru	1976	16.1	752.5	46.7	903.8
Dominican Rep.	1974	4.8	63.3	13.2	124.6
Malaysia	1974	12.3	291.3	23.7	428.1
Botswana	1975	0.7	15.2	21.7	61.8
Jordan	1975	2.8	50.0	17.9	68.5
Zaire	1972	25.6	278.2	10.9	599.6
Mexico	1975	62.3	530.6	8.6	887.7
Philippines	1974	43.8	331.0	7.6	493.9
Brazil	1974	109.2	752.9	6.9	955.9
India	1975	610.1	895.3	1.5	1,369.0
DCs					
Canada	1975	23.1	9,585.8	415.0	12,644.6
Australia	1976	13.9	3,350.4	241.0	4,895.2
South Africa	1976	26.1	3,800.6	145.6	n.a.
USA	1976	215.1	24,200	112.5	33,200

Source: Calculated from data in UN, *Statistical Yearbook 1977*; and UN, *Monthly Bulletin of Statistics* (ST/ESA/STAT/SER.Q/70).

a Countries selected on the basis of the importance of their mineral sector and the availability of separate data for the non-fuel mineral industry.
b In most cases the calendar year but for some countries the fiscal year ending in the year given.
c Calculated from national currencies applying the mid-period exchange rate of the respective year.

The LDCs' share of total world exports in recent years has been slightly more than 20 per cent for lead and zinc, in the range of 40-50 per cent for iron ore, manganese ore and copper, 65 per cent for phosphate rock, 78-80 per cent for bauxite and 90 per cent for tin. While the importance of individual commodities changes from year to year because of relative price movements, the five leading export minerals — copper, iron ore, bauxite, tin and phosphate rock — are by far the most significant, with copper alone accounting for nearly 40 per cent of LDCs' non-fuel mineral exports in the 1972-76 period (see Table 1.6).

The dominance of these few non-fuel minerals and metals in LDC exports explains the great importance of these commodities for countries which are major producers and exporters — Chile, Papua New Guinea, Peru, the Philippines, Zaire and Zambia for copper; Guinea, Guyana, Jamaica and Suriname for

Table 1.6. *Value of exports of the nine most important non-fuel minerals from LDCs*

	1972-76 average		1974-76 average		LDCs'
	Value million $	Share %	Value million $	Share %	Share of export %
Copper[a]	3,552	38.9	3,875	36.6	52.8
Iron ore[b]	1,692	18.5	2,059	19.5	40.2
Aluminium[c]	989	10.8	893	8.4	77.4[e]
Tin[d]	972	10.6	1,161	11.0	88.9
Phosphate rock	971	10.6	1,418	13.4	68.7
Zinc[d]	341	3.7	431	4.1	20.5
Nickel[d]	274	3.0	322	3.0	
Lead[d]	180	2.0	201	1.9	23.6
Manganese ore[b]	169	1.8	214	2.0	50.2
Nine commodities	9,140	100	10,574	100	
Five most important mineral export commodities	8,176	89.5	9,406	89.0	
Petroleum (for comparison)	79,290		113,295		91.2

Source: Division of Natural Resources and Energy, Department of Technical Co-operation for Development of the UN Secretariat, based on data from the World Bank and other sources.

a   Copper ores and concentrates, matte, cement copper, copper and alloys.
b   Ores and concentrates.
c   Bauxite, alumina, aluminium and alloys.
d   Ores, concentrates, metal and alloys.
e   Bauxite only.

bauxite; Mauritania and Liberia for iron ore; Jordan, Morocco and Togo for phosphate rock; Bolivia and Malaysia for tin; and Gabon for manganese ore (see Table 1.7). Non-fuel minerals account for as much as 96 per cent of total exports in some cases, although in general their proportion in LDC exports has been declining since 1972, reflecting increased exports of semi-manufactured and manufactured goods from some countries. At the same time, however, some individual LDCs (for example, Papua New Guinea and Guinea) have become more heavily dependent on mineral exports during this period, as the result of major new mineral projects coming into development.

The export earnings of most countries which are dependent to a large degree on exports of a single non-fuel mineral commodity have experienced sharp declines in recent years from the peaks achieved in 1973-74. Prices of copper, iron ore and phosphate rock have fallen, especially in real terms; these declines have only been partially and erratically offset by increases in byproduct prices (for example, gold, cobalt and molybdenum in the case of copper). While tin prices have reached high levels, bauxite prices have made only modest advances in real terms, and in fact declined during 1978.

Table 1.7. *Share of major minerals in exports of selected LDCs*

Country		Average share of major minerals (percentage)		
		1970-72[a]	1972-74[a]	1974-76[b]
Major mineral exports				
Copper	Zambia	96.6	96.3	96.5
	Zaire	71.5	73.3	66.6
	Chile	78.3	77.4	65.8
	Papua New Guinea	26.5	55.9	45.2
	Peru	43.9	55.8	35.8
	Philippines	17.7	15.9	11.8
Bauxite	Guinea	1.9	7.4	70.2
	Guyana	27.6	28.7	26.0
	Suriname	30.4	29.7	20.6
	Jamaica	25.5	21.3	18.4
Iron ore	Mauritania	82.2	90.3	88.6
	Liberia	72.7	67.0	70.1
	Sierra Leone	18.4	15.5	10.9
	Brazil	8.1	7.0	10.3
	India	8.0	6.5	5.5
Phosphate rock	Togo	32.3	45.3	66.3
	Morocco	27.6	30.1	55.5
	Jordan	19.7	23.9	35.2
	Tunisia	11.7	10.2	11.5
Tin	Bolivia	69.7	57.1	50.3
	Malaysia	19.1	14.1	12.1
	Rwanda	22.1	21.6	4.3
	Thailand	8.9	6.4	5.3
Manganese ore	Gabon	20.9	10.8	8.0
Total LDCs		8.5	5.8	4.6

Source: World Bank, *Commodity Trade and Price Trends* (various editions, Washington).

a   Bauxite, copper, iron ore, lead, manganese ore, phosphate rock, silver, tin and zinc.
b   Bauxite, copper, iron ore, lead, manganese ore, phosphate rock, tin and zinc.

Local Processing in LDCs

An increase in the share of raw material output that is locally processed to, for example, refined metal, semi-manufactures or even fabricated products, has for a long time been a primary objective of LDCs. Promotion of further local processing is also an objective of some of the mineral-producing states, notably Australia and Canada, which have large exports of raw materials and partially processed minerals. Some newly industrializing countries (for example, Brazil) are importing significant amounts of unprocessed raw materials, usually from other LDCs, for processing for the local market. Other LDCs such as the oil-exporting countries of the Middle East, are establishing mineral processing facilities which will use local energy supplies and imported raw materials, with the final products largely intended for export. Some LDCs, however, have cancelled or postponed plans for establishing local processing facilities because of the excess processing capacity currently available in the DCs (especially in steel, copper and zinc) and the difficulty in marketing refined metal as opposed to unprocessed raw materials.

Taking all these factors into account, there is a gradual increase under way, both in the share of LDCs' mineral products which are processed locally and in the proportion of LDCs' mineral output which is exported in processed form. For example, the share of world aluminium smelting capacity of LDCs (excluding CPEs) is expected to increase from 13.1 per cent to 21.1 per cent between 1977 and 1983. Similarly, LDCs' share of crude steel capacity is expected to increase from 9.3 per cent in 1977 to 15.0 per cent in 1983, and their share in copper refining capacity from 27.1 per cent to 30.3 per cent.[2] In all cases, however, the share of LDCs in mineral processing capacity will still be lower than their share in mine capacity in 1983, in some cases by a considerable margin (for example, it is expected that LDCs will account for 67.4 per cent of bauxite capacity in 1983 but only 36.4 per cent of alumina refining capacity and 21.1 per cent of aluminium smelter capacity; in the case of iron ore, the LDCs will have 44.7 per cent of mine capacity in 1983, compared with 15.0 per cent of crude steel capacity; and in the case of copper, the LDCs are expected to account for 58.9 per cent of mine capacity, 43.8 per cent of smelter capacity and 30.6 per cent of refinery capacity by 1983).

The impact of mineral processing activities on LDCs will vary, depending on the nature of the process, the economic situation of the country and the market structure for the commodity in question. In very broad terms, increased processing can generally be expected to generate some additional employment, additional government revenue, higher export earnings (though these may be balanced by the increased imports required for the processing plants, especially in the LDCs) and to create at least the possibility of additional linkages to the rest of the economy, both backward, involving the supply of goods and services for the processing plants, and forward, into the fabrication and manufacture of finished products. There are reasons for caution, however, in the establishment of local processing facilities; the need for imported inputs has already been mentioned. The high capital cost of processing facilities means that they are a very expensive method of job creation. The existence of relatively high levels of effective protection in the DCs for processed minerals, as opposed to ores and concentrates, may make marketing difficult in the absence of preferential treatment by the DCs. Where processing requires large amounts of energy (as in aluminium smelting) or of complementary materials (e.g. coal for integrated steelworks), the mere presence of abundant ores or concentrates will not be sufficient to make local processing economically viable unless the other inputs can also be obtained.

At present, processing capacity in the LDCs lags substantially behind mine capacity and behind their share of world reserves. Only in tin and lead is virtually all mine production in the LDCs processed locally; copper, zinc and nickel are intermediate cases, while the great bulk of bauxite and iron ore mined in the LDCs is processed elsewhere. While a number of LDCs have processing projects under way, there will be a substantial processing capacity gap in the mid-1980s.

There have been a number of recent developments, however, in expanding the processing capacity of LDCs. In the case of bauxite, for example, Guinea has been negotiating with Arab states (including Egypt, Iraq, Kuwait, the Libyan Arab Jamahiriya, Saudi Arabia, and the United Arab Emirates) for the establishment in Guinea of an integrated mine-refinery-smelter complex at Boké, at an estimated cost of $1.3 billion. Guyana has commissioned a feasibility study by the USSR of a 600,000 tons per year alumina refinery, while Brazil has undertaken integrated development based on local bauxite reserves and including such projects as the $400 million Alunorte alumina refinery, the $256 million Valesul smelter, and the $1 billion Albras smelter. Malaysia is planning two smelter projects with a total capacity of 200,000 tons per year, roughly parallel with its current level of bauxite production. A regional attempt at processing, involving Jamaica, Guyana, Mexico and Trinidad & Tobago has been under discussion, but now seems unlikely to go forward. India is planning a number of bauxite-processing projects, the largest of which is the $1.4 billion Orissa complex, involving an alumina refinery with a capacity of 600,000-800,000 tons per year and a 180,000 tons per year aluminium smelter. And in Indonesia final financing has been arranged for the $2.1 billion Asahan project which will have a smelting capacity of 75,000 tons per year by 1981 and 225,000 tons by 1984.

New processing projects are also under way for other metals. Bolivia, for example, is expanding the capacity of its Vinto tin smelter to 20,000 tons per year and is installing a plant to treat low-grade tin concentrates. These developments will enable the country to process all its tin concentrates locally, rather than sending them to the USA and UK for processing as in the past. Bolivia has also completed arrangements for the construction of a 24,000 tons per year lead smelter and refinery and is also planning a zinc treatment plant.

In the Philippines, a 126,000 tons per year copper smelter and refinery is scheduled to open in the early 1980s; until now, the Philippines has exported all its copper in the form of concentrates. Expansions of copper processing capacity are also planned by Peru and Zaire, both of which have received World Bank financing for these projects. A number of iron ore-producing countries are also increasing their processing capacity. While some of these developments represent efforts to supply the domestic steel market, others are designed to upgrade exports. For example, Chile's Compañía Acero del Pacífico is building a 3.5 million tons per year iron ore-pelletizing plant, which should have the effect of increasing foreign exchange earnings by $100 million per year. Venezuela plans to increase local steelmaking capacity from 1.2 million tons per year to nearly five million tons, some of which is intended for export to other South American countries.

A related development which gives iron ore-producing countries greater options in the sale of their output is the recent expansion of steelmaking capacity in the energy-rich countries, especially in the Middle East. For example, Saudi Arabia is proceeding with two major projects which will initially produce 4.3 million tons per year of sponge iron and one million tons of steel. In Iraq the 440,000 ton Khorr-al-Zubair steelworks has begun production, and a further 750,000 tons of sponge-iron capacity is under construction. The Umm Said works of the Qatar Steel Company began production in 1978 at a level of 400,000 tons per year. In some cases these steel plants use locally-mined iron ore, but in large part they will represent new markets for other LDC iron ore producers.

For many countries which are producers of raw materials, opportunities for processing within national boundaries are limited by technological and commercial realities. The size of the national or regional market may be too small to support a processing plant of optimum size, and additional transport costs and tariff barriers may make it difficult for the LDC to compete in the market for semi-fabricated and fabricated products in the DCs. The simple fact that processing plants in the DCs are closer to their customers and are able to respond to customer demand more quickly than processors some thousands of kilometers distant, gives the established plants in DCs a further advantage.

One recent development by which raw materials producers have moved into processing has been the establishment of joint venture facilities located in the DCs. Two recent examples are the continuous cast-copper-rod plants established in Germany by Codelco-Chile and a group of German companies, and in France by the Zambian copper producers together with a French firm. Such projects appear to overcome the problem of market access, but do not generate local employment or other benefits in the LDC in question.

For those LDCs that are large enough to provide internal markets of a size sufficient to support a processing plant, mineral production for the local market should be considered a desirable course of action. In the case of steel, for example, both Mexico and Brazil have industrial sectors that are already well developed, and both countries intend to become self-sufficient in steel by the early 1980s. Mexico, with a steel consumption of nearly six million tons in 1977, compared with a domestic production capacity of 5.5 million tons, has already nearly achieved self-sufficiency. Brazil, where steel consumption is estimated at 13 million tons for 1978, is continuing the rapid development of steelworks to keep pace with the growing domestic market. In addition, Brazil is undertaking a wide range of mineral processing projects, based largely on the country's own large population and rapid industrialization plans (although a portion of the output will be for export, primarily to other Latin American countries).

Several other LDCs also have the potential for mineral processing to meet local demand. In Latin America, Argentina already has a well-developed metal fabricating industry. In Asia, India has well-established steel and aluminium industries that produce for local consumption, as well as a range of planned projects for all metals industries. Other Asian countries with substantial plans for local processing in the context of national industrialization programmes include Indonesia and the Philippines.

In many cases, however, the economically efficient size of plants is too large for the limited internal markets of LDCs. Where a single mineral producing country does not have an internal market sufficient to justify plants of this size, there may be opportunities for regional cooperation.

Trends in Demand and Supply

In 1977-78, the demand for aluminium and copper exceeded the previous record levels of 1973-74; world consumption of primary aluminium was about 15 million tons in 1978, and consumption of refined copper was estimated at 9.5 million tons. Consumption of lead, zinc, tin and iron ore in 1978 approximately matched the previous record levels of 1973-74. Nickel and other steel alloy raw materials, on the other hand, have suffered considerable reductions in consumption levels, largely as a consequence of the difficulties faced by the steel industry in most DCs.

Where consumption remained at low levels, production was not always adjusted downward to match the new consumption levels, or it was adjusted only after large stocks had been built up. An extreme case is the example of nickel; output was eventually reduced by most major producers in 1977-78; but only after stocks in the hands of producers had reached more than double the normal levels. A similar stock build-up occurred in copper in 1976-77, before mine closings and production cutbacks restored a balance in the market. The production of iron ore and manganese was cut in some countries only when the physical limits of stockpile facilities were reached. In contrast, the demand for tin was restrained throughout 1977-78 by the unavailability of new supplies in the short term.

Some specific developments influenced supply, demand and price for certain metals. For example, cobalt production was interrupted by internal problems in Zaire, the major producing country, and total output in that nation for 1978 was 30 per cent below the normal level. An example of a metal where new applications have more than compensated for sluggish growth in the overall economy is molybdenum, for which demand remained strong in 1977-78.

The world-wide distribution of production capacity for some metals has undergone some changes, in particular as a result of new projects in the LDCs. In copper, Mexico and Peru substantially increased their capacity, through the Caridad and Cuajone projects respectively, and capacity was also added in the Philippines and Brazil among the LDCs, as well as in Poland. Copper capacity was reduced in the USA and Canada through market-related mine closings. In the case of nickel, new projects came onstream in Guatemala and Indonesia, and a significant expansion is under way in Cuba. Nickel mine production was reduced in Canada and Australia, the major DC producers. In iron ore, capacity was greatly expanded in Brazil and Mexico, and new pelletizing facilities have begun operating in Chile and India. In aluminium, bauxite capacity was increased in Guinea, while new smelters have begun operation or are under construction in Algeria, Bahrain, Dubai and Indonesia. The only metal whose production has become more concentrated in the DCs in the past two years is molybdenum, following the opening of a major new mine in the USA.

Major changes in capacity for 1979 include the opening of new copper mines in the Philippines as well as the start of full production from Caridad in Mexico. At the time of writing, the outlook for the Sar Chashmeh copper project in Iran, which had been due onstream late in 1978, was still uncertain. In bauxite, the largest anticipated increases will be in Brazil and Australia, while in the case of iron ore expansion programs continue in Brazil.

Price Movements

In broad terms, price movements for mineral commodities were more uniform in 1977-78 than earlier in the 1970s, though some individual minerals experienced either sharp price decreases or significant improvements. The price index established by the United Nations Conference on Trade and Development (UNCTAD) for the market prices of principal mineral exports of LDCs showed only small variations during the past two years; the index varied between 170 and 184 (1972=100) during the entire period, reaching the top of that range at the end of 1977 and again at the end of 1978.[3] A similar pattern is evident in the indices of world export prices of selected primary commodities and metals calculated by the UN Statistical Office. It should be noted, however, that prices of manufactured goods continued to increase, while mineral prices were relatively stable.

The apparent stability, however, conceals considerably wider fluctuations in the cases of some individual minerals. For example, the difficult situation in the steel industry in the DCs resulted in reduced demand for iron ore and for such steel alloy raw materials as manganese ore, nickel, tungsten and chromium. The prices of iron ore and manganese ore remained low during 1977-78, though they have recovered somewhat since. Sharp price reductions occurred in the case of nickel, a metal which had been characterized by very stable prices for many years. From a peak of $2.40 per pound in 1977 for refined (Class I) nickel, prices dropped to $1.80-$2.00 by the end of 1978, with corresponding reductions for ferronickel and other Class II products. Subsequently, the nickel price has risen sharply following the production cutbacks and the prolonged strike at the INCO mines.

The price of copper — by far the most important mineral export commodity, in terms of value, for LDCs — remained at low levels in 1977-78, although there was a strengthening in price in 1979. Several new pricing developments have occurred in copper. The American producer price, traditionally separate from the pricing in the rest of the world based on the London Metal Exchange (LME), was largely abandoned, as major US producers shifted to pricing on the basis of New York Commodity Exchange quotations, which closely follow those of the LME. In addition, LDC members of the Intergovernmental Council of Copper

Exporting Countries (CIPEC) have introduced new pricing formulas, including a premium over the LME quotation and the elimination of certain price-setting options for buyers. It is not clear at this time whether these changes will be a permanent feature of the copper market or merely transitory.

A number of other metals and minerals showed moderate to large price increases in 1977-78. The price of primary aluminium increased to a level of about 60 cents per pound by mid-1979. The price of lead rose sharply, to over 60 cents per pound by June 1979, considerably higher than the price of zinc. In contrast, the zinc price had been more than double that of lead as recently as 1974. Large price increases also occurred for molybdenum, tin and silver, reflecting strong demand.

The internal developments in Zaire, previously mentioned, had the effect of pushing the cobalt price to unprecedented levels. By early 1979 the producer price was $25 per pound, and prices of $40-$45 were reported for spot sales on the open market. In contrast, the producer price for cobalt during the boom period of 1974 was less than $4 per pound.

SOCIAL IMPACT OF MINING PROJECTS

Mining projects can have significant impacts on the structure of society, ways of life, immigration patterns and other social factors as well as on the physical environment. In some cases, these impacts are made even more pronounced by the typically remote location of mining developments, which are often isolated from existing communities and which require substantial new infrastructure. This section briefly reviews the major potential impacts of mining projects, especially those in LDCs.

Social impacts of mining industries may vary considerably from project to project and from country to country, depending on the size of projects and the relative importance of the mining sector in the national economies. Moreover, it is extremely difficult to quantify social costs and benefits deriving from mining activities, because of conceptual difficulties in measurement and a general lack of appropriate statistics. For these reasons, the analysis below is sometimes fragmentary and is limited to a relatively small number of countries and projects. The analysis attempts to shed some light on three major social factors: employment, training and education, and health.

Employment

The mining industry is often more capital intensive than manufacturing and other industries. The capital-labor ratio and the output-labor ratio depend, of course, on the size of mining operations. Large-scale mines with associated processing facilities tend to have substantially higher output-labor ratios than small or medium-sized mines. For example, in Peru the four large mining enterprises employ about 31 per cent of the total mine labor force but produce more than two-thirds of the metal output.[4] Output-labor ratios also depend on the type of mine operations. Underground mines are usually more labor-intensive than open pit mines. Table 1.8 compares value added per employee in mining and manufacturing industries in selected LDCs. All the countries in the table show higher value added per employee in mining than in manufacturing.

Table 1.8. *Employment and value added per employee in mining and manufacturing: selected LDCs.*[a]

Country	Year	No. of employees (thousands)		Value added per employee[b] (thousands of national currency units)	
		Mining	Manufacturing	Mining	Manufacturing
Zambia	1973	61.1	48.1	10.1	4.1
Zaire	1972	60.6	64.5	2.3	1.3
Malaysia	1973	54.6	206.2	8.7	7.4
Philippines	1973	42.0	538	60.4	20.9
Brazil	1973	65	3,199	53.2	42.6
Mexico	1975	47.9	1,708	138.5	111.3

Source: Calculated from data in *Statistical Yearbook 1977.*

a   Countries selected on the basis of the importance of their mineral sectors and relatively minor production of fuel minerals.
b   Since currency units are different, figures are not for international comparison.

In terms of job creation, small and medium-scale mining, where it is feasible, may be more desirable than highly mechanized open pit operations. The long-term secular decline in average ore grades, however, has necessitated large-scale capital-intensive mining operations in order to make exploitation of low grade deposits economically feasible. This trend can be observed not only in DCs but also in mineral producers in LDCs.

It is to be expected, therefore, that the mining industry will not contribute to job creation as much as it does to national income and to export earnings. For example, in Zambia, where the national economy relies heavily on copper production, only six per cent of total employment is in the mining and mineral processing industries. Similarly, the mining industry in Zaire accounts for only 6.4 per cent of total national employment. The data for bauxite-producing countries are even more striking. The bauxite and alumina industries in Jamaica, for example, account for only 1.2 per cent of total employment (compared to 15 per cent of GDP).

It should be noted, however, that these employment figures represent only the direct impact of mining employment. Most mines are located in remote areas which initially did not have any supporting facilities. Development of mines usually involves the construction of infrastructure, including roads, power plants, housing, schools, etc., which otherwise would not have been developed. Therefore, it may be misleading to conclude that the impact of mining on employment is minor by looking only at direct employment. Mining industries may generate substantial employment if all the indirect effects are taken into account.

Wage rates set by mining industries are generally high as compared to those in other industries. High wage rates can be explained partly by high labor productivity in the mining sector, resulting from the large amounts of capital per worker. In addition, the remote location of many mining operations, the limited availability of social services and amenities and the hard working conditions, especially in underground mining, may have to be compensated for by higher wage rates in order to attract the required labor force. Mine workers in many LDCs also have highly effective trade unions and strong bargaining power. Moreover, mining operations require engineers, scientists and skilled labor to handle increasingly complicated equipment. In countries in which trained skilled manpower is scarce, a large proportion of managerial, supervisory and technical positions may be filled by expatriates. Large differences between remuneration for expatriates and for national personnel still exist in the mining industries in many LDCs. For example, according to World Bank data, average salaries for expatriate staff in Zaire in 1973 were about Z1,800 per month, compared to an average of Z400 for Zairean staff and Z44 per month for Zairean mine workers.

Training and Education

Relatively extensive training programs are undertaken by virtually all large and medium-sized mining firms in DCs and LDCs. Even in the DCs, it is rare that all the required work force for a large mining operation can readily be found from a pool of experienced personnel, without the need for any training. Training and education are essential in the LDCs, especially where the general level of basic education is relatively low.

There are two basic objectives for training by mining enterprises in LDCs: (1) to develop the skills necessary for efficient operation and (2) to accommodate the manpower policies of the government, usually with the aim of maximizing employment of nationals. The first objective is directly related to the economics of the mining operation, because the overall costs of national employees tend to be significantly lower than those for expatriates.

Generally, there is a much higher turnover rate for expatriates as compared to nationals in mining projects. In the Zambian copper mines, for example, the annual turnover rate for expatriate employees in 1976 was 33 per cent, compared to 6.7 per cent for local employees.[5] The combination of high turnover rates for expatriates and government localization targets will usually prompt mining enterprises in LDCs to carry on extensive training programs.

Requirements for training depend on a variety of factors, including (a) the stage of mine development, (b) the scale of operations and level of technology, (c) the educational level of local people, and (d) labor turnover rates.

In most mines in LDCs, the majority of employees are recruited from the region of the country in which the mine is located. An already-trained labor force is often not available, either because of the remote location of the mine or because of a nationwide scarcity of industrial manpower. In many LDCs, 90 per cent or more of daily wage workers in the mines start out with virtually no training or experience.[6]

Consequently, most large-scale mines in LDCs conduct various training programs on a continuous basis. On-the-job training is the most commonly used and probably the least costly method but such training may be supplemented by a wide variety of additional programs, including adult literacy courses and basic education classes as well as formal education. For example, at the Cerro de Pasco mines in Peru (since nationalized and operating as Centromin-Peru) more than 3,000 out of a total of 11,800 daily wage workers were enrolled in formal training programs in 1973 in addition to those receiving only on-the-job training. In the case of countries where there is almost no existing industrial labor force, new mining industries will face enormous training tasks. For example, prior to the opening of the Bougainville copper mine in Papua New Guinea, the local inhabitants had engaged only in traditional subsistence agriculture and had never been exposed to industry. Therefore, special attention had to be paid to providing not only training in the skills required for the mining operations but also education for a transition from traditional ways of life. Since the start of exploration at Bougainville in 1967, the mining enterprise has conducted a massive training program. By the end of 1976, nearly 16,000 persons had undergone some kind of training, even though total employment at any one time is only 4,000.

Sometimes mining industries are partly responsible for the national education system in LDCs. For example, Gécamines, the state mining enterprise in Zaire, maintains 41 primary schools, seven secondary schools, a technical institute and six home economics teaching centers. Centromin, the Peruvian state enterprise, runs 67 schools in which 17,500 children of mineworkers are taught by more than 450 teachers.

As indicated earlier, one of the objectives of training programs is the replacement of expatriates with local people. Targets for employment of nationals are sometimes set explicitly in agreements between LDC governments and mining companies (current examples include Indonesia and Papua New Guinea). Other governments (for example, that of Peru) require mining enterprises to present training plans for government approval each year. In cases in which the mining industry is of major importance in the national economy and particularly where governments have majority equity holdings in the mining enterprises, mining industry training programs will usually be closely coordinated with national manpower planning and educational plans. For example, mine training programs in Zambia, carried out by the state-controlled Nchanga Consolidated Copper Mines Ltd and Roan Consolidated Mines Ltd, are coordinated with national employment policies through the Government's Mining Industry Manpower Service Unit. The companies' training programs are specially geared to the replacement of expatriates with Zambians and the proportion of expatriates in mining has decreased from 17 per cent in 1964 to seven per cent in 1976.[7]

The benefits produced by training and education in mining industries in LDCs can be significant. The extension of skills from the mining sector to other industries which require similar skills (e.g. manufacturing or construction) helps to increase the general availability of skilled labor. The impact of this external economy can be quite large if labor turnover in mining is fairly high and if skilled labor is scarce outside the mining sector. In addition, because mining training programs usually include long-term efforts to increase literacy and provide basic education, these programs have been a major force in some LDCs in improving general levels of education.

Health

The mining industry has long been considered one of the most hazardous industries. The International Labor Organization (ILO) recently estimated the frequency of on-the-job fatalities in eight countries (Germany, Guatemala, Hungary, Japan, Malaysia, Tanzania, USA and Zambia). In six of the countries (all except Guatemala and Malaysia) the frequency of fatalities in mining and quarrying was from 30 to 300 per cent higher than in manufacturing and construction.[8] Within the mining sector itself, the frequency of injuries and fatalities varies according to the type of operations. A Canadian study shows that the frequency of fatal and totally disabling injuries per million man-hours worked ranges from 0.13 in surface mining to 0.53 for underground metal mining and 0.58 for underground coal mining.[9]

In addition to accidents, mine workers may suffer occupational diseases to a greater degree than other workers. An association between mining dust and lung disease is common. Silica, asbestos and coal dust are often considered as major causes of pneumoconiosis. Lead, cadmium and beryllium can have toxic effects by entering through the lungs into the bloodstream. Asbestos and arsenic are apparently associated with cancer. A number of other lung diseases, such as chronic bronchitis and asthma, appear to be associated with exposure to dust. In addition, noise, vibration and exposure to radiation are other hazards of mining work that can cause serious occupational diseases.

The mining industry, because of its inherently hazardous work environment, has attempted to improve and strengthen safety programs. Mining enterprises normally aim at preventing accidents through the use of safety equipment as well as attempting to maintain acceptable air quality in working areas and providing adequate medical services, including regular medical examinations, for mine workers and their families. In the DCs, such efforts are often required by stringent regulations and enforced through frequent inspections.

Partly because of the requirements of their comprehensive safety programs and partly because of the frequent unavailability of medical services in the mine area, mining enterprises often operate hospitals or clinics and hire their own medical staff. According to World Bank data, for example, Gécamines in Zaire employs a medical staff of 175, including 40 doctors, and operates hospitals and other facilities with about 1,800 beds, for a work force of 29,000. By way of contrast, in 1972 there were 807 medical doctors and 73,000 hospital beds in all of Zaire, serving a population of 23 million. The data show that in this not atypical case the mining enterprise has provided comparatively good health care for its workers, as compared to nationwide standards.

The external benefits from health care services provided by mining industries can be considerable, although it is extremely difficult to measure them. If the emergence of a mining town means that people in the region can have access to modern medical care which would not otherwise have been available, the external benefits clearly accrue to the society.

LONG-TERM FORCES

The future of the LDC mining industry depends greatly on exploration, overall economic growth of the world economy, technological progress, and possibly on the rate of extraction of mineral resources from the ocean.

Exploration and Technological Progress

Low prices, high stock levels, increasing investment costs and financing problems have led during the past years to postponement of both new projects and expansions. This has taken the form of outright cancellation, suspension, or 'stretching' of investment programs.

The reasons behind such postponements are varied and not always easily identifiable. Some are clearly due to the fact that delivery times for equipment were longer than anticipated and to technical difficulties in mining and processing as, for example, with recent nickel projects (Greenvale in Australia and Marinduque in the Philippines). Depressed metal markets for extended periods, however, are probably the most important single reason for postponements; sometimes they tend to induce companies to 'prevent cancellation' by simply not starting even the exploration phase. The lack of funds, either before or during construction, has been instrumental in halting several recent projects, a problem that is normally exacerbated by the common over-run of costs during extended development periods.

Turning to exploration, in contrast to earlier years when smaller production rates and higher grade allowed the investigation of only a part of a deposit in order to prove up reserves for a specified period, usually 10 to 20 years, most deposits today are fully investigated in order to provide detailed data for developing the most efficient mining and beneficiation procedures. Adjustments at a later stage are the more difficult the larger the project. This tends to increase exploration costs during the early years of a project, as does the increasing effort necessary to find and delineate deposits in remote areas.

In most DCs, when faced with lower revenue, companies first cut expenditures for those activities, such as exploration, that do not contribute to sales, at least not directly and immediately. There are indications that exploration expenditures have declined, at least in constant money terms. If this trend continues for an extended period, problems of supply can emerge in the long run. The importance of continued exploration bears not only on the future global mineral supply but also on the future regional distribution of production. The traditional concentration of exploration in a few DCs appears to have remained unchanged or to have shifted even more towards them in recent years. In addition, exploration has increasingly concentrated on a few metals and minerals with apparent above average prospects, such as uranium, coal and molybdenum, and medium-size massive sulphide deposits while others were neglected. Low prices, increased stocks and other factors such as taxation, discourage investment because of insufficient return expectations; investment can also be delayed just because not enough cash flow is generated from which the required funds can be drawn when expectations improve. If the present practice of deferring capacity expansion continues for some time and if, simultaneously, some producing mines are closed, as has been the case in the past few years for some minerals, under-capacity could develop in a few years, with a consequent increase in prices and a new cycle of capacity expansion thereafter. If this stop-go behavior in certain minerals could be prevented, a stabilization of prices and revenue would be possible for the exporting countries.

In the past, technological progress has generally kept up with increased mineral consumption and the necessity to discover, mine and process lower-grade, deeper-lying and less beneficiable ores. Examples of major achievements abound. In the case of iron ore, fine-grained magnetic taconites, with grades as low as 25 per cent iron, as against over 50 per cent for 'direct shipping ore', have been successfully exploited on a large scale for 25 years. A new processing break-through − treatment of fine-grained, non-magnetic taconites − has proven its viability during more than two years of production at the Tilden project in Michigan. Direct reduction, an iron and steelmaking process that bypasses the traditional blast furnace, has been under consideration for more than a century but has reached commercial application only in recent years.

Another example of new processes developed and already brought to commercial scale is found in copper. The traditional concentration process, flotation of sulphide ores for subsequent smelting and refining, has been supplemented by processes for treatment of oxidized or mixed ores. Other developments − some at the commercial application stage, others still at the pilot-plant stage − include the hydrometallurgical treatment of sulphide concentrates (where the immediate product is cathode copper, thus bypassing smelting) and in-situ leaching.[10]

These examples illustrate the dynamism of technological progress and the response of technological development to economic and social requirements. This leads to the question of the driving forces behind technological innovation: the drive for as much self-sufficiency as possible in consuming countries − a long-standing practice in some, a more recent but growing concern in others; unprecedented concern over environmental protection, in some cases without regard to costs; increased knowledge of hitherto unknown types of mineral deposits that require new technology for exploitation; and the general striving for productivity gains and cost reduction because of the deteriorating quality of ore deposits and of rapidly growing energy costs.[11]

On the whole, hardly any new development is caused by one force alone, and progress in all fields, including technology, is inseparable from the general economic and social interaction within a country or the world.

Pollution abatement needs have induced the search for industrial application of various new technologies such as hydrometallurgical methods for copper and other metals, and the collection of sulphur dioxide in improved smelting processes and of hydrogen fluoride from phosphate plants and aluminium smelters. The development of hydrometallurgical processes to produce refined copper directly from sulphide concentrates noted earlier is at least partially motivated by concern over pollution.

Energy is of particular concern today since its costs have increased significantly during the past few years. The different energy consumption pattern for competing metals, such as copper and aluminium, can influence their substitutability over the long run. Energy availability and costs can also be decisive for the location of future processing facilities, in some cases to the disadvantage of countries that are primary mineral producers and which aspire to more local processing. Changed energy costs inevitably will accelerate the development of energy-saving technology in mining. How rapidly this takes place will depend on the trade-off of investment costs and energy expenditures. The development of energy-saving processes is clearly to the advantage of energy-deficient countries but makes little sense for those with energy surpluses, part of which are still being wasted, the flaring of natural gas being a case in point.

Many of the mineral deposits to be developed in the future are of lower grade, are less easily beneficiable, deeper lying and less easily accessible. Production costs will inevitably increase on the average if not counterbalanced by technological innovation. New technologies would be required even if mankind were to maintain the present consumption pattern. The desire for continued economic progress in all countries, especially the LDCs, implies rapidly increasing consumption of raw materials, which will be feasible only if technological progress remains strong. At present, research and development is virtually the monopoly of the DCs, adding to their power to influence world mineral developments. It is not so much the lack of arrangements for the transfer of technology that discriminates against LDCs in the long run; it is, rather, their limited capability to influence the course of technological development and to take part in the endeavor in order to ensure that innovations appropriate to their needs and resources receive adequate attention.

Ocean Mineral Resources

Undoubtedly the present increased interest in mining from the seabed will have a significant impact upon the global mineral industry and upon the mining industries of particular LDCs specializing in the production of those minerals which apparently can be recovered most easily from the ocean floor. Groups based in consumer DCs are already actively engaged in planning for exploration of these seabed resources.

Five consortia, including a large number of MNCs, have carried out large-scale prospecting and detailed exploration of prospective mining sites. Details of the consortia are reported in the general press and other publications.[12] The consortia have developed the necessary mining technology and are either in the process of testing the mining equipment or have already done so. They have probably selected suitable beneficiation processes and are expected to commence pilot plant tests in the near future.

One of the consortia — Ocean Management Incorporated, which includes INCO, the world's largest nickel-producing company, as well as firms from the USA, Japan and Germany — has decided to suspend further work and not to proceed with planned metallurgical tests. The reasons for this decision are said by INCO to relate to the poor market prospects for nickel and the continuing uncertainty about the legal régime that will apply to undersea mining. It appears, however, that other consortia take a more optimistic view. The Ocean Minerals group has announced tests of a mining system with a daily capacity of 1,000 tons of dry nodules, and this consortium plans to build a pilot plant to treat 50 tons of nodules per day over a period of from three to four years, at a cost of $4 million. The group reportedly plans to spend at least $150 million on ocean mining research and development in the 1978-81 period, in addition to some $60 million already spent on previous work.

There is general agreement that nodules to be mined in the 'first generation' operations will average approximately 1.3 per cent nickel, 1.1 per cent copper, 0.23 per cent cobalt and 25 per cent manganese. There are also strong indications that, because of the high cost of entry into ocean mining and the economies of scale that are likely, individual mining projects will need to have an annual capacity of not less than three million tons of dry nodules. Thus, assuming a recovery rate from processing of 90 per cent, each project would produce at least 35,000 tons of nickel, 30,000 tons of copper, 6,200 tons of cobalt and 675,000 tons of manganese annually.

At present world consumption levels, these amounts from a single project would represent about 20 per cent of the total demand for cobalt, five per cent for nickel, seven per cent for manganese and 0.4 per cent for copper. The actual impact, however, will be somewhat less, since demand will have increased by the time ocean-mining operations actually begin production in the 1980s. The impact will depend both on the timing of ocean-mining development and on the rate of growth in global consumption of the various metals. In both cases, considerable uncertainty exists. Past projections have uniformly been overly optimistic about the start-up date for ocean mining, which was originally foreseen as getting under way on a commercial scale in the 1970s. Similarly, recent projections of metal demand have been more conservative than those made in earlier years.

Reflecting these uncertainties, two alternative scenarios are presented for estimating the impact of ocean mining on land-based producers. As regards demand growth, 'high' and 'low' rates have been projected, as shown in Table 1.9.

Table 1.9. *Alternative demand projection for 1985, 1990 and 2000*

| | | Demand growth rate % | | Projected annual world demand[a] | | |
	Alternative	1975-85	1975-2000	1985	1990	2000
Nickel	A	3.1	2.8	905	1,054	1,314
	B	5.5	5.5	1,055	1,380	2,357
Manganese Ore	A	3.2	3.2	30,239	35,397	48,060
	B	4.3	4.3	30,987	38,247	58,269
Copper	A	2.9	2.8	11,341	13,084	16,839
	B	4.4	4.4	12,187	14,478	21,330
Cobalt	A	3.6	3.3	36,357	43,390	57,532
	B	4.9	4.9	37,810	48,026	77,488

Source: Calculations for alternative A made from data in W. Malenbaum, *World Demand for Raw Materials in 1985 and 2000* (Washington, D.C.: National Science Foundation, 1977); and for alternative B, from an extrapolation of historical growth rates.

a Units: nickel, manganese ore, and copper in thousands of tons; cobalt in tons per year. Since these are trend values, actual demand in any one year is likely to fluctuate.

Two alternatives have also been taken into account regarding the timing of ocean resource development: a rapid development case and a moderate development case. Although the rapid development case, which assumes two operations of three million tons (dry) each in 1985 and a total capacity of 16 million tons of (dry) nodules in 1990, must be considered unlikely, it has been included to indicate the potential impact if development activities are accelerated substantially in the very near future. The moderate development case is based on zero output in 1985 and four projects of three million tons of (dry) nodules each for a total of 12 million tons in 1990; for the year 2000 a doubling of the 1990 capacity was assumed in both cases, resulting in an annual production of 32 and 24 million tons of (dry) nodules, respectively.

Because production from ocean resources is considered unlikely before the late 1980s, the analysis is limited here to the years 1990 and 2000. The possible ranges of shares of supply from ocean mining are summarized below in percentages (the first number referring to the moderate development case and the second to the rapid development alternative).

| | 1990 Demand growth rate | | 2000 Demand growth rate | |
	High	Low	High	Low
Nickel	10-14	13-18	12-16	21-28
Manganese	16-21	17-23	21-28	25-33
Copper	0.8-1.1	0.9-1.2	1.1-1.5	1.4-1.9
Cobalt	52-69	57-76	64-85	86-115

It is obvious that the impact of ocean mining on the supply of copper, by far the most important of the four metals in terms of global production and export value, is at best marginal even if a rapid development of ocean resources and low demand growth rates occur simultaneously. On the other hand, cobalt would be severely affected under any assumption as soon as the first project started production. The markets for nickel and manganese will be moderately affected in the early years and increasingly so if ocean mining proceeds at the rate assumed here, or even more rapidly.

In addition to the uncertainties concerning the speed of development of ocean mining operations and the rate of metal demand growth, the impact of undersea mining may also be affected by the results of the UN Conference on the Law of the Sea, and especially by any quantitative limits set on ocean mining as the result of that Conference. Whatever the final determination, it seems certain that development of the new mining frontier on the ocean floor must be taken into account by mining LDCs.

CONCLUSIONS

In addition to the economic and social impacts discussed above, mining projects also are of prime interest for regional and national planning in most LDCs. The start of mining operations may involve major shifts in a country's infrastructure, including new transportation routes, new sources of power and new urbanized areas. In small countries, a major mining venture may generate more capital inflow than all other investments combined and may account for large proportions of gross domestic product, export earnings and government revenue. Mining is also an important part of planning for resource-based industrialization because of potential linkages between the mining sector and general economic development, both forward into mineral processing and metal fabrication, and backward into supply of goods and services for the mining industry.

The impact of mining projects is not limited to these economic and planning aspects. Increasingly, planners have become more aware in recent years of the potential social and environmental impacts of the mineral sector. Plans for mining projects in LDCs, whether those projects are carried out by state enterprises, national private capital or foreign firms, have increasingly stressed the employment of national personnel in all phases of the project as well as the related needs for education, training, and effective transfer of technology. In addition, greater attention is being focussed on health problems associated with mining, including problems that affect mine workers as well as the population of a country in general. Even though the above discussion has not dealt with all these aspects in full detail, they cannot be neglected if planning and project execution have the objective of contributing as much as possible to national development and to the growth of the standard of living of the entire population.

NOTES

1. *Mining and Manufacturing: Links in a Chain*, Mineral Bulletin MR-175 (Ottawa, Energy, Mines and Resources Canada, 1978), 6, 25.

2. *Joint study on international industrial co-operation* (UNIDO Publication, forthcoming 1980).

3. UNCTAD, *Monthly Commodity Price Bulletin* (December 1978). The index is a weighted average of the following minerals: copper − 41 per cent; iron ore − 18 per cent; phosphate rock − 11.1 per cent; tin − 10.9 per cent; aluminium − 10.6 per cent; zinc − 3.7 per cent; lead − 2 per cent; manganese ore − 1.9 per cent; and tungsten − 0.8 per cent.

4. R.F. Mikesell and E.H. Conant, *Know-how Transfers Through Employee Training: Cases of Natural Resources Industries* (New York: Fund for Multination Management Education, 1977), 14.

5. *Zambia Mining Yearbook 1976* (Kitwe: Copper Industry Service Bureau), 27.

6. Mikesell and Conant, *Know-how Transfers Through Employee Training*, 14.

7. *Zambia Mining Yearbook 1976*, 30.

8. *Occupational Health and Safety*, vol. 2 (Geneva: International Labor Organization, 1972), 900.

9. G.W. Gibbs and P. Pintus, *Health and Safety in the Canadian Mining Industry* (Kingston: Queen's University Center for Resource Studies, 1978), 32.

10. For a discussion of hydrometallurgical technology in relation to mining in developing countries, see, for example, L. Soto-Krebs, C. Molina-Vera and E. Domic-Mihovilovic, 'Progress in hydrometallurgy of low-grade copper ores', in UN Center for Natural Resources, Energy and Transportation, *Recent Advances in Mining and Processing of Low-Grade and Submarginal Mineral Deposits* (New York: Pergamon Press, 1976).

11. S. Dayton, 'The quiet revolution in the wide world of mineral processing', *Engineering and Mining Journal*, vol. 176 (June 1975), 87-194; W.R. Hopkins and A.J. Lyn, 'Anamax oxide plant: a new United States dimension in solvent extraction', *Engineering and Mining Journal*, vol. 178 (February 1977), 56-64.

12. For a recent listing see UN, Department of Public Information, *DESI Facts 79/1* (April 1979).

2

THE ALUMINIUM INDUSTRY
AND THE LDCs QUEST FOR EQUITY

C.E. Davis

Compared to other metals like iron, copper and tin which have been in use since antiquity, aluminium is in many respects 'modern', in that its commercial use has been fairly recent, being less than a hundred years.

The industry has grown from a dominance in the early years by three companies on both sides of the Atlantic — Aluminum Company of America (Alcoa) of the USA, and Aluminium Pechiney (Pechiney) and Swiss Aluminium Limited (Alusuisse) of Western Europe — to one in which there are many participants, including other transnational and smaller companies; Governments of DCs, CPEs, oil-rich States and even LDCs.

Notwithstanding these developments, the industry is dominated and to a large extent controlled by six major MNCs, variously called the 'Big Six' or (analogous to the 'Seven Sisters' in oil) the 'Six Sisters'. They comprise the three early ones mentioned above, i.e. Alcoa, Pechiney and Alusuisse, plus three later powerful additions: Alcan Aluminium Limited (Alcan), Kaiser Aluminum and Chemical Corporation (Kaiser), and Reynolds Metals Company (Reynolds).

Four of the six are North American centered — three in the USA (Alcoa, Kaiser and Reynolds), one in Canada (Alcan) and two (Pechiney and Alusuisse) in Western Europe.

These six companies are involved in all stages of the aluminium industry — from bauxite processing to aluminium fabrication. As Table 2.1 shows, together they own 50% of three of the major stages of the industry.

This dominance of the industry is not confined only to percentage ownership of the various stages of the industry. Perhaps more emphatically and importantly is their control of technology. To illustrate: most of the existing refineries and aluminium smelters have been built on technology provided by these six MNCs. Indeed, despite the existence of many new operators in the industries, these MNCs will be mainly responsible for providing technology for the new plants that are being built or planned.

It is interesting to note that, with the exception of the USSR, some companies from Japan and one or two 'small' US companies, such as Southwire Aluminum, the technology of the smelting phase of the industry is virtually controlled by the six major corporations.

Notes to this chapter may be found on page 60.

Table 2.1. *Approximate Ownership of Primary Aluminium, Alumina Refinery and Bauxite Capacities by the Six Major Aluminium Companies*[a]

Company	Aluminium Smelters	Alumina Refineries	Bauxite Mines
Alcoa	13.1	17.8	17.7
Alcan	11.2	10.3	6.8
Reynolds	8.4	8.0	6.0
Kaiser	7.8	9.1	13.2
Pechiney	7.1	6.7	4.9
Alusuisse	4.8	3.8	4.9
Total	52.4	55.7	53.5

a Summary of data from Stewart Spector, *Aluminium Industry Report* (6th September 1979) for aluminium, and Carlos Varsavsky, *Industry Studies of Non-Ferrous Industries* (Draft Report for UN Center on Transnational Activities) for alumina and bauxite.

Table 2.2. *Location of Aluminium Smelters, Alumina Refineries and Bauxite Mines in LDCs and DCs*

Location	Aluminium Smelters	Alumina Refineries	Bauxite Mines
LDCs	11.9	20.6	50
DCs	88.1	79.4	50

This applies to the development of new uses for metals, incorporating such sophisticated techniques as alloying, welding and the like.

The same can be said of the alumina stage where, with the exception of Hungary (rather than the USSR), they have virtual dominance over the Bayer technology.

Their technology dominance is not restricted to engineering and science but, very importantly, includes the area of marketing. Indeed, their dominance is such that a pessimistic word from them has made Governments defer plans for establishing aluminium-based industries and bankers hesitate to finance the establishment of these industries.

Apart from the dominance by the six major producers, the industry is charac- terized by concentration of the finishing stages in DCs, as is illustrated in Table 2.2. Bauxite mine capacity is evenly divided between DCs and LDCs, but this does not tell the full story, as within the LDCs the big producers (as well as other companies) own significant percentages of equity. Even when LDC Governments hold significant equity, production and marketing are still largely in the control of the companies. Two examples of this are: (1) the Republic of Guinea where the Government owns 49% equity but production is shared in its entirety by the HALCO consortium in which each party takes bauxite in pro- portion to its respective equity; (2) in Jamaica, the Government owns 51% of the Kaiser and Reynolds mining operations but production from these mines (for now and in the forseeable future) is determined not by the partnerships but the companies' needs.

Another feature of the industry is that the markets are located overwhelmingly in the DCs. This is understandable since aluminium consumption is correlated positively with a country's level of development. Nevertheless, LDCs are wholly exposed to the consumption patterns of the DCs.

For the time being, the aluminium industry is largely about bauxite and to some extent, alumina, and most plans for LDC development have to be laid on the basis of one or both of these commodities.

Bauxite is by far the most important aluminium raw material. Although there are alternatives, some of which are being used (e.g. nepheline-syenite and alunite), and research is being undertaken into others (e.g. kaolins, shales and anorthosite), the best critical opinion is that bauxite will continue to be the major and dominant source material for aluminium manufacture well into the twenty-first century.

The reasons for this are not very different from those advanced earlier by the author.[1] They include: (1) abundance; (2) availability; (3) considerable knowledge of the 'bauxite technology', the Bayer process; (4) the impact of increasing energy costs which serve to enhance (rather than worsen) the competitiveness of bauxite vis-à-vis alternatives; and (5) the capital costs involved in investing in alternative alumina producing or (if realizable) direct reduction methods.

Thus, the major issue for the producers of bauxite — particularly those LDCs to which it is a critical economic parameter — is not whether the resource is needed as a source of aluminium but whether greater benefits (inequity being assumed) can be derived from its exploitation.

Equity can be obtained in a variety of ways — some singly, some combined. They include: (1) greater direct revenues from exploiting the material; (2) the development of 'downstream' activities such as alumina processing, smelting and fabrication; (3) marketing diversification; and (4) the development of linkage industries.

The purpose of this paper is to discuss some of the problems experienced by LDCs in trying to achieve equity by using one or more of the approaches listed above. In addition, it will analyze the special effects of increased energy prices on current efforts to achieve equity.

The paper will draw heavily on the Jamaican experience since this is the area with which the author is most familiar, and also it typifies the situation of the majority of LDCs.

ATTEMPTS TO EARN GREATER REVENUES

Since the onset of the 1970s, spurred in part by the OPEC example (and effects) as well as by the consequences of other imported inflation, bauxite-producing LDCs have tried two main approaches to earn greater revenues from the industry. One (exemplified by Guyana) is the nationalization of the local industry; the other (exemplified by Jamaica) is by way of the imposition of levies.

Both approaches (especially the Jamaican) were initially very successful, due partly to the fortuitous circumstance of 1974 being a year of great demand for aluminium and partly to the inability of MNCs to mobilize alternative strategies within a short time frame. The MNCs were not happy with the levy, however.

Despite their discontent, the MNCs (perhaps anticipating that others would follow suit and that market demand would tend to create shortages rather than surpluses) duly signed agreements with the Government of Jamaica (Alcoa in 1976, Kaiser and Reynolds in 1977, and Alcan in 1978), *confirming* the levy rate of 7.5 per cent based on the price of primary aluminium.

Jamaica and the other Caribbean producers which obtained similar agreements — Dominican Republic, Haiti and Suriname — thus won the first round. They had gained acceptance for an important principle — a *meaningful* indexation (indexations had occurred before but had not been meaningful) between a raw material and the finished product.

Following this early success, a number of factors came into being, including: (1) the recession that began near the end of 1974 and which led to reduced demand for bauxite and alumina; (2) expanded mine production in Guinea and Australia; (3) differential attitudes to prices by bauxite producers in spite of the International Bauxite Association (IBA) and of the fact that some producing countries had equity in bauxite operations; and (4) MNC development of the technological ability to substitute one type of bauxite for another — hence the 'uniqueness' of (say) Jamaican bauxite for a particular alumina plant no longer held.

The effect of all this was a severe drop in production by the 'price leaders' — Jamaica, Dominican Republic, Haiti and Suriname — and increased production elsewhere (Table 2.3).

Table 2.3. *Bauxite Production ('000 metric tonnes) of Selected Countries 1974-1978*

Country	1974	1975	1976	1977	1978
Australia	19,994	20,958	24,085	26,074	24,300
Dominican Republic	1,477	785	516	722	757
Guinea	5,010	7,674	11,316	10,871	11,648
Haiti	641	522	660	588	565
Jamaica	15,166	11,570	10,306	11,433	11,739
Suriname	6,864	4,751	4,588	4,951	5,113

Notes
Data with the exception of Jamaica's are from IBA.
Data for Jamaica are from the Jamaica Bauxite Institute.

Guyana, which had nationalized its industry, found that it had to sell below prices that were normally desirable and in fact had to depend heavily on non-metal grade bauxite (of which it is a major producer) to carry the rest of the industry.

Jamaica, in attempting to 'hold the line', initially tried various *ad hoc* approaches such as rebates in special circumstances, pressures inside the IBA and bilaterally with other bauxite producers. The prospect of continued reduction in production, of possible closures of some operations, and disinvestments, however, forced Jamaica to renegotiate the levy set in 1974 and to introduce a new basis[2] dependent on production by each company, and an aluminium price which varied to as much as 30 per cent less than what had been proposed in 1974. (The formula was structured so that production had to be close to capacity and the metal price very high to get reductions over 20 per cent).

The irony of it all is that while these modifications were being made, the parent companies of the MNCs operating in Jamaica in 1978 and 1979 recorded their greatest overall profits for a long time (Table 2.4).

Table 2.4. *Income and Revenues by the Four Major North American Aluminium Companies 1975-1979 (million $)*

	1975	1976	1977	1978	1979
Alcoa					
Net Income	64.8	143.8	195.2	312.7	504.6
Revenues	2,306	2,924	3,416	4,052	4,800
Alcan					
Net Income	35.0	44.0	201.5	289.4	427.5
Revenues	2,313	2,671	3,058	3,711	4,380
Kaiser					
Net Income	94.7	44.5	112.1	145.5	232.2
Revenues	1,578	1,852	2,180	2,466	2,900
Reynolds					
Net Income	60	75	86.3	117.8	177
Revenues	1,731	2,132	2,392	2,829	3,300

In addition, Jamaica's general economic problems and its acceptance of the IMF program resulted among other things in a devaluation of its currency from J$1 = US$1.10 to J$1.78 = US$1, with the consequence that earnings from the industry were further eroded. Moreover, contrary to what the IMF may have expected, bauxite exports did not rise as a result of devaluation.

ATTEMPTS TO DEVELOP DOWNSTREAM ACTIVITIES

It goes without saying that an economy accrues more benefits with each further stage of processing of a particular commodity. For example, the contribution to foreign exchange earnings of the alumina-exporting sector of the Jamaican industry (excluding levies and royalties which are the same whether bauxite is processed or exported) is approximately three times that of the bauxite-exporting sector for the same volume of bauxite mined. To illustrate the value-added point in another way: the relative values of bauxite, alumina and aluminium at current rates (very little bauxite is in fact marketed) are in the ratio 1:3:10. It has therefore been a major element of policy for bauxite and alumina producers to try to increase further processing in their respective countries.

Bearing in mind its lack of indigenous energy resources, which ruled out the establishment of aluminium smelting, Jamaica as early as 1974 planned an alumina plant of ca. 600,000 tonnes per annum capacity to supply alumina for smelters in Mexico (with which it was to be associated) and Algeria; and to Trinidad & Tobago and Guyana in a regional smelter plan to be based respectively on natural gas and hydro-electric power from Trinidad & Tobago and Guyana, and bauxite (alumina) from Jamaica and Guyana.

Notwithstanding much deliberation, including several meetings at the levels of Heads of Governments, Ministers and technocrats, neither the smelter in Mexico nor the regional one got off the ground. Although it is difficult to ascribe precise reasons to these failures to implement, the following appeared significant from the author's vantage position.

(1) The lack of certainty by oil/gas-rich States in determining:
   (a) the use to which they wished to put their oil and gas; and
   (b) how much they wanted to charge for it.
(2) The painting of a pessimistic scenario (by MNCs among others) with respect to aluminium demand/supply and price in the early 1980s made all new projects look risky.
(3) The unwillingness of the various parties to recognize that such projects need some level of 'subsidy' (compare this with the US Government's support of Kaiser and Reynolds in the early years) before they are fully established. Hence, producers of bauxite (alumina) on the one hand, and energy on the other, expected the maximum from their respective resource.
(4) The high capital costs (including technology) required for these projects vis-à-vis alternative uses that would provide more employment in countries facing chronic unemployment and, presumably, more foreign exchange earnings.

In retrospect, the deferral of these projects proved to be a serious miscalculation. The market for aluminium has been strong and prices have been good. Further, it is expected that the trend will hold at least until the end of the 1980s. Perhaps more importantly, the plants would have been constructed during times of relatively low inflation rates as against the current high rates.

One LDC — albeit an oil-exporting one — which did not make this miscalculation was Venezuela. Notwithstanding its enormous financial strength, Venezuela experienced sufficient pressures to also defer its project. The country proceeded with its plans, however, and completed the project in spite of some setbacks. VENALUM now produces metal for export, and the industry is the second highest earner of foreign exchange for Venezuela.

Both Mexico and Trinidad & Tobago have now reactivated their smelter plans and it is expected that these will be implemented. As a consequence, Jamaica may be able to proceed with further alumina expansion plans.

Guyana has been discussing the financing of its massive hydro-electric and smelter program with the World Bank, but in view of its scale and the pace at which institutions like the World Bank analyze such projects, early implementation is not anticipated.

Apart from the prospects of supplying alumina to Mexico and Trinidad & Tobago, Jamaica has been having some success in establishing an independent alumina plant. This is a consequence of agreements with: (a) the USSR to supply 250,000 tonnes per annum; (b) Algeria, 150,000 tonnes per annum; (c) Iraq, 150,000 tonnes per annum. At the time of writing, the contract with Iraq has been signed. That country has gone further and given Jamaica a 'soft' loan of US$50 million towards the project. In addition, Algeria has agreed in principle to take an equity in the plant, principally to lessen the financial burden on Jamaica.

The developments with respect to this plant show that much can be achieved when LDCs cooperate among themselves. Although hurdles such as financing the rest of the project still have to be cleared, the fact that this cooperation has been achieved is a major step forward and may represent an unprecedented breakthrough.

ATTEMPTS AT MARKET DIVERSIFICATION

Given the structure of the world aluminium industry, bauxite and alumina-producing LDCs face an imposing task in getting new markets. Yet, if they are to break from the stranglehold of utter dependence on the MNCs and on the markets of a few countries, they must diversify their market base. Some of the difficulties they faced are the following.

(1) The relatively small capacities owned (e.g. Guyana owns an alumina plant of 300,000 tonnes per annum, and Jamaica's small equity ownership in two alumina plants amounts to 100,000 tonnes per annum), versus the large capacities held by the major companies. Hence, from the point of view of pricing, they are up against stiff competition from the majors who (depending on their marketing strategies) can price on the basis of average or marginal cost considerations.

(2) Their alumina is sourced from one location, compared to the diversified locations of the majors. Alcoa, for example, can feasibly deploy alumina from its plants in Australia, Suriname, Jamaica or the USA so as to minimize transportation costs to a particular location; on the other hand, an LDC such as Guyana must of necessity supply from one source.

(3) Several of the majors have their own shipping lines (e.g. Alcan, Alcoa, Reynolds); as a consequence, they are much less vulnerable to the often volatile freight markets. An LDC may in some instances have to supply contracts on a cif or c&f basis.

These considerations have proved crucial in LDC attempts to diversify market outlets. As mentioned earlier, Guyana met severe competition in its attempts to market bauxite and alumina and had to price accordingly. In fact, some of its marketing has been done through a major broker, Philipp Brothers of New York.

Even LDC plans to produce aluminium (a more easily marketable commodity than bauxite and alumina) have met with stringent terms such as heavy discounting by MNCs and by various companies in developed countries. This problem has now abated somewhat, however, due to the current strong market for aluminium.

ATTEMPTS TO DEVELOP LINKAGE INDUSTRIES

The establishment of linkage industries has been a basic strategy for LDCs seeking equity from the industry. One that has been given much consideration in Jamaica is the establishment of a caustic soda plant to supply the requirements of the industry. The value of the product used by the Jamaican industry is in the order of US$40 million per annum, a significant amount in an industry where the value-added outside of the levy is currently less than $125 million.

Evaluations have been made of the electrolytic process but Jamaica's lack of indigenous energy resources and the high cost of energy, mean that it is unlikely to be viable.

The older (and largely discarded) Solvay Soda-Ash process is now being examined as a possible alternative.

The inability to develop the aluminium industry in the Caribbean Community, where at least one member has adequate oil and gas, is further evidence of the failure of LDCs to implement certain programs that are well within their capability.

THE IMPACT OF ENERGY

The aluminium industry is a heavy user of energy. The production of each tonne of metal (from about 1.95 tonnes of alumina) requires about 15,000 kilowatt hours of electricity. This has had a major influence on the location of aluminium smelters and, with the escalation in energy prices, the influence will become even greater.

For several bauxite-producing countries, the price of energy — even before the OPEC 1973 increases — rules out the possibility of building aluminium smelters. While Jamaica has toyed with the idea, the fact that it had to compete with cheap hydro-electric and other energy sources elsewhere has made the proposition (despite some early optimism) unattractive. There are two obvious disadvantages: the cost of imported oil and, unlike Japan, the lack of a local market.

Apart from totally ruling out any consideration of smelters, in some LDCs the increases in the price of oil have had many negative effects.

In the first place, a significant percentage of foreign exchange earnings are used to pay for oil. The Jamaican case (admittedly perhaps the most extreme) serves to illustrate the point. In 1974 (after the first round of major OPEC price increases and the imposition of the production levy), Jamaica earned a total of some US$285 million from the bauxite and alumina industry ($185 million from levies and royalties and $100 million from miscellaneous local expenditures such as wages, salaries, etc.) and purchased its oil requirements for some $140 million.

In contrast, it is estimated that in 1980 total earnings from the industry will be in the order of $325 million (due to reduced production, lower levy and devaluation) while the oil bill (on the basis of 1979 level of imports) will be about $320 million.

In order to pay for oil as well as for other vital raw materials, food, drugs, etc., Jamaica has had to borrow heavily to supplement its foreign exchange earnings. The effect of all this is reflected in the estimates for 1980 which show that debt repayment is in the order of $335 million. In addition, oil ($320 million) and non-oil imports (which have been severely restricted) ($396 million) will leave a major foreign exchange deficit which has to be supplemented by further borrowing.

Other major bauxite-producing LDCs such as Guyana, Suriname and Guinea, are oil importers and must undoubtedly be feeling similar (if not as devastating) effects as Jamaica.

One direct consequence which the heavy borrowing has on the development of the local aluminium industry is that the lowering of the country's credit rating makes it more difficult to finance projects.

The escalation in the price of energy has another major effect on the pattern of development of the industry. Other than in earlier years, most of the major developments are now taking place outside the major market economies, two of which constitute Jamaica's major markets for bauxite and alumina, viz: North America and Western Europe. Rather, developments are taking place and/or are being planned in Australia, the Middle East, Venezuela and Brazil (as well as the USSR).

The building of smelters in Australia, Brazil and Venezuela offers no market opportunities for countries like Jamaica which are restricted to exporting only bauxite and alumina of the range of aluminium commodities, since the others have considerable reserves of bauxite and plan to exploit them.

The only real opportunities open in this current situation are the Middle East and the USSR.

Jamaica has been making some progress in these areas but has of necessity to modify its approaches as a result of the long and expensive freight distances.

CONCLUSION

The discussion above highlights some of the imposing problems which the LDCs face in seeking equity from an industry of which many of them form part but from which the benefits have been almost minimal.

The grudging acceptance of the principle of a meaningful indexation of the raw material to a finished product and actual increased revenues have enabled some LDCs at least to survive. There has also been a much greater awareness of the industry, and the development of a technological base.

Attempts to gain equity through fuller integration have met with frustration due, among other things, to the weakening of the LDC resolve to push on with the projects and to the massive capital outlays necessary vis-à-vis employment.

The escalation of energy prices has contributed to the difficulties: (1) by eroding the foreign exchange reserves of some LDCs; (2) as a consequence, by putting them heavily in debt, thus eroding their financial credibility; and (3) by enhancing developments in energy-rich countries, some of which have bauxite and alumina, thereby restricting marketing opportunities for LDCs who can only produce these commodities.

All these problems, however, should not cause the LDCs to despair, but rather to find ways for further analysis so that they may evolve suitable strategies by which to achieve equity. The first of these strategies should be to come to cooperation among themselves.

NOTES

1. *Alternatives to Bauxite* (Special Publication Geological Society of Jamaica, 1974).
2. This is detailed in Jamaican Government Ministry Paper No. 46 of 1979.

3

THE STRUCTURE OF THE WORLD COPPER INDUSTRY

R.F. Mikesell

A substantial portion of the world's copper production is in the DCs, which in recent years have been producing about 45 per cent of the output of the market economy countries (MECs), as contrasted with 55 per cent for the LDCs. This is an important fact to keep in mind in discussing questions such as the potential for cartels and international commodity agreements in copper. It might also be said that the number of copper producing countries in the world is expanding; and with the entry into the market of Panama, Iran and Argentina, together with substantial expansion of production in the future by Papua New Guinea (PNG) and Mexico, the predominant position of the principal CIPEC countries — Chile, Peru, Zaire and Zambia — will be eroded.

There are several mines that are likely to come onstream between now and 1985, including the Sar Cheshmeh mine in Iran and La Caridad in Mexico, which are virtually completed. These will eventually be joined by new mines in PNG, Panama, Argentina and Chile, for which the feasibility studies have either been completed or are in process.

Concentration in copper mining has decreased markedly in the past 30 years or so. Shortly after World War II four mining firms accounted for about 60 per cent of world output (excluding the USSR) and eight firms for 70 per cent of world output. By 1974 the four largest private copper producers — Kennecott, Newmont, Phelps Dodge and Riotinto Zinc — had a majority ownership interest in less than 19 per cent of the mine copper output of the MECs, and ten privately owned companies had a majority interest in less than 35 per cent of the world's mine copper output from the MECs. Ten other privately owned companies are majority owners of an additional ten per cent of the copper output of the MECs.

Russia and the East European CPEs as a group are self-sufficient in copper. Poland, which is the largest CPE producer after the USSR, has been expanding copper producing capacity rapidly and may become an important exporter of copper to the MECs in the next decade.

Much of the material in this chapter has been taken from R.F. Mikesell, *The World Copper Industry* (Baltimore: The Johns Hopkins University Press for Resources for the Future Inc., 1979).

Notes to this chapter may be found on page 69.

In contrast with bauxite and some of the other minerals, there is a high degree of processing of copper in the LDCs, particularly at the smelter stage. Refining is still concentrated in the DCs, but the LDCs smelt and refine over half of their own mine output.

The copper industry is far less vertically integrated than the bauxite-aluminum industry and, among the LDC copper producers, government-owned or controlled mining enterprises tend to dominate. There are, of course, a number of countries where foreign investors produce all or the bulk of the copper output, as is the case with Indonesia, Peru and PNG. Government enterprises constitute the principal producers, however, in Chile, Zaire and Zambia.

THE NATURE OF THE MARKET FOR COPPER

The world copper industry is on the whole fairly competitive with most of the copper entering into international trade sold at prices governed by quotations on the LME. Even in the USA, where the dominant primary copper producers have been able to set their own prices, often at levels well above or below prices in the world metal exchanges, producers' prices have recently followed rather closely prices quoted on the London and New York metal markets.

Copper entering into international trade takes the form of concentrates containing 25 to 30 per cent copper, blister copper which has been smelted and contains 98 per cent or more copper, and refined copper. Most copper is sold on the basis of annual contracts for delivery, but with the price paid by the buyer at the time of delivery varying with the current price on the LME. For concentrates and blister, refining and/or smelting charges are deducted by the buyer, but the seller will be given credit for byproducts such as gold or silver frequently contained in copper concentrates. Copper prices have been subject to very sharp fluctuations, mainly as a consequence of variations in demand generated by the business cycle, speculative buying, or buying by consumers in anticipation of rising prices. Once inventories have been built up to a substantial level, consumers may draw down inventories for a considerable period with the expectation of a further decline in prices. Inventories are held all along the line, not only by producers and consumers of refined copper, but also by consumers of semi-fabricated products and even of fabricated copper products. This contributes to rapid shifts in the demand for copper. Gyrating copper prices have led to a demand for International Commodity Agreements (ICAs), negotiations for which have been going on at UNCTAD in Geneva for some time, or to collusive action on the part of producers for the establishment of a world producers' price, perhaps something like the US producers' price established by the large American primary copper companies.

CHARACTERISTICS OF WORLD SUPPLY

Copper mining is characterized by a long gestation period between the initial outlays for exploration and the beginning of commercial production. A good example is the Cuajone mine in Southern Peru, which only recently went into production as one of the largest copper mines in the world, producing nearly 180,000 metric tons of copper annually. Although the existence of copper mineralization in the area where the mine is located has been known for decades, the claim was acquired by a US mining firm from a local Peruvian prospector in the 1940s, and a couple of million dollars was spent on exploration. Intensive exploration did not begin until the early 1960s, however, and the feasibility study and the decision to construct the mine were not made until 1969. Mine construction began in 1970 and required nearly seven years to complete. The original cost estimate was $350 million, but it actually cost over twice that amount. This is perhaps an extreme case, but for a large mine ten to 12 years between the initial expenditure and the beginning of commercial production is not at all unusual.

Each of the several stages in mine exploration requires a separate decision as to whether to go ahead with additional investment expenditures, culminating in the feasibility study covering geological, engineering and economic analysis required for a final decision to construct the mine. Even at this point a favorable decision on the feasibility of the mine will not insure its construction until the financing has been mobilized, long-term contracts for the output negotiated and, in some cases, the mine development agreement has been negotiated with the government. In recent years, however, companies have been demanding an agreement with the host government before undertaking intensive exploration which requires outlays running to millions of dollars.

As more copper ore bodies are discovered and developed, exploration must necessarily become more difficult, costly and sophisticated in terms of the techniques required for finding commercial deposits whose existence is not observable by traditional surface methods of exploration. Exploration involves a high degree of technology, much of which is the property of large mining MNCs. Exploration activities in LDCs have declined considerably in recent years and this has been a subject of considerable concern by the mining industry, governments and the UN, which has held several conferences on the subject recently. Although copper producing capacity in the LDCs has been growing during the 1970s at a faster rate than capacity in the DCs, much of the new capacity being developed consists of ore bodies that were identified and explored decades ago by the mining MNCs. Considerable work in identifying ore bodies has also been done by the UNDP, but the UN, including the UN Revolving Fund for Exploration, lacks the resources for the intensive exploration required to determine whether a deposit is commercially feasible. For large mines, exploration costs through the feasibility study may range from $20 million to $30 million, and much of this is very high-risk capital.

With the exhaustion of older high-grade ore bodies, most of the new mines coming onstream consist of large porphyry deposits of relatively low grade, which necessarily require very large mine complexes costing a billion dollars or more. This has complicated the problem of financing – a subject that will be taken up later. With reduced interest on the part of mining MNCs in exploration and development, there is major concern as to whether the copper and other mineral resources of LDCs will be developed at a rate warranted by their comparative advantage and their need to expand exports. In the case of copper at least, if output does not expand in LDCs, there are plenty of copper reserves in DCs.

Some of the copper producer DCs are experiencing constraints on increasing capacity as a consequence of environmental restrictions. Three principal environmental problems may be cited. First, copper smelters pollute the air with sulfur dioxide and other gases and they are being forced either to reduce emissions by the use of expensive equipment, or to close down. Secondly, open pit copper mines may be a beautiful sight to miners, but most people regard them as ugly scars on the land. Finally, in the USA at least, large amounts of federal lands have been removed from exploration and development for natural wilderness areas and parks.

Many LDCs are more willing to accept the environmental consequences of mining than developed countries, and this is particularly true for smelters which LDCs seem anxious to have and which DCs want to avoid. Environmental restrictions on traditional pyrometallurgical smelting have helped to encourage the development of hydrometallurgical methods based on leeching and electrolytic processes. These processes are still in the experimental stage, but show considerable promise in reducing pollution in the copper industry. All of the factors that have been discussed above, including the low level of exploration, the high and increasing costs of copper mines, the problem of financing, and the environmental consequences of mines and smelters, raise questions regarding the rate of expansion of copper producing capacity in relation to demand over the next couple of decades.

The supply of copper tends to be relatively inelastic in the short run, largely because of the high overhead costs and long gestation period of copper producing capacity. This is, of course, one of the reasons for the sharp movements in copper prices with changes in demand.

CHARACTERISTICS OF DEMAND

One of the reasons why an investment of a billion dollars or more in a new copper mine entails substantial risks is to be found in the uncertainties relating to the long-run demand for copper. In the author's *The World Copper Industry*, projections are reviewed of the annual rates of growth in demand for copper from 1977 to 1990, or the year 2000. Projections ranged from 2.8 per cent per year by W. Malenbaum (a wellknown scholar from the University of Pennsylvania), to 4.3 per cent per year by the UN, about four per cent per year by the US Bureau of Mines, and 3.6 per cent per year by the World Bank. The rate of growth in demand by the DCs is generally projected at a much lower rate than in the past, about four per cent over the 1955-57 period, while the rate of growth for LDCs is expected to be considerably higher, partly because the rate of growth in their GNP is likely to be higher and partly because of the higher rate of growth of consumption of electrical appliances and the expansion of telecommunications and other copper-using industries.

Some of the projections are based on extrapolations of past trends adjusted for expected changes in the rates of growth of copper-intensive industries. The more disaggregated the demand analysis, the better the results are likely to be, provided the growth projections and the production functions of copper using industries are correctly anticipated. Important also is the elasticity of substitution between copper and other materials such as aluminium, and the expected prices of these substitute materials.

The projected rate of growth of copper consumption is substantially less than that of aluminium and its raw material bauxite, and aluminium is the principal rival of copper in many industrial uses. Projections for the rate of growth in demand for aluminium are 50 to 100 per cent higher than those for copper. Because there are many substitutes for copper, the long-run price elasticity of demand for copper is relatively high, and because the world is endowed with large copper resources widely dispersed among DCs and LDCs, the long-run elasticity of supply of copper is also fairly high.

Another factor influencing the demand for primary copper is the high proportion of copper scrap in the total supply of copper consumption. In the USA at least, scrap constitutes almost half of copper consumption — see chapter 17. Higher prices of copper and the encouragement of scrap collection throughout the world could increase substantially the contribution of recycled materials to consumption. Moreover, the world's copper resources, including both reserves and probable and hypothetical reserves, appear ample to satisfy world demand for many decades in the future. Copper resources on land will eventually be supplemented by the large amounts of copper in seabed nodules, which alone could nearly double current measured reserves of copper.

There are a number of technological developments which may greatly affect the demand for copper. One of these is the future of optic fibers in communications, while another is the demand for lighter materials in automotive radiators.

THE POSSIBILITY OF A COPPER CARTEL

It is necessary now to analyze the possibility of a copper producers' cartel, or more broadly, the ability of a group of copper producing countries acting in collusion to control world copper prices. The ability of a group of producers of a commodity such as copper to increase substantially the revenue of the group by limiting production or exports in order to achieve an increase in the world price depends on several technical factors as well as non-technical ones. The technical factors may include the proportion of the world's supply controlled by the producers' cartel in the commodity, the price elasticity of world demand for the commodity in question, and the elasticity of supply with respect to price of non-members of the cartel. These variables may be put in a formula for determining the elasticity of demand for the output of a cartel as follows:

$$E_{dc} = \frac{1}{m} \times E_{dw} - \frac{1}{m} \times (1-m) \times E_{sr}$$

where E_{dc} = elasticity of demand for the output of the cartel;
       m = portion of world output supplied by the cartel;
       E_{dw} = elasticity of world demand for the commodity;
       E_{sr} = elasticity of supply of non-cartel sources of the commodity.
Unless E_{dc} is less than unity, any cutback in sales by the cartel will not increase its revenue.

There are various possible groups of countries suggested as potential members of a producers' cartel in copper. The most frequently mentioned group is comprised of the regular members of CIPEC (Chile, Peru, Zambia, Zaire, Indonesia). CIPEC's associate members (Australia, Mauritania, PNG and Yugoslavia) are not subject to the decisions of CIPEC with respect to exports, but it is conceivable that some of them might join a cartel. It should be emphasized that CIPEC is not now a cartel and so far as is known there is no agreement among members to try to control world prices by supply cutbacks. Efforts were made in 1974 and 1975 to stem the decline in world copper prices by reductions in production or exports, but without success.

Although the world demand for copper is estimated to be quite inelastic with respect to price over the short run, say -0.2 to -0.4 (the short run being regarded as less than a year), the elasticity of world demand for copper is generally estimated at between -0.5 and -1.0 for a period of two or three years. It might not pay a cartel to increase its revenues by raising world prices for only a year or so if by doing so it would stimulate an expansion of world supply which would result in much lower prices later on.

At the present time, the regular members of CIPEC control about 30 per cent of the output of copper of the MECs. Assume that the elasticity of world demand for copper over a two-year period is -0.5 and the elasticity of supply of non-CIPEC is 0.3 (estimates which are in line with those made in recent econometric studies).[1] Utilizing these figures in the above formula results in elasticity of demand for CIPEC's output of -2.1, which would mean that in order to increase the world price by one per cent the CIPEC countries would need to reduce their output by 2.1 per cent. This, of course, would be disastrous from the standpoint of CIPEC's revenue, which would decline substantially with, say, a 20 per cent cutback in exports. Even in the unlikely event that CIPEC could form a producers' cartel that would include all the LDCs, it would not be able to sustain a price rise which would improve substantially their revenue for more than a couple of years, following which supplies from DCs would increase so that the cartel would need to reduce its exports progressively in order to sustain the cartel price, with a consequent loss in revenue.

The same principles can be applied to prospective producers' cartels in other non-fuel minerals. A cartel among the major producers of manganese, cobalt or chromite could probably be fairly successful for a number of years on technical grounds, but there are political factors which limit the possibility of forming cartels. A manganese cartel involving South Africa, Australia, Brazil, India and Gabon would consist of rather strange bedfellows. The same could be said of a world chromite cartel consisting of South Africa, Turkey and the USSR.

AN INTERNATIONAL COMMODITY AGREEMENT IN COPPER

In part because of the infeasibility of controlling world prices through collusive action — something that not all LDCs agree upon in any case — those LDCs which export copper have concentrated their efforts on the formation of an ICA in copper which would include both producing and consuming countries, both DCs and LDCs. The type of ICA which is being negotiated in UNCTAD would involve a buffer stock rather than primary reliance on export and import quotas. A number of LDCs, however, believe that a buffer stock should be supplemented by controls over production, something generally rejected by the USA and Canada.

The negotiations in UNCTAD have revealed certain disagreements regarding an international copper buffer stock even though most of the DCs appear now to support such an arrangement in principle. First, the DCs want a buffer stock arrangement that is capable of moderating sharp rises in copper prices as well as maintaining prices above a floor, and they believe this should be done wholly by means of buffer stock purchases and sales, and not supplemented by export restrictions by the producer countries. Spokesmen for the LDCs have argued that it will be necessary to supplement a buffer stock by controls over production or exports, since otherwise the buffer stock would be too costly. By too costly they mean too large a financial fund to support the price above a floor. But if a price is supported by quantitative controls, the buffer stock will not accumulate enough of the commodity to prevent the price from penetrating the ceiling price. There are also differences of opinion regarding how a floor price should be determined and whether it should be tied to the international price index.

Several econometric studies have been made for simulating the operation of a copper buffer stock over historical periods, including the 1970s when prices were subject to wide fluctuations. The purpose of these studies is to determine the size of a buffer stock in terms of both money and copper metal that would have been necessary to maintain copper prices within a range of ten or 15 per cent above and below the long-term trend. One of the most interesting of these studies was that prepared by Charles River Associates (CRA) for UNCTAD.[2] The study was designed to answer the following questions: (1) would procedures utilizing a buffer stock and supply restrictions have stabilized prices in the 1953-76 period; and (2) what would the buffer stock or supply restrictions cost and how large would the stocks or supply restrictions have to be?

In brief, the results of the CRA study were scarcely encouraging to those advocating the use of a buffer stock for maintaining price fluctuations within reasonable margins. Using a number of simulations based on several possible rules governing the buffer stock operations, the CRA study found that for every simulation the LME copper wirebar broke through the ceiling in the mid-1960s, and that any rigid *a priori* rules would have proved unsuccessful. The CRA study found that a stock with unlimited resources of money and copper would have sold some 22 million tons of copper (about $24 billion at 50 cents per pound), over the 1964-76 period in order to maintain the ceiling price on a slowly rising trend. Since only a fraction of this amount would have been accumulated by the buffer stock manager prior to 1964, it seems obvious that a buffer stock operation capable of maintaining the ceiling price under almost any fixed decision rules would not have been feasible. Nor would supply restrictions have helped; they would only have made the problem of maintaining the ceiling price more difficult.

It seems clear from the CRA and other studies that reducing the magnitude of copper price fluctuations by means of a buffer stock can only be successful if the buffer stock manager is given very wide latitude in adjusting the reference price on the basis of his perception of the long-run equilibrium price, or trends in that price. But one of the difficulties of buffer stock operations in the past has been that minimum prices and ceiling prices have been established by a political decision on the part of the members of the ICA, and the buffer stock manager is not given sufficient money or stocks of commodities to maintain the price within the minimum-maximum range. In fact, according to the CRA study, maintenance of a copper price within any fixed range would not have been feasible in terms of either the financing or the stocks of copper that might have been made available.

What then is the answer to the problem of widely fluctuating copper prices that affect the economies of countries, some of which depend on copper exports for more than two-thirds of their foreign exchange income? Short of establishing a world copper authority which would include copper industries of both DCs and LDCs, a high degree of price stability does not seem to be possible. Some of the instability during the 1970s can be traced to US government price controls, which led to a sharp divergence between the free market and the US producers' prices for copper. It is quite possible that a copper buffer stock with limited goals and great flexibility might have moderated copper price movements, which led to a nearly tripling of copper prices between early 1973 and the spring of 1974, followed by an equally precipitous decline by the end of 1974.

CONCLUSION

World copper production and reserves are widely dispersed geographically and, although the largest and highest grade copper resources are in the LDCs, these countries will require large amounts of foreign capital and technology to expand their output in line with their resource base. There is little likelihood that any group of countries will be able to establish an effective cartel in copper for more than a short period of time. Moreover, there are serious obstacles to achieving stability in the world price of copper by means of an ICA.

NOTES

1. See R.F. Mikesell, *The World Copper Industry* (Baltimore: Johns Hopkins University Press for Resources for the Future, Inc., 1979), 209-212.
2. *The Feasibility of Copper Price Stabilization Using a Buffer Stock and Supply Restrictions from 1953 to 1976* (Prepared for United Nations Conference on Trade and Development. Cambridge, Mass.: Charles River Associates Inc., 1977).

4

LDCs AND THE MARKETING AND DISTRIBUTION
OF IRON ORE

C.D. Rogers

This paper reviews briefly developments in consumption, production and trade in iron over the past quarter-century so as to place current problems in a longer-term perspective.[1] It traces the emergence of an international market for the commodity and the increasing importance of developing countries as suppliers of iron ore.

Against this background, it discusses the system of marketing and distribution of iron ore and the manner in which that system has responded to the changes in the international market. It also assesses the control over the market exercised by consumers of iron ore and investigates the implications for LDCs of this market power in the light of current structural changes in the market.

Questions specifically related to pricing policies are discussed elsewhere.[2]

REVIEW OF THE WORLD MARKET

Demand for Iron Ore

The steel industry is the main consumer of iron ore with about 95 per cent of world production of ore being consumed in the manufacture of steel. The remaining five per cent is consumed in a wide variety of uses, of which the manufacture of cement is the most important. Thus, the demand for iron ore is immutably linked to the performance of the steel industry in the short run, while over the longer term, technological advances in the iron and steel industries determine both the amount of iron ore required to produce a unit of steel output and the qualitative requirements for the ore.

Reliable information pertaining directly to iron ore consumption is not available but information on pig iron production provides indirect evidence of iron ore consumption since the patterns of both are essentially similar. An increasing problem with this measure of iron ore consumption is the growing extent to which iron ore is consumed directly in steel making, particularly through the direct reduction process.

The production of pig iron is heavily concentrated in the DCs and the CPEs of Eastern Europe, which in 1977 together accounted for some 88 per cent of

Notes to this chapter may be found on page 83.

world production. The share of the LDCs was about seven per cent of the world total, with China as the other significant producer.

The EEC, Japan, and the USA account for about 90 per cent of pig iron production within the DCs and represent the major markets for internationally-traded iron ore, although this is a relatively recent development. In Western Europe, France and Spain, which were significant exporters in 1955, have become net importers, while other major consumers, such as the UK and West Germany, have seen domestic production of ore decline significantly as a proportion of consumption. The USA has remained a major producer but has become increasingly dependent on imported ores, which now furnish over one-third of consumption requirements. In the case of Japan, the emergence of a steel industry itself is a comparatively recent development and the absence of a domestic supply of iron ore has resulted in Japan becoming the largest single importer of iron ore over the course of just two decades.

In the CPEs of Eastern Europe steel production has grown faster than the world average. The increase in the demand for iron ore, however, has been met essentially from the reserves of the USSR and the region has been almost self-sufficient in iron ore throughout 1955 to the present. Given the size of the reserves of the USSR this situation is likely to continue in the foreseeable future, although transportation problems may cause some local difficulties which offer limited opportunities for import penetration from outside the region, especially from LDCs.

Even within LDCs the consumption of iron ore is heavily concentrated in Asia (principally in India, and North and South Korea), and in Latin America (principally in Brazil, Mexico and Argentina). These six countries account for 85 per cent of pig iron production in developing countries. The world steel economy, however, seems poised at the beginning of a period of substantial structural change. The recessionary conditions experienced in Western Europe, and to a lesser extent in the USA, have not generally been felt by developing country producers and the next ten years may well see a marked increase in the proportion of the world's steel produced by such countries. This process will involve not only an increase in output from existing producers but also a number of other countries becoming major suppliers, e.g. Venezuela. Such a re-shaping of the world steel industry will necessarily re-fashion the geographical pattern of the demand for iron ore as well as providing a stimulus to change in the system of marketing and distribution, as will be discussed below.

Supply of Iron Ore

Early industrial development was based on the exploitation of an iron and steel technology with these industries inevitably occupying a central role. Indeed, a necessary but not sufficient condition for industrial development was access to adequate supplies of iron ore. Thus, the production of iron ore was much more geographically restricted than the distribution of iron ore reserves. After all, iron ore remains one of the most abundant minerals found in the earth's crust. As noted above, until comparatively recently ore production took place to serve essentially local or regional markets.

The emergence of Japan as a major steel producer and hence iron ore consumer, broke this regional pattern of production and trade. Japan was located some distance from existing producers and needed to develop new sources of supply. At the same time, demand in Western Europe was outstripping the traditional sources of supply. Ore reserves in West Germany and the UK were being depleted and it was necessary for future growth of ore consumption to be met from elsewhere. Even in the USA where substantial reserves of iron ore continued to exist, the poor quality of much of them created a climate conducive to increased import penetration.

It was against this background that a rapid expansion of new sources of supply took place from the middle 1950s, with the exploitation of reserves in India, West Africa, Brazil and Australia. In 1955, 85 per cent of iron ore production took place in Europe, the USA and Canada; by 1977 this proportion had fallen to under 55 per cent.

In particular, there was a significant increase in the share of the LDCs in iron ore production, from about ten per cent of world production (actual weight) in 1955 to over 25 per cent by 1977, facilitated by their substantial high-grade ore reserves. The number of LDCs producing in excess of two million tons of iron ore (actual weight) per annum increased from four to twelve over the same period. This internationalization of trade in iron ore was fostered by changes in shipping, in the fields of vessel size and port facilities, which led to a substantial fall in unit freight costs for the transportation of iron ore in the period 1960-70.[3]

A major feature of this geographical spread of production was its impact on the quality of iron ore available to world markets, with the new sources of supply generally being of a higher iron content. In addition, iron ore reserves were exploited in countries which were not consumers, and the increase in ore production thus represented in large part an increase in the amounts available for export. The proportion of world production (actual weight) which was exported rose from 24 per cent in 1955 to 43 per cent by 1977, and the value of these exports from $700 million to $5,500 million.

There was a corresponding increase in the scale of production within producing countries. Indeed, technological developments in iron ore mining were characterized by increased emphasis on large-scale production — more powerful shovels, larger trucks, high capacity crushing and screening plants, more flexible conveyor systems and more widespread blasting patterns. Whereas mines of over one to two million tons per annum were few and far between in 1955, mines producing five to ten million tons per annum are quite common now and production of as much as 50 million tons per annum is being planned in one instance — Carajas in Brazil — based on a single deposit.

Changes in ore mining practice have affected the physical specification of the ore supplied to the market. In particular, the increased mechanization of mining has reduced the possibility of selective mining and so has increased the amounts of lower grade material available, especially from open-cast operations. This in turn has led to greater need to concentrate and beneficiate the ores so as to achieve a marketable quality, despite the general increase in the quality of ores exploited.

Technological change in pig iron production has also resulted in the need for a better prepared blast furnace burden through blending and beneficiation and the increased use of sinter and pellets. Thus, the consumption of ore subject to some initial processing has increased, with the proportion of run-of-mine ore in total iron ore consumption falling from over one-half in 1955 to under one-quarter at present. The demand for pellets has been especially strong in those countries producing relatively low-grade ores, i.e. North America and the USSR, which together account for about three-quarters of world consumption of pellets.

The impetus to the development of agglomeration has therefore come both from the production side through the increased availability of ore fines consequent upon changed production techniques, and from the consumption side through the need for an improved blast furnace burden. The result has been an increase in the use of agglomerated ores, mainly sinter and pellets, in the manufacture of pig iron. Sinter accounts for over 75 per cent of the production of agglomerated ores but because of its friable nature is not widely traded internationally, although Japan has recently been experimenting with the import of sinter from the Philippines, apparently with success. International trade has generally been confined to more expensive but less commonly used pellets.

The production of pellets amounted to only 1.5 million tons in 1955 but increased to 46.5 million tons by 1965 and to 167 million tons by 1976. In 1976, 54 per cent of world production took place in the USA and Canada, 19 per cent in the USSR, and nine per cent in developing countries. Originally, the technique was to make use of ores which were too fine even for sintering, but its growth has developed from the use of ores which could otherwise have been sintered.

With pellet prices being significantly higher than the prices for unprocessed ores, the contribution that pelletization could make to foreign exchange receipts is well demonstrated. The high energy input, however, indicates that the technology may only be appropriate to LDCs with adequate and cheap domestic supplies of energy. In addition, there is increasing evidence of consumer resistance to pellets in the face of substantial price increases, which indicates that their market might be smaller than was at first thought. Nevertheless, pellet production is attractive for exporting LDCs, not least because of the contribution it might be expected to make to reducing unit shipping costs[4] and increasing foreign exchange earnings.

The other important development in ore processing is the exploitation of the direct reduction process, and there are a number of reasons why this has attracted so much attention in recent years.[5] The high capital cost of new blast furnace plants and the large size of their optimum utilization means that for many developing countries intending to produce relatively small quantities of iron, the pre-reduction process may result in lower unit costs of production.

Secondly, the pre-reduction process allows coke to be replaced as the main reducing agent by a variety of alternatives. Finally, the fluctuating price of scrap, the problems of residual elements in the scrap and, especially in developing countries, its limited availability, have encouraged the search for a scrap substitute. Indeed, it has been suggested that 'spare capacity in the pre-reducing plants could lead to commercial quantities of pre-reduced iron becoming available on the market which could help to stabilize the scrap market.'[6]

At the present time it is difficult to assess the rate at which direct reduction technology might be employed in steel production. The current recession in the world steel industry and the consequential excess capacity existing in certain countries does not represent an encouraging backcloth against which to introduce a new technology. Indicative of this are the delays recently announced with respect to several investment projects involving direct reduction technology.

THE SYSTEM OF MARKETING AND DISTRIBUTION

Ownership and Control

The primary purpose of this section is to describe the organizational structure of the marketing and distribution system for iron ore. In the absence of an existing detailed account of the system, the information presented here is drawn from a wide variety of sources, both formal and informal. The description will indicate the relationships which exist between firms operating in the sector and in some instances will reveal the extent to which MNCs may exert control through the activities of subsidiaries. In other cases, the links between MNCs are more tenuous. Although their existence reveals the potential for widespread collusion in the marketing and distribution of iron ore (if not the potential for control of the sector to be exercised by a small number of dominant firms), it has not proved possible to establish the extent to which these dominant firms exploit this potential.

We shall now deal in turn with the role of each of the main organizational groups in the industry: the steel companies, the merchant companies, and the independent producting (often nationalized) companies, and then assess the impact of these three groups on each other in determining the effect of these inter-relationships on the world market for iron ore.

Trade between the CPEs of Eastern Europe, together with that of the Asiatic CPEs, is excluded from the analysis partly because, at a superficial level, the system of marketing and distribution in socialist countries is well understood, and partly because information is not available which would permit a deeper and more complete analysis.

Due to the widespread availability of iron ore in commercial quantities, its production is frequently depicted as being a geographically diverse operation in comparison with other major metals: the leading ten countries in 1977 accounted for 84 per cent of world production. The USSR is the largest producer with 29 per cent of world output and China has six per cent of world output. If output from the CPEs of Eastern Europe and Asia is excluded, the leading ten countries still accounted for 84 per cent of output from LDCs and DCs together.

Data compiled from company, rather than country, figures reveal a concentration of production among leading companies. In 1977, shipments from the largest ten ore mining companies accounted for slightly less than one-third of world output and for almost half of world output if CPEs of Eastern Europe and Asia are excluded.[7] The steel companies and merchant ore companies jointly seem to have accounted for over half the iron ore produced outside those CPEs.

The Role of Steel Companies

The primary importance of steel companies derives from their role as buyers of iron ore; as we have stated, about 95 per cent of iron ore production is consumed in the manufacture of iron and steel. Although iron ore has some other uses, e.g. as a chemical or in the manufacture of cement, these are collectively unimportant when compared with the demand from steel makers.

The steel industry is highly concentrated; in 1976, the largest 50 companies produced over four-fifths of the total steel production, excluding that of European and Asian CPEs. The largest 20 companies produced over half this output, the leading ten companies over one-third, and the leading five companies about one-quarter. Thus, the number of buyers of iron ore on the world market is extremely limited. Indeed, their concentration may be even greater than the figures for steel companies would suggest in so far as in Japan, which accounts for over one-third of world iron ore imports, steel companies tend to import through the medium of specialized trading firms, and in West Germany buying is conducted by two specialist companies acting for the steel companies.

The steel companies, however, are also important suppliers of iron ore. Historically, most steel companies (with the exception of those in Japan) have developed their own iron ore mines as the basis of their requirements. As their consumption of iron ore has grown, they have tended for various reasons to increase supplies from other sources. One important source for such supplies is the merchant ore companies which will be discussed below.

In North America, the market for iron ore can be considered to be a single one, with the national boundary between Canada and the USA having no decisive effect on the pattern of development of the industry. Although differences in national practices and legislation have from time to time influenced the pace of development on one or other side of the border, they have not had a significant impact on the structure of the distribution and marketing system for the commodity.

In effect, the major steel companies have an Iron Ore Division or a Raw Material Procurement Division which, *inter alia*, is responsible for the management of subsidiary iron ore mines. In many cases, they operate through the medium of wholly-owned subsidiary companies, e.g. Bethlehem Steel Corporation owns Marmoraton Mining Company, Inland Steel owns the Caland Ore Company and the US Steel Corporation owns Quebec Cartier. Ownership of Canadian mines by American interests is commonplace. Further, steel companies have often joined together to own and control iron ore resources. Thus, Reserve Mining Company is 50 per cent owned by Armco Steel Corporation and 50 per cent by Republic Steel Corporation. In other cases, specialist mining companies are owned by consortia of steel companies and/or specialist merchant companies. A paramount example of this kind of arrangement is the Iron Ore Company of Canada which in 1977 shipped five million tons of direct shipping ores, 11 million tons of concentrates, and 16 million tons of pellets, which in total represented over half of Canadian production of iron ore in that year. The Iron Ore Company is owned by a group of nine companies (of which Hanna Mining with a 27.24 per cent interest is the major partner), including six steel companies (of which Bethlehem Steel has the largest share with 19.42 per cent of the equity). The implications of the joint ownership of mining facilities with merchant companies are discussed more fully in the next section.

In addition to their activities in North America, the American steel MNCs have developed subsidiary companies in South America. With the nationalization of such companies in Venezuela (and of Marcona Corporation in Peru which was owned by US mining interests), such activities have ceased, but the steel companies have equity shareholdings in mines in Liberia and Australia as well as the Canadian holdings discussed above.

In Europe the pattern is a little different,[8] although steel companies own a number of mining enterprises. In France, the most important iron ore producing country, ore mines are owned by the steel companies; in the majority of cases a single company has a controlling stake in the equity of the mine. In a number of cases, the mine is 100 per cent owned by a single steel company; in other cases several companies participate in the equity but one partner has a share of 50 per cent or greater. In a minority of cases no single steel company has a controlling interest. The mines in turn usually sell to a variety of steel company buyers and it is significant that in many cases the pattern of deliveries (by company) does not match the pattern of equity participation. Thus, the inter-relationships of steel companies in iron ore mining in France are more complex than would be suggested from an examination of equity participation. Outside Europe, European steel companies have equity shareholdings in iron ore in Brazil, Canada and Liberia.

In Japan, the steel industry has developed with minimal local resources of iron ore and steel companies thus do not directly control supplies. The typical pattern is for steel companies to obtain their requirements through specialist merchant companies, with the result that a few buyers are responsible for imports. Like steel companies elsewhere, however, Japanese steel companies have direct equity investments in mining, notably in Australia and Brazil.

Apart from their influence as buyers and suppliers of iron ore, the steel companies of Europe and North America often own, or control through associates, captive tonnages of shipping, or maintain chartered fleets. US Steel operates through an associate company, Navios Corporation, Bethlehem Steel operates through its Interocean subsidiary, and Italsider through Sidermar, while the British Steel Corporation operates a fleet of chartered ore carriers and also owns selected ships. In effect, North American and European steel companies thus have some direct interest in shipping.

In Japan, although their influence is less direct, steel companies still maintain effective control over shipping in a manner that makes the realities of practice similar to those elsewhere. Usually, control is exercized by steel companies through a system of cargo guarantees which they effect with the shipping companies owning the vessels. These cargo guarantees generally cover a major part, if not all, of the ship's life and serve to tie the vessel to the needs of the steel company.

The Role of Merchant Companies

The rapid growth of the steel companies made it difficult for them to match their requirements with supplies of iron ore from their own captive sources, and they began to have recourse to specialist merchant companies as a means of procuring marginal requirements and of disposing of surplus supplies. As the size of efficient steel plants and ore mines continued to increase, the problem of matching requirements with supplies became more difficult for steel companies, thus further increasing the role of merchant companies. The phenomenon of merchant ore companies, which to a certain extent is peculiar to North America, has had a number of implications for the organization and structure of the world marketing system for iron ore.

Although these merchant companies own and control a sector of the mining industry in North America, they also participate with steel companies in the development of ore facilities in Latin America, Africa and Australia. The most important companies are Cleveland Cliffs Iron Company, Hanna Mining Company, Oglebay Norton Company and Picklands Mather and Company International. In North America and increasingly elsewhere, notably in Australia, such merchant companies become more and more important as owners, individually and collectively between themselves or with steel companies, of iron ore mining facilities. In a growing number of cases, no single company has a controlling interest in a mining enterprise. Thus, the extent of control of supplies could be based on the apportionment of supplies in proportion to the extent of participation.

Merchant companies play a greater role than simply allocating supplies and helping determine prices. In particular, their equity participation in mining ventures makes them important sources of finance to the iron ore mining industry. In this role they frequently provide the central organizational support to a joint mining venture. Initially, as in Canada, and in Latin America before nationalizations, such joint ventures were between combinations of steel and merchant companies. More recently, the concept of the joint venture has been extended to include local participation, either through companies and/or individuals as in Australia and Brazil, for example, or through the host government or its nominee, as in Liberia.

In this central role in the development of an ore mining project, the merchant ore companies often provide the necessary skills for geological exploration work and undertake project feasibility studies. Further, once a project is underway, a merchant company is frequently appointed to manage the project. In such ways, the influence of the merchant companies may well extend beyond their apparent influence derived through equity participation.

Like the major steel companies, many of the merchant ore companies own or control a fleet of ore-carrying vessels. Their interests thus also extend to the maritime transportation of iron ore.

Two further aspects need to be noted in the assessment of the importance of specialist merchant ore companies. Most of the above discussion has been based on the experience of companies located in North America, although increasingly active in other continents. In Europe, however, similar companies exist (such as Exploration and Bergbau GmbH, which has interests in Brazil and Liberia) and are becoming increasingly important in the development of ore resources, especially in Africa. The International Division of the British Steel Corporation, for example, is increasingly becoming involved in mining ventures and is capable of supplying a wide range of expertise. Similarly, the Swedish company Gränges plays an important role in the Liberian Iron Ore Ltd. In the case of Japan, where imports of iron ore are arranged through specialist trading companies, such companies have increasingly become involved (along with direct participation by Japanese steel companies) in the provision of equity finance to mining ventures, especially in Australia and Brazil.

Finally, notwithstanding this dominant role of the specialist iron ore merchant companies, the increasing complexity of mining together with the greater financial requirements has caused the entry of a number of specialist mining companies with limited previous experience in the iron ore or steel industries: companies such as Amax Inc. which, through the Amax Iron Ore Corporation, has an interest in Mt Newman in Australia; and Consolidated Gold Fields which, through CGF Iron Pty Ltd, has an interest in Mt Goldsworthy, also in Australia. It is perhaps too early to assess the significance of this development other than to note that it broadens the role of some mining MNCs into the iron ore mining sector.

The Role of Independent Companies

The definition of an independent iron ore company is no easy one. Although it would be analytically attractive to describe it as being a company without formal links with either the specialist ore companies or the steel companies described in the foregoing section, this requires further clarification. In general, but not always, the ore companies described in this section are nationalized companies, such as CVRD in Brazil, CVG Ferrominera Orinico CA in Venezuela, the South African Iron and Steel Industrial Corporation Limited, Luossavaara-Kiirunavaara AB (LKAB) of Sweden, and Société Nationale Industrielle et Minière of Mauritania. In many but not all of these cases the companies, or the governments of the countries concerned, have developed or are developing steel-making facilities. Such companies may therefore be regarded as conceptually similar to the iron ore divisions of the major steel corporations described in an earlier section. The main difference rests in the operational principle that these companies tend to be net sellers of ore, whereas those described earlier were net buyers of ore. Even here, the distinction is not perfect since there have been occasions in the past when certain US steel companies have been net sellers of ore, but these have been marginal sales and made to other US steel companies. In spite of certain similarities, there seems to be ample justification in terms of behavioral differences, for examining this group of iron ore mining companies independently from those already discussed.

The significant feature of these companies is that they need to arrange for the sale of their production on world markets without any formal relations with buyers or with other sellers. As such, their influence tends to be limited to the size of the disposals they might have available. In some instances this influence is considerable. CVRD is the largest iron ore mining company in the world with shipments in 1977 of 46 million tons, equivalent to 5.5 per cent of total world production, or 8.8 per cent of world production excluding CPEs of Eastern Europe and Asia. In recent years CVRD, as a very low-cost producer, has emerged as the pacemaker in establishing the price level on world markets in the round of annual price negotiations. Other independent producers are in a much weaker position; being faced with higher unit costs than CVRD and much smaller outputs, they are forced to follow developments in world markets, having neither the size nor relationship to influence negotiations.

CVRD has one of the largest fleets of ore carriers, including ore-oil ships, and has received considerable state support in establishing its shipping arm, Doce-nave. India may also be considered to have captive shipping through its state-owned shipping line but most independent producers have no control over maritime transportation.

In many cases, independent ore mining companies own insufficient technical skills and need to obtain these from the engineering and specialist service divisions of merchant or steel companies for the adequate development of their resources. This relates not only to exploration and feasibility studies but also intrudes on decisions as to local processing; for example, Kobe Steel's involvement as the builder of a pellet plant in Mauritania.

In certain instances, these independent companies have been formed by the nationalization of existing mining companies owned and operated by steel MNCs or merchant companies. In these instances it is interesting to observe some of the operational changes that have taken place subsequent to the modifications of the structural relationships between buyers and sellers in the world iron ore market. In turn, this has some implications for the institutional forms that nationalization can take.

In the case of Venezuela, the government had involved itself for a number of years with a policy of modification and adjustment of export prices for iron ore, such that by the end of 1974, when the industry was nationalized, export values were unilaterally established by the Venezuelan government and adjusted according to changes in domestic prices in the USA. Further, in the year following nationalization, the companies continued to operate in their own right to ease the transportation process.

This contrasts somewhat with the situation in Peru where the government nationalized the activities of the Marcona Mining Company, an American company exploiting iron ore resources. The government had had little previous direct involvement with the industry and difficulties were experienced both with maintaining production levels following nationalization and also, and perhaps more importantly, with retaining sales contracts on the terms which had previously been undertaken directly by Marcona.

Summary and Conclusions

The importance of the steel companies in the marketing and distribution of iron ore derives primarily from their influence as buyers. This fundamental position is reinforced by their ability to control the supply of ores either from mines wholly under their ownership and direction or from mines owned jointly with other steel companies and/or merchant ore companies. In the context of the world market for iron ore, the interests of the independent merchant companies tend to be virtually analogous with those of the steel companies, who in turn are buyers for the whole output of the merchant companies. The interests of the latter are closely and inseparably linked to those of the steel companies.

The influence of these merchant and steel companies extends beyond the production of ore to include all questions of technical engineering assistance and even financial aid, embracing many companies that are otherwise independent. The steel and merchant companies are also important in determining the location of ore processing facilities – in producing or consuming countries – and for determining priorities in research and development expenditures on processing. In particular, this might explain why little attention has been devoted to obtaining less friable forms of sinter, which would make it possible to transport sinter over long distances and permit the development of its manufacture in ore producing countries.

In discussing the impact of control over supplies of iron ore that might be exerted by merchant companies or consortia of merchant companies and steel companies, it is necessary to distinguish two sets of factors: the first is quantitative; the second relates to price considerations. In an industry where economies of scale are important and where unit costs of production can be maintained at low levels by operating mines at or near capacity, owners of iron ore mines will be especially concerned to maintain production levels. Where mines are owned by steel companies, the latter will have an additional incentive to favor their own subsidiaries when determining their procurement policies. Although this tendency will be strongest with regard to wholly-owned subsidiaries, it will also operate in those instances where the steel company has a minority equity stake in the iron ore producing company, at least in comparison with other ore producers. Thus, with regard to assigning priority to supplies, the steel company is likely to favor supplies from subsidiaries, whether wholly or partly-owned, as against supplies from other sources.

In the case of pricing policy, however, the distinction is somewhat different. A mine which is a wholly-owned subsidiary of a merchant or steel company may undertake transfer pricing with respect to its output. In cases where a number of companies share the ownership of a mine, and particularly where these companies are located in different countries, the potential for transfer pricing is reduced significantly.

By exerting their monopsonistic power, the steel companies and merchant ore companies are able to influence the prices charged by independent producers and, if need be, to price their own supplies somewhat differently. The relationship between the pricing policies of these different groups of producers will be the subject of more detailed discussion in a further paper.

Control over shipping gives the buyers control over freight costs (the cost of maritime transportation is often over 20 per cent of landed prices) and over the timing of shipments, and influences the preference for fob rather than cif contracts.

Thus, although the importance of 'captive' supplies appears to have diminished with the nationalization of mines in several countries, the dominance of the steel companies has remained entrenched, if it is not enhanced. The situation continues to be that almost all aspects of the marketing and distribution of iron ore are controlled by the buyers. The widespread influence of the buyers through all aspects of the trade makes it difficult for ore-producing LDCs to increase their control over their domestic resources through the nationalization of production facilities, as the experience of Peru clearly shows. It is true that an independent producer, CVRD, has emerged as the pacesetter in the pricing of iron ore, but this situation is not inimical to the interests of the steel companies. As possibly the lowest cost producer in the world, aggressively interested in raising its market share, CVRD exercizes pressure to lower world prices, a situation which buyers welcome. At the same time, the steel companies can protect their own subsidiaries, if necessary, from any harmful effects of lower prices by differential pricing.

Implications for Producer LDCs

The growth of the world market for iron ore has allowed many LDCs to enter the market and to become producer-exporters. In many instances, the development of the industry has made a significant contribution to foreign exchange earnings and to the provision of economic activity and employment within these societies. The ability of such countries to enter world markets has been facilitated by the availability of higher grade deposits giving possibilities for production economies of scale which, when exploited, lower unit production costs and enable these producers to undercut other producers and to increase sales and output. This process has been greatly enhanced by improvements in the shipping of bulk cargoes which have reduced the barriers to market access previously posed by distance.

Although this increased LDC participation in the iron ore trade has brought benefits to these countries, problems remain, and in some cases have increased, as a consequence of the process described above. In particular, the LDCs have benefitted to a much lesser degree from increased shipping and the further processing of ores. It would seem that the continued dominance of the industry by large industrial MNCs located in DCs has inhibited a restructuring of the industry beyond the tapping of new sources of supply. The long-term amelioration of this situation requires a restructuring of the world shipping industry together with the development of new centers of iron ore consumption, which would serve to break down the existing power structure in the world industry.

With regard to the existing problems of producers, these derive almost exclusively from the continuing fall in real prices for iron ore and the impact of this on the financial viability of existing projects as well as the implications for the development of future new sources of supply. Over the post-war period the fundamental influence on iron ore prices has been the marginal unit cost of supply from the newest ore fields. The industry has witnessed staggering productivity improvements with consequent falls in unit cost and prices. The result of the pricing policies pursued in international markets, however, is that the benefits of these productivity improvements have passed primarily to the consumer.

New or field developments are now required to be very large scale in order to earn sufficient scale economies to permit entry to the market. As a result, the additional supplies on world markets from the start-up of new projects, especially but not exclusively in periods of depressed demand, often tend to displace existing supplies. Further, the dampening effect on world prices puts pressure on margins in existing mine developments where large-scale capital investments have been made.

Problems are especially acute in certain countries which have absorbed unit price declines by expanding export volumes and thus have managed to obtain continued growth in export receipts. In a number of cases it is no longer possible to continue to increase export volumes, and the results of continuing falls in real prices must manifest themselves through a decline in export receipts (expressed in real terms). The consequences are especially severe for countries for whom iron ore is a major contributor to export earnings (e.g. Mauritania and Liberia).

In addition, the costs of new ore-field developments are now so large (over three billion dollars for Carajas in Brazil) that they are extending beyond the competence of mining companies, steel companies or host governments. Thus, the financing of mine projects has become of major concern to all parties. One positive consequence is that the international companies are now much more prepared to work with host governments in determining appropriate solutions to the problem, and this represents an opportunity for host governments to gain more control over mine development.

A further consequence is that costs of exploration for iron ore deposits are reduced relatively, such that the financial costs are no longer the obstacle they once were for many developing countries. There are now real opportunities for financing increased expenditures related to exploration for mineral resources. Indeed, it is interesting to contrast the situation prevailing with respect to minerals with that existing in the oil industry. In the latter it is by no means uncommon for some companies to specialize in exploration and, upon discovery of exploitable reserves, to sell the production rights to another company more specialized in production, or to allow the host government to negotiate a separate concession with respect to production. It may well be the case that the heavily vertically-integrated structure of the world iron ore industry and the dominant role of the steel companies has inhibited the search for viable iron ore deposits, especially in LDCs.

It would seem, however, that continued expansion of iron ore production, through commissioning a series of new developments each with a lower unit cost of production than its predecessor, is now effectively constrained by the sheer magnitude of the financial expenditures involved and by the adjustment problems caused to the world industry from such large discrete amounts being added to world supply. It is against this background that a reassessment needs to be made of the whole structure of marketing and distribution for iron ore, with special attention being paid to the level of real prices.

NOTES

1. A fuller discussion of these developments is to be found in a recent report issued by the UNCTAD secretariat on 2 August 1977, *Iron Ore: Features of the World Market* (Document TD/B/IPC/IRON ORE/2. Related statistical material is in document TD/B/IPC/IRON ORE/AC/4).
2. C.D. Rogers, 'Long-Term Procurement Contracts, with special reference to iron ore', chapter 8 in this volume.
3. See UNCTAD, *Maritime Transportation of Iron Ore* (TD/B/C.4/105/Rev.1; United Nations Publication, Sales No. E.74.II.D.4).
4. *Ibidem*.
5. R. Scholey, 'The Present Situation Regarding Pre-Reduced Iron and Coke-Making Technology', *Proceedings of the Sixth Meeting of the International Iron and Steel Institute* (8-12 October 1972).
6. *Skilling's Mining Review* (29 January 1977), 67.
7. Based on information in *Skillings' Mining Review* (8 July 1978), 8 and 9. There are problems, however, in allocating output between companies where a mine is jointly owned. For example, *Skillings'* allocate the whole of the output of the Iron Ore Company of Canada to Hanna Mining, even though Hanna own only 27.24 per cent of the equity. Hanna, however, are also managing agents for the project.
8. For a description of the European industry see, Agence européenne d'informations, *Le minerai de fer et l'Europe* (Brussels, 1978).

5

TRENDS AND PROSPECTS IN NICKEL

W. Gluschke

STRUCTURE OF THE INDUSTRY

Nickel is primarily used in various ferrous and non-ferrous metal alloys, although important quantities of metallic nickel are also used in electroplating and iron and steel castings; minor amounts of nickel compounds are needed by the chemical and petroleum industries (catalysts), and for insecticides, ceramics and coinage. In alloys, nickel imparts strength, durability, toughness, and resistance to corrosion, oxidation and change at high temperatures. As one of the major steel alloying metals, it is exceeded in volume of consumption only by manganese and chromium. Typical of this metal's versatility and potential is its use in 'super alloys' in jet engines and in nuclear energy applications, in cryogenics, and in nickel-containing batteries.

Nickel Products and Uses

Stainless steel accounts for about 40 per cent of all intermediate nickel uses, followed by nickel-plating (16 per cent), high nickel alloys (12 per cent) and iron and steel casting (nine per cent) (see Table 1). During the past two decades, growth rates for nickel use in stainless steel and electroplating have been considerably higher than those for other uses.

In terms of end-use, it has been estimated that about two-thirds of total nickel consumption is used for capital goods for the chemical, petroleum, construction and pipeline industries, and one-third for consumer durables, particularly automobiles and household appliances and utensils.

The varying characteristics of nickel ores require different production technology; the main processes and the resulting products are shown in Fig. 1. Energy consumption is much higher for the treatment of lateritic ores because these are not amenable to physical concentration. The higher cost of processing is compensated for in part by large-scale, open-pit mining, while almost all sulphide deposits are to be mined underground.

The views expressed here are those of the author and do not necessarily reflect those of the organization by which he is employed.

Notes to this chapter may be found on pages 99-100.

Table 5.1. *Intermediate and Final Uses of Nickel in Market Economies*

Intermediate use	Volume (thousands of tons)	Market share (%)	Final use	Market share (%)	
Stainless steel	216	41	Chemical industry	30	
			Consumer durables	30	
			Vehicle construction	15	
			Building and construction	4	
			Other (power generation, etc.)	21	100
Electroplating	84	16	Automotive industry	55	
			Household appliances	10	
			Furniture	10	
			Fittings	5	
			Other	20	100
High nickel alloys	64	12	Chemical and petroleum industry	25	
			Industrial furnaces	25	
			Aviation industry	15	
			Other (turbines, auto-motive industry, etc.)	35	100
Structural alloy steels	53	10	Oil and gas pipelines, air-craft construction	44	
			Vehicle construction	21	
			Building and construction	23	
			Other (machinery, tools, etc.)	12	100
Cast iron and steel	48	9	Agricultural machinery, chemical industry and plants, etc.	50	
			Furnace and boiler indus-try, glass and similar industry, etc.	50	100
Other intermediate uses	64	12			

Source: G.C. Hesse and M.S. Martin, *Nickel Industry Study* (Toronto: Canavest House, 1975); data refer to the situation in 1974.

The entry of new producers from outside the traditional countries from the early 1950s onward, the development of new steel-making technology (e.g. argon oxygen decarbonization-AOD) and other processes, new end-uses, and the increasing exploitation of lateritic nickel occurrences, have resulted in the development of new products. There are now more than 15 products, designed to meet the specific needs of the industry, which have in part taken the place of the traditional forms of pure nickel. For convenience, these different forms are classified loosely according to grade. Products that are essentially 100 per cent nickel (e.g. pellets, cathodes and briquets) form a group known as Class I, while products with lower nickel content (e.g. ferronickel and nickel oxide sinter) form the Class II group.

Fig. 5.1. *Generalized Flow Chart for Major Nickel Production Processes (Land-based deposits)*

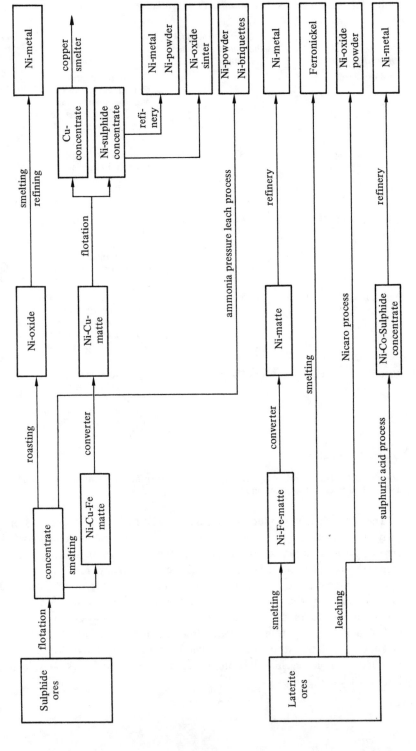

At present, somewhat less than 50 per cent of world (excluding the CPEs) nickel consumption is in the form of Class II products, up from about one-fourth ten years ago. According to estimates prepared by AMAX,[1] Class I nickel consumption has grown only 0.3 per cent annually, while that of Class II products increased by 9.0 per cent. It is also expected that growth rates for Class II nickel consumption will be lower in the future, with its potential market consistency of 90 per cent of nickel used in stainless steel and alloy steel and half of the nickel consumed in ferrous castings.

Concentration in the Industry

The structure of the international nickel industry has changed during the last 30 years. While over 95 per cent of the total finished nickel production in the MECs came from three companies in 1950 — INCO, Falconbridge Nickel, and Société Le Nickel (SLN) — these companies provided only approximately 55 per cent in 1976 and are expected to account for less than 50 per cent of projected capacity in the 1980s. Including the CPEs, these three companies already represent less than half the world output. The change is particularly sharp for the largest single producer, INCO, whose share dropped to around 30 per cent and is likely to be even lower in the 1980s though its total production has grown in absolute terms. The reason for this development is that various new companies have entered the industry since the early 1960s. These include Western Mining in Australia; various Japanese companies, primarily affiliated with steel producers; AMAX in the USA and Botswana; and Larco in Greece.

Additional companies have plans to instal productive capacity in the future, among them Anglo-American Corporation, which already has some interests in nickel-producing companies in South Africa, and American and European steel companies (the US Steel Corporation and Hoogovens in Indonesia; Thyssen and other companies of the Federal Republic of Germany, through a common subsidiary, in Brazil), and Billiton, a subsidiary of the Royal Dutch/Shell Group, an oil company, in Colombia (Cerro Matoso).

The major trend of diversification and a decrease of concentration is also very obvious in the case of mine and intermediate (matte) production, since most of the major companies have integrated operations from mining to smelting and/or refining. Notable exceptions are the Japanese companies, which import large amounts of ore and intermediate products from New Caledonia and other countries, and AMAX, which imports matte for its Port Nickel refinery (USA) from Botswana, Australia and other sources. The three traditional producers (INCO, Falconbridge and SLN) have refineries in Western Europe, close to one of the major markets (INCO in the UK, Falconbridge in Norway and SLN in France).

The CPEs as a group have traditionally been self-sufficient; production has increased with consumption. Since the early 1960s a major part of Cuban production is exported to other member countries of the COMECON. As it is likely that these countries will remain self-sufficient in the future — and there are no known reasons why they should not be able to do so — they are unlikely to have any major impact on the changes affecting the future structure of international industry. One exception is Cuba which, if present expansion plans of about 100,000 tons per year planned for completion by 1990 are realized, will enter the international market as one of the major exporters.

This diversification of production of nickel to at least ten independent companies or groups of companies with significant capacity is likely to introduce more competition into the market. It should not be overlooked, however, that the position of the major producers, even though it is being weakened because of the entry of newcomers, is still extremely influential because they are the principal sources of technological know-how, finance and marketing expertise. The entry into the nickel industry by new companies can be difficult and costly, as can be seen from the many difficulties experienced by recent projects, such as those in Selebi-Pikwe in Botswana and Greenvale in Australia; technological problems, either in processing or mining, have resulted in considerable cost overruns and delays in production start-up.

The influence of the major companies is also greater than their production shares indicate. Both INCO and SLN have minority participation in Japanese companies, and some of the major producers participate in the consortia formed to develop ocean mining.

Trade and Pricing

Nickel is internationally traded in semiprocessed form (ore, concentrate or matte) and in refined form (including ferronickel) as shown in Fig. 5.1. Semiprocessed nickel is either shipped between mining and processing facilities of the same company, but in different countries, or between independent companies. Independent transactions take place primarily with Japanese nickel smelters, which import ores and concentrates from New Caledonia, Indonesia, Australia and Canada.

The patterns of refined nickel trade are somewhat more complex but basically represent shipments by INCO, Falconbridge, SLN and other companies from Canada, Norway, the UK and other countries to the major industrial MECs; Western Mining of Australia mainly supplies Western Europe, while Japan imports only small quantities of refined metal. Cuban exports are for the most part directed towards the member countries of the COMECON, but expansion plans may result in increased exports to MECs, as mentioned before.

Primary nickel is sold by producers or their agents at prices established by the producers and changed infrequently. The posted prices (also known as producer prices) of pivotal grades maintained by the major companies are identical or comparable in the principal markets. The nickel-content prices of the various forms of nickel differ slightly, with the price of nickel contained in ferronickel about five per cent below that of pure nickel.

The domination of one company in the market has expressed itself in the mechanism of price determination and in the level of prices. With few exceptions, INCO has set and published prices, and the other producers have followed; this was the case until August 1977, when public price quotes were discontinued for some time.

In addition to the producer price, there is a smaller open market for the sale of secondary nickel as well as primary nickel. The latter has been fed by the USSR and other CPEs, by independent producers in MECs, and by merchants or consumers who re-sell the metal. The prices in this market fluctuate heavily. In some years in the past, when primary nickel supply has been extremely tight, the demand for open-market nickel and for pure nickel scrap has been very strong and prices have invariably commanded a large premium over the producer price. More recently, nickel is also traded on the LME.

During the post-war period, prices increased from $0.35 per lb in 1946 to $0.74 per lb in the late 1950s to $2.41 per lb in mid-1977, or an average of over six per cent per year. In mid-1977, however, prices started to fall rapidly and most companies stopped publishing list prices because heavy discounting made them virtually meaningless. At the end of 1977, prices were generally quoted a few cents above $2.00 per lb for Class I products and at about $2.00 for Class II products. Only slightly higher prices were quoted at the end of 1978, but because of heavy competition, the prices actually realized were reported to have been even lower. In February 1979, INCO and other companies reintroduced published price quotation. Since then, nickel prices have increased sharply to over $3 per lb. This rapid increase is as unprecedented as was the decline over the last years.

DETERMINANTS OF DEMAND AND DEMAND OUTLOOK

The consumption of nickel depends on the general level of economic activity, the development of new uses for nickel, trends in substitution both towards and away from nickel, and — as far as the demand for primary nickel is concerned — on the level of recycling. The sensitivity of nickel demand to changes in the business cycle is due to nickel's use in capital goods and consumer durables, including many products vital for military requirements. As a result, the forecasting of future demand for nickel, which is primarily a derived demand, is subject to considerable margins of error.

Substitution

Without doubt, there has been some substitution for nickel in the past, partly because nickel has been in short supply over extended periods. Although substitutions are possible in almost all cases in which nickel is used, many of these substitutes either have less desirable properties, are more expensive, or are produced in small quantitites in relation to total nickel use. In addition to direct substitution, there is the possibility of indirect substitution, namely, the replacement of nickel containing steel by other products, for example, plastics or aluminium.

Nickel producers, however, do not seem to be seriously concerned. One reason is that the increased use of new alloys need not necessarily be achieved at the expense of nickel. More important still, nickel is used in many modern technologies (aerospace, aeronautics, marine, nuclear, desalination, pollution control) that generally are characterized by high demand growth rates. Most nickel-producing companies, particularly in Canada, have extensive research and development programmes geared to the finding of new uses and the adaptation of nickel manufacturing technology to changing conditions.

Recycling

Secondary or scrap sources of nickel form a significant component of nickel supply (see Chapter 14 *infra*). Though data on the consumption of these different types of scrap are insufficient and not always comparable, industry sources indicate that on average prompt industrial and old scrap account for 20-30 per cent of the nickel feed for steel and alloy producers. The largest source of secondary nickel that appears on the market is stainless steel scrap, which is an internationally traded commodity. This is almost invariably used to make stainless steel, while nickel alloy scrap is used to produce nickel alloys and nickel-based superalloy scrap is used to make superalloys.

The presence of scrap markets with flexible prices means that the volatility of demand for primary nickel is accentuated. On the downturn of the business cycle, demand for nickel slackens off, while the flow of home and prompt industrial scrap continues for some time at the higher level. New scrap flows account, therefore, for a greater share of total nickel production when there is a downturn in the general economy; then during an upswing in demand, a larger share has to be provided by primary production.

Demand Outlook

In the last 25 years, consumption of nickel has grown at over six per cent, more than that of any other major metal during the post-war period, with the exception of aluminium. Recent oversupply, reduced prices and a slackening in the growth of general economic activity, however, have convinced almost all the organizations and companies which have published projections in the last few years that future increases will certainly be lower; they disagree, as is natural, by how much. Selected recent forecasts are shown in Table 5.2.

The average projected consumption in 1990 of about 1.3 million tons compares with a 1978 consumption of 714,000 tons and an estimated level of 740,000 tons in 1979 (Table 5.3). More recent projections agree that an even lower growth rate of demand is to be expected for the 1980s.

Table 5.2. *Selected Consumption Forecasts for Nickel*

Sources	Forecast period	Projected growth rate[a] %	Projected consumption in 1990[a] (thousands of tons)
Peters[b]	1972-1985	3.9	1,190
Stanford Research Institute[c]	1974-2000	4.6	1,550
Canada[d]	1975-2000	4.5	1,390
United States Bureau of Mines[e]	1975-2000	3.4	1,110
Federal Republic of Germany[f]	1976-1990	3.8	1,130
Average		4.0	1,274

a In some cases, projected growth rates or consumption in 1990, or both, were calculated from data for 2000 or other years, applying the given growth rates.
b H.D. Peters, *Nickel – Vorkommen, Production, Bedrafsdeckung in Rahmen der Weltwirtschaft* (Essen: Verlag Glückauf, 1975).
c IRS International, *World Mineral Availability, 1975-2000*, Vol. 8 (July 1976).
d Department of Energy, Mines and Resources, *Nickel* (Mineral Policy Series, MR 157. Ottawa, 1976).
e US Department of the Interior, Bureau of Mines, *Nickel 1977* (Mineral Commodity Profiles No. 4, Washington, D.C., 1977).
f Bundesanstalt für Gewissenschaften und Rohstoffe (Hannover) and Deutsches Institut für Wirtschaftsforschung (Berlin), *Untersuchungen über Angebot und Nachfrage mineralischer Rohstoffe – X Nickel* (Stuttgart: E. Schweizer Bart'sche Verlagsbuchhandlung, 1978).

SUPPLY FACTORS AND TRENDS

Resources

Nickel resources occur on land and, as 'manganese nodules', on the floor of the oceans. This section deals with land-based resources.

Land-based nickel deposits occur as two main types of ore which require a separate technology for extraction from the naturally formed minerals: sulphide and oxide ores; the latter are also commonly called lateritic ores because they are formed by weathering or 'laterization'. Since they occur near the surface, they can be mined by open-pit methods, while virtually all sulphide occurrences require deep underground mining. Known sulphide ores are concentrated in only a few countries, mainly in Canada (Sudbury district), the USSR, Finland, Australia and southern Africa. They are often associated with copper. Lateritic ores occur mostly in tropical and subtropical regions, mainly in the LDCs; they may be associated with cobalt and minor concentrations of other metals.

Total economically recoverable resources of nickel amounted to approximately 64 million tons of contained metal in 1978 (Table 5.4). Another 125 million tons of additional resources are believed to exist, though they are considered to be sub-economic at present.

About 45 per cent of the resources in producing mines contain sulphide ore,[2] but the share of lateritic resources in deposits not yet being exploited but considered to be economically exploitable is over 90 per cent; of all resources about

Table 5.3. Consumption of Nickel, 1967-1979 (Thousands of tons)[a]

	1967	1968	1969	1970	1971	1972	1973	1974	1975	1976	1977	1978	1979[c]
Federal Republic of Germany	31.0	35.4	36.8	40.9	34.3	43.0	54.8	61.2	42.8	56.4	53.9	67.4	
France	28.7	30.7	31.8	36.1	32.2	31.3	29.6	40.5	31.9	33.5	35.8	36.0	
Italy	14.4	17.4	16.2	19.8	18.0	21.0	23.2	20.0	17.0	22.0	23.0	24.5	
United Kingdom	30.5	33.1	32.5	37.5	31.0	30.0	31.5	33.5	27.0	30.5	30.5	32.0	
Austria	5.0	4.3	5.0	5.6	3.0	3.9	5.3	5.2	4.3	4.2	5.4	5.5	
Sweden	15.5	16.5	16.1	23.1	19.0	22.6	26.8	31.9	22.0	24.0	17.5	21.0	
Spain	1.6	2.0	2.9	3.1	3.1	4.3	5.3	6.2	5.0	6.4	8.2	8.8	
Other Europe[b]	4.9	6.3	6.6	7.1	7.0	8.1	9.6	10.6	11.0	10.7	10.2	15.0	
Europe[b]	131.6	145.7	147.9	175.2	147.6	164.2	186.0	209.1	161.0	187.7	184.5	210.2	220
India	1.2	1.1	1.3	1.7	2.5	1.7	1.5	2.8	3.3	3.5	5.6	6.0	
Japan	50.0	59.3	74.7	99.3	90.6	87.7	113.6	115.9	83.3	115.0	97.3	99.0	
Other Asia[b]	0.5	0.6	0.4	0.5	1.1	1.3	2.2	2.7	1.6	3.4	4.1	3.9	
Asia[b]	51.7	61.0	76.4	101.5	94.2	90.7	117.3	121.4	88.2	121.9	107.0	108.9	105
Africa	4.0	4.0	4.0	3.6	3.5	3.2	5.0	6.0	6.0	5.0	5.2	5.2	
USA	157.7	144.5	136.6	149.1	133.2	156.9	182.1	194.5	132.9	152.7	146.0	173.5	
Brazil	0.9	1.0	0.9	1.6	1.5	0.9	5.3	6.6	3.9	4.7	5.2	6.3	
Canada	8.0	10.2	13.2	15.0	11.3	12.5	10.8	11.6	11.3	11.5	9.0	11.5	
Mexico	0.1	0.2	0.2	0.7	0.6	1.2	0.8	0.7	3.0	4.0	2.5	2.7	
Other America	0.5	0.8	0.7	0.8	0.8	1.6	1.5	1.7	1.8	1.6	2.3	2.0	
America	167.2	156.7	151.6	167.2	147.4	173.1	200.5	215.1	152.9	174.5	165.0	196.0	

Australia and Oceania	3.5	3.0	2.9	4.1	3.9	3.6	5.0	4.8	2.3	4.3	4.3	5.3	
MECs	358.0	370.4	382.8	451.6	393.6	434.8	513.8	556.4	410.4	493.4	466.0	525.6	550
USSR						100.0	100.0	105.0	115.0	121.0	125.0	127.5	
German Democratic Republic						8.0	8.0	9.0	9.0	10.0	10.5	11.0	
Poland						5.0	5.0	7.0	7.5	7.8	8.0	8.5	
Romania						2.9	3.2	4.0	5.0	6.0	6.0	7.0	
Czechoslovakia						7.0	7.0	8.0	9.0	10.0	10.4	11.0	
China						20.0	18.0	18.0	18.0	18.0	18.0	19.0	
Other CPEs						2.4	2.5	3.3	3.5	3.9	3.9		
CPEs	115.0	120.0	120.0	125.0	130.0	145.3	143.7	154.3	167.0	176.7	181.8	184.0	190
WORLD	473.0	490.4	502.8	576.6	526.6	580.1	657.5	710.7	577.4	670.1	647.8	709.6	740

Source: Metallgesellschaft AG, *Metal Statistics, 1967-1977 and 1968-1978* (Frankfurt, 1978 and 1979).

a Including nickel content in ferronickel and nickel oxide sinter.
b Excluding CPEs.
c Preliminary estimates (as of January 1980).

Table 5.4. *Economically Recoverable Nickel Resources by Socio-Economic Groups of Countries (1978) (Metal content)*

	Total		Sulphide ores		Laterite ores	
	Thousands of tons	*Share %*	*Thousands of tons*	*Share %*	*Thousands of tons*	*Share %*
LDCs[a]	39,550	61.6	1,100	5.7	38,450	85.8
DCs	14,700	22.9	11,100	57.2	3,600	8.0
CPEs[b]	9,950	15.5	7,200	37.1	2,750	6.2
WORLD	64,200	100.0	19,400 (30.2%)	100.0	44,800 (69.8%)	100.0

Source: Bundesanstalt für Geowissenschaften und Rohstoffe and Deutsches Institut für Wirtschaftsforschung, *Untersuchungen über Angebot und Nachfrage mineralischer Rohstoffe – X Nickel* (Stuttgart, 1978); US Bureau of Mines; and files at the Department of Technical Cooperation for Development, UN Secretariat.

a   Including Cuba.
b   Excluding Cuba.

70 per cent are laterite deposits. This clearly indicates that incremental land-based supplies will primarily be from oxide ores.[3] This also suggests that the increase of the share of LDCs in future supplies of primary nickel, discussed later in this paper, is inevitable because of the regional distribution of resources. These countries as a group account for almost two-thirds of the total economic resources, while DCs and CPEs possess about 23 per cent and 16 per cent, respectively, of these resources. In contrast, the LDCs accounted for only one-third of installed mine capacity in 1978, while the DCs and CPEs accounted for 42 per cent and 23 per cent respectively.

Known economic resources of nickel are concentrated primarily in a few countries. New Caledonia, the USSR, Indonesia, Canada and the Philippines each have more than ten per cent; together, these countries account for over 70 per cent of the world total.[4] The remaining resources are distributed among a number of countries, such as Cuba, Brazil, Greece, the Dominican Republic, Guatemala, Colombia, Venezuela, Zimbabwe, South Africa, Botswana, India and Yugoslavia. Many others probably have the potential for discoveries of nickel deposits if and when adequate exploration is carried out.[5] These opportunities should be carefully evaluated, taking into consideration not only such deposit criteria as the ore tonnage and the grade but also transportation conditions, the development of reliable processing technology and the availability of investment finance.

The global resources are clearly sufficient to support the growth in demand projected in this paper well beyond the end of this century; in the case of nickel, exhaustion is definitely not a threat.

Regional Distribution of Production

In the early 1950s, Canada produced over two-thirds of the total primary nickel, virtually all of the remainder being accounted for by the USSR (about 20 per cent), New Caledonia (under six per cent) and Cuba — at that time a new producer (about four per cent). Since then, various other countries have become producers or have expanded considerably their originally very small capacity: Cuba in the 1950s; Greece, Finland and Australia in the 1960s; and the Dominican Republic, Indonesia, the Philippines, Botswana and Guatemala during the 1970s. Additional production capacity is under consideration in Colombia, Brazil (in addition to the present low level), Yugoslavia and possibly Venezuela, besides other countries with long-term prospects. At the same time, production capacity has been expanded in various countries, particularly in New Caledonia, Australia, the USSR and South Africa, among others. The result is a decline of the Canadian share to about 30-35 per cent at present. The number of producer countries has increased considerably, leading to a much lower degree of concentration in the primary production of nickel. This trend is expected to continue throughout the next decade, major expansions being envisaged in New Caledonia, Indonesia, Greece, the Philippines, Cuba, Australia, Brazil and the USSR. It is possible that Canada's share may fall to below 25 per cent in 1990, even though output may be higher than at present in absolute terms.[6]

By socio-economic groups of countries, the share of the LDCs (including Cuba) has been increasing in the past and is likely to continue to grow in the future (see Table 5.5). Their share is expected to surpass that of the DCs during the 1980s while the share of the CPEs (excluding Cuba) is likely to remain about the same.

Table 5.5. *Mine Production of Nickel by Socio-Economic Groups of Countries 1952-1978 (Thousands of tons, metal content)*

	1952		1962		1972		1975		1978	
	Tonnage	*Share %*	*Tonnage*	*Share %*	*Tonnage*	*Share %*	*Tonnage*	*Share %*	*Tonnage*	*Share %*
LDCs[a]	19.6	10.5	59.8	16.1	192.4	30.9	243.7	32.0	198.8	31.7
DCs	129.2	69.2	225.8	60.9	312.9	50.0	372.7	49.0	264.2	42.2
CPEs[b]	37.8	20.3	85.3	23.0	119.6	19.1	144.6	19.0	163.7	26.1
Total	186.6	100.0	370.9	100.0	624.9	100.0	761.0	100.0	626.7	100.0

Source: Metallgesellschaft AG, *Metal Statistics*, various issues.

a Including Cuba.
b Excluding Cuba.

The distribution of smelter and refined production (ferronickel, oxide sinter briquettes, powder, etc.) is less concentrated by country, since part of the Canadian and New Caledonian production is exported to Western Europe and Japan before it is refined. The share of the DCs, however, is higher than their share of mine production and, unlike the latter, has shown a slower limited decline during past years. This is primarily because of the rapid increases in Japanese capacity during the 1960s. Although no major expansions of capacity

Table 5.6. *Production of Refined Nickel by Socio-Economic Groups of Countries, 1955-1978 (Thousands of tons, metal content)*

	1955		1965		1970		1974		1978	
	Ton-nage	Share %	Ton-nage	Share %	Ton-nage	Share %	Ton-nage	Share %	Ton-nage	Share %
LDCs[a]	3.7	1.5	16.7	4.0	35.5	5.8	99.3	14.2	88.5	14.5
DCs	190.8	79.6	286.1	69.0	420.5	69.3	428.0	61.2	348.2	56.4
CPEs[b]	45.1	18.8	111.7	26.9	151.1	24.9	172.6	24.7	179.8	29.1
World	239.6	100.0	414.5	100.0	607.1	100.0	699.9	100.0	616.5	100.0

Source: Metalgesellschaft AG, *Metal Statistics*, various issues.

a Including Cuba.
b Including Cuba.

are expected in Japan and Canada (the largest producer), the share of the DCs is not expected to decrease as rapidly as their share of mine capacity because of planned capacity expansions in some European countries, Australia and the USA. The share of the CPEs (excluding Cuba) has remained about constant at one-fourth of the world total, a higher share than that of mine production capacity, reflecting imports of ore and matte. Table 5.6 summarizes these trends.

Investment Costs

The low consumption rates from 1975 to 1977, below those of 1973 and 1974, the accumulation of large stocks in the hands of producers, the deterioration of prices in 1977 and 1978, and sharp increases in investment and energy costs, have combined to discourage the development of new production capacity in virtually all MECs. Very few major projects, such as FENI in Yugoslavia and expansions in Greece and possibly New Caledonia, will commence production in the early 1980s; this is in contrast to the second half of the 1960s and first half of the 1970s, when major new projects came on stream or were started.

Because of the complexity of nickel production processes, as illustrated in Fig. 5.1, and the variety of intermediate products, investment costs for individual projects are difficult to compare and should more realistically be seen in the context of all production costs. A comparison of a number of projects being realized and under investigation for future development reveals that a modern project for the exploitation of lateritic ores requires approximately $8 to $9 per lb annual nickel capacity in 1979 prices or $300-$500 million for a medium-sized project of a capacity of approximately 20,000 to 25,000 tons per year.[7] This includes expenditure for infrastructure (energy generation plants, etc.).

Additional investment will become necessary for new projects to satisfy the increasing demand for nickel, to replace exhausted mines and obsolete plants, to provide for pollution abatement measures and for continuing exploration. Based on the projected growth rate of four per cent per year until 1990, and assuming an average capacity utilization of 90 per cent, 30,000-35,000 tons of annual capacity will have to be added on the average each year, requiring between $560 and $660 million annually or $6.7-$7.9 billion for the 12-year period starting with 1979 and extending to 1990 (in 1979 prices).[8] This estimate excludes costs for replacement capacity, exploration and pollution control measures in existing mines and plants. Naturally, the expenditure would not be equal in each of the years because of the 'lumpiness' of investment in a few large projects.

Potential Supplies from Ocean Resources

Estimates of resources of nickel and other metals contained in manganese nodules vary considerably because of the proprietary nature of most of the data and the lack of publicly available information. According to a more recent calculation of resources that would be economically exploitable under conditions expected to exist when the first projects come on stream, there are 23 billion dry tons of nodules which, at an average nickel grade of 1.26 per cent (and 1.0 per cent copper, 0.25 per cent cobalt and 27.5 per cent manganese), contain about 290 million tons of nickel.[9] This is much more than the economically recoverable land-based resources and about double the total estimated land-based resources. Even if this estimate exaggerates the amount of nickel present in ocean resources, there can only be one conclusion: total resources are huge and sufficient for any exploitation rate envisaged at present. Needless to say, extensive exploration is required to delineate the resources under consideration for mining in the coming decades.

Because of this uncertainty, and uncertainty about future consumption growth rates, an estimate of the potential contribution of ocean resource exploitation to nickel supplies should be considered not as a forecast but merely as an indication of possible impact. For a more complete analysis see the section 'Ocean Mineral Resources' in Chapter 1.

PROSPECTS AND OUTLOOK

In the MECs the international nickel industry has experienced a number of years of low consumption levels, production cutbacks in most major producer countries and prices that have gone below total production costs for some mines. The fall in consumption in 1975, reaching the lowest level since 1971, and the subsequent rather tentative gains, combined with sharp increases in investment costs, have resulted in a situation where most major producing companies, with the exception of INCO, operated at a loss.

A comparison of projected demand, as outlined above, and probable additions to primary production capacity indicate that a substantially reduced capacity surplus is likely by 1982 and approximate equilibrium between demand and supply could be reached by 1985 (see Table 5.7). One should, however, be

Table 5.7. *Projected Nickel Demand-Supply Balance for Primary Nickel, 1979-1985[a] (Thousands of tons)*

	1979	1980	1981	1982	1983-85
Announced additions to mine capacity		56	16	23	50[b]
Total primary capacity at year's end:	830	886	902	925	975[c]
Projected consumption	550[d]	615[d]	660[d]	710[d]	800[c]
Required mine production[e]	578	646	693	745	840[c]
Required primary capacity[f]	635	711	762	820	924[c]
Capacity surplus (+) or deficit (-)	+195	+175	+140	+105	+5[c]

a   Excluding CPEs but including Cuba and Yugoslavia.
b   Assuming that about two-thirds of the total announced additions to capacity will actually be realized.
c   End of period.
d   Assuming a more rapid annual growth rate until 1981; thereafter a 5.0 per cent growth rate has been assumed until 1985, which should compensate for the low consumption level in the base year 1978.
e   Assuming a 5 per cent loss between mine and refined production.
f   Assuming an average utilization rate of 90 per cent.

aware of the possibility of delays; if these occur, it would mean that additional capacity would be necessary, which could probably be provided by expanding existing mines. Furthermore, the real productive capacity of INCO has always been difficult to estimate; in its annual report for 1977 the company states that its Canadian capacity is only 210,000 tons per year because of environmental restrictions. In spite of this, INCO's capacity has been assumed in Table 5.7 to be 250,000 tons per year. For the period 1983-85, only about two-thirds of announced capacity additions have been assumed actually to commence production during that period. Finally, it should be recalled that production can be considerably below capacity, as was the case in 1978, when capacity utilization was around 65 per cent in the MECs. Therefore, even though excess capacity may exist for several more years, production and consumption can be balanced much earlier if present reductions are continued by the major companies. Actually, stocks, which at one time were equivalent to almost nine months' consumption, have declined considerably.

New nickel projects are relatively large in order to be able to benefit from economies of scale and to provide the heavy investment for infrastructure necessary due to the remote location of many deposits; financing is therefore likely to be one of the most serious obstacles to the development of new nickel projects. Total investment costs for major projects are unlikely to be below $300 million for a medium-sized project and could reach one billion dollars. The economic risk involved in such projects could deter many investors and lenders and would require some caution from the countries interested in proceeding with such projects.

In fact, very few major projects are expected to come on stream during the next few years. On the other hand, various new projects are under consideration for development during the 1980s; at present they are either in the feasibility stage or awaiting a decision to start construction, or they need additional time for feasibility evaluation. But it is by no means assured that even those for which financing has been arranged will actually be developed according to the planned time schedule.

Production costs for projects exploiting sulphide ores and laterite ores are in part sensitive to different influences. Lateritic projects, because of the much higher energy requirements for treatment of the ore, could suffer if energy has to be imported at an increasing cost. Sulphide ores, on the other hand, because they are mostly mined underground, require relatively higher labor costs and are therefore more sensitive to wage increases. Both lateritic and sulphide-based projects have suffered from the rapid escalation of investment costs in recent years, which have resulted in a disadvantageous capital cost situation for new projects in comparison with those completed several years ago. Companies with existing production facilities, for example the traditional major producers, can more easily afford to develop new projects than other firms because they can average-out production costs for the initial years.

As a general rule, small or medium-sized projects will probably contribute more efficiently to economic development in most LDCs than large projects. This tends to favor projects based on sulphide ores. Furthermore, these ores often contain copper and other associated recoverable minerals, and prospective revenues are therefore less dependent on the price fluctuations of a single metal. And, finally, the lower energy consumption per unit of output makes these projects less vulnerable to energy costs that are beyond the control of most developing countries. Although sulphide ores are less widely distributed than laterite occurrences, systematic exploration is likely to yield results in some countries, as has been shown by the recent success of a UN exploration project in Tanzania.

NOTES

1. See chapter 9 *infra* and also L.G. Bonar, 'The changing options of adding nickel to steel' (presentation to *Metal Bulletin*'s First International Ferro-alloy Conference, Zurich, October 1977).
2. Earlier reports mention a share of more than 50 per cent. The change since then was caused by a start-up of projects in Australia, the Dominican Republic, Guatemala, Indonesia and the Philippines, among others.
3. Virtually all projects announced for future development are on the basis of lateritic ores.
4. Cuba also has very large resources; not enough information was available, however, to include most of these resources in the 'economically recoverable' category.
5. For example, nickel discoveries have been made in Burundi and, more recently, in the United Republic of Tanzania, in the course of UNDP-financed mineral projects executed by the Department of Technical Cooperation for Development of the UN Secretariat.
6. Excluding possible production from ocean resources.
7. *Prospects for the Development of the Raw Materials Base for the Nickel Industry* (Report of the UN Secretary General, E/C.7/102, 30 March 1979).

8. On the basis of an average of $8.50 per lb annual capacity.
9. A. Archer, 'Resources and potential reserves of nickel and copper in manganese nodules' (contribution to the UN Expert Group Meeting on Sea-bed Mineral Resource Assessment, New York, 28 November-1 December 1977).

6

STRUCTURE OF THE WORLD TIN INDUSTRY

D.J. Fox

The discovery of bronze, an alloy of tin and copper, over five thousand years ago, gave man the power to advance beyond the Stone Age and attached a value to tin which it has never lost. Throughout history, the prospect of finding fresh deposits of tin has drawn miners and traders into the distant corners of the known world. The separation of mine from market, of producer from consumer, is a long-established trait of the world tin industry. The sources of the tin traded today lie almost exclusively in the tropics and its destinations are virtually confined to the temperate world: a case of the developing world responding to the demands of the industrialized world. Such a clear-cut dichotomy endows the trade in tin with a political importance not shared by all metals. It is not by accident that tin is the subject of the most successful, most durable and most comprehensive inter-governmental commodity agreement reached to date, a pioneer agreement designed to mitigate the harsher aspects of world trade in raw materials. The agreement is particularly important since tin is unusual in possessing a market which has grown more slowly than that of almost any other metal in recent years while, at the same time, the economies of a number of important producing countries depend very heavily upon their sales of tin on the world market.

Tin is one of the rarer of the common elements in the earth's crust, as scarce as uranium or tungsten. Lead is seven times, copper thirty-seven and zinc fifty-five times as abundant. Areas of the earth's crust physically rich in tin form belts of differing geological ages in which the tin has distinctive characteristics and affiliations. One such belt now straddles the south-eastern coast of South America and the once contiguous south-western coast of Africa: it runs northwards to embrace Rio Grande do Sul in Brazil, Nigeria and perhaps the concentrations of tin in Iberia. A second belt runs through Central Africa from Natal to Uganda parallel to that of the Atlantic. A third originates in the elbow of the Andes and includes Bolivia, Rondônia, Guyana, and perhaps extends to the Atlas mountains in North Africa. Bolivia is also part of the great circum-Pacific tin belt which begins in the Argentine, follows the line of the Andes, and extends by way of the Central Mexican deposits and those of the western cordillera of North America, to run down the Seward peninsula in Alaska and to terminate in north-eastern Siberia. A second arc of the belt runs from the Yunnan province of China southwards through Burma and Thailand to Malaysia, Indonesia and, perhaps, to coastal Australia.

The three European tin belts — that which includes Galicia, Brittany and Cornwall; that which runs from the Massif Centrale to Tuscany; and that of the Erzebirge — are several orders of size below those of the Pacific rim.

These broad geographical and geological associations define the context in which the economic deposits of tin have been worked in the past and the present and circumscribe the situations in which the economic reserves of the future are likely to be found.

TIN PRODUCTION

Tin deposits which have proved their economic worth are confined to certain parts of these tin-rich belts. A digest of current production figures is offered in Table 6.1, which clearly shows the dominance of a few countries. A high degree of concentration upon a few sources has been a lasting feature of the international tin picture. A century ago, Cornwall was still the single most important tinfield and, together with the new Australian mines, produced half the world's tin; the long-established workings in Malaysia and the Dutch East Indies accounted for four-fifths of the remainder. By the end of the 19th century output had more than doubled and Malaysia had won the premier position she has maintained (except during the Japanese occupation in World War II) ever since. With the Dutch East Indies (now Indonesia) and Thailand, she was responsible for three-quarters of the tin reaching the world markets. The advent of Bolivia as a major producer slightly diminished the hegemony of South-east Asia but the normal pattern has been for two-thirds of all tin produced to emanate from this corner of the world. Malaysia alone has met one-third of the world's requirements of tin during the 20th century. It is difficult, if not impossible, to find a parallel amongst other non-ferrous metals of such a long period of dominance of a significant metal market by a single country. Another remarkable feature of Table 6.1 is the complete absence of any significant production by the United States: this deficiency gives tin a strategic importance not shared by many other metals.

Within *Malaysia* the main tin belt runs on a strip about 600 km long and 80 km wide between the Main Range with its granite core and the west coast. Almost all the tin worked is allumial or elurial material: there is one important lode mine. The Kinta Valley north of Kuala Lumpur remains the focus of mining and has provided half the tin to come out of Malaysia. It was known as a source of tin to Arab writers in the ninth century and Chinese were mining tin in Malaysia well before the modern period. It was fighting between rival Malay, Thai, and Chinese miners which brought British intervention in 1873. With intervention came rapid change: the first steam engine used in the mining industry was introduced in 1877 and the first European mining company in the Kinta Valley was launched five years later. In the early 20th century there were about 250,000 miners, mainly Chinese, working the tinfields of Malaysia. It was the adoption

Table 6.1. *Tin Production*

Major Producing Countries	Production in tonnes 1968	Production in tonnes 1978	Cumulative % of world total 1978	% Change 1968-78	% Production consumed abroad 1978
Malaysia	76,274	62,650	25.0	14.5	99.5
USSR	24,000*	33,000*	38.2	37.5	0
Bolivia	19,568	30,881	50.5	4.4	99.6
Thailand	23,980	30,186	62.5	25.9	98.7
Indonesia	16,940	27,410	73.4	61.8	98.4
China	20,000*	20,000*	81.4	0	15.0*
Australia	6,642	11,716	86.1	76.4	66.9
Brazil	1,865	11,000*	90.5	59.0	55.0
Nigeria	9,804	4,011	92.1	59.1	98.0
Zaire	6,264	3,450	93.5	45.9	98.0
S.Africa	1,866	2,886	94.7	54.7	0
UK	1,827	2,831	95.8	55.0	0
World	227,000*	250,700*	100	10.4	

Source: International Tin Council, *Monthly Statistical Bulletin*.

* Estimates from *Mining Annual Review* (1979).

in 1906 by Chinese miners of a European idea — mining by gravel pumps using monitor jets — that proved one of the spurs to the expansion of production in the 20th century. The second innovation, again from Europe, was the arrival in 1912 of the first tin dredge. Dredging had long been used in mining other alluvial ores, particularly gold. The more capital-intensive requirements of dredging kept this part of the industry mainly under the control of European companies whereas the cheaper, smaller-scale, more flexible gravel-pump operations remained largely in Chinese hands. By the late 1930s European companies had grown to account for two-thirds of Malaya's tin output: early growth in production from dredges was achieved by increasing the number of dredges; after the 1920s it was achieved by increasing the size of the average dredge.

The Second World War, subsequent guerilla activity and the wariness of the London capital market and the international mining companies to invest in an independent Malaya, dealt heavier blows to the dredging side of the industry than to the gravel-pump sector. Certainly by 1977 only one-third of the country's tin was being won from dredges, compared with one-half from the less mechanized, yet more resilient, Chinese-owned section of the industry. During 1978 the gravel-pump operators were able to react quickly to take advantage of the exceptionally high tin prices with a speed of response seemingly not open to the dredge companies.

Malaysia illustrates one of the features of the tin mining industry which distinguishes it from that of most other metal industries. That is the large number of working units of diverse ownership. The dispersed nature of the alluvial deposits clearly helps to permit a variety of independent operations. Even within the pattern of company ownership no real move towards a private monopoly has ever emerged. In the early 1960s the Anglo-Oriental group of companies provided about 25 per cent of the country's output and the top three groups 45 per cent; yet the leading 35 companies in 1972 were responsible for only 40 per cent of Malaysia's tin and the largest single unit supplied less than one-twentieth of the national total. The weakening position over the last quarter century of the European companies, vis-à-vis the Chinese, helped to preserve what elsewhere might be called a relatively unstructured situation.

This situation began to change in the 1970s as a new indigenous element, the Malaysian government, entered the arena. In 1976 the Malaysian Mining Corporation (MMC), a holding company whose stock is jointly owned by the Malaysian government (71 per cent) and Charter Consolidated (24 per cent), bought out the holdings of the London Tin Corporation, which included the Anglo-Oriental group in Malaysia, and the holdings of Associated Mines. By 1979 MMC was not only producing 30 per cent of Malaysia's tin but was operating two companies in Thailand and had inherited interests in Nigeria. The internal significance of this grouping extends beyond the first entries as principal characters of the government and of a multinational onto the tin mining stage. In 1979 MMC was actively entering into joint mining development projects with the separate states within the Malaysian Federation, thereby deepening the involvement of public funds in the Malaysian tin industry. It was also entering the business of selling tin directly to customers in violation of the practice normal in tin, but unusual in many other metals, of selling through the established metal markets in Penang, London and New York.

Tin production in *Indonesia* is more restricted in location: almost all comes from two islands, Bangka and Belitung (Billiton) off the east coast of Sumatra at the southern end of the great train of commercial tinfields of South-east Asia. The Bangka deposits have yielded approximately two-thirds of Indonesia's output since working first began 250 years ago and continue to do so today. Since 1900 Indonesia and Bolivia have run joint seconds in the world tin production stakes, although Indonesian production during the last quarter-of-a-century has fluctuated more widely than has that of Bolivia. Indonesian ore, like Malaysian, is almost entirely alluvial and has relied on a largely Chinese labor force: mechanization of the industry by the adoption of the gravel pump and the dredge came in the 1920s, a little later than in Malaysia, but the technology soon conquered the hand-pick and boosted production if not employment. Dredges and gravel pumps continue today to share production in equal proportions. It is noteworthy that two-thirds of the current dredge production comes from offshore deposits, a source more important in Indonesia than in any of the other tinfields of the world; three-quarters of the tin taken on land is from gravel pumps. It is not only in the substantial exploitation of offshore deposits that Indonesian mining differs from Malaysian. A major distinction lies in the very long history of government involvement in the Indonesian industry. It began in 1722 when the Dutch obtained a monopoly of trade in the metal, and expanded when the Government of the Dutch East Indies took over the Bangka mines in 1816. Subsequently, the Dutch Billiton Company obtained a minority shareholding in the state mining enterprise and, in effect, operated the mines until Indonesia became independent in 1959. The Dutch connection, a symbol of the old colonial days, was severed, at least temporarily, during the late 1950s, and ownership of the Indonesian tin industry was completely vested in the new state. For a variety of reasons, some technical brought about by a loss of metallurgical and managerial expertise on the nationalization of the mines, some political including the pogroms against the Chinese and the imposition of insensitive army control, and others more obviously reflecting a national economy on the slide, tin production plummeted; it reached a low point of below 13,000 tonnes in 1966. Since then joint ventures with foreign companies have been encouraged, new tin dredges (including the largest in the world) have come into commission, and fresh off-shore tin reserves have been discovered. Production in 1978 was over twice that in 1966 and the portents for a continued improvement, at least in the short term, appear good.

Thailand has produced as much tin as Indonesia during the last decade, almost all of it from alluvial and eluvial deposits similar to those of neighboring Malaysia. Yet as recently as the 1950s her output was only one-third of that of Indonesia and in the first quarter of this century it was only one-quarter. This slower, if steadier, pace of development may seem surprising in view of Thailand's early (1907) application of off-shore dredging. An explanation probably lies in the greater reluctance until recently of European and American companies to invest in always-independent Thailand rather than in the seemingly more secure erstwhile colonies further south. But whatever investment she lost before World War II, Thailand was spared the sometimes painful adjustments to political independence required of all her neighbors and her tin mining industry has boomed. In the meanwhile the tin dredges, which are in the main creatures of the larger, often European-owned, companies, reduced their share of production from over half in the 1950s to less than a quarter in the 1970s. And, as in Malaysia and Indonesia, the smaller, generally Chinese-owned, gravel pump and hydraulicking operators expanded output to the extent that in the late 1960s they accounted for two-thirds of all production. But today their fraction is only one-third as a new category of producer has arrived on the scene. This is the suction boat. There are now probably about 3,200 suction boats working the tin-rich bed of the Andaman Sea. Most are domestically owned and worked by small-time operators — either Thai or ethnic Chinese — hoping to make a quick fortune. Until recently those who made their fortunes frequently did so by smuggling their concentrates overseas, thereby avoiding Thai domestic taxes. Indeed, the sharp rise (by an estimated 25 per cent) in tin production figures for Thailand between 1977 and 1978 may be mainly because of much stricter policing of the mining waters. In spite of the seemingly favorable trend in Thai tin production brought about by the advent of the suction boats, the relatively low recovery rates (40 per cent) of material sorted by these boats is a source of concern to the officials of the long-established Ministry of Mines. In their eyes the boats are depleting reserves which might be worked more efficiently by dredges. The role of the Thai government in the mining industry is increasing. It has become reluctant to renew the off-shore leases of foreign-owned dredging companies and the official Off-shore Mining Organization is acquiring an increasing proportion of those leases. The old foreign-owned companies are rapidly becoming mere contractors for the Off-shore Mining Organization, while others are going into junior partnership with Thai-owned companies.

The tin mines of *Burma* continue the tin belt northwards. Production reached an annual level of 6,000 tonnes before World War II, but the industry has never really recovered from the disruptions of the Japanese invasion and post-war independence and is insignificant today. Neither have the formerly French-owned mines in *Laos* been able to recover their full capacity under communism.

The other major producer in South-east Asia is *China* with an estimated output of about 20,000 tonnes per year. Although the deposits are extensions of the Malay-Thai tin belt and lie in the contiguous parts of Southern China, there are many significant differences that distinguish the Chinese tin industry from that of its neighbors. In the first instance only the minority (40 per cent) of tin is won from alluvial deposits. These are the deposits of the eastern tin zone in the Fuhochung district of Kwangsi province. Dredges are few and good gravel pumps are rare: the technical level of operations is at least twenty years behind that of Malaya. The reasons for this backwardness are fairly obvious. Malaya, Thailand and Indonesia collared most of the European capital that went into the mechanization of alluvial mining in South-east Asia in the first third of the century. By the time these other demands had been sated the Sino-Japanese war had begun and, as subsequent events in China have shown, the opportunity for outside capital had been lost, perhaps for good. The majority (60 per cent) of China's tin is won from lode mines in the Kuchiu area of Southern Yunnan. The mines reach depths of 900 meters underground and conditions are primitive by the standards of Cornwall. In 1938 the mines employed about 100,000 men to produce about 10,000 tonnes of saleable tin. Since World War II and the communist revolution only fragmentary information has become available about the industry, much of it collated by the US Bureau of Mines. The expectation is that the application of expertise won in the lode mines of Cornwall and Bolivia and on the dredges of Malaya could usefully be employed to increase current production substantially. And with the Chinese openly seeking overseas technical assistance, not only can expanded production be anticipated but also a lifting of the mists that shroud our knowledge of her tin industry.

The other Asiatic producer about which less is known than one would wish is, of course, *Soviet Siberia*. The best available estimate of current production is, again, provided by the US Bureau of Mines which believes that the USSR produced 33,500 tonnes of tin in 1978, a rise of 3,550 tonnes since 1974. These figures place the USSR in second place in the 1978 international production table. Fifty years ago Soviet production was negligible — say between 1,000 and

3,000 tonnes — and the present output has been generated by an intensive exploration program and a disregard for mining costs which could be prohibitive in a free market economy.

Bolivia offers the closest parallel to the harsh working conditions in the tin fields of the USSR. High altitude negates the ameliorating effects of low latitude. Bolivian miners work in the cold, oxygen-starved environment of the high Andean cordillera. Few mines are below the 4,000 m contour line and some are above the permanent snowline; the mountains are arid and treeless. As in the USSR, most of the tin comes from underground mines and many of the veins are lean and unwilling to release their tin. It is Bolivia that has been squeezed out of second place in the production stakes by the USSR, if the American estimate of Soviet production in 1978 is correct. In recent years Soviet technology has been imported in an attempt to ease some of the tin mining problems of Bolivia, but the metallurgical problems are difficult in both countries. Bolivia appears over the top in her ability to produce tin whereas the trend of Soviet production is upwards.

Harsh conditions mean that mining is a seasonal task in many of the three-to-five thousand workings of the so-called small miners. Such seasonal mining operations usually form an adjunct to peasant farming. Although only responsible for nine per cent of Bolivia's tin production in 1978 this primitive section of the mining economy accounts for half the miners listed in the country's somewhat hazy employment figures. They are a category of miner which would be an anachronism in almost any other mining country; the methods employed are those described by Agricola and familiar, for example, to the mediaeval tinners of Devon and Cornwall.

The great bulk (70 per cent in 1978) of Bolivian tin is won from commercial mines employing methods and equipment more in keeping with Bolivia's position as one of the world's leading suppliers of tin during the 20th century. Many of these mines are direct descendants of the silver mines which made Upper Perú famous in colonial days. They are mines which were revitalized by a new breed of local entrepreneurs who rose to the fore in the heady days of the first half of the century when fortunes were won by applying the technology of, in particular, British hard-rock tin mining to the fat ores of Andean Bolivia. Simon Patiño is the most famous. His fortune was founded on his tin mines at Catavi, Huanuni and Colquiri; he subsequently broadened his interests to include half the world's tin smelting capacity and added financial holdings in Malayan and other tin companies. The other Bolivian mining empires of Aramayo and Hochschild were of domestic importance but are remembered now only by association with that of Patiño. The nationalization of the Big Three mining groups was one of the many and early accomplishments of the Bolivian Revolution of 1952. The Corporación Minera de Bolivia (Comibol) formed to run these mines has had a trouble-racked history, partly because of misfortune and inherited difficulties, partly through difficulties of its own making. The mines were in poor state when nationalized; the removal of sources of capital and overseas technical assistance and the milking of early profits to help build a fledgling oil industry compounded early problems. Comibol, responsible for over half the country's export income, was rescued from the brink of bankruptcy in the late 1950s only by accepting substantial injections of American aid and direction; the controlling position that the Bolivian miners' unions had gained in the affairs of Comibol was sacrificed on the altar of national economic survival. The miners have remained the most important body of organized labor in the country and a political force with which successive governments have always had to reckon. Some have chosen to rule by martial law; others have bought peace with higher wages. Higher wages have sometimes coincided with a fortuitous rise in world tin prices; at other times payment has only been possible in a devalued Bolivian currency, such is the importance of tin in the life of Bolivia.

In no other country is the tin industry such a potent political, social and economic force. The difficulty for Comibol, as for the country, is to balance the requirements of efficient tin mining under the conditions laid down by the world tin market with the role of the tin industry as the only significant source of external wealth in an impoverished economy. The facts that Comibol has not fallen victim to the vicissitudes of the last 27 years and that the same handful of mines have continued in production, are remarkable tributes to their powers of survival. But whatever the relative successes of the past, Comibol is soon to face a severe test. The great underground mine at Catavi is running out of ore. For over half-a-century Catavi has been the world's largest tin mine and alone has accounted for over one-quarter of Bolivia's production. But its premier position is about to be overtaken by the Renison Bell mine in Australia. The average grade of ore leaving the Bolivian mine has fallen from the already low figure of 0.53 per cent in 1973 to average only 0.39 per cent in 1978; Catavi lost $8 million in 1978. Drilling to test the possibility of turning it over to open-cast mining has shown that even this final solution is not open to Comibol. The latter has nothing to take Catavi's place, either in the tin economy or as a source of employment for the 30,000 dependent upon the mine.

There is no substantial commercial private mining sector to soak up unwanted labor and to make good lost production. There are about 17 private tin mining companies in Bolivia and this sector has proved itself remarkably resilient in recent years. It has demonstrated an innovative ability not paralleled in the state sector and is, in general, a more efficient producer of ore. The most remarkable success of recent years has been the re-introduction of tin dredging, first amongst the gravels of the Pazña valley and secondly in the even less hospitable canyon of the Pilcomayo. But dredging will never play anything but a minor role in what is essentially a traditional lode mining country. Although the better-run mines have a history of capital and technical expertise supplied from British and American sources, it has been noticeable over the last decade that these exogenous ties have been weakened. In particular, the W.R. Grace Company has deliberately divested itself of its Bolivian mining properties which have been taken over by indigenous Bolivian interests.

Brazil, to the chagrin of her smaller neighbor, has not only discovered substantial deposits of eluvial tin just across Bolivia's eastern frontier in Amazonia, but has been successful in attracting capital with which to develop them. The deposits are associated with granites younger than those in Bolivia; they are situated in the hot, low-lying selva of the Amazon forests. Once made accessible by feeder roads from the new trans-Amazon highway system there is little technical difficulty in exploiting the Brazilian deposits and her production of tin-in-concentrates is six times what it was a mere decade ago, although still only one-third of that of Bolivia. Development began in the late 1960s with a tin-rush of individual *garimpeiros* soon replaced by the more systematic and, by implication, less wasteful, mechanical working of the deposits by substantial mining corporations. These companies included W.R. Grace, Billiton, and the Patiño interests in conjunction with the national development bank (BNDE). In 1979 the geographical area worked for tin by mechanical mining was extended beyond Rondoñia to the Alto Xingu region and to Nova Roma in Goias. Cynics fear that the new black tin coming out of the forests, like the natural rubber and Brazil nut brought out earlier this century, will provide only a fleeting bonanza to these remote regions.

The other tin producer in the same class as Brazil is *Australia*. It, too, produced between 11,000 and 12,000 tonnes of tin-in-concentrates in 1978. Australia, too, was producing much more than (in fact, twice as much as) a decade ago and was expecting to continue to expand production. As in Brazil, all tin mining in Australia is in the hands of private companies, many with outside financing. Unlike Brazil, 80 per cent of Australia's tin comes from underground mines and tin mining has a century, rather than a decade-and-a-half, of history behind it. Australia first rocketted to importance in the 1870s: the skills of Cornish immigrant miners, put out of work at home, helped her to assume briefly the mantle of world leader. Yet it is only in the last 15 years that Australia has returned to being a significant producer again. Seventy per cent of Australia's production today comes from the Renison, Aberfoyle and Cleveland mines in Tasmania and the hard-rock open-cast Ardlethan mine in New South Wales; the rest comes from small mines and alluvial workings in Queensland, New South Wales and Western Australia. Renison has been rejuvenated since 1964 by Consolidated Gold Fields. The Australians have been more successful in recovering tin from low-grade vein deposits than have the Bolivians who face similar mining and metallurgical problems.

Cornwall, too, saw a revival in its time-honored tin mining activities in the 1960s and early 1970s with fresh capital being sunk in the two remaining mines (Geevor and South Crofty) of the 24 that were working at the close of the First World War; Wheal Jane is to re-open in 1980. Cornwall occupies a more important place in the world tin picture than its current production would suggest. The Cambourne School of Mines remains the Alma Mater of many of the world's hard-rock tin miners and many of the innovations in tin processing still originate in Cornwall.

The major African producers, on the other hand, have suffered a decline of over one-third in output during the last ten years, a trend at variance with that of any other continent or region. In 1968, *Nigeria* produced 10,000 tonnes of tin-in-concentrates; in 1978 the figure was under 4,000 tonnes. An absence of reserves cannot be blamed for this decline. Difficulty in attracting mine labor is a partial answer: this is a difficulty partly brought upon the industry by its own reluctance (not necessarily a social mistake) to substitute machines for men. A further partial explanation lies in the reorganization that the heretofore private, mainly British, mining companies have undergone in the last few years. Sixty per cent of the capital of such companies has been acquired by Nigerians and the Nigerian Mining Corporation as part of a national policy now virtually completed. The reorganized Amalgamated Tin Mines of Nigeria remains responsible for about half of the country's tin but has been unlucky in its attempts with draglines to remove the over-burden from the sub-basalt deposits; other companies are reluctant to embark on new ventures until the amalgamations of existing units have been completed and the policies of the new controllers are established.

In *Zaire* production is half what it was in the late 1960s; this in turn, was half what it had been during the 1950s, the last decade of Belgian colonial rule in the Congo. No other tin mining area of substance has had such a rapid rise and fall in output. It was during the 1930s that metropolitan capital was put into Belgian tin mining companies funded to work concessions originally granted to the railway company. The deposits are relatively numerous though individually small in extent; only alluvial and eluvial ore is worked. Peak production (15,000 tonnes per year) occurred during the privileged conditions of World War II, and since then there has been a stepped decline. Both capital and skilled personnel are obviously difficult to attract into Zaire. The recently elaborated new mining plan is mainly aimed at restoring confidence in the much more important nationalized copper industry, but it also sheds light on the difficulties that any joint venture in Zaire might anticipate.

Several generalities follow from the preceding survey of tin producing countries. The first is the remarkable degree of concentration of the industry. One country, Malaysia, produces a quarter of the world's tin: three produce one-half; and the leading five countries account for three out of every four tonnes of tin produced. This is a higher degree of concentration than found in the other three older non-ferrous metals − copper, zinc and lead − and indeed in iron ore itself; it is comparable to that found in the bauxite and nickel industries, both newer elements on the world industrial scene than tin. Equally remarkable is the degree of concentration in particular regions of the world: in particular South-east Asia where half the world's tin is produced. It is remarkable that there is no tin in North America. The major source of tin in the western hemisphere is Bolivia and the USA has had a difficult time nursing that economy through the troubles of the 1960s and 1970s.

The impression of unbalance is confirmed when viewed against patterns of world trade. The three leading South-east Asian producing countries supply two-thirds of the tin which enters world trade; with Bolivia they are responsible for four-fifths. None of the major consumers of tin, with the exception of the USSR, are self-sufficient in the metal; none of the major producers of tin consume more than a small fraction of the tin they produce. It is only in China, and in Brazil and Australia in the third division of producers, that domestic demands make many substantial inroads on the tin produced at home.

The tin produced and traded in the MECs is essentially a product of the Third World. The average per capita income of the Big Four producers (that is, excluding the USSR and China) was $467 in 1976. The average income of all tin producing countries, weighted to take account of the size of their production, was higher at $1,130. In contrast, the average income of the tin consuming countries, weighted by the amount of tin they consumed, was more than four times higher, at almost exactly $5,000. The world, as seen from the vantage points of the producers, is an unfair one: their tin is undervalued to the degree that the standard of living of their citizens falls below that enjoyed by citizens of the consuming countries.

Half the world's tin is produced by state-run enterprises and part of the remainder is produced by private companies in which the state plays a significant role. The move in recent years has been towards public ownership of national tin mining industries. This move has not been at the expense of the big mining MNCs since they have not been as involved in the mining of tin as they have of other allied metals. In fact, the MNCs have become more closely involved with tin once the process of nationalization has got under way and their management skills have been called upon. The degree of success of the state mining corporations has been mixed. It is possible that the relatively small scale of individual tin deposits mitigates against the success of large corporations whose scale can make them insensitive to the specific requirements of individual sites. The effect of growing public ownership in the tin industry on the availability of capital for investment is equally unclear. International governmental aid may be more readily available to a national enterprise than to one in private hands and even compensate for exclusion from access to domestic and overseas private capital. Attempts by the American government to rehabilitate Bolivia's nationalized industry were conditioned by the political need to sustain a country thought important to American security; at a purely economic level the consultants found the private sector much more worthy of capital injection. Signs suggest that the real weakness of those nationalized tin mining corporations whose functioning is open to inspection lies in their inability to develop new reserves. It has not always proved easy for politicians to appreciate the need for, and to justify, the expenditure of scarce funds on chancy exploration ventures at the expense of achieving more immediate results in the frequently limited lifetime of a national government. Once the error of sacrificing expenditure on exploration is appreciated, a role frequently emerges for the mining MNCs, which can normally bring to bear a much wider experience in the establishment and development of new reserves than that possessed by the nationalized concern. And by restricting their role to the discovery and proving of fresh reserves, they avoid the popular odium of being cast as international robbers of national inheritances more interested in private gain than public benefit. It is still easy, nevertheless, for mining MNCs to become scapegoats for bad government or find themselves *persona non grata* with new regimes, and the corporations have to be careful in safeguarding themselves against the consequences of bad faith of successor governments. In general, the international mining houses command more resources than do even the larger organizational units in the tin mining economy. The three largest units outside the USSR are the Indonesian PT Tambang Timah corporation with a tin production of 24,000 tonnes in 1978, Comibol (21,500 tonnes), and the Malaysian Mining Corporation (19,000 tonnes), with turnovers that fell within the range of US$250 to 300 million. In contrast, Consolidated Goldfields (with a 36 per cent interest in the Renison mine) had a turnover of almost $2,000 million, as did Kennecott Copper and Asarco; the aluminium giants — Alcoa, Kaiser and Reynolds — all exceeded that figure; and the turnover of the big steel companies dwarfed even those, By comparison even large tin corporations are relatively small fry in the international mining pond.

The average working unit in tin is also relatively small. The biggest underground mines — Catavi in Bolivia, Renison in Tasmania — each handled about 600,000 tonnes of rock in 1978 and Renison produced 5,300 tonnes of tin worth about $67 million; the biggest tin dredge is capable of an annual throughput of eight million cubic metres and a production of 1,500-2,000 tonnes of tin. But the number of mines producing 1,000 tonnes of tin a year can be counted on the fingers of a pair of hands and the 105 dredges operating in South-east Asia in 1978 each produced an average of only 360 tonnes of tin-in-concentrates valued at about $4.6 million. The gravel pumps are much smaller units: 1,200 were working in 1978, each producing an average of 44 tonnes of tin with a market value of $572,000. Nor is productivity high, even excluding the peasant miners. The average underground miner produces 1.7 tonnes of tin a year; his counterpart on a dredge 2.2 tonnes; and gravel pump operators only one tonne of tin per worker.

THE PROCESSING OF TIN

Tin ore is low-grade ore. About one-quarter of the tin produced is from lode mines and emerges from the ground in material that nowadays is considered rich if it contains one per cent tin. The average grade of ground worked by many Malaysian dredges is currently as low as 0.2 lb/yd^3 or seven parts in every 100,000 by weight. The mill handling material from the Ardlethan open pit in Australia treated 588,975 tonnes of material to recover 1,715 tonnes of tin in 1978, a return of one tonne of tin for every 343 tonnes of material handled; in 1977 the ground worked assayed between 0.2 and 0.3 per cent of tin. These grades are perhaps 25 per cent below those of ten years ago.

The lean grade of most ores makes for particular problems in processing concentrates. All the ore is turned into concentrates at the minehead, on the dredge or, in general, at the site of production. This means that the concentrating mills are dispersed and handle relatively small volumes of ore. Some are highly efficient, being precisely adjusted to the particular characteristics of the local ore; others are inefficient. The processes employed are in large part mechanized versions of the gravitational sorting techniques employed by the pre-industrial miners of Europe. These ancient techniques are more widely employed in the tin industry than in those of other non-ferrous minerals, partly because cassiterite has a relatively high density compared with the ores of most other mineral ores and makes the old process more effective in tin. As yet there has been very little application of non-gravimetric methods in the tinfields of the world. This means that the processing of ore is still one in which the individual skill and attention of the mill worker can materially affect recovery rates; automation plays only a negligible role to date. Techniques long employed in the processing of other minerals have made little headway in the modern tin mining industry. Flotation is employed in a few of the mills attached to the underground mines where the head carries a more complex range of minerals and where fine grinding is needed to liberate the cassiterite fragments. Volatization has so far gained only very limited application: it is expensive of energy and has yet to prove economical in the market economies outside the USSR.

The tin smelting industry is more footloose in its location. Historically, heavy transport costs have meant that tin concentrates were smelted on the spot, but the cost of transporting bulky ores has fallen. With the advent of the steamship it became economical to transport concentrates from the mines perhaps half-way around the world to feed the smelters of the new industrial powers of 19th century Europe. Smelters could grow large and enjoy economies of scale. The tin smelters have traditionally been independent of both the mines and the tin-consuming industries. Tin smelting has been a toll arrangement in which a service was provided to the tin producers for a fixed charge independent of the price of tin. The smelters have traditionally helped to even-out the cash flow of mining companies by advancing money on the strength of concentrates held. Marketing has not been a function of the smelters.

The distribution of smelters at the end of the first half of the 20th century illustrates their freedom to locate almost at will. Half the world's tin smelting capacity was situated in the tinfields — notably in Malaya — and the other half in the industrial world — notably in the former imperial countries of Western Europe. The smelters in Singapore and Penang, financed by British capital, drew upon Malay production (thanks to an export levy on concentrates) and that of Thailand. Bolivian and Nigerian concentrates came to Britain; half of Indonesia's concentrates were smelted in the Netherlands and those from the Belgian Congo in continental Europe. Perhaps the most interesting and exceptional development during the first half of the 20th century was the entry of Simon Patiño into the tin smelting field in 1912. By the late 1930s Patiño companies controlled half the world's tin capacity. But the smelters remained separate entities and were not integrated backwards into the mining companies. The relationships between producer and smelter and between smelter and consumer have been weaker in tin than in other mineral industries.

The last twenty years has seen a move to closer financial and geographical ties between the smelters and the mines. No self-respecting tin producing country now feels it can be without its own smelter. Economic arguments quantifying the anticipated savings in shipping costs of transporting metal rather than more bulky concentrates, the transfer of the value added in the smelting process, the savings in foreign exchange, and the possible roll-on effects within other sectors of the economy, have all been used to justify a domestic smelting industry. Studies to date suggest that these economic arguments are not necessarily conclusive, but this is frequently irrelevant. The building of a domestic tin smelter has been a political decision and its accomplishment a matter of national pride.

New state-owned smelters have been opened in Indonesia and in Bolivia in the 1970s and now smelt a majority of the domestic concentrates there produced. Two new smelters were opened in Nigeria in 1961; a new privately-owned smelter opened in Thailand in 1965, and Brazilian smelters have expanded their capacity to process the new tin coming from the Amazonian fields. Some Chinese concentrates are still smelted outside the Republic but no Soviet tin is smelted abroad. Many long-established smelters in Europe have closed and world smelting capacity remains above requirements. As recently as 1958 half of the world's tin production (excluding that of the CPEs) was smelted in Europe; 1958 was the last year in which the production of tin metal was greater in Europe than in Asia. Ten years later, Europe still produced one-quarter of the world's tin; by 1978 it produced under one-eighth. Two-thirds of the world's tin concentrates is now smelted in Southeast Asia. Malaysia has the largest output, producing 72,000 tonnes of tin in 1978. Thailand (29,000 tonnes), Indonesia (26,000 tonnes) and Bolivia (16,000 tonnes) were next in order, and in the same category as the USSR (31,000 tonnes) and China (20,000 tonnes). Brazil (9,500 tonnes) overtook the UK (8,500 tonnes) as a producer of tin metal in 1979. Only 11 per cent of the world's tin in 1978 was smelted outside the producing countries.

THE TRADE IN TIN

The shift to domestic smelting has reduced the volume of world trade in concentrates, but increased that in tin ingots. In 1977 only about 42,000 tonnes of tin-in-concentrates, or one-sixth of the world's production, entered world trade compared with, for example, 58,000 tonnes in 1970. The addition of a further 10,000 tonnes to Bolivia's domestic smelting capacity before the end of 1980 can only reduce trade in concentrates. This new capacity will raise that available in the world to 400,000 tonnes per year — a capacity 60 per cent in excess of that required.

There is now four times as much metal as concentrates entering the world trade in tin. Although exports of imported tin metal from the USA, the UK, Malaysia and Singapore are included in world trade figures, their impact on the essential trade pattern is negligible. The links between producer and consumer have become more direct now that most production is smelted at home. For example, in 1967 Europe exported 27,000 tonnes of metal; ten years later the figure had been reduced by 10,000 tonnes. The leading exporters of tin metal in 1977 were Malaysia (63,179 tonnes), Indonesia (23,521 tonnes), Thailand (23,295 tonnes) and Bolivia (12,478 tonnes): they accounted for over three-quarters of the total supply. The countries of destination were more numerous. The USA (48,338 tonnes) absorbed over one-third of the total and the EEC countries (46,000 tonnes) another one-third. Japan (28,200 tonnes) accounted for two-thirds of the residue. The rest of the world took up the remaining 10 per cent.

THE CONSUMPTION OF TIN

Table 6.2 shows the geographical pattern of consumption of primary tin (that is, newly-smelted tin metal, as distinct from secondary tin which is reclaimed from scrap, mainly in alloy form, and used again). Twenty years ago the USA used one-third of the world's tin; today she consumes about one-quarter. The actual figure reached an all-time high of 61,175 tonnes in 1966 but by 1978 had returned to the same level (47,000 tonnes) that it had been twenty years earlier. The nine countries which now make up the EEC used 52,300 tonnes in 1958, 49,667 tonnes in 1968, and 49,941 tonnes in 1978: in proportional terms,

Table 6.2. *Primary Tin Consumption, 1978*

	Tonnes
US	47,000
USSR	33,000*
Japan	28,973
China	15,000*
West Germany	13,465
UK	13,189
France	10,264
Italy	6,800
Canada	5,005
Brazil	5,000
Others	55,600*
Total	233,300*

* See Table 6.1.

Western Europe's share of manufactured tin has dropped from about one-third twenty years ago to one-fifth today. Consumption in Europe as a whole has risen following the probable doubling of consumption within the USSR, however, and the share of Europe (including the USSR) has remained remarkably stable during the period at about 47-48 per cent of the world total. Japan has doubled (to 12 per cent) the proportion of the world's tin she uses in spite of a relative decline since 1973. Changes in the share of Asia in world tin consumption are almost entirely due to the predominant role of Japan. Nevertheless, if one makes assumptions about the situation within Mainland China it is a notable fact that one-quarter of the world's tin is now consumed in Asia compared with one-fifth twenty years ago. Yet the average American continues to use 4.5 times his fair share of the world's tin, the average Japanese four times (1.8 in 1958) and the average West European three times (four in 1955). In contrast, that half of the world's population which lives in Asia, excluding Japan, uses only one-fifth of their notional allocation of the world's tin. This fraction is, however, higher than the one-seventh of twenty years ago.

Regional changes in the proportions of tin consumed can be related to the well-known strengths and weaknesses of particular industrial economies. A more remarkable feature of world tin consumption, however, is the lack of change in the gross amount consumed: this has not risen in line with other global indicators of world economic growth. In 1900 about 100,000 tonnes of primary tin were absorbed by world industry. Consumption reached a peak of about 185,000 tonnes in 1929, falling to about 155,000 in 1939. It returned to the 1939 level in 1950 and is currently about 220,000 tonnes a year. Consumption by the MECs averaged 141,000 tonnes during the 1950s, 170,000 tonnes in the 1960s, and 191,000 tonnes in the 1970s. The rate at which the free market for tin has grown slacked from two per cent to 1.3 per cent per annum between 1950 and 1970; consumption in 1978 was exactly the same as in 1970. These growth rates are very much lower than those measuring the demand for the older non-ferrous metals — lead, zinc, copper, aluminium — or, indeed, for steel.

An analysis of the uses to which tin is put suggests some of the reasons for what to producers is a disappointing trend. Tinplate remains the most important single absorber of tin and 40-45 per cent of the world's production is used in the manufacture of 'tins' for the canning industry, an adjunct of the world's steel industry. The preserving of food and drink is clearly a growth industry and, although tinplate has suffered competition from other packaging materials — plastics, paper, aluminium and glass — output has doubled every twenty years since 1900, from a little under one million tonnes of tinplate in 1900 to over 14 million tonnes in 1977. The fact that tin consumption has not matched this rate of expansion is partly explained by the replacement in tinplate manufacture of the old hot-dipping process (in which the steel was dipped into a bath of molten tin) by electrolytic coating. The latter allows much greater control over the thickness of the coating; it has reduced the thickness of the average tin coating to one-third of what it was thirty years ago. Were an adequate substitute for tin to be found, the tinplates mills, with their loyalties to the steel industry and not the tin industry, would not hesitate to switch from tin. The fact that almost half the world's tin production depends upon a single usage is never far from the forefront of tin producers' minds.

The second important usage of tin is in solder. Again, tin is used as a minor constituent of a bi-metalic product: in this case lead is the principal constituent. The industrial need to make joints and connections has, of course, risen during the century and no satisfactory substitute has been found to date for tin in solder. Refinements in the technology of manufacturing have meant much more careful control over both the amount of solder used and the amount of tin needed in the alloy, and these have more or less counter-balanced any tendency towards an enhanced demand. The remaining one-third of world tin consumption is partly in the form of other alloys, including the traditional ones of bronze and pewter and the industrial white metal alloys used in bearings, and partly in industrial chemicals and petrochemicals. Only very rarely is tin used as a major constituent of a finished article.

A proportion of the world's tin is recycled. Most of the tin reclaimed from discarded primary usages is from alloys such as bronzes, brasses, solders, bearing and type metals, and is used again, in alloy form. The UK is the most expert at reclaiming secondary tin (at least according to statistics — it is a difficult area to monitor successfully) and in recent years has accounted for about one-third of the 10,000 tonnes of tin entering the free world economy in this fashion. Scope to increase this total remains and during times of emergency tin has been recovered from old tinplate scrap: but normally the prices of both scrap steel and secondary tin do not warrant the cost of reclamation.

The prospects of a dramatic increase in the consumption of tin in the foreseeable future are not rosy. The US Bureau of Mines has forecast that American consumption of tin is likely to rise at a rate of only 0.3 per cent per annum for the rest of this century. The requirements of the US tinplate industry are likely to fall from being over one-third to becoming under one-quarter of the total tin consumed and, partly as a consequence of this changed pattern of demand, secondary tin is likely to provide a higher proportion (say 20 per cent) of tin requirements. The same source believes that the probable annual growth during the next twenty years in world demand for primary tin will be at a rate of only one per cent (and that of secondary tin 1.9 per cent). In tonnages these rates yield a most probable global demand of 306,000 tonnes of primary tin in the year 2000, supplemented by 47,000 tonnes of secondary tin. There is a real possibility, however, that demand may actually fall. The anticipated low rate of growth of demand for tin is in contrast with the higher rates anticipated for almost all other metals. The only metals for which lower rates of growth in the USA are anticipated are mercury and thallium. The demands for copper (2.9 per cent), iron-in-ore (1.6 per cent), both lead and zinc (1.9 per cent), nickel (3.0 per cent) and tungsten (4.6 per cent) are expected to rise in line with the expected growth in GNP (3.3 per cent) and in the rate of industrial production (3.7 per cent), both of which variables were used in modelling the demand for metals.

INTERNATIONAL CO-OPERATION IN TIN

The historically low rate of expansion in the market for tin and the relatively pessimistic outlook for growth during the next twenty years; the strong dichotomies apparent between the characters of the supplying countries and those of the consuming countries; the central importance of tin in the export economies of the producing countries and its relative insignificance in the trading accounts of the importing countries; the growing investment of national capital in the mining and smelting of tin; the greater difficulty of attracting private investment capital into tin than into other metals; these and other considerations combine to make the world trade in tin a matter more strongly charged with political interest than that of many other raw materials.

This interest has been given concrete form in the operations of the many international tin agreements (ITA) which have been in existence for most of the last fifty years. The first ITA was a product of the world economic slump and came into force in 1931. It was an agreement amongst producing countries to limit the amount of tin entering the market by using a buffer stock to adjust supply to demand and thereby maintain a reasonable tin price; it was moderately successful and served as a useful model for the deliberations of the International Tin Study Group after World War II. By 1954 the International Tin Council (ITC) had been formed and since 1956 has administered a succession of five-year ITAs.

The aim of the ITAs has been to ensure that the wider political interests of the producing and consuming countries are taken into account in the world trade in tin. Their interests include the alleviation of social distress in the producing countries during times of reduced demand for tin, the prevention of excessive fluctuations in the price of tin, the provision of bases for longer-term planning, and the ensuring of adequate supplies of tin at reasonable prices at all times. Clauses in successive ITAs have adumbrated the need to maintain the export earnings of producing countries, to review the disposal of non-commercial stocks, and to promote the efficient development and exploration of new resources. One of the strengths of the ITAs has been that all the major producers which enter world trade have been signatories to the agreements. Brazil is the only current exception but may join the Sixth Agreement in 1981. One of the more recent features of the ITAs has been the fuller involvement of the consuming countries. At first the USA was the only notable outsider but the strong recovery of the West German and Japanese economies quickly made their absences felt. The changing climate of world opinion and the rise of producer-rings in other raw materials fields have meant that all the big consumers including the USSR have now been netted by the ITC and all are bound by the ITAs.

The direct way in which the ITC attempts to influence the tin market is by the use of the twin weapons of a buffer stock and export control. The size of the buffer stock, 20,000 tonnes of tin or its cash equivalent, has been too small to achieve completely the balance sought. It has, for example, had no tin in stock since January 1977 and has been ineffective in clamping down on price rises. It is expected that the buffer stock will be expanded when the next five-year Agreement becomes open for signature in 1980. Export control has not been popular with some producers. A very important indirect weapon has been the influence that ITC has been able to muster to prevent distortion of the market by the dumping of tin surplus to the strategic requirements of the Russians in the late 1950s and of the Americans more recently. The American strategic stockpile contains 200,000 tonnes of tin and if released could have a very depressing effect upon tin prices. With legislation pending requiring the USA to dispose of 35,000 tonnes of tin, the ITC has been heavily exercized in trying to ensure that such a release would have no deleterious affect on the economies of the producing countries.

It is difficult to be dogmatic about the effect of the various ITAs on the world tin industry. The general view is that they have worked reasonably well. The fact that they have been in force continuously for a quarter-of-a-century and that the numbers of interested parties adhering to them has increased is testimony in itself. Although there is some sabre-rattling among producers in favour of an OPEC-like cartel, it is generally expected that a sixth five-year agreement will come into force in 1981. The yardstick against which the performance of the ITAs is most frequently measured is the price of tin which is established on the three tin markets: London, Penang and New York. The prices are established competitively in the light of supply and demand. In this respect, tin resembles gold and tungsten and differs from metals such as aluminium and steel, whose prices are set by producers; it also differs from copper, lead and zinc which are sold both on producer-controlled markets and on the LME and New York Commodity Exchange. A review of the prices of tin and other non-ferrous metals in the USA during the period since 1956, the year in which the first post-war ITA came into force, reveals that, using the average price in 1955-57 as a base of 100, the average price of tin in 1977 was 601.7; of copper 179.6; of lead 200.8; of nickel 336.3; of zinc 277.7, and of aluminium 199.6. Thus, in spite of a flagging demand, the price of tin has not slumped relative to other metals, rather the reverse. It also suggests the possible depressing effect on the market that a release of the marginal supplies of tin held in the US stockpile could have. Calculations of the range through which the price has fluctuated during each of the years since 1956 suggests that the ITAs have damped down the worst of the fluctuations from which the metal suffered in pre-ITA days. Between 1956 and 1977 the highest price of tin on the Penang exchange in any given year averaged only 13 per cent above the average price of the year, the lowest price was only ten per cent below that average figure.

The Tin Agreements have their critics, the most vociferous internal critic being Bolivia which is in the forefront of moves to create a producers' cartel. Bolivia's dissatisfaction stems from many sources but is partly a consequence of her heavy dependency upon tin. Exports of tin have supplied over half Bolivia's foreign exchange earnings for decades and no other country is so vulnerable to changes in the price of the metal. She taxes tin more heavily than most producers and in some years derives one-third of governmental income from levies on the metal.

High prices are more important to Bolivia than to any other producer because her production costs are higher than those of any other supplier to the world market. Figures recently released by the ITC and showing comparative production costs for mid-1978, give the following values (in Malaysian dollars per picul, or 133.33 lbs): Bolivia $1.685; Malaysia $1,304; Indonesia $1,303; Thailand $1,191; UK $1,145; Australia $1,101. Bolivian costs are half as much again as those of the other hard-rock mining districts of Cornwall and of Australia. The importance to Bolivia of belonging to an organization which, its critics say, tends to fossilize production patterns, is clear. The figures for Australia suggest something of the benefits to be won by heavy private investment on a scale more normally associated with other metals. Under the umbrella of the ITAs Bolivia has survived, Australia has grown fat, and a dialogue has been maintained between producers and consumers. Thanks to the ITC, the activities of the tin industry are better understood than are those of most other metals and the characteristics that make the tin industry unique are better documented.

REFERENCES

W. Fox, *Tin: The Working of a Commodity Agreement* (London, 1974).
K.L. Harris, *Tin: Mineral Commodity Profile 16* (Bureau of Mines, US Department of the Interior, 1978).
International Tin Council, *Monthly Statistical Bulletin*.
——, *Tin Statistics* (1967-1977).
——, *Statistical Yearbook* (1968).
——, *Technical Conferences on Tin* (1967, 1969).
Mining Annual Review (London, 1979).
Tin International (London, monthly).

PART II

CHANGING RELATIONSHIPS BETWEEN
MINERAL PRODUCERS AND CONSUMERS

MARKET STRUCTURE AND BARGAINING POWER

M. Radetzki

The purpose of this paper is to study how market structure affects the bargaining power and ultimately the division of benefits from trade between buyers and sellers. Three international mineral markets – for bauxite, iron ore and copper – constitute the cases on which the analysis is based.

In all three markets, a major proportion of overall supply originates in the developing countries, and the paper centers on how LDC exporters are affected by differing market conditions. To the extent that definite conclusions on the chosen issue can be reached, they will suggest the direction of market reforms aimed at increasing LDCs' benefits from their participation in the international exchange of the three commodities.

THE THREE COMMODITIES COMPARED

In 1975, about 80 million tons of bauxite, 900 million tons of iron ore, and 7.3 million tons of copper metal were mined. Aluminium is a new metal experiencing a much faster growth in demand than iron and copper which explains the dynamic expansions of bauxite output. The 1975 production of aluminium was about three times the 1960 level. For both copper and iron ore, the production level had less than doubled over the corresponding period.[1]

World trade has recently constituted around 40 per cent of overall output for the three materials. Bauxite trade expansion has been slowed down by increasing local processing into alumina in several major producing countries. In value terms copper trade is much higher than trade in bauxite and iron ore. Table 7.1 provides summary data on the value of world exports as well as on the exports of LDCs for the three products.

International trade in copper is truly global. The unit value of copper, whether in the form of concentrate or refined metal, is high, and even very long transport adds little to total costs. Consequently, one finds considerable trade flows from each of the three major exporting areas – South America, Southern

Reproduced with the permission of IPC Business Press from *Resources Policy* (June 1978).

Notes to this chapter may be found on page 142.

Table 7.1. *Gross Exports, Average Annual Values 1973-1975 (million $)*

	Bauxite	*Iron ore*	*Copper*
World	529	4285	7487
Of which developing countries	376	1707	3965

and Central Africa and the Western Pacific Rim — to Europe, Japan and the USA.[2]

The unit values of bauxite and iron ore are much lower, and transport charges weigh more heavily in the total cif price. Before 1960 there was no world market in these commodities. Even in the mid-1970s, bauxite and iron ore trade has a regional character. Most of Australia's supplies of these commodities are sent to Japan; Caribbean bauxite has a natural market in the USA, while that produced in West Africa is usually sold in Europe. Europe also buys most of West Africa's and Brazil's iron ore, while US import requirements of iron ore are largely met by Canada and Venezuela.[3]

In the past 15 years, with the introduction of huge ore carriers and the establishment of efficient bulk handling facilities at major ports, it has become economically possible to ship the two commodities over much greater distance. As a result, the regional markets are gradually being merged into one single world market.

More than 80 per cent of the traded supplies of the three commodities end up in the world's industrial centers — Western Europe, the USA and Japan. The dependence of each of these areas on imported supplies varies considerably. In Japan 90-100 per cent of domestic requirements for the three materials have to be bought from abroad. In Western Europe, import dependence is around 50 per cent for iron ore and bauxite, but nearly 90 per cent for primary copper. The USA is almost self-sufficient in copper, but imports 30 per cent of its iron ore needs and more than 90 per cent of the raw materials for aluminium.[4]

The availability of old scrap reduces the degree of import dependence described by the above figures. About 25 per cent of overall iron and copper metal consumption is satisfied from such scrap. In aluminium, the figure is considerably lower — perhaps about five per cent.[5]

Scale economies are considerable in the production of the three materials, and an increasing share of world output is produced in giant mining operations. Both in terms of tonnage and investment requirements, the largest scale is required for the exploitation of iron ore deposits located far away from the sea and in areas where infrastructural facilities have to be built up from scratch. An annual production capacity of ten million tons, and a total investment of $1.5 billion[6] or more is often required to make such projects economical. When deposits are nearer to the sea, or when use can be made of existing infrastructures, the scale can be considerably smaller, with investment needs not exceeding $100-200 million. A similar distinction can be made for bauxite deposits, though both the capacity and investment figures would be no more than half of that required for iron ore. In the case of copper, a major proportion of the additions to world supply result from projects with a production capacity above 100,000 tons of metal content, and with investment requirements above $500 million.[7] Numerous economic projects with capacities of no more than 30-50,000 tons, and total investment needs from $100 upwards have also been developed in recent years, however.

Specialized organization skills and advanced technology are required for building a modern mine, but neither of these is monopolized. Given the availability of financial resources, both a government of an LDC and a firm with no earlier mining experience can buy the talents needed from the international market to develop deposits of bauxite, copper or iron ore, and to run mines, although former experience in such activities is likely to make these operations cheaper and more efficient.

MARKET ARRANGEMENTS

Bauxite

About 75 per cent of world bauxite output originates in six countries, with Australia and the Caribbean supplying more than half of the total.[8] The material is used almost exclusively for aluminium production.

The world aluminium industry is a tight oligopoly, dominated by six MNCs, of which three are domiciled in the USA. These firms are fully integrated, occupying strategic positions in the industry from raw materials production to marketing both the metal and metal products. Considerably more than 50 per cent of non-socialist world capacity of bauxite, alumina and aluminium is under their control.[9] Through a variety of consortia arrangements, one or several of these firms are associated with practically all new projects of international significance within the industry.[10]

The oligopoly has a strong hold over the market for aluminium metal and metal goods. Prices of aluminium in the world market are tightly controlled by the firms, and the official quotations show a high degree of correspondence and stability. There exists a small free market for aluminium, in which metal from the USSR and other minor sources is offered. Prices in this market fluctuate in consonance with those of the LME quotations for other non-ferrous metals.

Production costs of bauxite in the mid-1970s have been estimated at $6-12/ ton, and ocean transport varies between $3 and $15 per ton, depending on length of the haul, the higher figure constituting an extreme. Total delivered cost of bauxite, excluding taxes and government levies in exporting countries, amounts to between $10 and $25 per ton.[11] About five tons of bauxite are required to produce one ton of aluminium metal. With aluminium metal prices varying between $750 and $1100 per ton in recent years,[12] bauxite costs (excluding taxes) constitute no more than 5-15 per cent of the refined metal price, and still less of the aluminium product price.

Prices are ordinarily a major guide for determining the division of benefits between buyer and seller, but the international bauxite market constitutes an exception. Only very fragmentary information is available on the prices of arm's length sales. For the major share of international bauxite trade, export prices consist of quotations internal to the MNCs.[13] These quotations are adjusted upwards or downwards, often without reference to levels of cost or value, with the sole motive of helping the firms attain their global profit maximization objective.

The structure of the integrated aluminium industry and the artificial nature of most price quotations suggest that, for a major share of bauxite trade, the real trading partners are the governments of exporting countries and the companies, and that taxes and other government levies assume the role ordinarily played by prices in dividing the benefits between buyers and seller. Bargaining power will therefore be reflected in the ability to influence the fiscal conditions on which the integrated foreign investors are permitted to exploit bauxite in producing and exporting countries.

Iron Ore

Seven exporting countries and six importing nations account for more than 80 per cent of world trade in iron ore.[14] About 20 per cent of the total consists of internal transactions between mines and steel mills under the same ownership. Half of the rest is sold under short term (one year) contracts, which are regularly renewed. Many stable trade relationships extending over decades are based on such annual contractual agreements. The remaining 40 per cent of iron ore exports are transacted on long-run contracts, over 10-15 years. The long-run contracts became a common feature of the international iron ore market from the early 1960s, when a number of new large-scale mines were opened up in Africa, Australia and Latin America. The international investors who provided finance for these ventures commonly required that the new mines sign extended delivery contracts with steel producers in the industrialized centers, to assure an adequate cash flow during the period of loan repayment. By the time the contracts ran out, and the loans had been repaid, the mines commonly converted to selling their production on an annual contract basis.

Though the distinction in terms of contractual arrangements between old and new mines continues to prevail, the difference in substance between long-run and short-run contracts has been reduced in the present decade. Whereas in the 1960s the long-run contracts ordinarily specified the price at which the product would be sold throughout the contract period, more recently, as a result of the high inflation which has prevailed, the contracts usually provide for annual bilateral renegotiations of the price levels. Spot trade is not an important feature in the iron ore market.

Substantial foreign ownership still remains in the world iron ore industry. In the past 15 years, however, governments have acquired a strong equity interest in the iron ore mines of most exporting countries, and have extended their control over the industry by various other means. One result has been far-reaching coordination of the export efforts at the national level. Conditions for exports from countries like Brazil, Peru, Venezuela and India are closely supervised by the national governments. In Australia, too, government approval is usually required for major export contracts. There are not many iron ore exporting countries where the private miners are free to enter into contractual agreements independently of government. For all practical purposes, therefore, the market concentration among sellers is as high as that among exporting nations.

The steel industry, which consumes 95 per cent of all iron ore, is also heavily concentrated, both among and within nations. International iron ore purchasing is even more concentrated. In Japan, the UK and Belgium, the entire purchase needs are handled by one single agency. The German steel mills are represented in the ore market by only two organizations.[15] Even though antitrust legislation prevents formal collusion in the US steel industry, the concentration on the buying side is nevertheless high, in view of the dominant position of the largest steel producers in that country. The emergent degree of concentration among iron ore buyers and sellers appears to be equally high.

More than 90 per cent of world steel production is consumed locally. The oligopolistic market structure in the major steel producing countries, as well as outright government intervention, help maintain relatively stable internal steel prices in the short run.[16]

In the DCs, the iron ore used to produce one ton of steel usually contains no more than 0.6 tons of iron,[17] while the rest is provided by the use of old and new scrap. Taking the representative cif price of iron ore of about 60 per cent Fe content, delivered at North Sea ports in 1975-76 at $20/ton, and the domestic German steel price in that period at about $300/ton,[18] the iron ore cost is seen to constitute less than ten per cent of the final product price of the steel industry.

The short-run contracts as well as the price levels of the long-run contracts are renegotiated once a year. Each negotiation is a bilateral deal, involving one selling and one buying organization. The outcome of each depends heavily on information from other negotiations carried on simultaneously, or concluded in the recent past. As a result, there is a certain convergence in the cif prices of comparable qualities of iron ore in each consuming area.

Copper

Six developing countries and Canada account for more than 80 per cent of net world exports of copper, while Western Europe and Japan take an equally high share of global imports.[19] International vertical integration is not common in the copper industry, and exports, whether of refined or unrefined metal, almost always consist of arm's length transactions.

As in the case of iron ore, the government of several exporting countries have acquired strong control over their copper industries, through equity ownership or otherwise.[20] This has resulted in considerable concentration of the decision units responsible for copper exports. Thus, almost all the export trade of Chile, Zaire and Zambia is handled in each country by a government-owned copper marketing organization. In Peru, marketing of copper is tightly controlled by the government, while in Papua New Guinea, all copper production originates from one mine. Only in Canada and the Philippines (22 per cent of net world exports), among the major exporting countries, is copper trade decentralized to several individual mines.

Substantially more than half of net world exports of copper are in the form of refined metal.[21] Refined wirebars and cathodes are bought by the copper fabricating industry, which shapes them into a variety of forms, and sells them to copper using manufacturing industries. The degree of concentration in copper fabrication is considerably lower than among the copper exporters. Even the largest fabricating concerns have capacities for copper absorption far below the output and sales of the major producing units.[22]

A major share of refined copper is sold to independent fabricators, without forward links. The value added by such fabricators to the raw material is fairly limited, and 80-90 per cent of the value of the fabricated products is represented by the refined copper itself.[23]

Some copper using manufacturing industries have acquired their own fabricating facilities. In such cases, it is difficult to provide a general assessment of the share of the copper input in the value of the final product sold, since this would vary between products and industries.

Unrefined copper in international trade is bought by smelters and refineries in the industrial centers of the world. There are considerable economies of scale in processing, and the important buyers of unrefined metal, located in five countries only, are at least as highly concentrated as the exporters.[24]

Quite frequently, the smelter and refiners that import unrefined copper are integrated forward into fabricating. The copper raw material costs would constitute about half of the fabricated product price for an establishment combining a smelter, a refinery and a fabricating plant.[25]

A high proportion of world trade in unrefined copper ends up with Japanese smelters,[26] many of which constitute the backward integration end of elaborate industrial complexes which include a variety of manufacturing industries. The unrefined copper purchased by such establishments obviously constitutes a relatively limited share of the value of the final product which they sell.

Refined copper is sold on the basis of annually negotiated bilateral contracts which specify quantities and brands. They also stipulate that current quotations on the LME should be used to determine the price of contractural shipments. Unrefined copper is mostly sold under long-run contracts extending over many years. Here too, the LME quotation is used as a basis for pricing, though deductions are made for the cost of processing the material.

The LME is a truly marginal market for refined copper. Its physical turnover is commonly no higher than 5-10 per cent of world trade. Part of the physical transactions is for secondary refined copper from numerous small suppliers, though buyers and sellers of primary metal use the Exchange to dispose of marginal surpluses, or to satisfy marginal deficits.[27] The marginal character of this market undoubtedly adds to its price instability, at least in the very short run. The most important variations in copper prices are not the very short-run ones, but those which coincide with the business cycle. During industrial booms the LME prices tend to be high, and conversely during industrial recessions. It is far from obvious that these business cycle-induced price movements in copper are exaggerated by the marginal nature of the LME.

MARKETS STRUCTURE, BARGAINING POWER AND DIVISION OF BENEFITS

This section considers how the differences between the three markets are likely to affect the bargaining power and hence the division of benefits from trade between the parties involved. Trade is transacted in a variety of ways in each market, and we focus attention on the dominant modes only. In the case of bauxite we consider the exports internal to the integrated multinational firms. In iron ore we discuss sales based on short-run and long-run bilateral contracts between independent parties. In copper, we deal exclusively with the trade transacted under short-run and long-run contractual arrangements. Our attention is centered on how the supplying LDCs fare from the exploitaton and exports of natural resources located within their borders.

Where nationally-owned firms produce and export the minerals to foreign companies, the definition of trading parties is unambiguous. When dominant foreign interests are involved in the exploitation, however, the issue becomes blurred, even when the export transactions are of an arm's length nature. This is because a share of (after tax) profits accrues in the end to foreign rather than national subjects. Given the large and increasing national equity interest in iron ore and copper mining in LDCs, and the fact that a substantial share of mineral rents are nationally appropriated through profit tax or other government levies, we choose to regard the mining companies as one of the two trading parties in these two minerals, even where foreign equity interests are involved.

When exports take place within vertically integrated MNCs, the prices are ordinarily set within an overall corporate strategy, aimed at maximizing global profits. In view of the foreign control, and the arbitrariness of the emergent turnover and profit figures, it would be less appropriate in such cases to regard the extracting subsidiary as one of the two parties in the transactions involving an LDC's mineral assets. A more reasonable approach, adopted in our treatment of the bauxite market, is to view the entire foreign corporation as the buying party, and the host government as the selling party. The ability to extract taxes for the right to exploit the resource will then assume the role ordinarily played by prices, in dividing a large share of the benefits from the relationship between the two parties.

The 'benefits from trade' is a tricky concept to define. Simply stated, the benefits consist of such desirable and valued items as would disappear if the trade relationship were discontinued. In the case of commercial firms, whether privately or publicly owned, the benefits can consist of additions to profits, increased security of supply, or reduction of commercial or political risks. In the case of governments, which ordinarily pursue a wide array of objectives, the benefits can assume a great variety of forms. In addition to increased tax income, they could consist of additions to employment or foreign exchange. Access to technology, financial markets and entrepreneurial talent, as well as opportunities to train nationals, as a result of the trading or investment relationship would also ordinarily be regarded as benefits.

However, the above begs a number of questions. An assessment of benefits from a given trade relationship requires a comparison with a situation when that relationship no longer exists. But the ensuing reduction of benefits will obviously depend on the prospects of replacing the former trade relationship with a new one. Furthermore, while instantaneous losses from breaking up the trade flows may be substantial, the damage will be reduced over time with the expansion of alternative domestic activities, increasing use of substitutes, etc. We will not venture further into these complications. In most of the following discussion we adopt a highly simplistic, qualitative rather than quantitative approach, with a heavy emphasis on those benefits which express themselves through profits and government revenues.

That a market structure provides a biased advantage to one of the two trading sides does not necessarily imply that the advantage is always used. Failure to do so may depend on inexperience, commercial ignorance, political constraints or other factors. Factual levels of prices, profits and tax incomes, as well as changes in these levels, will therefore have to be treated with great caution as a proof of biased market arrangements. Our analysis of the three markets has to be more in terms of the potential rather than actual division of benefits from trade, which could be attained within each market.

Economic Theory and the Market Structure

The three market structures briefly described above are all variations of an oligopoly-oligopsony situation. In this sub-section we scan economic literature for a type of analysis which would help determine how the division of benefits from trade might be affected by the differences between the markets we study. Price theory, the theory of industrial organization and the theory of bargaining are the three fields which first came to mind as possibly relevant to the issues we wish to disentangle. Experimental economics, too, have treated problems akin to the ones dealt with here, and we shall look at the insights that this part of the economic discipline can provide.

Price Theory

Much has been said by this theory about the prices that emerge under conditions of perfect or monopolistic competition, oligopoly and monopoly among the sellers (buyers). What makes it less applicable to our problem is the implicit assumption in most cases that perfect competition prevails on the other side of the market. The results emerging from price theory analysis, therefore, become less helpful in treating our special problem.

The only case treated by price theory where explicit assumptions are made about the structure of the market *both* on the selling and the buying side is that of bilateral monopoly. Even then, the price theoretical approach does not help in obtaining definite conclusions insofar as price determination is concerned. Price theory is of no help in determining the bilateral monopoly price level beyond stating that, dependent upon the bargaining strength of the two parties, price will settle within the range bounded by the high price which would prevail in a monopoly—perfect competition relationship, and the low price which would emerge in a perfect competition-monopsony situation.[28]

Theory of Industrial Organization

From our point of view, industrial organization theory suffers from the same weakness as price theory, in that it ordinarily only studies one side of the market, and implicitly assumes conditions of perfect competition on the other.[29] In those circumstances, the usual finding that concentration within an industry in most cases leads to an increase in the sales price level above competitive equilibrium[30] does not carry us far towards substantive conclusions relevant for the markets we study. The resigned quotation from Scherer about the inability of industrial oranization theory to disentangle the oligopoly-oligopsony issues, is illuminating:

> When power in sellers' markets is countered by power in buyers' markets, almost anything can happen. Buyers *may* be able to exploit their power to secure lower intermediate product prices, and they *may* pass the resultant savings on to consumers. But when suppliers are powerful or when competition in end product markets is weak, monopoly or monopsony gains are likely to be trapped somewhere in the production and distribution pipeline. With presently available evidence we are limited to such statements about *possibilities*; not enough is known to make confident judgments about *probable* patterns.[31]

Theory of Bargaining

This has provided useful advice and insights into behavioral patterns in so-called two-person zero-sum games.[32] Such games are helpful, for instance, in determining price levels emerging in bilateral monopolies. But game theory has much less to offer on the strategy of action in non-zero sum games, where the division of interests is combined with mutual dependence. Relatively few non-zero-sum games admit to formal mathematical solutions.[33] Our problems are neither two-person nor zero-sum. Several independent decisionmaking units operate on each side of the three markets we study, and the arrangement of their relationships is likely to have a heavy impact on the sum of potential gains. The complexity of the bargaining models required for treating such intricate cases and the meager conclusions that can be derived from the formal exercises suggest that bargaining theory too, has limited applicability to the task pursued here.

Experimental Economics

This method has been used to test behavioral patterns and emergent trade conditions in bilateral monopoly with equal and unequal strength, in varied oligopoly situations, as well as in competitive markets.[34] Interesting insights have been obtained on the impact of varying such conditions as the information available to the participants, the form of bidding, and the presence or absence of contact between the trading partners. Some of these are relevant to our study — e.g. the finding that better informed bargainers tend to agree to less favorable terms,[35] or that those who bid actively in a market tend to end up with a less advantageous deal than those who adopt a wait and see attitude.[36]

There is an obvious need to make each experiment sufficiently specific to permit derivation of clear-cut and meaningful conclusions. Our search of the literature on experimental economics has not succeeded in finding experiments which describe conditions similar to those prevailing in the three markets under study.

It is possible that a fruitful approach to disentangling our problem would be through economic experiments, in which the structure of the bauxite, iron ore and copper markets was reproduced. Such experiments would require time and resources beyond the scope of this study, however.

The conclusion emerging from this brief scan is that the issue dealt with here cannot be tackled mainly by recourse to any one of the branches of economic discipline discussed above. Each of these will certainly be of help in clarifying specific detailed aspects, but the main argument will have to rely on common-sense rather than on available theoretical constructs, or on unequivocal results of empirical investigations and economic experiments.

We turn then to a simple practical approach, which we hope will lead to improved understanding of the impact on trading partners of the structural differences between the three mineral markets.

Factors in the Market Structure Affecting Division of Benefits

The following discussion is structured around five factors likely to affect the division of benefits between the two trading sides. It first considers the degree of *market concentration* among buyers and sellers respectively. It goes on to analyze the *ability* of the trading parties *to inflict losses* on one another. Then we consider how the *varying share of the raw materials in final product prices* could affect the division of benefits between the trading parties. In this context, it becomes necessary to consider the degree of vertical integration among the firms on the buying side. The fourth point discusses the *structure of the market in which the final product is sold by* the raw material buyers, and the possible impact of this market structure on the division of benefits in the raw material market. Finally, we compare the *process of negotiation* through which agreements on trade are reached, in an attempt to deduct whether the differing approaches are likely to tilt the balance of advantages one way or another.

Market Concentration

The literature on price theory and on industrial organization attaches considerable importance to concentration for wielding market power. Where there is a significant difference in the degree of concentration between buyers and sellers, the more concentrated side will usually be in a stronger position to impose its will on the conditions under which trade takes place.

Concentration is high in the three markets under study. However, whereas the degree of concentration seems to be about the same among the buyers and sellers in the bauxite and iron ore markets, there is a marked difference in favor of the sellers in the case of copper.

In heavily and evenly concentrated oligopoly-oligopsony markets, like those for bauxite and iron ore, bargaining skill and collaboration within the group of sellers or buyers will be very important for improving the terms of one side against those of the other. High concentration, coupled with bargaining skill and ability to collaborate, have long been prevalent on the buying side in these two markets. On the selling side, on the other hand, these features have only recently emerged. In 1974, Jamaica drastically raised its levies on bauxite. The government take was increased from around $2/ton to nearer $15 ton. The Jamaican government thereby absorbed most of the locational rent resulting from the low cost of transporting its bauxite to the US market.[37] The Jamaican move was the starting signal to a closer collaboration and an intensive exchange of information between the major bauxite exporting countries. This collaboration has been institutionalized by the creation of the International Bauxite Association. In the case of iron ore, supply decisions, until recently managed by individual mines, are now handled at the national level, and under government guidance and supervision in most cases. The result has been a considerable increase in the degree of concentration as compared with the late 1960s, when, for instance, the new Australian mines were acting individually and without coordination. This development, in turn, has facilitated the setting up of the International Iron Ore Association, which is to help bring about coordination of the exporting nations' future policies.

In view of the longstanding concentration and implicit collaboration among the buyers, and the recent moves in that direction on the selling side, it is reasonable to expect that the two markets have been and still are tilted in favor of the buyers. If this supposition is correct, one could expect improvements for the sellers in coming years, consequent upon the changes just described. The increased rates of taxation in some of the bauxite exporting countries may be the first sign of a move towards a new balance in the bauxite market, more favorable to the exporters.

The uneven concentration in the refined copper market is not a new phenomenon. Though the decision units were different, concentration among exporters was also very high before the many nationalizations of the copper sector in Africa and Latin America in the past decade. Considering market concentration alone, one might argue that the sellers have failed to take full advantage of their superior market power, by relegating the price determination to an outside institution like the LME.

Where unrefined copper is concerned, concentration would probably be higher on the buying side, in view of the scale economies in smelting and refining. Though the prices applied in the sales of unrefined copper are LME based, determination of deductions to cover the cost of processing gives the buyers ample opportunities to use their negotiating power and superior technical knowledge to their advantage. The strong urge among copper producers in the developing world to integrate as far as the refining stage can probably be explained as a wish to overcome the existing imbalance in these respects.[38]

Ability to Inflict Losses

Ability to inflict losses on the other party is an important factor in determining the outcome of trade negotiations in the three minerals markets. The bauxite situation is different from the other two. The users of bauxite, by their direct investments in extraction in the exporting countries, are much more tied to these countries than would be the buyers of iron ore or copper. By threatening to nationalize the companies' investments, the exporting countries' governments have the power to extract a better deal than what would be feasible if such investments did not exist.

In the absence of direct investments in the exporting country, the demand curve of a bauxite consuming company indicates its highest acceptable bauxite cost level. When investment funds have been committed, it will ordinarily be preferable for the company to get even a strongly reduced return on that capital rather than face outright nationalization. Thus the maximum bauxite cost that the company will accept when threatened by nationalization will equal the level of its demand curve *plus* the opportunity cost of the capital invested, per unit of bauxite capacity. In this way, the negotiable range within which the exporting country's unit returns can vary, is widened upwards. The level finally agreed will ultimately depend upon the skill in bargaining, and it is by no means certain that the exporting country will wish or be able to make full use of the additional leverage resulting from the foreign ownership.

The ability to inflict losses through nationalization or threats of nationalization is limited both in value and time. Once the foreign assets have been taken over, the threat ceases to exist. Also, a company that is unable to earn the opportunity cost of the capital invested in a bauxite exporting country will be cautious about reinvestments and will avoid new investments to create additional capacity in that country. As the foreign-owned capacity is reduced over time, the threat of nationalization will gradually lose its force. The existence of foreign assets in bauxite extraction can be viewed as a potential one-time advantage to the governments of exporting countries.

Integration, concentration and collaboration in the world aluminium industry provides the companies with a high degree of market control which can be used as a counter-threat against the governments. So long as they are in control, the companies can threaten to reduce production, and thereby government revenue in those countries whose fiscal measures make bauxite exploitation less economical. When the government decides to take over the production facilities, it will still be dependent on the oligopoly for selling the product, since there are not many sizeable and independent bauxite buyers. The companies' control of the market gives them a powerful negotiating weapon, not available to the buyers of iron ore and copper.

Easy access to financial resources will reduce vulnerability to outside threats, and will consequently strengthen bargaining power. Though no clearcut difference can be discerned between the three markets in this respect, it is probable that the importers, who are more fully integrated into the industrial and financial structures of the rich world, have an advantage over the exporters.

Losses can be inflicted on the opposite party by various means, one of which is unilateral price decisions. It can be argued that the trade partners in the copper market have reduced their reciprocal ability to inflict losses on one another by removing the price decision to the LME.

Ability to inflict losses will increase and bargaining power will improve with an increasing degree of dependence for the opposite party on the trade in question. If my trading partner cannot survive without continued trade, he will be more willing to make concessions than if he has other endeavors to fall back on when the opportunities in one field are reduced.

A very heavy dependence on bauxite, iron ore and copper characterizes all the companies acting in the three markets. On the selling side, the iron ore or copper mines are rarely diversified, and depend entirely on their trade in these materials. On the buying side, too, dependence of the aluminium and steel producers as well as copper fabricators on each of the three materials is very strong, though diversification in some cases should make this dependence less than complete.

Another type of dependence of considerable significance for the bargaining power is becoming increasingly relevant as the governments of exporting countries take over more and more of the control over their mineral industries. This is the national dependence on each one of the three commodities. Importing countries can be disregarded in this context − their governments seldom aspire to control the industries concerned. Furthermore, the economies of the major importing countries are so diversified that the import value of any of the three commodities constitutes a very small share of the total.

The dependence and degree of vulnerability of the exporting countries can be expressed differently. Dependence may be high in terms of export earnings, contribution to the government budget, or employment. We limit our discussion to dependence in terms of export earnings. Table 2 lists the countries which are heavily dependent on exports of each of the three commodities. Since a fast increasing share of bauxite is processed into alumina before exports from major supplying countries, alumina has been added to bauxite when measuring national dependence. Australia is not listed, despite its dominance in the bauxite and iron ore markets, because its overall exports are highly diversified, and the two commodities account for a small proportion of its total trade.

Table 2 indicates that only 10 per cent of world traded supplies of iron ore originate in countries heavily dependent on exports. Mauretania and Liberia are likely to suffer from the double weakness of being unimportant global suppliers, and simultaneously extremely dependent on iron ore. Hence they could face serious problems in withstanding bargaining pressures from buyers. Major exporting countries like Brazil, Australia, Canada and India, on the other hand, can

afford to be tougher in trade negotiations, since their iron ore sales account for
only a small proportion of total exports.

Table 7.2. *Country concentration of exports in three mineral commodities (average annual values for 1972-1974)**

	Commodity share of country exports (%)	Cumulative share of gross world exports (%)
Bauxite and alumina		
Guinea	86	9
Surinam	83	22
Jamaica	62	47
Guyana	41	53
Haiti	11	54
Iron ore		
Mauretania	75	3
Liberia	67	9
Sierra Leone	11	10
Swaziland	11	10
Copper		
Zambia	93	16
Chile	73	33
Zaire	67	43
Namibia	61	44
Papua New Guinea	56	48
Peru	29	53
Philippines	15	57
Mauretania	15	57
Cyprus	11	58

*   In view of the large price differential between bauxite and alumina, the cumulative share
of world exports for these materials is based on volume in terms of aluminium content.

Note: Only countries where the share of each of the commodities amounts to at least 10%
of total exports have been listed.

Source: For iron ore and copper, IBRD, *Commodity Trade and Price Trends* (1976 edition,
Reports No EC 166/76).
For bauxite and alumina, the figures are my own assessments, computed on the basis of a
variety of World Bank data.

The structure of bauxite/alumina and copper exports presents a different picture. Almost half of the traded supplies comes from countries where these commodities account for more than 50 per cent of total trade. Like Mauretania and
Liberia, such countries are likely to be vulnerable to bargaining threats, where
their minerals exports are at stake. Of course, the bauxite/alumina and copper
exporters' bargaining position is strengthened by their greater importance in
overall world supply.

Share of Raw Material Cost in Final Product Price
The reason for taking up this point is the supposition that a raw material buyer
will be determined to press hard for a maximum of concessions from his supplier

when the raw material cost constitutes a high proportion of his total cost. He may be more lax in his attitude towards his trading partner when the raw material is a relatively unimportant cost item in relation to the final product sales price.

The share of the raw material cost in final product price depends on two factors. First, it will tend to be higher the more processing is undertaken before the material is sold. Second, it will be negatively related to the value added created by the buyer. The higher the value added per unit of sales, the less important will be the raw material cost to the buyer. Buyers with far-reaching forward integration will therefore ordinarily be less affected by the price changes of raw materials bought, and will find it easier to absorb such changes in their total costs.

When scrutinizing the organization of the three mineral markets, we found that delivered bauxite and iron ore costs commonly constituted no more than about 10 per cent of the metal ingot price. In the case of copper, we found the proportion far higher. It was assessed at 80-90 per cent for the large proportion of refined deliveries to independent fabricators, and around 50 per cent for copper concentrates sold to metal processors, integrated forward into fabricating.

A 10 per cent increase in the raw material cost would add about one per cent to the cost of producing steel. The whole of the cost rise could be absorbed without difficulty, by temporarily reduced profits in the steel industry. After all, a one per cent input cost increase could be neutralized by less than six months of ordinary productivity gains, and would hardly be worth negotiating fiercely.

A similar increase in the raw material cost would have a still smaller impact on the aluminium industry, because much of the output sold by the six multinational aluminium firms has been processed beyond the metal ingot stage. The small share of raw material costs in final product price explains why the aluminium companies have succeeded in coping with the near-doubling of bauxite costs resulting from the tax increases in the early 1970s in Jamaica and some other Caribbean countries.

At the other extreme, the unintegrated copper fabricating industry would have considerable difficulties in absorbing a 10 per cent increase in copper prices. Such an increase would equal 50 per cent or more of the value added created by the fabricators. Were copper prices to be determined in direct negotiations between copper producers and fabricators, the latter could be expected to put up a very hard fight against any rise. In current circumstances, there is nobody to fight with, since the price level is determined authoritatively by the LME. The great exposure of copper fabricators to variation in copper prices is certainly one important explanation to the common practice in this industry to base its sales prices on current LME copper quotations.

Type of Market in which the Raw Material Buyer Sells his Product
The buyer is likely to negotiate more stubbornly against increases in his raw material costs where he has to absorb these himself, but he will be more amenable

to accept the seller's demands in situations where the cost increase can be passed on by way of higher prices on his sales. The rationality of this argument is obvious — in the former case his profits will be directly affected by the increase in costs, in the latter they will not. From this point of view, it would be an advantage to the sellers of the primary product to trade with processors who have a strong monopoly or oligopoly hold over the market where they sell their products. What differences can be distinguished between the conditions prevailing in the markets where the buyers of bauxite, iron ore and copper dispose of their final products?

Market power is probably greatest among the aluminium producers. The aluminium oligopoly has a tight control of the metal price, and exerts considerable influence over aluminium products too. Despite the great concentration among steel producers at the national level, steelmakers have less freedom to pass on cost increases to their customers, because in several of the major steel producing countries governments exert an overt or covert influence over steel.[39]

The situation is less obvious than would appear from a cursory glance at arrangements in the case of refined copper sold to independent fabricators. It is true that fabricators by tradition price their products on the basis of copper purchase costs. This does not necessarily signify a high degree of power on their part in the fabricated product market. The role of the fabricators in the chain from copper mining to the copper containing final consumer goods is very limited. This is apparent from the small value added created by the fabricating industry. The fabricators neither gain nor lose on their copper deals. They could therefore be regarded as mere intermediaries who shape the copper metal on behalf of the copper using manufacturing industries. These industries bear the entire impact of variations in copper prices. Hence, it would not be unreasonable to see them rather than the fabricators as the true buyers of copper. With this view, a more correct assessment of the power of copper buyers in the final product markets would have to include a scrutiny of the conditions under which the copper containing final products are sold.

Identification of the products sold by the electrical, building and other copper using industries would be a sizeable undertaking. A scrutiny of the market conditions under which those products are sold would be further complicated by existing national differences in the organization of these industries. There is no scope for such an assessment within this paper.

The Process of Negotiation

It may be instructive to take note of some common features in trade negotiations in the three markets. First, it seems to be a rule that each negotiation is bilateral, involving only one seller and one buyer. Second, in all three cases, negotiations end up with an agreement specifying both quantities to be traded and prices (or taxes and other levies) to be applied. Third, there is a certain stability in the arrangements, in that agreements are always of at least one year's duration and frequently much longer.

Two key factors distinguishing the negotiating conditions in the three markets can be identified. First, in the bauxite market negotiations are between governments and commercial organizations. In the other two markets, both sides are represented by commercial firms (whther private or publicly owned). Second, price levels (or taxes and levies) are determined directly through the process of negotiations in the case of bauxite and iron ore. In copper, the standing agreement is to use LME prices, and there is no bargaining about price levels.

In the case of iron ore and copper, where commercial organizations (both private and public) face each other in the negotiations, a certain community of interests is likely to emerge between the bargaining parties. Each of them pursues the same kind of goals; both probably rely on similar sources for the information on which negotiations are based; both speak the same commercial language, and are likely to have an understanding of each other's problems. As a result, it should be relatively easy to limit the scope of negotiations to a few key issues and to narrow down the feasible ranges within which agreements can be reached.

The parties negotiating with each other in the case of bauxite are much less similar. The governments of the exporting countries are interested in promoting broader goals than those pursued by the companies. This, along with the different background of the negotiators, probably makes it harder to narrow down the issues and to identify the areas where compromise is possible. For these reasons, negotiations in bauxite are likely to be more complex and to take longer to resolve. This greater complexity need not make the negotiations more prone to breakdown. The increased number of variables brought into the discussion by the government should open up additional means of reaching agreement.

Governments not directly involved in commercial operations are likely to be slower in perceiving changes that occur in the market. This will probably constitute a disadvantage in their relations with the companies exploiting and exporting the bauxite, for while the companies will be quick in pointing out such market developments that warrant a change to their advantage in the arrangements with the governments, they are likely to withhold the opposite type of information.

As long as the company has direct investments to defend in the exporting country, the government will be able to maintain an upper hand in any negotiations by the implicit or explicit threat to use its power to nationalize. We discussed earlier the limitations of this government advantage.

The role of the government administration in the negotiations changes substantially after the hegemony of the integrated foreign firm has been broken, and mineral extraction has been transferred to national hands. The nationally owned company established to run the activities taken over from the foreigners ordinarily assumes the responsibility to negotiate trade terms with foreign buyers, and the government's role is reduced to one of supervision and control. Nationalization ordinarily brings an end to the government-company bargaining relationship and introduces company-company negotiations instead. This happened in numerous cases, both in iron ore and copper, after the waves of nationalizations in the Third World in the late 1960s and early 1970s.

A number of consequences follow from the arrangement between the exporters and importers of copper to take the LME prices as a basis for their transactions. This arrangement simplifies negotiations, since there is ready agreement from the outset on this key issue – the annual copper contract negotiations are a very smooth and unheard-of affair, which contrasts considerably with conditions in the other two markets.

Acceptance of the LME prices has the advantage of a uniform price level for all sellers and buyers. The prices (or government levies) emerging from bilateral negotiations in iron ore and bauxite may well show significant differences from one trade deal to another. The irritation and the feeling of having been cheated on the price to be applied, are avoided by the 'objective' price mechanism in the case of copper.

With a neutral and uniform price, determined separately from the bilateral contract negotiations, there is in principle little possibility for the exporters or importers of copper to take any initiatives with regard to prices. This neutrality would tend to work to the advantage of the weaker side in the market. When price is determined by bargaining, the stronger side will tend to push it towards the limit of a wide feasible range. There will be less scope for using bargaining power to push prices around in a pricing arrangement like that in copper.

In practice there are of course possibilities for groups of copper exporters or importers to influence the LME prices to their advantage in the short term. Physical turnover on the LME is limited, and a few well timed sales or purchase orders could have a significant effect on price developments. Traders on the LME claim that concerted action of this kind is uncommon. An attempt, for instance, by the buyers to influence the LME prices could easily lead to retaliatory action of the same kind by the sellers. Awareness of the advantages of the LME as a neutral pricing medium may have discouraged such attempts.

In distinction from the arrangements in the other two markets, the organization of copper trade reflects instantaneously all emerging changes in supply and demand. The LME is a marginal market, with nervous prices, which tend to react strongly even on small overall changes in the world copper economy. The choice of the LME cash prices at the time of delivery as the pricing medium has created a sharp and at times inconvenient instability in the prices of internationally traded copper. But then, this inconvenience could easily be overcome by pricing contractual copper trade on the basis of monthly or even semi-annual average prices on the exchange.

CONCLUSIONS

After scanning relevant branches of economic literature, we may conclude that there does not exist a body of theory suitable for clarifying how the existing difference in the oligopoly-oligopsony structure of the three international mineral markets is likely to affect the division of benefits between the trading partners.

In the absence of established analytical tools, we have adopted an informal approach, in which the markets are scrutinized with reference to five factors which appear relevant and important for determining the division of benefits in each. The scrutiny is in no way exhaustive — the list of relevant factors could certainly be made considerably longer. The approach chosen is highly simplistic, and must be seen as a first attempt to delineate the issues involved.

We have noted the bargaining strength that can be derived from a high degree of market concentration, and conclude that the recent tendencies towards greater concentration and collaboration among the suppliers in the bauxite and iron ore markets are likely to increase their ability to negotiate better trade terms.

We have observed that the governments of the bauxite exporting countries have an additional bargaining leverage in the form of a threat to nationalize the bauxite mines now owned by the integrated multinational aluminium firms. The advantages of this leverage are limited both in value and time, and disappear completely once the government decides to execute its power to nationalize.

We have noted the high vulnerability of countries very heavily dependent on exports of mineral commodities to pressures from buyers, supported by threats to cut trade. A reduction of such national dependence would widen the options open to these countries, and thus improve their negotiating position.

Commonsense suggests that raw material buyers will bargain less fiercely with their suppliers when raw material costs constitute a small share of their final product price, and when these costs can be passed on to final consumers. Our analysis suggests that the bauxite buyers are best placed in this regard, with a consequent bargaining advantage to the bauxite suppliers.

Our discussion on the process of negotiation and the procedure through which prices are determined fails to reach a definite conclusion as to which of the three approaches is most beneficial to the suppliers. The arrangement between the sellers and buyers of copper to use LME prices for all trade deals considerably simplifies the negotiating procedure, and equalizes the price level for all transactions at a given time. We also note that this arrangement prevents the refined copper suppliers from using the strength arising from their high degree of concentration to push prices upwards in trade deals with the less concentrated copper fabricators.

The results emerging from the preceding discussion are disappointing in that they fail to provide clearcut indications as to which of the three market organizations would be preferable from the point of view of the exporting side. It may be that the differences in structure of the three markets are not crucially important to the outcome of the terms at which trade takes place. Our inability to reach conclusions could be because the bargaining strength and the division of benefits between the trading partners are predominantly determined by other factors than the features and variations of the market structure, on which the discussion of this paper has centered.

NOTES

1. UNCTAD, 'Consideration of International Measures on Iron Ore' (TB/B/IPC Iron Ore/ 2/Add.1, 8 August 1977, mimeo); and Metallgesellschaft, *Metal Statistics*, several issues.
2. World Bureau of Metal Statistics, *World Metal Statistics*, recent issues.
3. IBRD, 'Prospects for Exports of Bauxite/Alumina/Aluminium from Developing Countries', *Commodity Paper* No. 12 (10/74, mimeo); and Malmexport, 'Report on Iron Ore — Past Trends 1950-73' (Stockholm, 1975, mimeo).
4. The figures have been derived from a variety of sources, in particular Metallgesellschaft, US Bureau of Mines, and 'Report on Iron Ore'.
5. US Bureau of Mines, 'Mineral Facts and Problems 1975 Edition', *Bulletin 667* (Washington, 1976).
6. All investment cost figures given in this paragraph pertain to the dollar cost levels about 1975.
7. Mine and concentrator only.
8. Metallgesellschaft, *Metal Statistics*.
9. IBRD, 'Market Structure of Bauxite/Alumina/Aluminium and Prospects for Developing Countries', *Commodity Paper* No. 24 (3/77).
10. US Bureau of Mines, 'Mineral Facts and Problems 1975 Edition'.
11. IBRD, 'Market Structure of Bauxite/Alumina/Aluminium and Prospects for Developing Countries'.
12. IBRD, 'Commodity Trade and Price Trends', Report No. EC/166/77.
13. IBRD, 'Prospects for Exports of Bauxite/Alumina/Aluminium from Developing Countries'.
14. Malmexport, 'Report on Iron Ore'.
15. Author's interview with Malmexport AB (Stockholm, 1976).
16. L. Friden, *Instability of the International Steel Market* (Stockholm: Beckmans, 1972).
17. UNCTAD, 'A Comparison of World Prices of Iron Ore and Steel 1950-1970', UNCTAD CD/Misc 58 (October 1974, mimeo).
18. IBRD, 'Commodity Trade and Price Trends'.
19. CIPEC, *Statistical Bulletin 1976*.
20. R. Prain, *Copper, the Anatomy of an Industry* (London: Mining Journal Book, 1975).
21. *World Metal Statistics*, recent issues.
22. 'Copper 1974', a *Metal Bulletin* special issue.
23. Figures based on material compiled by the International Wrought Copper Council.
24. 'Copper 1974'.
25. Figures based on material compiled by the International Wrought Copper Council and on reports issued by the Commodities Research Unit.
26. *World Metal Statistics*, recent issues.
27. Commodities Research Unit, 'The Pricing and Marketing of Copper' (a report for CIPEC, 1969, mimeo).
28. K.J. Cohen & R.M. Cyert, *Theory of the Firm* (New Jersey: Prentice Hall, 1965).
29. J.S. Bain, *Industrial Organizations* (New York: Wiley, 1959); G.J. Stigler, *The Organization of Industry* (Homewood: Irvin, 1968); or E.M. Scherer, *Industrial Market Structure and Economic Performance* (Chicago: Rand McNally, 1970).
30. Bain, *Industrial Organizations*.
31. Scherer, *Industrial Market Structure*, 252.
32. A Rapoport, *Two Person Game Theory* (University of Michigan, 1966).
33. T. Schelling, *The Strategy of Conflict* (London: Oxford University Press, 1963).
34. L.E. Fouraker & S. Siegel, *Bargaining Behavior* (New York: McGraw Hill, 1963); Symposium on Experimental Economics', *Review of Economic Studies* (1969); and V. Smith, 'Effects of market organization on competitive equilibrium', *Quarterly Journal of Economics* (May 1974).
35. L.C. Cummings & D.L. Hartnett, 'Bargaining behavior in a symmetric bargaining triad', *Review of Economic Studies* (October 1969).
36. Smith, 'Effects of market organization'.
37. This argument is based on data contained in Note 9.
38. For a fuller discussion of this point, see M. Radetzki, 'Mineral Processing in LDCs', reproduced in this volume as Chapter 13.
39. G. Manners, *The Changing World Market for Iron Ore 1950-1980* (Baltimore: Johns Hopkins, 1967).

8

LONG-TERM PROCUREMENT CONTRACTS, WITH SPECIAL REFERENCE TO IRON ORE

C.D. Rogers

Pricing policies for minerals generally reflect the structure of ownership and control which characterizes each market. This paper will describe in general terms the method of pricing under each type of market structure in the iron ore industry and then will continue to discuss the implications of these diverse methods for the total world iron ore market, with particular attention to the interrelationship between the markets. Discussion will focus on the role of long-term procurement policies and the implications of their development with respect to market stability and contract design. The experience in the international iron ore market seems of enhanced importance given the increased advocacy of long-term sales contracts as solutions to problems currently being encountered in other mineral markets.

Iron ore is not a homogeneous commodity and this in turn means that there can be no unambiguous price for the commodity (see my Chapter 4 *supra*). Unlike several other major metals, iron ore is not traded on a commodity exchange and there exists no reference grade, uniform standard, or fixed contract for the commodity against which price movements could be gauged. Comparisons between iron ore prices are, therefore, generally made in terms of prices per metal (Fe) unit contained in the ore. Even here, however, comparisons need to be conducted with caution in order not to be misleading — premiums will often be paid if an ore has specific metallurgical, physical or chemical properties of value to the buyer or discounts made if the ore contains unwanted impurities which will add to the buyer's costs.

In very general terms, iron ore is sold in three broad physical specifications: lumps for use directly in the iron furnace; fines generally needing to be sintered by the buyer before use in the iron furnace; and pellets, a bonded form of ore sometimes manufactured at mine which contains other additives and generally reduces associated processing costs at the furnace stage. Reflecting both relative production costs to the producer and value to the buyer, pellets are generally the most expensive, and fines the least expensive of these three categories.

Further, iron ore is generally, but not always, sold on an fob basis. Exceptions to this will be indicated in the subsequent sections. Buyers, however, procuring supplies from different sources try to equalize landed cif prices which,

---

Notes to this chapter may be found on page 152.

in turn, means that suppliers from distant sources need to charge lower fob prices to remain competitive in cif terms. The substantial fall in maritime freight rates over recent decades has aided suppliers distant from the main consumption centers of Europe, Japan and the USA, but one paradox of this fall in freight rates is that, because of the longer distances involved, they still account, in some instances, for up to 40 per cent of landed prices.

Essentially, there are three marketing modalities (producer pricing, an annual contract market and a long-term contract market) in the international iron ore market which broadly reflect existing differences in ownership and control. Although the emphasis of this paper is directed towards the role of long-term contractual arrangements, there must be some introductory discussion of the other modalities in order to arrive at a proper understanding of long-term contracts and their place in the world market.

PRODUCER PRICING

Where the iron ore mine is wholly owned by the buyer, i.e. a steel company, then pricing policies need not follow economic logic and possibilities for transfer pricing exist. In the case of iron ore, however, these possibilities are much restricted in comparison with other commodity markets. This is primarily because most wholly-owned mines are located in the same country as the buyer and are consequently under the same fiscal regime.

In fact, little is known about producer pricing and the extent to which such prices vary in comparison with other prices. It is the case, however, that most such mines have high production costs in relation to other mines and the output would often not be competitive except for its proximity to the point of consumption and the desire of consumers to maintain some control over supplies.

MERCHANT COMPANIES

Merchant companies work in very close relationship to their customers and although such companies, especially in North America, post prices, it is known that discounts are offered to regular customers with little public indication of the size, extent and regularity of such discounts. The evidence that is available concerning such purchases suggests that these prices are both more stable and generally higher than other world prices for iron ore.

As with producer prices, a major explanation for this lies with both the higher production costs of such ores and the willingness of consumers to pay a premium to guarantee access to supplies. The physical nearness of these supplies to the consumers serves to facilitate such pricing policies, while access to supplies is guaranteed through the close commercial relationships existing between merchant companies and purchasers reinforced by the common political umbrella covering their operations.

CONSORTIUM COMPANIES (JOINT VENTURES)

The enormous start-up costs associated with new mine developments has resulted in there being a growing tendency for steel companies to join together to finance new iron ore mining activities, which has implications for the pricing of iron ore. Unlike many wholly-owned subsidiaries, these mines generally have very low unit costs of production but are frequently located substantially further from the point of consumption. Further, since the partners in the venture are frequently located in different countries this makes the practice of transfer pricing both more intricate and less likely. Rather, fob prices are likely to be established which cover costs of production and earn a reasonable return on capital employed. Different participants may well be charged different fob prices to reflect differences in maritime transportation costs. It is also the case that venture partners located a distance from the market would be more inclined to negotiate a contract containing cif prices than venture partners near to the source of production who would favor fob prices. Thus, the basis for pricing provisions in contracts may be as much, if not more, disputed between venture partners from different consuming countries, as between such venture partners as a group and the host government or its agent.

Supplies from joint ventures are likely, therefore, to be sold at fob prices frequently below those from wholly-owned subsidiaries. Like prices from wholly-owned subsidiaries, however, there is a tendency for these prices to be relatively stable over the short and medium terms, although changes in the longer-term competitive position will need to be reflected in price movements. Such sales, however, are usually made on the basis of a long-term contract and the terms and conditions of such contracts are discussed more fully below.

ANNUAL CONTRACTS

The increasing recourse to long-term contracts has meant that a smaller proportion of world iron ore sales has taken place in the traditional way through annual contracts, a method of sale which is analogous to spot sales in other metals markets. Traditionally, buyers have purchased on an annual basis those requirements which cannot be met from their own resources but, with the development of long-term contracts, buyers have additional supplies to which they are committed and their purchases on annual contracts have generally fallen.

Experience in the 1970s, when long-term contracts had become a major element of purchase plans, reveals some disturbing tendencies. In 1974 and 1975, when supplies of iron ore were tight, prices of Swedish Kiruna D ore, a major supplier to the annual market, rose to record levels (prices in 1975 were 91 per cent higher than the level in 1973). Recorded price rises were substantially greater than those re-negotiated under long-term contracts or experienced in the North American domestic market. In the recessionary conditions of 1978, the price of Kiruna D fell substantially more than prices in long-term contracts or in the North American domestic market.

In effect, buyers have supplies from subsidiaries which, as far as possible, they take in order to keep such mines operating at full capacity, so keeping unit production costs at a minimum. Secondly, buyers have undertaken long-term contractual commitments which, as far as possible, they are required to honor. Thus, in times when economic activity is at a high level, subsidiary mines cannot provide additional supplies since they were previously operating at full-capacity and long-term contracts provide only a small margin of flexibility. The bulk of additional requirements, therefore, must come from increased purchases on the annual market. Conversely, in recessionary conditions, the need to maintain production levels in subsidiary mines and the inflexibility of contractual obligations undertaken in long-term contracts means that the reduction in purchases is concentrated on the annual market. In this way, the bulk of economic adjustment is concentrated on the annual market and, as the size of this market declines relatively, the instability so produced increases.

LONG-TERM CONTRACTS

As implied above, long-term contracts have become increasingly the most important modality for the selling of iron ore. It is estimated that over 60 per cent of iron ore entering international trade is now sold on the basis of long-term contracts and the actual figure may be nearer to 70 per cent. The situation with respect to long-term contracts is, therefore, central to any understanding of the pricing of iron ore on world markets.[1]

The development of long-term purchase contracts for iron ore has taken place primarily over the last two decades following the large-scale recourse of Japanese importers to this method of purchasing requirements. Since then it has been increasingly employed by European importers and to a lesser extent by American importers. It is popularly employed in conjunction with shipments from joint ventures discussed in the previous section. Trade between socialist countries essentially takes place within the confines of long-term contractual arrangements but little is known about the terms of such contracts or the principles determining such terms other than that the contracts establish quantitative sales and purchase obligations at fixed prices with provision to adjust such prices at intervals (often every two years) in the light of changes in prevailing economic conditions. It seems likely that, in practice, adjustments in contract prices generally follow the price trends established in the world iron ore market.

Essentially, the Japanese import contracts, which have established themselves as models in the world market, were envisaged as providing a general planning framework covering approximately 90 per cent of Japanese iron ore requirements. They were not envisaged by the Japanese as rigid, legally binding, contracts in a European sense. As such, they enabled the buyer to ensure adequate supplies of raw materials as requirements increased and allowed investment decisions in the steel industry to be more soundly based, covering not only quantitative requirements but also likely supply costs.

To the producers, they guarantee off-take, increasingly necessary as the scale of mining increased, making reliance on a spot market more hazardous. The increase in the scale of mining also faced producers with problems of financing such mine developments − estimated development costs of between $3-4 billion for the Carajas ore field in Brazil being the extreme example. This increase in development costs, beyond the financial capability of even the steel MNCs, was a major incentive for the undertaking of joint ventures, which in turn utilized long-term sales contracts to allocate supplies between participants. Such contracts, guaranteeing both quantities and prices (and hence revenues), provided collateral to the banking community to secure the loans necessary to undertake the mine development. Thus, mining companies with insufficient financial resources to develop new product facilities could enter into sales contracts with respect to the prospective output from the development and on the basis of such contracts raise the funds from the financial community (particularly the Eurodollar market) to finance the mine project. Long-term sales contracts became during the early 1970s an important element in the ability of the mining industry to attract sufficient finance to permit the continued rapid expansion of output.[2]

In practice in recent years the principle of long-term contracting has come under strain from a number of directions. Consumers faced with a recession, deeper and more prolonged than anticipated, have been unable to continue to receive the quantities they had contracted and have been obliged to seek renegotiation of contracts with smaller tonnages. Producers have found costs rising much faster than they anticipated and have sought a re-negotiation of contracts to raise prices in line with increases in production costs. Finally, the choice of an adequate numeraire in which to express prices has become increasingly troublesome given the instabilities of the international currency market and especially of the US dollar, the traditional numeraire. With such pressure on both the quantities and prices of long-term contracts, their value as collateral has been doubted and consequently the problems of financing mine development have been highlighted.

Long-term purchase contracts were designed to provide a stable framework to promote the long-term development of the world iron ore industry while taking sufficient account of changes in short-term circumstances. It is with the need to secure the appropriate trade-off between these competing objectives that a more detailed review of the development of Japanese purchase contracts is undertaken below. Effectively, such contracts have three elements which will be considered separately and in turn: provisions relating to prices; to quantities; and to shipping.

With regard to prices, the early contracts generally fixed prices for three to five years, and sometimes even longer. Although these provisions were maintained through the late 1960s and early 1970s, the inflationary pressures forcing up production costs and the decline of the US dollar meant that in 1973-74 widespread re-negotiation (upwards) of prices took place. Subsequently, prices have been fixed for a maximum of two years and in reality price reviews have frequently taken place at annual intervals. In the case of one contract with a Canadian supplier, prices were fixed in relation to movements in North American domestic prices.

Although contracts specify tonnages to be delivered over the life of contracts (contracts have a life of between five and 20 years, with the average contract covering ten years), most contracts have a provision for tonnage options of ±5 per cent to ±10 per cent (in some extreme cases ±20 per cent), almost always at the buyer's option. It has been suggested that this mechanism has been used by consumers to promote excess capacity. For example, a contract is negotiated for the sale of 100 tons ±10 per cent at the buyer's option. The seller now tends to provide 110 tons of capacity in case the buyer chooses to exercise that option. The buyer, however, exercises his option to buy only 90 tons, thus leaving the seller with 20 tons of unsold ore which he needs to dispose of on the free market. This, in turn, forces down world prices and the buyer enters into a new purchase contract with a new supplier at a lower price, fixed with reference to the lower world price. Although it is difficult to document sufficient evidence to totally substantiate this assertion, it is true that in the majority of cases where buyers have exercised their option, it has been to take a smaller, not a larger, tonnage.

In recent years the recessionary conditions existing in the world steel industries have meant that purchasers have been unable to take up all their contracted tonnages, even within the flexibility margins existing in the contracts. In some instances shipments have fallen to 60 per cent of contracted volumes. Thus, pressure for re-negotiation has originated from the purchasers' side with respect to volumes, at a time when vendors have been seeking re-negotiation of prices.

The majority of contracts are on fob terms, although an increasing number, especially with Africa and Brazil, divide the quantity, e.g. 60 per cent fob, 40 per cent cif. There are two sets of issues here. The first are the standard economic arguments that cif contracts would augment exporters' export receipts and foreign exchange earnings and would facilitate their entry into the shipping industry. The second set of issues may be even more important and relate to the questions of control. Fob contracts allow the buyers to make the arrangements for shipping and put them in control of the physical provision of shipping. Again, it has been informally alleged that in recent years when buyers have been reluctant to take contracted tonnages, ships did not arrive on occasions; and on other occasions, sailing times between importers and exporters have doubled. The importance of control over shipping was demonstrated a few years ago when, in a dispute between Australia and Japan over sugar contracts, vessels loaded with the disputed sugar anchored off the coast of Japan and the argument was resolved essentially in favor of Australia.[3]

The fundamental problem is to build into long-term contracts enough rigidities to make them valuable as planning aids (for physical planning or financial planning), while retaining sufficient flexibility to enable them to respond to changes in underlying market conditions, especially in situations where strict adherence to contract conditions would introduce considerable economic distortions into the market and would involve one or both of the parties in unreasonable, unforeseen costs. This would seem to suggest the need to develop contractual flexibility in such arrangements.[4] It is in this sense that improved contract design has an important role to play in providing a new generation of long-term contracts that fulfil these requirements.

Although contracts have three separate elements, they combine together to constitute binding agreements under which unfavorable pricing provisions may be compensated by favorable quantitative or shipping arrangements. It is therefore, difficult to consider the pricing provisions of long-term contracts in isolation from these other aspects. It does seem, however, that the more frequent price revisions are not consistent with the early optimism regarding the benefits provided by this means of sale. In addition, the contribution of long-term contracts to increased price stability needs to be evaluated in the context of the whole of the international market for iron ore and not just in the context of that part of the market covered by such contracts.

CONCLUSIONS

This paper has attempted to describe the main modalities for marketing iron ore. In so doing, it has brought out the inter-relationships between the iron ore markets as parts of a totally global system. It is clear that much more work needs to be done to develop a model of the world market and a concept of the world price that satisfactorily takes account of these inter-relationships.

Although short-term price instability is not the major price problem, it is clear that some of the apparent benefits of increased market stability resulting from an extension of long-term contracting are offset (possibly more than offset) in a global sense by the consequent destabilization of the shrinking annual market, which increasingly bears the brunt of economic adjustment. In addition, long-term contracting is continuing to evolve as it adjusts to changing economic circumstances. In particular, the more frequent revision of both price and quantity provisions has lessened the degree of market stability contained within the long-term contract sector. Further, the increased flexibility within such contracts raises important issues with regard to contract design to achieve the specified objectives and has relevance to commodities other than iron ore.

Nevertheless, increased recourse to long-term contracts is being advocated for a variety of primary commodities and especially mineral materials. Long-term contracts can contribute to the amelioration of some of the problems facing exporters of mineral materials, especially from LDCs. Apart from their potential contribution to enhanced market stability, they can assist with the provision of mine finance, and intrinsically involve access to markets. Iron ore represents a major commodity for which long-term contracts have been used for many years and it is surprising that so little attention has been directed to the experience of this market with regard to the operation of these contracts, especially since this experience has been gained over a period when world commodity markets have been especially volatile.

The preliminary conclusion which emerges from an examination of this experience is that market stability has been improved in that segment of the world market covered by long-term contracts but at a cost of increased instability in other parts of the world market. Further, long-term contracts have gradually become more flexible and so have lost some of their other qualities; in particular, they are less acceptable as loan collateral.

The existence of different pricing arrangements in the world market for iron ore is of particular relevance given the concentration of different pricing methods within different countries. Thus, almost all Canadian exports are producer priced, almost all Australian sales are under long-term contract, and almost all Swedish sales on annual contract. With different price movements in each market, it is clear that individual producers will be in substantially different positions, and will form different views with regard to whether or not increased use of long-term contracts has enhanced or diminished market stability. Essentially, similar differences exist between individual consumer countries where most US imports are related to US producer price, most Japanese imports being under long-term contracts, and the EEC having a more balanced import structure.

These conclusions, however, are particular to iron ore and depend heavily on the market structure prevailing in that industry. Their relevance to other primary commodity markets, even for mineral materials, needs to be evaluated carefully against the institutional arrangements existing in each individual market. For example, although the bauxite/alumina/aluminium industry has many parallels with the iron ore industry (they are both bulk commodities, experiencing increasing economies of scale in mining, and sharing problems of obtaining adequate mine finance), the differences in the two industries, with the bauxite/alumina/aluminium industry being much more vertically integrated and more dominated by MNCs, suggest a different role for long-term procurement contracts and consequently a modified form of such contracts. Secondly, in an industry such as copper, where the number of buyers and traders is much greater than is the case for iron ore, there exists a much enhanced role for the metal markets as a sales medium, and a much subjugated role for long-term contracts. Even in this case, however, one can envisage increased recourse to appropriately designed long-term contracts as a means of improving market stability, albeit in conjunction with other tools.

There does seem to exist a strong *prima facie* case that increased use of long-term procurement contracts could make a substantial contribution to easing the difficulties being faced by LDC producer-exporters of mineral products. Further, it is a solution available to private companies, to nationalized industries or to governments, and accommodates a wide variety of legal structures of both producers and consumers.

There is evidence that consumers concerned with the need to guarantee supplies of raw materials are now actively considering long-term procurement contracts as a possible instrument for improving access to supplies. In the particular case of iron ore, several European interests have noted the lower prices being paid by Japanese importers and are considering long-term contracts, collectively negotiated, as a means of increasing that bargaining power. The Federal Government in Australia has recently expressed the concern of vendors with regard to the exercise of monopsonistic power in this market.

All of this suggests that long-term contracts might be more generally applied in the future than they have been in the past and also suggest reasons why a new generation of contracts might be necessary. A further consequence of such a development is that it would separate production and sale of the commodity from exploration. It is quite likely, therefore, that a parallel development would be a new approach to the question of the assignment of mineral rights and the financing of exploration activity. This is a topic, however, which is beyond the scope of this paper.

POSTSCRIPT – PROBLEMS IN CONTRACT DESIGN

No view has emerged with regard to the relative priority to be afforded to price stability as against stability in traded volumes or stability of revenues or expenditures. Indeed, is stability of any of these to be defined in terms of total global market stability or of stability of particular markets, defined either geographically or functionally? There are both theoretical and empirical issues which have not, as yet, received adequate attention.

This is one aspect to be resolved in future contract design. Equally important is to restore in contracts the qualities that will permit long-term procurements to be recognized again as adequate collateral against which loans will be made to finance mine development. This seems to limit the flexibility that will be tolerated in such contracts, although the exact restrictions that this will impose have yet to be tested by the market. One approach would be to place a floor to pricing/quantity provisions leaving contract variations free to move only above this floor. A second approach would be to reinforce the collateral qualities by including government guarantees in the contract provisions – guarantees by government of vendors or purchasers or both. It is worthwhile considering, therefore, the circumstances in which such governments would be prepared to offer appropriate guarantees.

In considering the optimum flexibility of contracts one will need to take account of inflationary or other upward pressures on production costs which, without some consequential adjustment of contract prices, would result in the bankruptcy of productive enterprises. In the same way, improved provision for downward revision of contracted tonnages seems necessary in severe recessionary periods. In both instances, the contract will require vendor and purchaser to share in an agreed and equitable manner the additional costs of making the required market adjustments.

The question of an adequate numeraire to replace the US dollar in such contracts is theoretically easier to solve. The national currencies of the participants could be used, in agreed proportions or, where costs (e.g. investment costs) are incurred in a third currency, this too could be included in an agreed proportion. Thus, the price to be paid would be expressed in a fixed basket of two, three or more currencies. An alternative approach would be to choose a 'neutral' numeraire such as Special Drawing Rights.

The complete solution to the problems of contract design, however, requires a more careful articulation of the economic circumstances that the long-term contract is an instrument in resolving. The experiences of the international iron ore market provide useful insights with regard to these problems and the response to them has considerable relevance for other mineral markets also considering the adoption or extension of long-term contracts as a trading instrument.

NOTES

1. For a review of long-term contracts in the context of Australian-Japanese trade, see Ben Smith, 'Long-term contracts for the supply of raw materials', in Sir John Crawford and Sabivo Okita, *Raw Materials and Pacific Economic Integration* (London: Croom Helm, 1978), 229-270. Also Ben Smith, 'Security and stability in minerals markets – the role of long-term contracts', *The World Economy*, Vol. 2 (January 1979), 65-75.
2. For a general discussion of the problem of financing mining developments and the potential role of long-term procurement contracts see e.g. David Levine, 'Developing countries and the $150 billion Euromarket financing problem', *Euromoney* (December 1975), 14-23; Nicholas Ferguson and Graham Haclin, 'Is there enough money in mining?', *The Banker* (September 1976), 1011-1015; and Gordon Haworth and J. Terry Aimone, 'How major new mines will be financed in the future', *Mining Engineering* (September 1977), 30-32. For a discussion of the response of the World Bank Group to the problem, see Lester Nurick, 'Multilateral financing', *The Journal of International Law and Economics*, Vol. 12, No. 2 (1978), 217-226.
3. *The Economist* (22nd October 1977), 98.
4. For a discussion of the general issue of providing for contractual flexibility in international law, albeit in a slightly different context, see Thomas Walde, 'Revisions of transnational investment agreements: contractual flexibility in natural resources development', *Lawyer of the Americas* (1978), 265-298.

9

CHANGES IN THE NICKEL MARKET

O. Jarleborg

Like all metal markets, the nickel market is subjected to major changes under the influence of the present business climate, but also of decisions taken several years ago. In this paper we shall consider the present situation of the market, the ways in which it has developed, and its likely future. In fact, any attempt to bring that future into proper perspective requires an examination of the past and a comparison with the present. The focus will therefore be on three particular years: 1950 (the past); 1978 (the present); 1984 (the future).

Since 1950 the share of sulfide ores, generally mined underground in temperate climates, has declined relative to that of oxide/silicate ores, generally mined by open pit methods in tropical or semi-tropical climates (see Figures 9.1 and 9.2). These trends will continue in the future with an even greater percentage of nickel being derived from oxide/sulfide ores. This has significance not only with respect to the geographical distribution of nickel production — most strikingly seen in the decline of the Canadian contribution to total production from 91 per cent in 1950 to 37 per cent in 1978 — but also with respect to the nature of the total mineral resources which can be obtained from operating nickel mines. The geological properties of the sulfide ore deposits allow beneficiation techniques to be utilized and also usually permit the recovery of other minerals as by-products, whereas oxide/silicate ores are not amenable to beneficiation and provide only minor by-products, if any. (For further details upon the changing base of nickel production see Chapter 5).

If these geological/geographical observations are to be translated into economic terms, we need to ask what these facts mean in terms of costs and, ultimately, in terms of pricing.

(i)   Less and less of the ore mined will be amenable to beneficiation — thus large physical plants and increasingly large capital investments will be necessary;

(ii) less and less of the ore mined will provide by-products — thus there will be less revenue per ton of ore;

(iii) more and more of the ore mined will be located in remote LDCs — thus large infrastructure investments will be required;

(iv) mining costs and labor costs may be lower than in the past;

Figures to this chapter may be found on pages 158-176.

(v)   unit energy cost will be much higher than in the past.

As sources of nickel have increased since 1950, so have the number of companies in the nickel industry. In fact, while in 1950 the market was overwhelmed by one or perhaps three major producers (INCO, Falconbridge, and SLN) which together produced 98 per cent of the world's refined nickel production, today their share has declined to 55 per cent (see Figure 9.3). Since the mid-1960s other producers have persistently gnawed at the production share of the 'Big Three'. In fact, had it not been for the 1972 Falconbridge expansion in the Dominican Republic and, most recently, INCO's two 1977 expansions to Indonesia and Guatemala, the combined share of the 'Big Three' in 1984 would be 47 per cent rather than the anticipated 55 per cent.

A major outgrowth of the expanded nickel industry has been the number of nickel products that are made available to nickel users. In 1950, there were essentially three such products: carbonyl pellets produced by INCO, electrolytic nickel produced by INCO and Falconbridge, and rondelles produced by SLN. These products, which were the result of their current production technology, satisfied consumer requirements until the early 1960s. In the late 1950s and early 1960s, however, production technology changed, resulting in the volume availability of ferronickel and nickel oxide sinter. At the same time, the steel industry realized that high-purity nickel was not essential for their operations and that these new forms were not only acceptable but even more economical. Thus the 1960s saw the advent of nickel oxide sinter and a variety of grades of ferronickel. At the same time, the period 1955-75 saw the introduction of yet another form of high purity nickel with briquettes being offered by five producers. By 1984, it is possible that another five to ten nickel products will be introduced, bringing the total by that time to well over twenty-five.

These products are classified according to grade into two broad categories: Class I are products which are essentially 100 per cent nickel and Class II are products with a lower nickel content. Figure 9.4 shows that very little Class II nickel was used during the 1950s. This changed dramatically during the 1960s and early 1970s when Class II usage grew at an average rate of nine per cent per year. By 1978 consumption of Class II products accounted for roughly 45 per cent of total nickel consumed, while over the same period growth in consumption of Class I nickel products was minimal. These developments were due to:

(i)   availability – i.e. more companies made Class II products available and wanted to sell them. It is worth mentioning that during the 1960s the natural product to make from oxide/silicate ores was ferronickel;

(ii)   pricing – i.e. producers made their prices attractive in order to sell Class II products;

(iii) technological developments – i.e. during the late 1960s and early 1970s the use of Class II products was made easier than in the past.

AMAX has estimated that by 1984 the split will be the reverse of what it is today, i.e. consumption will be divided as follows: Class I 45 per cent, and Class II 55 per cent.

Of interest now is the Class I/Class II split by major geographical areas, which vary significantly. First, however, we shall examine the changing trends in total nickel consumption by major geographical areas.

Figure 9.5 shows that during the period 1950-1969 total Western Bloc nickel consumption grew at an average annual rate of 6.8 per cent, slightly less than the 8.0 per cent average annual growth rate in Western Bloc stainless steel production. This period, of course, was one of exceptional economic growth, particularly in Western Europe and Japan.

Yet during the 1970s Western Bloc nickel consumption grew at only 2.5 per cent annum, while stainless steel production grew at only 4.4 per cent, as shown in Figure 9.6. Through 1984, AMAX expects nickel consumption and stainless steel production to grow at about 4.6 per cent and 5.0 per cent per year respectively. Figures 9.7, 9.8 and 9.9 show that much of the growth in Western Bloc nickel consumption was attributable to the phenomenal growth experienced by Japan, which showed an average annual rate of 26.7 per cent between 1950 and 1969.

During the 1970s, with the maturation of the Japanese economy and the nationalistic trends in LDCs, the Japanese growth rate (as shown in Figure 9.10) dropped to a mere 1.5 per cent per year. It is not expected that this will continue as the Japanese economy adjusts to world economic changes: growth in nickel consumption should then return to a more realistic 4.1 per cent.

The Class I/Class II split by major geographical areas (see Figure 9.11) shows that since 1964 American consumption of Class I products has declined at an annual rate of 1.4 per cent, while consumption of Class II products has enjoyed a growth of 5.2 per cent per year over the same period. Of the estimated 380 million pounds consumed in the USA in 1978, 68 per cent was in the form of Class I and 32 per cent in the form of Class II. By 1984 it is expected that the Class I/Class II split will be 56 and 44 per cent, respectively.

The Japanese Class I/Class II split (see Figure 9.12) shows a considerable difference to that of the USA. Japanese consumption of Class I products has grown at an average annual rate of 4.1 per cent over the past twelve years and that of Class II products at 9.7 per cent per year. Of the estimated 226 million pounds of nickel consumed in Japan in 1978, 29 per cent was in the form of Class I while 71 per cent was Class II — the reverse of the US proportions. The major reason for the high proportion of Class II products consumed in Japan is that 76 per cent of it is consumed by the steel industry, the biggest user of Class II nickel. By 1984 it is expected that the Class I/Class II split will be 25 and 75 per cent, respectively.

The Class I/Class II split in Western Europe is indicated in Figure 9.13. Although Class I/Class II growth rates vary from country to country, overall West European consumption of Class I products has grown marginally over the past twelve years, while consumption of Class II products has shown a fairly healthy growth rate of 11.3 per cent over the same period. Fifty-six per cent of the estimated 465 million pounds of nickel consumed by Western Europe in 1978 was in Class I products while 44 per cent was in Class II products. In 1984 it is expected that this split will be about 42 per cent and 58 per cent, respectively.

Class II production and consumption growth are not expected to continue at their former high rates. These were temporary, due to the changeover that was taking place among consuming industries. Historically, as shown in Figure 9.14, production of Class II products grew at an average annual rate of 6.7 per cent but by 1984 it is expected that Class I and Class II production will be roughly equal, in accordance with market conditions.

Since 1950, patterns of Western Bloc nickel consumption have shifted with respect to geographical areas and intermediate-use markets. In 1950 when total Western Bloc nickel consumption was 290 million pounds, the US consumption of 196 million pounds accounted for 68 per cent of the total. Post-war consumption in Japan was miniscule, while West European consumption accounted for 27 per cent. Others accounted for the remaining five per cent.

By 1978, the US share of total Western Bloc consumption had declined to 32 per cent; the Japanese share had increased to 19 per cent, the West European share to 40 per cent, and Others to nine per cent. By 1984 nickel consumption by Others is expected to take an even higher share of the Western World's total, whereas the share of the USA will decline. More specifically, in 1984 US consumption will account for 29 per cent of the total, Japanese consumption for 19 per cent, West European 40 per cent, and Others 12 per cent (for these changes see Figure 9.15).

Some mention has been made of the intermediate-use markets of nickel consumption. These can be classified into six major categories: stainless steel, alloy steel, non-ferrous wrought alloys, foundry products, electroplating and catalysts/chemicals. Nickel consumption in each category varies by geographical area (see Figure 9.16), a distribution that has altered only slightly over the last quarter-century. In each case, however, consumption by the steel industry (the stainless and alloy steel categories) accounts for the majority of nickel consumed. For the Western Bloc as a whole, consumption in stainless steel accounts for 43 per cent of the total; nonferrous alloys 21 per cent; alloy steel 11 per cent; electroplating 12 per cent; foundry products eight per cent; and catalysts/chemicals five per cent. It is important to remember that these categories depend on capital spending and, in particular, on producer's fixed equipment.

More important than the historical growth rates for each category of intermediate use which, of course, vary by geographical area, are the recent shifts in some of those trends. For example, the emphasis on smaller, lighter cars with plastic and/or rubber bumpers will certainly contain the growth of nickel consumption in electroplating. Indeed, this has already taken place. Production of nickel-free ferritic stainless steels may also adversely affect nickel consumption in stainless steel to some slight degree.

On the other hand, some factors could exercise a positive influence on consumption, i.e. the increased usage of high nickel and superalloys by the energy industry; the increased usage of nickel/copper alloys in marine and ship-building applications; and increased usage in powder metallurgical applications.

Since the boom came to an end in the summer of 1974 the supply of nickel has exceeded demand (see Figure 9.17). This is due in part to the severe drop in consumption in 1975 — the worst since the Great Depression. It is also due in part to the fact that the producers as a whole were not very responsive to the fall-off in consumption and did not cut back production adequately. Cash flow demands and the need to run-in new plants resulted in increased production, and producers were burdened with excessive inventories (see Figure 9.18). As a result, total inventories were pushed above the upper band of the equilibrium level, eventually leading to intense price competition. Obviously, bargain prices did not help the producers. Consumption has steadily improved since 1975, however, except for a slight decline in 1977 (see again Figure 9.17).

At the end of 1977, producers' refined inventories approximated 780 million pounds of which 400 million were considered excess. Every major producer announced that production would be curtailed in 1978 and by the second half of the year these cutbacks were realized. Lay-offs of over 3000 employees, extended summer vacations, and an INCO strike were experienced in Canada; mines were closed in Canada, Australia and Zimbabwe; a fifty-day wildcat strike occurred in New Caledonia in protest against lay-offs and proposed wage reductions. In general, smelters and refineries operated at about 55 per cent of capacity. Voluntary and involuntary production cutbacks helped to decrease excess inventories but so did a better than expected ten per cent increase in nickel consumption to almost 1.2 billion pounds in 1978.

The supply/demand balance in 1978, including the usual net imports from Cuba and the USSR of approximately 50 million pounds, resulted in a drawdown in producers' inventories of approximately 190 million pounds to 590 million pounds or six months' demand. In an industry where about 4.5 months of producers' refined inventories are required to maintain equilibrium, a further drawdown of 1.5 months is necessary. If producers continue to act rationally, and barring a severe economic recession, equilibrium can be restored and they will be in a better position to face the challenges of the 1980s (see also Chapter 5). Assuming a five per cent average growth rate of the nickel market (see Figure 9.19), an additional mine capacity of 25,000 tonnes per year will be needed from 1982 onwards. As the leadtime for bringing a mine into production is approximately five years, decisions must be taken now in order to avoid shortages in the late 1980s.

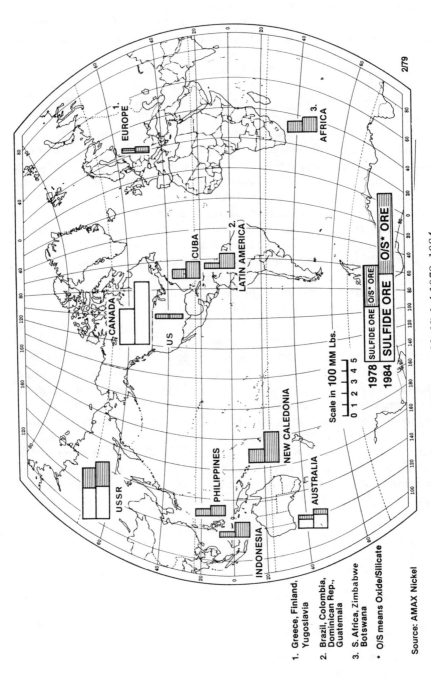

Figure 9.1. *Estimated World Mine Production of Recoverable Nickel 1978, 1984*

1. Greece, Finland,
   Yugoslavia

2. Brazil, Colombia,
   Dominican Rep.,
   Guatemala

3. S. Africa, Zimbabwe
   Botswana

* O/S means Oxide/Silicate

Source: AMAX Nickel

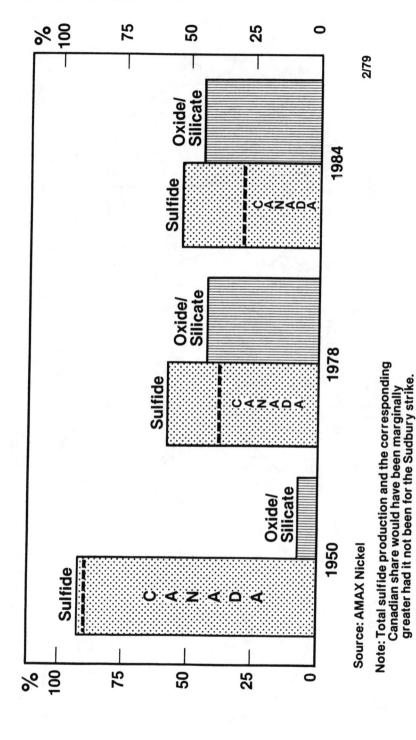

Figure 9.2. *Mine Production of Nickel by Type of Ore*

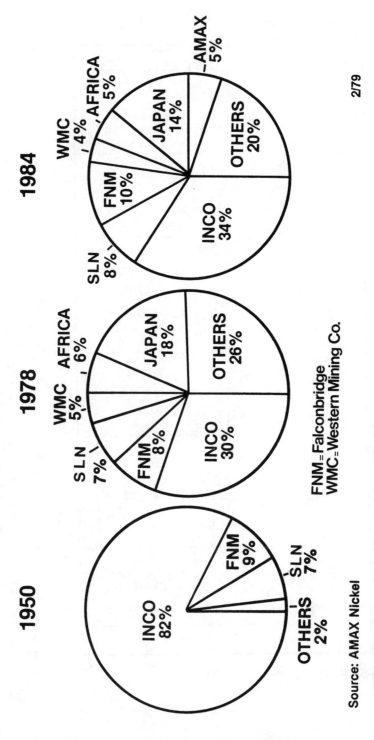

Figure 9.3. *Refined Nickel Production by Supplier*

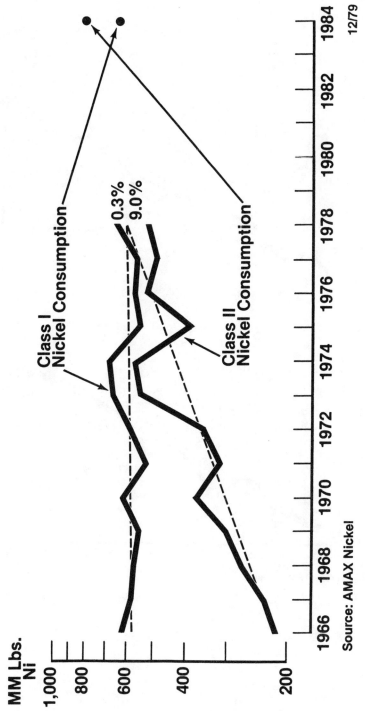

Figure 9.4. *MECs Nickel Consumption by Class*

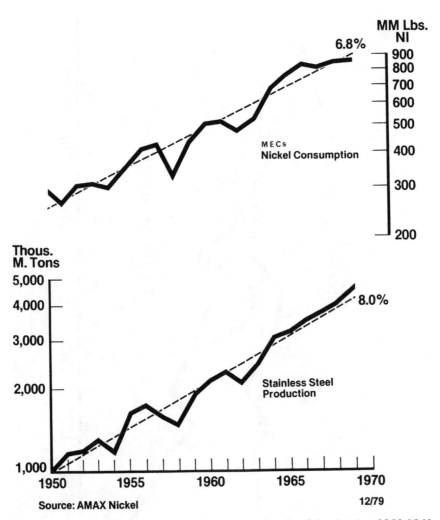

Figure 9.5. *MECs Nickel Consumption vs Stainless Steel Production 1950-1969*

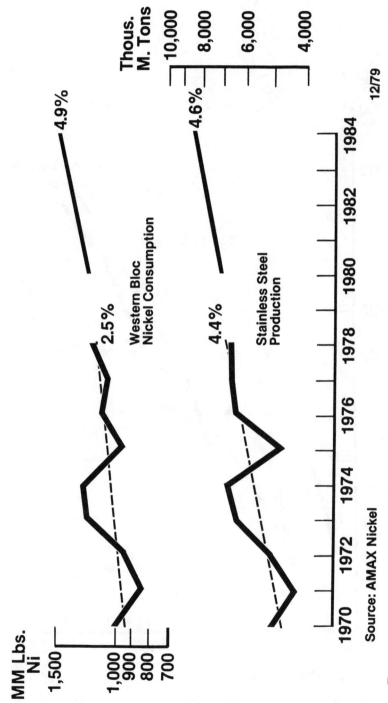

Figure 9.6. *MECs Nickel Consumption vs Stainless Steel Production 1970-1978*

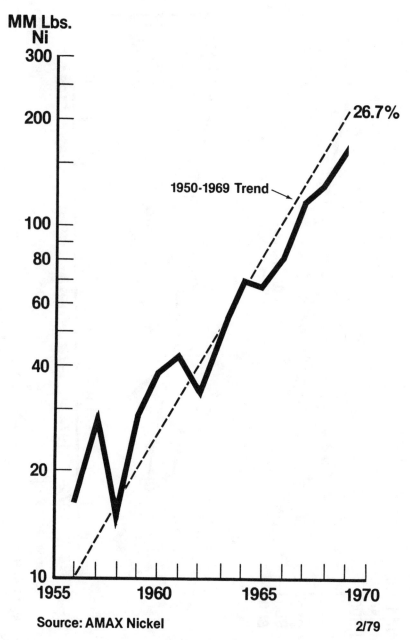

Figure 9.7. *Japanese Nickel Consumption 1955-1969*

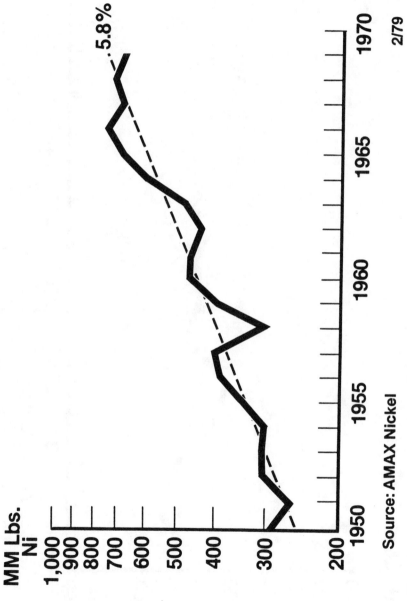

Figure 9.8. *MECs Nickel Consumption Excluding Japan 1950-1969*

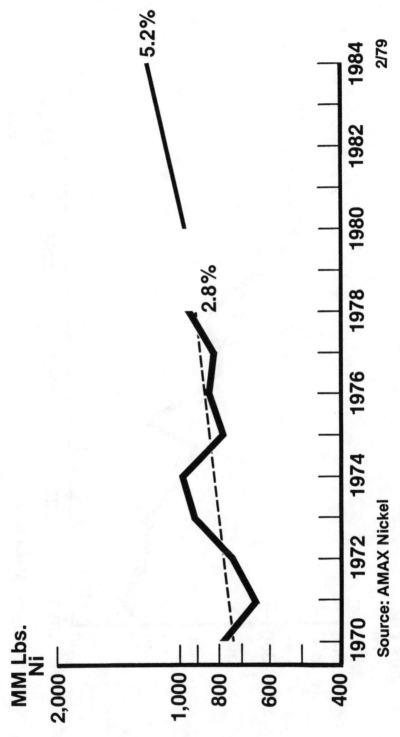

Figure 9.9. *MECs Nickel Consumption Excluding Japan 1970-1978*

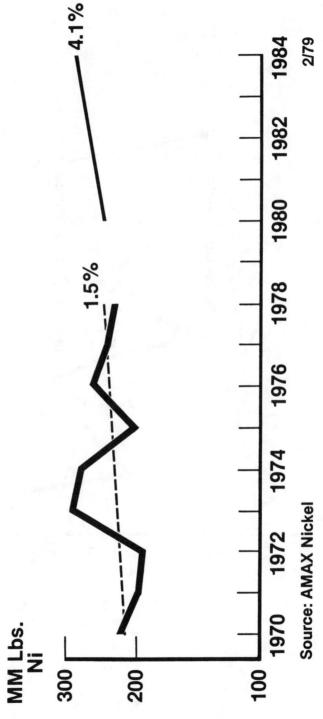

Figure 9.10. *Japanese Nickel Consumption 1970-1978*

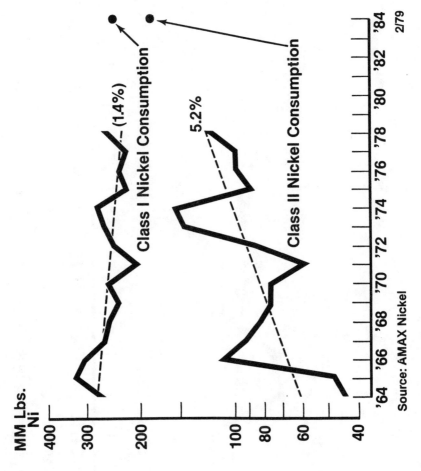

Figure 9.11. *US Nickel Consumption by Class*

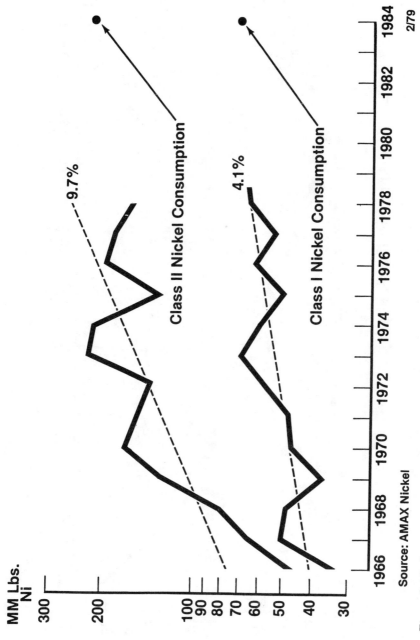

Figure 9.12. *Japanese Nickel Consumption by Class*

2/79

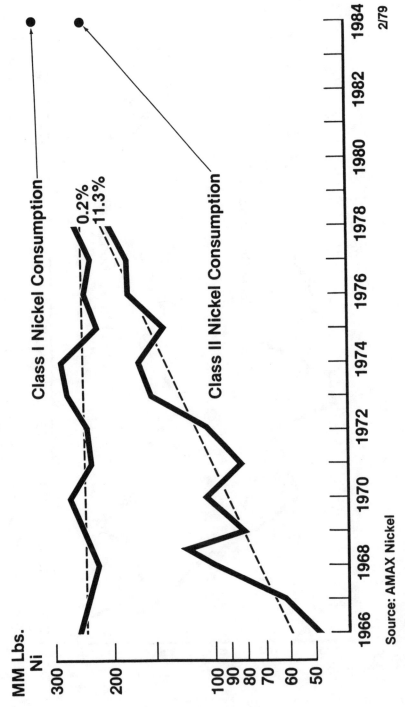

Figure 9.13. *Western European Nickel Consumption by Class*

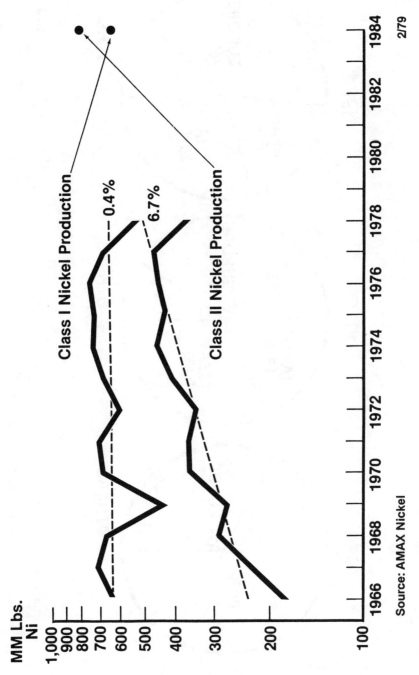

Figure 9.14. *Nickel Production by Class*

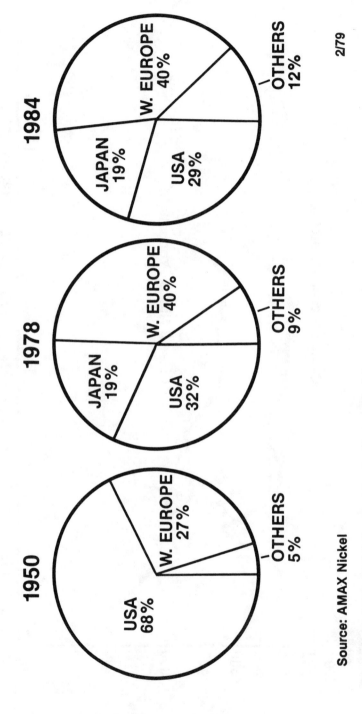

Source: AMAX Nickel

Figure 9.15. *MECs Nickel Consumption by Geographical Area*

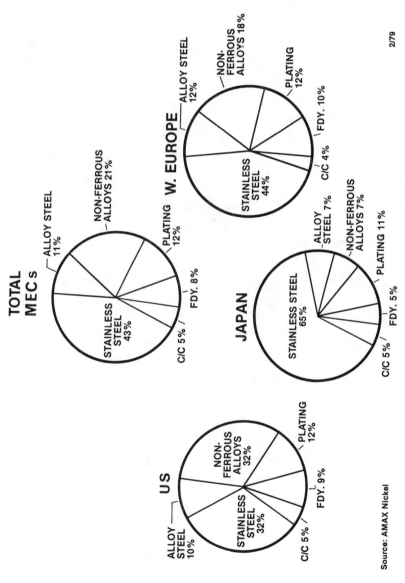

Figure 9.16. *Nickel Consumption by Intermediate-Use Market in 1978*

Source: AMAX Nickel

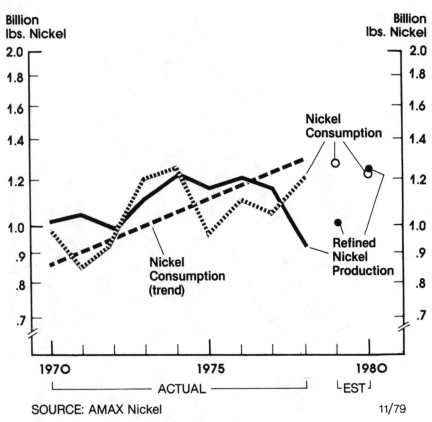

Figure 9.17. *MECs Nickel Production and Consumption*

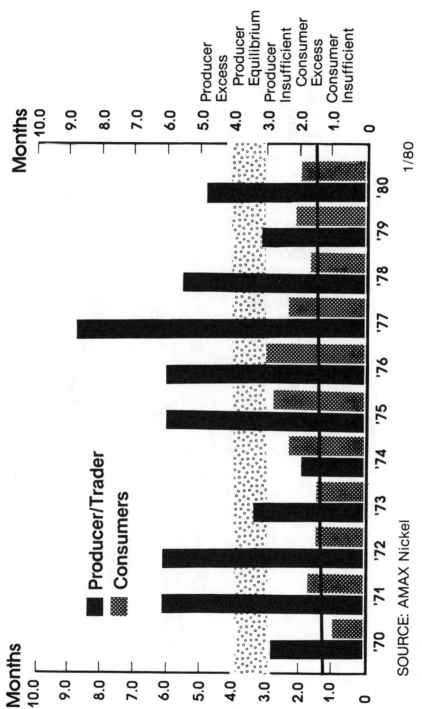

SOURCE: AMAX Nickel

Figure 9.18. *MECs Refined Nickel Inventories at Year End in Months of Demand*

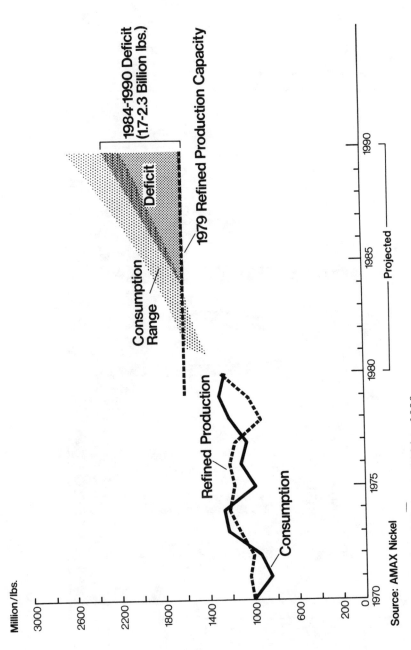

Source: AMAX Nickel

Figure 9.19. *Nickel Shortages 1984 to 1990*

10

FOREIGN FINANCE FOR LDC MINING PROJECTS

M. Radetzki and S. Zorn

While the overall demands for financing for mining projects in LDCs during the 1980s are not very great by comparison with worldwide financial resources — one estimate is that some US$4.4 billion (in constant 1977 dollars) will be required annually[1] — these demands pose real problems for many individual countries. Traditionally, mining operations have been financed through equity investment and the generation of cash flow from ongoing production. More recently, in the late 1960s and 1970s, 'project finance', involving a mixture of syndicated bank loans, export credits and equity contributions from MNCs, became a significant source of LDC mining funds. As a result, however, of the increasing capital requirements of major mining projects, and the changes in the world financial system in the late 1970s, these mechanisms by themselves are unlikely to prove adequate to the task of funding all the LDC mining projects that are economically viable. New approaches, therefore, are receiving increasing attention.

PROSPECTS FOR INTERNAL FINANCE

One obvious source of funds for LDC mining projects would be the LDCs themselves. More specifically, one might look for financing to the following: (a) state mining enterprises; (b) private capital; (c) national mineral development banks; and (d) direct budgetary appropriations. Each of these potential sources of funds, however, has severe limitations.

As regards state mining enterprises in the LDCs, there are three such firms listed among the 300 largest companies outside the USA — Cia. Vale do Rio Doce (CVRD) of Brazil, Codelco-Chile, and Zimco, the state holding company for the Zambian copper industry. There are also significant state mining com-

This article is an abridged and edited version of material which appeared in M. Radetzki and S. Zorn, *Financing Mining Projects in Developing Countries* (London: Mining Journal Books Ltd, 1979). The views expressed are those of the authors and do not necessarily reflect those of the organizations by which they are employed.

Notes to this chapter may be found on page 197.

panies in a number of other countries, including Centromin (Peru), Gécamines (Zaire), Comibol (Bolivia), Hindustan Aluminium (India), PT Timah and PT Aneka Tambang (Indonesia), and ENAMI (Chile).

In a few cases, notably CVRD in Brazil and Codelco in Chile, these firms are financially strong and generate significant amounts of cash from their ongoing operations. In many other cases, however, the state mining enterprises are in very weak financial positions, unable even to finance the necessary investments to maintain existing levels of production.

As for private domestic capital, that appears to be a significant factor only in a few countries, notably Mexico, Brazil, the Philippines, Malaysia and India. Few LDCs have either a strong domestic capitalist class or well-organized capital markets. And even where these exist — as in Brazil, for example — the very large cost of new mining projects puts them beyond the capacity of private capital alone to develop. In those few cases where private capital has been especially important, this has been at least in part the result of geological accidents that permit the development of relatively small mineral deposits. This is the situation in the copper industry in the Philippines and the tin industry in Malaysia, for example.

A further limit on the potential utility of private domestic capital is that such funds tend to be invested in projects that promise high returns and short payback periods. The long-term view required for investment in a large-scale mineral operation is not normally characteristic of LDC investors, who see opportunities for greater and faster gains in real estate transactions, import and export trade, and similar ventures.

In a few LDCs, governments have established national mineral development banks which fund exploration activities and provide finance for smaller-scale mining development. The most prominent examples are Cia. de Pesquisas de Recursos Minerais (CPRM) in Brazil, the Banco Minero in Peru, and the Comision de Fomento Minero in Mexico. While these agencies, and others like them in a few additional countries, have great value in stimulating the development of smaller projects, it is clear that their financial resources are not likely to be adequate to the needs of a major, large-scale mining project.

Similarly, the prospect of direct budgetary appropriations by LDC governments in support of large-scale mining projects offers at best a limited potential. In view of the limited employment creation potential of most mining projects (as opposed to agriculture, for example), and in view of the availability of mineral finance from outside sources (as discussed below), it is often difficult for a government to justify the decision to invest directly in mining, using scarce budget funds.

CHANGING PATTERNS OF FINANCE

Historically, only a small proportion of the total capital required for mining projects in LDCs has come from non-equity, non-internal sources. For the period up to 1960, informed estimates are that close to 90 per cent of total capital requirements for LDC mining were met either by private investment or by internal generation of cash from ongoing operations.[2] While this generalization hides the important fact that some key mining enterprises — for example, the Zairean copper industry and Cerro de Pasco in Peru — were started on the basis of loan finance, and that internal cash generation was often aided by the low-taxation policy of the colonial governments in many locations, it is still accurate to say that the basic source of capital for LDC mining projects up until the mid-1960s was private external capital supplied by the large mining companies. In addition, in such integrated industries as steel and aluminium, the MNCs frequently invested backwards, using a combination of equity and loans from parent companies to subsidiaries, to assure themselves of the raw material (iron ore and bauxite) supplies required.

As the scale of projects grew, however, even beyond the capacity of the large mining MNCs to finance, 'project financing' became established as a major technique for funding LDC mining projects. Without attempting a precise definition of project financing, one can say that it contains the following basic elements:

(a) reliance on the anticipated cash flow of the project itself to repay the debt, rather than reliance on the overall credit of the project sponsors;

(b) a matching of several different sources of finance to the needs of the project, rather than reliance on a single source of funds; and

(c) a sharing of the risks involved, usually by syndicating the project loan on as wide a basis as possible.

Other typical features of what by now has become 'traditional' project finance include the role of a leading bank as organizer and manager of the finance, the provision of completion guarantees by the project sponsors to ensure that the venture actually comes into production at the anticipated level, and the linking of the loan repayments to firm long-term sales contracts for the output of the project.

In the past few years, however, traditional project finance has run into difficulties. First, the overall size of mining projects has continued to grow; second, high rates of inflation have increased the incidence of cost overruns and uncertainty associated with mineral financing; third, LDC debt has increased to high levels, and many commercial banks are becoming doubtful about the wisdom of further loans to at least certain countries. For all these reasons, it appears that the basic project finance packages typical of the early 1970s will be less common in future, and that more complex arrangements will be required.

Until the 1970s, the mining MNCs were clearly the single most important factor in LDC mining finance. In the 1970s, however, their role as direct sources of equity capital diminished. There appear to be two reasons for this trend. Firstly, the increased concern of LDCs about sovereignty over their natural resources, resulting in substantial government equity positions in many LDC mining projects and in nationalization of some foreign-owned ventures, has given the mining companies a perception of higher risk levels in LDCs. Secondly, even if the mining MNCs were willing to put substantial funds into the LDCs, the size of individual projects has grown, while the companies' own financial ability is in most cases significantly less than it was a decade earlier.

One response of both the LDCs and the mining companies to the emergence of sovereignty over resources as an area of concern has been an attempt to separate mining companies' provision of technical skills from an equity risk. This separation can occur through the use of joint ventures, in which the mining MNC may have only a minor equity stake but acts as operator of the project, responsible for planning and execution.

This pattern may be an adequate solution to mining companies' increasing fears of the political risk in LDCs, but it offers no solution to the financing problem. Firstly, the major commercial banks often insist that a mining company, with technical qualifications that the banks consider adequate for the project, have a substantial equity stake. Secondly, many mining companies themselves consider the return on a service management contract inadequate, compared to the potential return on a successful equity investment.

A further effect of the withdrawal of many of the mining MNCs from LDC operations is that it leaves no source of the high-risk capital required at the very earliest stages of mining projects — for general exploration and initial proving of deposits. Whereas in some cases LDC governments or state enterprises may be able to finance project development, once the existence of a commercially viable orebody has been confirmed, it is considerably harder for a government that may be in need of funds for a variety of other meritorious projects to commit large sums of money for exploration with no real assurance of any return at all on the investment.

Looking to the future, the insistence of banks and other financial institutions on a continuing role for technically qualified mining companies appears to ensure that these companies will be a part of many LDC projects. It is likely, however, that the mining companies will wish to put as little money of their own at risk as possible. Thus LDCs will have to look increasingly to other sources for high-risk exploration funds, and will be able to involve mining companies only when the existence of what is at least potentially a commercially profitable deposit has been proven.

In addition, much of the finance provided by the mining companies themselves can be expected to be in the form of advances, loans, and preference shares, rather than equity risk investments. While investing money as loans rather than equity does not guarantee the mining company that it will earn a return on its investment, especially since in most cases the mining company advances are subordinated to debt from other sources, such an arrangement does improve the overall security of a company's participation in a project (though possibly at the expense of a higher return). The overall trend, then, is to shift the risk in mining projects to the governments of the LDCs.

Project Finance

In the late 1960s and early 1970s, project finance loans were available for periods of up to 12 or even 15 years. More recently, the typical loan repayment period has been reduced to five to seven years, although increasing liquidity in the Eurodollar market in 1978 pushed average maturities up to eight years.[3] The shorter payback period obviously imposes greater cash flow burdens on new mines, especially if they come into production when the market for their products is depressed.

In view of the general wariness towards further bank lending to LDCs, it can be expected that the repayment period for project loans will not generally return to the relatively long timespans characteristic of earlier lending.

Interest rates for the commercial bank loans involved in project financing tend to be at a floating rate, reflecting a spread between the banks' own cost of borrowing and the rate paid by the borrower. At present those projects being considered by the banks are offered at rates of 0.5-1.0 per cent above the London interbank offering rate (LIBOR). The spread will vary with the strength of overall loan demand, and with bankers' perceptions of the risk involved in LDC mining projects. Thus, commercial bank project loans will tend to be somewhat more expensive in the future than they have been over the past decade, taking into account the generally elevated level of all interest rates (including LIBOR) in the wake of high inflation in recent years.

The lead banks in mining finance have also tended in recent years to tighten requirements for equity participation in projects. Whereas in the early 1970s loans-to-equity ratios of 3:1 were acceptable to the banks, this ratio is now being set at 2:1 or even less. In addition, project sponsors are tending to be held to more stringent completion guarantees in many of the loans currently being negotiated.

Increasingly, project loans also involve deficiency agreements, whereby the project sponsors become directly liable for any debt service not met by the project itself. Thus the earlier trend to limit the responsibility of parent companies through project financing appears to have been reversed.

Project financing, and especially the commercial bank loan segment of such financing, will remain a significant feature of LDC mining projects, but the conditions imposed on project loans by the commercial banks, in respect of interest rates, payback periods, and particularly the stringency of completion guarantees, will tend to be fairly rigorous. As a result, commercial bank lending may look less attractive to sponsors of LDC projects.

Recently, export financing and supplier credits have become important elements in the financial package of most new mining projects, particularly those in LDCs. It has, in fact, become common for the export finance component to be the first to be negotiated, because of advantageous financial terms typically associated with such financing.

Export credits are available from all of the OECD countries, usually involving fairly long repayment periods and fixed interest rates. In addition, export credit schemes normally involve a government guarantee mechanism, sometimes as part of the same system that ensures equity investments in LDCs and sometimes through a separate government agency.

The export credit schemes of the DCs tend to be fairly similar in their terms. A 'gentleman's agreement' among the major export credit-giving countries in

1976 set standard minimum requirements of a 15 per cent down payment, and minimum interest rates of 7.5-8.0 per cent. As of 1977, the average interest rates on typical export finance loans from major industrial countries were as follows:

Canada	9.3 per cent
France	8.2 per cent
Fed. Rep. Germany	8.6 per cent
Italy	9.2 per cent
Japan	8.7 per cent
United Kingdom	8.9 per cent
USA	8.45 per cent[4]

Interest rates usually vary over a relatively narrow range. In the US Eximbank scheme, rates range from eight per cent for loans of up to six years to a maximum of nine per cent for loans of 14 years. Generally, credits are limited to five years for 'wealthy' countries, but to 10 years or more for the LDCs.

Despite the attractiveness of the export finance schemes, several problems prevent their full application to the entire range of LDC mining projects.

Firstly, the system is relatively rigid. Export credits for terms longer than five years are governed by the Berne Convention, which requires inflexible and rapid commencement of repayment. Thus, if technical problems reduce expected cash flow in the early years of a project's life, the inflexibility of the export credit arrangements may act to increase the financial pressure on the project.

Secondly, export credits have a limited application to the mining phase of projects. Typically, a large open-pit mining project will incur only 45 per cent of its costs in imported capital equipment and services that qualify for export credits. If only a portion of this 45 per cent can be financed through the export credit institutions, this may mean that only 35 per cent of the total cost can be met through this mechanism. The proportion of imported goods and services is much higher for smelter and refinery projects.

Thirdly, export credits are obviously not applicable for projects in those countries with sizeable domestic mining equipment industries of their own. Mexico, Brazil and the Republic of Korea are current examples of such countries, and other LDCs have ambitions, expressed in their development plans, to build mining equipment industries. Thus, over time, the scope for export credit financing in the LDCs may decrease.

Fourthly, export credits are always dependent on the guarantee of the exporting country government. In the case of LDCs which are judged uncreditworthy by the guarantee institutions in the DCs, no guarantee will be provided, even if a particular mining project is otherwise financially viable. Similarly, there have been instances in which LDCs were not granted guarantees because of political differences.

Fifthly, export credit financing commitments have tended to grow more rapidly than the capital base of the export finance institutions. In the USA, for example, Eximbank loan commitments increased by 300 per cent from 1967 to 1977, while the agency's capital and reserve increased by only 25 per cent. While this increasing loan-to-capital ratio is a general feature of the Western banking system over the past decade, it appears to be especially marked in the case of the export financing agencies, raising the question of whether these agencies are adequately capitalized.

Despite these difficulties, the general view of bankers involved in mining finance appears to be that the relatively long-term, fixed-rate export credit system is an essential element in mining finance for LDCs. There is no evidence that the importance of this element in the total universe of funds available for mining projects will decrease in importance over the next decade.

Investment Guarantees

Most of the major DCs have established some form of investment guarantee scheme covering, *inter alia*, mining investments in LDCs by companies from the DCs. Since they cover both equity and loan investment, these schemes facilitate the procurement of finance and the assembly of complete financial packages for mining projects in LDCs. The role of such schemes must therefore be considered in a comprehensive review of mining finance.

The oldest and largest of the insurance systems is the Overseas Private Investment Corporation (OPIC), an agency of the US government, which was established in 1948.[5] The Japanese and Federal Republic of Germany schemes were established between 1956 and 1960, while others in Western Europe and in Canada and Australia began operation in the late 1960s or early 1970s.

The basic political risks insured are those of expropriation, civil war, or other disturbances, and limitations on the transfer of funds. Details of the different national insurance schemes are shown in Table 10.1.

Most of the insurance programmes restrict coverage to those LDCs where a bilateral investment agreement has been executed between the DC and the host government. These agreements are usually intended to promote private investment by protecting the investor against discriminatory legal and administrative action, both as compared to the local business community and as compared to investors from other countries.

The agreements normally do not provide automatic protection against nationalization, but generally the host country is required to undertake to provide fair compensation without undue delay (exactly what constitutes fair compensation is often a matter for strenuous debate, and occasionally for arbitration). The investment agreements can be either in a very detailed form, dealing with a number of specific issues (as in the case of those negotiated by the Federal Republic of Germany), or more general, expressing general intentions and establishing procedural mechanisms for resolving disputes (as in the case of those negotiated by the USA). All the schemes provide cover for both equity and loans, and in some cases cover the value of licences, services, royalties and know-how payments.

The coverage is subject to some limitations. For example, each of the schemes has a limit on the total amount of coverage that can be provided world-wide, determined by the extent to which the sponsoring government is prepared to

Table 10.1. OECD Countries' Investment Guarantee Schemes (A Summary of Characteristics)

	Risks insured a) expropriation b) war c) transfers	Geographic coverage a) worldwide b) LDCs only c) countries with bilateral investment agreement only	Type of investment a) equity b) loans c) licences and royalties d) others	Eligibility criteria a) development effort b) export promotion c) global ceiling	Coverage of principal and earnings a) initial investment b) reinvested earnings c) remitted earnings	Coverage in case of loss – basis for evaluation	Annual premium (% of current amounts)
Germany Treuarbeit A G 1960	a) b) c)	b) c) in prin-	a) b) c)	a)	a) 100% b) 50% c) 8% p.a. for up to 3 years	'Going concern' value not exceeding capital brought in	0.5% for the three risks together
Belgium Office National du Ducroire (OND) 1971	a) b) c) and catastrophic risks in some cases	a) c) in principle	a) b)	a) b) c) $23.5 million	a) 100% b) 50% c) 10% p.a. for up to 3 years	Phasing out on a case to case basis	0.75% for the three risks together
Denmark Agence Danoise pour le Développement International (DANIDA) 1966	a) b) c)	b)	a) b) c)	a) b) c) $85 million	a) 100% b) c) 8% p.a. for up to 3 years	Financial statements	0.5% for the three risk together

France (PFCE) 1971	a) b) c)	b) c) in principle	a) only, in principle b) long-term loans from shareholders	a) b)	a) 100% b) 50% c) 25%	Financial statements	0.7-1.0%
Netherlands Netherlands Credit Insurance Co. (NCM) 1969	a) b) c)	b) c) in principle		a) b)	a) 100% b) 50% c) 8% p.a.	Limited amortization during last five years coverage	0.8% for the three risks together
UK (ECGD) 1972	a) b) c)	a)		a) c) $650 million	a) 100% b) 100% total covers c) 100% limit: 200%	Financial statements	1% for the three risks together plus 0.5% as stand-by amount
USA (OPIC) 1948	a) b) c)	b) c)		a) c)	a) 100% b) 100% total covers c) 200% limit: 200%	Financial statements; phasing out for large and sensitive projects	a) 0.6% (expropriation) b) 0.6% (war) c) 0.3% (convertibility) plus 0.25% as stand-by amounts
Japan (MITI) 1956	a) b) c) and credit risks in some cases	a)		a)	a) 100% b) 100% c) 10% p.a. and up to 100% over the project life	Financial statements	0.55% for the three risks together; 0.7% including credit risks

Source: Radetzki and Zorn, *Financing Mineral Projects*, 95.

underwrite the coverage. In addition, most schemes limit coverage in any one country; OPIC, for example, does not permit more than ten per cent of its outstanding coverage to be in any single country.

From the point of view of host countries and of mining companies and lenders, there are several drawbacks to the insurance schemes as they apply to mining projects. For example, many of the national schemes are simply too small to cope with the massive investments currently required in new mining projects. These schemes are intended to operate on a more or less commercial basis; they have in fact managed to do so, and have even reduced premium rates over time, but only by rejecting some large projects that posed potential threats to their solvency.

Another difficulty in the insurance programmes is the increasingly typical multinational consortium organization of large LDC mining projects. In such a consortium of companies from different countries, risks can be shared, and access to a wider range of financing facilities can be obtained. The use of a consortium also, from the point of view of the mining MNCs, permits the maximum political leverage to be exercised against the host government. But use of the consortium approach may make it more difficult to arrange political risk insurance, since some members may be able to obtain guarantees while others may not.

Also, the insurance schemes generally do not deal adequately with 'creeping expropriation', in which the terms under which an investor originally undertook a project are subsequently altered to his disadvantage by the host government, but without removing the investor's formal ownership. Examples of this situation include increases in tax or royalty rates, restrictions on employment of non-nationals, restraints on investment, sales, and purchases, and the acquisition by the host government of an increased but still minority, equity share on especially favorable terms. Because in these situations there is no clear point at which the insurance coverage becomes operative, there may be no repayment at all for the investor.

For all these reasons, the effectiveness of investment and loan insurance in directing funds into mining projects in LDCs has been less than the sponsors of the insurance programmes might have hoped for.

Consumer Credits

Loans for mine development from countries highly dependent on mineral imports — notably the Federal Republic of Germany and Japan — have been a significant feature of mining finance for some time.

In Germany, Kreditanstalt für Wiederaufbau (KFW) has been the most significant agency for extending finance tied to long-term supply agreements. Since the early 1960s, KFW has participated in financing at least twelve mining projects in LDCs, Canada and Australia, with the aim of assuring long-term supplies for German industry. Such loans are usually extended for 10-15 years, at fixed interest rates. Projects in which KFW has been involved include the Selebi-Pikwe copper-nickel development in Botswana and the Nanisivik lead-zinc mine in Northern Canada. The financing package for Selebi-Pikwe was linked to a 10-year purchase contract from Germany for the copper and nickel produced by the project.

Japanese interest in financing mine development tied to supplies has been equally active. Much of the recent development of the porphyry copper mines in the Pacific Rim region has involved Japanese finance, and most of the Pacific Rim (Papua New Guinea, Philippines, British Columbia, Chile and Peru) new production has gone to Japanese consumers.

Japan has also been involved in financing mining development through the Overseas Mineral Resources Development Corporation (OMRD), a government enterprise that participates with the major Japanese mining and trading companies on a 50-50 basis in new mining projects. OMRD is the major shareholder in the Mamut copper project in Malaysia, whose 30,000 tons per year output goes to Japanese smelters, and has a 40 per cent interest in the Frieda River copper project in Papua New Guinea. It is also involved in several large South American projects, including the Michiquillay operation in Peru.

A final example of the importance of consumer financing is the recent FENI ferronickel project in Yugoslavia, which involved a credit of $35 million from Poland, out of a total project cost of $171 million, linked to a supply contract between the FENI project and a Polish government agency.

The outlook for consumer credits is somewhat clouded because of decreasing concern in the major importing countries over security of minerals supply. It is not clear at present what degree of continued support agencies like KFW and OMRD will receive in the near future for further supply-linked projects, in view of the current excess supplies and large inventories in many metals. Consumer credits, however, have certain advantages, both from the host country point of view and from the lender's point of view. The credits are commonly offered for long time periods, and by their nature assure a continuing market for the mine's production. From the lender's point of view, the link between finance and sales makes it possible to set up a segregated account into which the proceeds of the contracted sales can be paid to the amount required to meet debt service on the loan.

THE ACTIVITIES OF INTERNATIONAL AGENCIES

That the World Bank and the regional development banks have not been major factors in the global mining finance picture to date, is indicated in Table 10.2. Nonetheless, these international agencies are important for several reasons. Firstly, public international financial agency loans are concentrated in those 40 per cent of mining investments that occur in the LDCs. Secondly, the funds tend to be focussed on a few key projects which can be of great importance to the economies of particular LDCs. Thirdly, international agency funds often serve as catalysts for much larger loans and investments from other sources. Thus it has

Table 10.2. *Lending for Non-Fuel Minerals and Energy Development, 1971-76 by the World Bank, the Inter-American Development Bank, and the Asian Development Bank*

	IBRD/IDA July 71-June 76		Inter-Am Dev. Bank Jan 72-Dec 76		Asian Dev. Bank Jan 72-Dec 76	
	($ million)	%	($ million)	%	($ million)	%
I. Non-fuel minerals	252	1	39	0.7	5	0.2
II. Energy development	3065	13	1349	24	553	24
Coal and gas	–	–	10	0.2	99	4
Power	3065	13	1349	24	454	20
Total of I and II	3317	14	1398	25	558	24
Total Loans	23216	100	5671	100	2307	100

Sources: World Bank, Statements of Loans and Credits, March 31, 1977; Inter-American Development Bank, Document No. GN-1152/4, March 23, 1977 (*Documento del Banco Interamericano de Desarrollo Solamento Para Uso Oficial*); Asian Development Bank, *Statements of Loans as of December 31, 1976* and *1976 Annual Report.*

been estimated that, in the 1957-75 period, direct World Bank funds accounted for only 1.0-1.5 per cent of mineral sector investment in the LDCs, but that those projects in which the World Bank played a part accounted for 6.0-8.0 per cent of such investment, taking into account total loans and investments in all projects where the World Bank was involved.[6] In these projects, the World Bank funds, on average, accounted for 23 per cent of total project cost; the remainder was met by other lenders and equity investors.

A recent internal examination of World Bank/IDA activities in the minerals sector estimated that total lending for LDC non-fuel minerals projects could reach one billion dollars over the five-year period 1977-81.[7] This level of funding would allow participation in two or three major projects per year, assuming a continuation of the 20-25 per cent level of total project cost represented by World Bank funds. Using an estimate of four billion dollars annually as a likely figure for total capital needs in LDC mining projects, the World Bank could be expected to be directly involved in about one-quarter of all major LDC projects.

Lending at the planned level would appear to be of considerable significance for LDC mineral industries. The basic financial problem for LDC projects does not appear to be an overall shortage of investment funds, but rather specific problems associated with packaging these funds in a way consistent with the development of the mining projects. In particular, the higher debt levels in major new projects often create strains in the early years of project life between lenders, equity investors and the host government, all of whom are anxious to obtain rapid and substantial returns from the project. Where the use of World Bank funds permits a more orderly organization of debt service, or where it attracts additional finance on advantageous terms, the World Bank (or regional development bank) funds may have an importance greater than their numerical value would indicate.

In addition to the World Bank/IDA lending, the International Finance Corporation (IFC) has also played a significant role in smaller mining projects. From 1957 to 1975 it participated in nine such projects, involving total financial commitments by the IFC of $119 million. For the five years beginning in 1977, however, the expected level of IFC investment in mining projects will be $50-75 million annually, which will be spread over projects where the total investment, including the IFC share, may equal $400-500 million per year.[8]

The regional development banks have not been particularly active in the minerals sector. For the coming years, however, there appears to be significantly greater interest in mining finance in the Inter-American Development Bank (IADB) – in some cases both the World Bank and the IADB are involved in the same projects. Examples of this increased interest are the current Centromin expansion project in Peru and the Caraiba Metais smelter and refinery in Brazil.

International Agency Lending in Practice

In this section several cases are presented in which international agency finance has been involved. They illustrate the way in which these funds fill in particular gaps in financial packages for mining projects and support borrowing by state enterprises that might not otherwise have access to credit markets.

Selebi-Pikwe

This Botswana project, as structured in 1972, used long-term international funds for all infrastructure requirements, as well as concessional finance for a good share of production facilities. The project's original financial structure is shown in Table 10.3.

Table 10.3. *Financial Structure for Selebi-Pikwe ($ million)*

Infrastructure		
World Bank 20-year loan	32.0	
US AID 30-year loan	6.5	
Canadian IDA 50-year loan	29.0	
Other loans	4.5	
Total infrastructure		71.0
Production		
Equity and sponsors' advances	46.6	
Indust. Dev. Corp. of South Africa 10-year loan	18.0	
Kreditanstalt für Wiederaufbau 10-year loan	68.0	
Total production		132.6
Total project		203.6

Source: Radetzki and Zorn, *Financing Mineral Projects*, 111.

Clearly, Selebi-Pikwe would not have been developed unless international agency financing had been available; infrastructure costs alone were one-third of the total estimated project cost. It appears that a major factor in the assembling of the concessional finance for the project was the lack of alternative investment opportunities in the country; Selebi-Pikwe was seen as virtually the only project in any sector that might offer an avenue towards self-sustaining growth.

In the event, the project has turned out to be in very serious financial trouble, because of low copper and nickel prices and because of severe technical problems in achieving the designed capacity. International agency funding, linked with finance from bilateral agencies, appears in this case to have permitted development of a project that would not otherwise have been developed. The net benefits to Botswana from this situation have yet to be quantified.

Centromin

The expansion programme for this government-owned mining complex in Peru, involving a major enlargement of one mine plus construction of a mine water treatment plant, involved finance granted in 1975 by both the World Bank and the IADB.

In this project both the World Bank and IADB loans are for a total of 15 years, including grace periods of four-and-a-half years in each case. The interest rate on the World Bank loan is 8.5 per cent, but Centromin will also pay 1.5 per cent guarantee fee to the Peruvian government, bringing the cost of the funds to Centromin to ten per cent. For the IADB loan, interest is at a rate of eight per cent. The loan from COFIDE, the Peruvian government's own development finance agency, is for a term of ten years, including a four-year grace period, and carries an interest rate of eight per cent.

In view of the high level of Peruvian public borrowing from foreign commercial banks, it is not entirely clear why commercial bank project finance was not available to the Centromin expansion project. The long payback periods available from the international agencies, however, give the project a distinct advantage over those which have been financed by commercial banks.

Gécamines Expansion

This Zairean project is similar to the Centromin project outlined above; all external finance comes from international agencies or aid institutions. In outline, the financing plan is shown in Table 10.4.

Table 10.4. *Financing Gécamines' Expansion Program ($ million)*

External finance		
World Bank loan	100.0	
Libyan Arab Foreign Bank loan	100.0	
European Investment Bank loan	20.0	
Total external finance		220.0
Equity		
Gécamines–cash penetration		240.4
Total financing		460.4

Source: Radetzki and Zorn, *Financing Mineral Projects*, 113.

All the loans, which were approved in 1975, are for terms of 15 years, including four years' grace. Interest on the World Bank and Libyan loans is at eight per cent, plus a two per cent guarantee fee to the Government of Zaire, making the cost to Gécamines equal to ten per cent. The interest rate on the European Investment Bank loan is 10.5 per cent.

Equity requirements in this case are considerably higher than in the other examples and, in fact, because of low copper prices and technical difficulties in its existing refining operations, Gécamines has been unable to generate cash at the rate required for the project. As a result, some elements in the expansion programme have been delayed.

All these projects share certain features, which might be seen to raise questions as to the effectiveness of international agency financing in promoting viable projects. Firstly, in each case the international agency funds either were necessary if the project was to proceed at all or gave the project a distinct advantage, as compared to similar projects awaiting financing. Secondly, in all three cases the financial results to date have not been satisfactory, and have been far from the projections made at the time the loans were granted.

While these conclusions do not indicate that international agency lending for large-scale mineral projects is inappropriate, they do suggest that the goals of projects using such lending need to be clearly specified, and that projections of cash flow from the projects should be critically scrutinized.

Other Roles for International Agencies

In addition to providing large amounts of finance for major mining projects, international financial agencies have at least three other significant roles in relation to LDC mining projects. These are:

(1) acting as a catalyst for the involvement of other participants;

(2) providing technical assistance in the early stages of project development; and

(3) undertaking general surveys that can lead to the identification of viable mining projects.

IFC equity investments in smaller mining projects — ordinarily in association with both foreign and host country capital — are notable examples of the catalytic role that international agencies can play. In IFC projects, the agency is often seen to give a stamp of respectability to the project, which then makes it easier to obtain further equity and loan commitments. The World Bank's emphasis on co-financing is another example of the importance of this catalytic effect.

A second field in which international agency involvement can assist viable projects, without risking the funding of non-viable ones, is in technical assistance early in the process of project development. While World Bank or other international agency participation in high-risk exploration activity is unlikely, several possibilities for useful World Bank involvement to facilitate the raising of risk money are available. The first would be direct World Bank participation in the negotiation of mining agreements between host countries and foreign investors. Such involvement might be seen by the foreign sources of capital as providing some assurance of the stability of the agreement, thereby inducing the foreign investor either to provide more risk capital than he otherwise would, or to insist on a slightly lower projected rate of return in view of the added security offered by the World Bank participation. This approach might also be accompanied by at least tacit understanding that the World Bank would consider favorably a request from the project sponsors for financing of some portion of investment needs if the project proved to be viable.

A second possible role for the World Bank at this stage would be the provision of loans to the host country for its share of exploration and feasibility study expenses in a joint venture where an agreement with a foreign investor had already been negotiated. In view of the high-risk nature of these activities, it would probably be necessary for the foreign partner to provide some guarantee to the World Bank in the event the project did not proceed.

Finally, the World Bank could further extend its program of undertaking special surveys relating to mineral development on behalf of the LDC governments. Some 25 of these surveys have been conducted to date, ranging from national mineral potential assessments in Bolivia and Upper Volta to less comprehensive work, such as reviews of the market prospects for particular minerals. This type of general technical assistance would obviously strengthen the bargaining position of LDCs and should make it possible to obtain finance on more advantageous terms than would otherwise be available.

UN DEVELOPMENT PROGRAM

A significant source of finance at the exploration and feasibility-study stage — particularly for those LDCs that for one reason or another did not experience mining company investment — has been the UN Development Program (UNDP). The UNDP and its predecessors have financed more than 120 mineral exploration projects, at a total cost of more than $100 million. Most of the UNDP-financed projects have been located in remote areas, with difficult access; more easily accessible zones with favorable geology have typically been able to attract exploration commitments from the mining MNCs.

While the list of significant deposits discovered or proven in the course of UNDP-sponsored exploration work is impressive, the overall level of resources that has been available through this program has been relatively small, compared to the amount of exploration undertaken world-wide by the major mining MNCs. On average, UNDP spending for exploration and feasibility studies has been six million dollars per year; in addition, another four million dollars per year has been contributed to these efforts by the governments of the LDCs where explorations were carried out. Thus, in total, annual exploration budgets have been approximately $10 million, although the 1979 spending level is nearly $20 million. This is a substantial amount, but probably would only equal the annual exploration budget of a single major mining MNC. Thus the effect of the UNDP projects has been to supply the equivalent of another large mining house, but one which concentrates all its exploration effort on the LDCs, as opposed to the typical patterns of existing mining companies, which normally spend from 75 to 100 per cent of the exploration budgets in the DCs.

The level of finance that has been provided through the UNDP, however, is suitable for exploration and initial feasibility studies, and not for detailed engineering studies or mine and plant construction; funds for these latter purposes still need to be found elsewhere. The UNDP projects may improve the ability of LDCs to attract this additional finance, however, by lessening the risks involved. Similarly, the recently started UN Revolving Fund for Natural Resources Exploration offers a further source of exploration finance. At the end of 1978, the Revolving Fund had five exploration projects under way or completed and approximately ten more being prepared. Total funds involved in these projects, if all were actually executed, would exceed $10 million.

The primary difficulty in establishing the Fund as a major source of exploration financing has been the hesitancy of LDC governments to make commitments to the level of repayment, via royalties, that the Revolving Fund management has considered necessary to ensure that, over a period of time, the Revolving Fund actually does revolve. For example, countries have been asked to pledge to pay a royalty of two per cent for up to 15 years where Revolving Fund exploration results in a mine being developed; in the view of some governments, the most attractive exploration areas can attract better terms from mining companies than from the Revolving Fund. In any case, the overall policies of the Revolving Fund are due to be reviewed within the UN system, and the Revolving Fund may become an important source of exploration financing in future.

ALTERNATIVE SOURCES OF FINANCE

In this final section several possible additional sources of mining capital for LDCs are discussed. None of these sources is completely new in the sense that mine financing has never been undertaken by the organization concerned. The financing precedents which have been set, however, are quite recent. Although the evolution of certain existing organizations into sources of mine finance is certainly in an early stage, it does perhaps offer the future possibility of a significant new pool of capital funds which mining interests in LDCs might seek to tap.

Oil Companies and Countries

The high profitability of oil companies in recent years and their large cash flows have led to a number of these companies becoming involved in non-fuel mineral projects. This involvement has occurred in two ways. Firstly, a small number of companies have set up new mining subsidiaries and entered into all phases of mineral exploration, evaluation, and production.

Examples of this kind of involvement include Exxon, which has focussed its mineral exploration effort in North America, and Amoco Minerals, a division of Standard Oil of Indiana, which has taken substantial equity positions in several projects, including Tenke-Fungurume copper mine in Zaire, and the Ok Tedi prospect in Papua New Guinea.

The second kind of oil company involvement has been through purchase of operating mining companies or of their stock. The most significant case is the purchase of Billiton by the Royal Dutch/Shell Oil Group which has made Billiton a major factor in LDC mining projects, including the Cuajone copper development in Peru, the Trombetas bauxite project in Brazil, and an offshore tin dredging development in Indonesia.

Other oil company acquisitions of existing mining companies include the purchase of the Disputada copper mine in Chile by Exxon, the takeovers of Anaconda by Atlantic-Richfield and of Copper Range by Louisiana Land and Exploration Co. in the United States, as well as the purchase of a 20 per cent interest in AMAX (which in turn still holds a 49 per cent interest in Roan Consolidated Mines in Zambia) by Standard Oil of California.

Oil companies setting up their own mineral divisions or (as in the case of Billiton) injecting sizeable amounts of new capital in older mining and metal companies, clearly provide a new source of capital for mining projects. In addition, it can be argued that the greater familiarity of oil company managements with operations in LDCs, as compared to mining company managements, may lead to a less restrictive view of potential investments, less hampered by perceptions of greater risk in LDCs.

On the other hand, oil companies have traditionally looked for very high rates of return on their successful projects, to compensate for the large amounts spent in unsuccessful exploration; this history of seeking high returns may deter some investments in marginal projects.

The advantage that oil company participation brings to mining projects is twofold. Firstly, additional cash tends to be available as direct equity, from the large cash flows of the oil companies. Secondly, the credit ratings of oil companies are generally higher than those of metal mining companies, and hence it is easier for those companies to raise funds for mining projects than it would be for mining companies with questionable credit ratings.

A possible parallel to the funds invested in metal mining by the oil companies may arise from the surpluses generated by some oil-producing countries ('petrodollars'). These funds are very large and so hold the potential for being a major source of capital investment, for mining in LDCs as well as for many other purposes. As yet, however, the evidence that petrodollars will make a large, identifiable contribution to the needs of LDC mining finance is uncertain.

Much of the liquidity in the Eurocurrency market is provided by deposits of surpluses from oil-producing nations. In particular, the very largest banks — those that tend to be the lead banks in mining project finance — are by far the largest recipients of petrodollar deposits. This recycling of petrodollars through the commercial banking system has clearly made some funds available for LDC mining finance, though it is impossible to determine how much the commercial banks would have cut back on project lending had the petrodollars not been deposited with them.

More directly, there have been a few cases in which Arab states have made funds available for specific mining projects. Two of the most significant are the $100 million loan from the Libyan Arab Bank to the Gécamines copper expansion project in Zaire and the 1977 grant of $100 million from the Government of Saudi Arabia to the Sultanate of Oman for development of a copper project in the latter state.

In general, Arab investment policy has been relatively conservative, avoiding mining projects because of their high risk factor. In our assessment, based on the relatively few examples of direct oil-producing country mining financing, such financing will continue to be rare, and to be concentrated in a few locations (as in Oman) with close ties to the oil-producing states. By far the more significant impact of petrodollars will be through the liquidity that they give to the Eurocurrency market, and through more general assistance to LDC governments (either bilaterally or through contributors to international agencies like the World Bank/IDA or the IMF) which allows those governments to include mining projects in ongoing overall development plans.

Insurance Companies

Like the oil companies, insurance companies in many DCs are major sources of capital. In particular, the stable and predictable financial structure of insurance companies (as opposed to commercial banks whose deposits are for relatively short terms) allows them to consider very long-term lending. Such lending can clearly be advantageous to mining projects that usually carry a heavy debt service burden in the early years of production.

In LDCs, there are two major mining projects that have relied on insurance company financing. These are the Ertsberg (Gunung Bijih) copper project in Indonesia and the Falconbridge Dominicana nickel mine in the Dominican Republic.

These financings illustrate both the advantages and disadvantages of insurance company financing for mining projects in LDCs. The major advantage, clearly, is the long term of the loans, 22 years in the case of Falconbridge. On the other hand, interest rates tend to be high, and the security and guarantee arrangements demanded by the insurance companies are extremely stringent. Moreover, insurance company funds have thus far been available only to projects in which all the equity was held by private companies, and not by the host governments.

Merchant Finance

The role of metal merchants is often not clearly understood by those involved in mining finance. In particular, traditional sources of finance like the commercial banks have tended to insist on purchase agreements, where required, with ultimate consumers rather than with merchants. Yet a sales contract with a merchant may be as good or better security for a mine than a contract with a smelter (as shown by the example of Pacific Rim copper producers being forced to cut back on their contracted deliveries to Japanese smelters in 1974-76).

In addition to providing an outlet for the sale of mine production, merchants have recently become involved more directly in LDC mining finance. In the Marinduque nickel project in the Philippines, the merchant firm of Philipp Brothers provided ten million dollars in bridging finance and working capital, as an advance against deliveries of production. While this amount was relatively small in relation to the total cost of the project, it was a key element in the overall financial package required to bring Marinduque into production.

While the capital available to merchant firms is limited, in comparison with the amounts potentially available through insurance companies, or oil companies, the combination of marketing knowledge and useful bridging finance which merchant firms may bring to projects can be helpful.

Equipment Leasing

Equipment leasing is a technique that has been widely used in the USA, but rarely in LDCs. A recent example of a coal project in the USA indicates how it could be applied to other mining projects. In the case of the coal project, the mining company has leased equipment valued at $100 million from a commercial bank, for a 25-year lease term at an effective interest rate (amortizing the original capital cost over 25 years) of less than six per cent. In turn, the bank can gain from the depreciation deduction it is able to take on its income tax (banks typically have few depreciable assets) and thus can offer the lower interest rate on the lease. Had the mining company borrowed the funds and bought the equipment, it would have had to pay 9.5 per cent interest and put up 25 per cent of the total cost as equity.

The same financing advantages might apply to equipment leases from banks in the USA and other DCs to mining projects. While the example of the 25-year lease at six per cent interest may be extreme, leasing should offer scope for longer-term financing at relatively low rates. Though there are current discussions about operating a $25 million tin dredge in Indonesia on a lease basis, leasing in mining remains a largely unexplored option so far.

CONCLUSION

The preceding review of the various sources of capital for mining projects in LDCs indicates some of the problems that face those countries with major mineral potentials. Only in rare cases will the funds for mineral development be available internally; more often, an LDC will have to seek external finance of some kind. While the absolute amounts of finance needed for mineral development, on a worldwide basis, are well within the capacity of the international financial markets, the terms on which finance may be made available for any one particular LDC project may be less than totally satisfactory from the viewpoint of the host government. In the case of Eurocurrency borrowing, for example, repayment periods may be quite short, creating the potential for severe cash flow problems in the case of minerals whose prices are subject to large fluctuations. Similarly, in the case of direct equity investment by mining MNCs, the desire of the latter for a high discounted cash flow rate of return and a relatively rapid payback period may conflict with the host government's desire for a reasonable flow of tax revenue from the commencement of production. Export credits may unreasonably tie a host government to a particular supplier. And international and new sources of mining finance do not yet appear adequate to meet the demand for funds. Thus, although the world as a whole does not face any shortage of funds for mineral development, competition among LDCs to obtain funds may have the effect of weakening those countries' bargaining position vis-à-vis the suppliers of finance.

NOTES

1. M. Radetzki and S. Zorn, *Financing Mining Projects in Developing Countries* (London: Mining Journal Books Ltd, 1979), 30.
2. *Minerals: Salient Issues* (Report of the Secretary-General to the 5th session of the Committee on Natural Resources, May 1977, UN document E/C.7/68).
3. *New York Times* (3 December 1978), F.1.
4. Bureau of National Affairs, *Daily Executive Report* (5 January 1977).
5. For more extensive analysis of OPIC, and new programs adopted recently, see Chapter 13 *infra*.
6. International Bank for Reconstruction and Development, *Minerals and Energy in the Developing Countries* (Washington, 1977), 37.
7. *Ibidem*, 34.
8. *Ibidem*, 38.

11

MINING AGREEMENTS AND CONFLICT RESOLUTION

R.F. Mikesell

The world's mining and petroleum industries have changed enormously over the past decade. In 1965 all of the world's great copper mines were owned by a handful of mining MNCs, while most of the petroleum production outside the United States and Canada was in the hands of the Seven Sisters. Today, although mining and petroleum MNCs still play an enormous role in production and marketing, the ownership and control of much of these resources have passed to governments of LDCs. Gone are the long-term mining and petroleum concessions that gave the foreign holders complete freedom to produce and market, while paying only a modest royalty. The bulk of the rents in the form of a surplus over cost are now being captured by the governments of the producing countries.

PETROLEUM AGREEMENTS

As early as the 1950s, governments of petroleum-producing countries began demanding a 50-50 split of net revenues between the petroleum companies and the governments. This was regarded as a radical development but, in effect, the governments of the producing countries were asking only for the same share that the US government and the governments of other DCs had been obtaining in the form of corporation taxes on the revenues of the oil companies derived from abroad. MNCs did not object too much to being taxed by the governments of LDCs so long as the tax did not exceed that on net corporate income imposed by the governments of the parent companies, since taxes paid abroad were generally creditable against taxes owed to the home governments. Most LDCs decided that they could raise their corporate income taxes to the 50 per cent level without impairing foreign investment.

The governments of LDCs were not satisfied with capturing those rents that otherwise would have gone to the home governments of the foreign investors. In petroleum, the 50-50 split was replaced by 60-40 and beyond in favor of the

---

In the preparation of this chapter, the author has drawn heavily on two of his own publications: *New Patterns of World Mineral Development* (Washington: British-North American Committee, 1979); and *The World Copper Industry* (Baltimore: Johns Hopkins University Press for Resources for the Future, Inc., 1979).

Notes to this chapter may be found on page 209.

governments. In mining, income taxes and other levies also captured progressively higher shares of the rents. In addition, the governments of both mining and petroleum-producing countries began demanding a share of the equity in the investments to be provided by the foreign investors at a nominal price and paid for out of profits on the acquired shares. By the end of the 1960s, governments of petroleum and mining countries were demanding a majority equity position, together with tax rates that captured the bulk of the rents. Failure to accord to the demands of a host government often meant expropriation of the foreign investment. In many petroleum-producing countries the foreign companies became little more than suppliers of services, with the payments for their services depending upon the outcome of expenditures for exploration and development. Moreover, exceptionally high rewards for the risk takers have been progressively whittled down by demands for contract renegotiation. Since the several-fold increases in petroleum prices engineered by the OPEC governments, gross revenues of the petroleum companies in favorable geological areas have been high enough to justify risky investments, with the host governments receiving up to 85 per cent of the net earnings from the operations.

The revolution in mining and petroleum came with the political and economic independence of the LDCs. Government control over natural resources is a strong characteristic of nationalism, and foreign investors in the resource industries have been a target of nationalistic movements, at least since the Mexicans nationalized their petroleum industry in the 1930s. Economic nationalism has presented many governments of LDCs with a dilemma. On the one hand, if they eliminate foreign investment in their resource industries entirely, or establish conditions that keep out foreign investment, they cannot maximize their revenues for economic development. On the other hand, if they offer attractive terms to foreign investors, the government may lose the next election or be overthrown by a military coup. Since failure to obtain sufficient revenues to satisfy the growing aspirations of the public is likely to result in the overthrow of the government in any case, governments cannot rest comfortably on either horn of this dilemma. There are good examples of this situation in the South American countries, including Argentina, Brazil, Chile and Peru, among others. Middle-of-the-road governments seeking some accommodation with foreign investors have been overthrown by left-wing governments that have nationalized the country's resource industries — only to be overthrown by rightist regimes because of economic failure. Peron ruined a thriving petroleum industry in Argentina by throwing out the foreign investors. In 1958 President Frondizi brought back the foreign petroleum companies and made Argentina self-sufficient in petroleum, but he was accused of selling out the country and was replaced by a more left-wing government in 1963 which cancelled the contracts with the private petroleum companies. The cycle was later repeated with a military regime again bringing in the private petroleum companies, but this policy was reversed when Peron returned to Argentina in 1972. The Argentine government is again seeking to negotiate contracts with foreign petroleum companies for the development of their oil, and the Peruvian government under President Bermudez reversed the previous foreign investment policy of his predecessor, General Velasco, in favor of attracting foreign investors into both petroleum exploration and mining.

Essentially the same pattern of repression and expropriation of foreign investment in the resource industries, followed by efforts to attract such investment, has occurred in Brazil and Chile in response to the interplay of economic and political forces. Today the pendulum in most LDCs seems to be swinging in favor of greater participation by foreign investors in both petroleum and mining. Following their unfortunate experiences in LDCs, however, many resource companies are reluctant to make investments in these countries unless the expected rewards are unusually high.

The bargaining position of governments has been far stronger in the case of petroleum than in the case of mining, especially since the several-fold increase in world petroleum prices as a consequence of the operation of the OPEC cartel since 1973. In the OPEC countries, 100 per cent or majority government ownership and service contracts or production-sharing contracts with foreign petroleum MNCs tend to dominate; but whatever the formal arrangements, control over output and prices has shifted from the petroleum MNCs to governments.

In non-OPEC countries where production is often insufficient for exports and large producing areas do not exist, petroleum companies have considerably more bargaining strength. MNCs are very anxious to obtain crude oil to supply their downstream markets the world over and tend to be less interested in finding and producing oil in countries where potential reserves are relatively small, costs are high — as well as risks — and there is little chance of producing oil in amounts beyond what is necessary to supply the domestic market. The companies may be more interested if they have refinery and retail outlets in the country, but this is not always the case. For example, in Peru production-sharing arrangements have been made with petroleum MNCs which provide for a 50-50 split at the wellhead between the government petroleum enterprise and the foreign petroleum MNCs, with the government enterprise paying all the local taxes. In the case of one agreement made in 1978 for exploration in the Peruvian jungle, the split was 75-25 in favor of the company for the first 12 million barrels. Of course, the petroleum company puts up all the capital for exploration and development. In contrast, Indonesia's production-sharing agreements have been providing for an 85-15 per cent split in output in favor of the government, since there are large fields and producing wells and the bulk of the output is available for export. Also, risks are lower when companies bid for contracts in areas where the reserves have been determined by exploration.

Frequently governments arrange for competitive bidding for contracts with companies to explore for and produce oil, with the contract going to the company that offers to pay the largest bonus, which often may run into many millions of dollars. In some cases, as in Argentina, competitive bidding is on the basis of how much the foreign company is willing to spend for exploration and development of a particular area that is put up for bidding. Competitive bidding for contracts or leases is used in many countries, including the USA, in the leasing of areas for offshore exploration and development.

The bargaining strength of the host government and the foreign enterprise is perhaps more equal in mining than in petroleum under conditions of the petroleum market today as contrasted with the market for most non-fuel minerals. Modern mining agreements have emerged from conflicting policies and objectives of the foreign investor and the host government. In many cases, existing agreements are the result of a renegotiation of the older agreements characterized by 100 per cent foreign ownership and control. Where the renegotiations have failed, however, there have been expropriations of the properties of foreign investors. By and large, these expropriations have proved disadvantageous to both sides. In other words, since both the host government and the foreign investors need one another, it seems feasible that in most cases solutions could have been worked out which would have been more beneficial to each side than outright expropriation.

In the following section the conditions generally desired by the foreign investor will be listed and contrasted with the conditions frequently demanded by host governments. Approaches to reconciliation of these often opposing positions will be considered and illustrated through the examination of several actual agreements that have been negotiated in the past three or four years.

Conditions Generally Desired by the Foreign Investor

The 'ideal' contract conditions generally desired or demanded by the foreign investor are the following.

(1) Majority equity ownership.

(2) Full control over production, employment, investment, purchases of materials and equipment, marketing and distribution of earnings.

(3) Tax provisions that will enable the foreign investor to earn and repatriate the capitalized value of his investment, including the repayment of external indebtedness, within a relatively short period of time, and a corporate tax rate that does not exceed that imposed by the home country of the parent company.

(4) Foreign exchange arrangements that permit the foreign investor to hold sufficient export proceeds abroad to meet all external obligations, including those arising from current foreign purchases, and to remit dividends and authorized capital repatriation.

(5) Freedom to make payments to the parent company, or to other foreign firms, for technical services and the use of patented processes and to import equipment and materials from any source so long as the prices and quality are competitive.

(6) Exemption from import duties of equipment and materials employed in construction and operations.

(7) No export or production taxes or royalties, and guarantees against the imposition of new taxes or other legislation or regulations that would affect the operation and profitability of the investment that did not exist at the time of the investment agreement or were not specified in it.

(8) Guarantees against expropriation or demands for contract renegotiation during the life of the agreement.

(9) Negotiation of an agreement covering exploration, production and operations before any substantial exploration outlays.

(10) A minimum of tenure of the life of the mine, often at least 30 years after the initiation of commercial production.

(11) In the event of expropriation, a guarantee of full compensation based on replacement cost of assets or present value of projected earnings.

(12) Arbitration of disputes arising in the implementation of the contract by an independent arbitration agency such as the International Chamber of Commerce or the International Center for the Settlement of Investment Disputes of the World Bank.

This list could be extended, but it probably includes the most important initial demands of the foreign investor.

Conditions Demanded by Host Governments

The governments of host countries also usually insist on certain 'ideal' conditions from their point of view for foreign investments in their resource industries. Although these demands differ from country to country and from time to time, they frequently include the following.

(1) Majority government ownership, or the option to acquire a majority of the equity at some time following the exploration period; and in some cases, the option to acquire 100 per cent of the equity after a certain number of years of operation with compensation to be made at book value and often in long-term bonds.

(2) Gradual replacement of all expatriate personnel by nations, and the establishment of training programs designed to achieve localization targets in accordance with rigid timetables.

(3) A high excess profits tax on accounting profits in any year resulting from higher than anticipated market prices, with no carry forward and no accelerated depreciation.

(4) Repatriation of all export earnings to the central bank and the application of existing foreign exchange regulations to the foreign investor.

(5) Government control over marketing of the products.

(6) Domestic processing of minerals and gradual expansion to downstream operations.

(7) The right to demand contract renegotiation whenever the government decides that changes in the contract are in the national interest.

(8) Full application of all national laws to foreign investors with no guarantee against changes in the legislative framework in contracts with foreign investors.

(9) The settlement of all disputes between the government and the foreign investor through national judicial procedures and the rejection of any form of international arbitration.

Some or all of the government policies and conditions set forth above are likely to be incompatible with those regarded as essential by foreign investors. Without compromises, new investments in resource industries are unlikely to be made. In recent years, there have been some new and imaginative contractual arrangements that go a considerable distance toward meeting certain of the policy objectives of host governments while at the same time satisfying minimum requirements of the foreign investor. Thus, compromises, short of either side's 'ideal' positions, are being made in the negotiation of major new mineral investment agreements, as shown by the following recent examples.

INNOVATIVE FEATURES OF SOME RECENT MINE DEVELOPMENT AGREEMENTS[1]

The Papua New Guinea-Bougainville Copper Agreement (1974)

The 1974 renegotiated agreement between the Papua New Guinea (PNG) government and Bougainville Copper Ltd represents an attempt to deal with a possible future contract renegotiation in an orderly manner. It also contains some tax provisions designed to protect the company from the effects of inflation on the tax rate.

During the first year-and-a-half following the beginning of commercial operations of the Bougainville mine, profits were exceedingly high in relation to what they were expected to be at the time of the negotiation of the mining agreement in 1967. This was the result of higher than expected prices of both copper and gold, an important by-product. Although profits declined sharply with the fall in copper prices after mid-1974, the high initial profits led to a demand by the PNG government for a renegotiation of the contract. The 1974 agreement provided for a review and possible contract renegotiation every seven years. The language of the review provision suggests that changes in the agreement are to be made only on the basis of mutual consent. The arbitration arrangement, which provides for the appointment of a third arbitrator from a panel of five arbitrators to be nominated by the president of the ADB, would appear to safeguard the company against being forced to accept highly unfavorable conditions at the time of this periodic review.

The 1974 agreement provided for a normal rate of corporate tax (36.5 per cent as of 1978) on corporate income up to 15 per cent of the capitalized value of the investment (adjusted for future additions to capital investment), and a 70 per cent corporate tax rate on taxable income above this amount.[2] Since the capitalized value of the original investment does not change (except for capital replacements), a continuous high rate of world inflation might mean that a substantial portion of the taxable income would be subject to a 70 per cent corporate tax rate, while the real value of this income in, say, 1974 prices may not have risen. Provision is made, however, for an adjustment of the tax formula in favor of the company under conditions of 'abnormal inflation' (defined as an annual increase in the US consumers price index in any tax year that exceeds by 20 per cent or more the average rate of increase in that index in the five years ending with the tax year). Although the tax laws provide for payment of taxes in PNG currency, i.e. the kina, the tax formula provides for an adjustment with a change in the dollar value of the kina and, in addition, provides for an adjustment in the tax rate in the event that the value of the dollar in terms of Special Drawing Rights (SDRs) varies more than 10 per cent from such value in November 1974.

The Broken Hill Proprietory Agreement on Ok Tedi (1976)

The Broken Hill Proprietory (BHP) Agreement with the PNG government in 1976 for the exploration and development of the Ok Tedi copper mine illustrates the introduction of the discounted cash flow rate principle in tax arrangements. The negotiation of this agreement followed a long and ultimately unsuccessful negotiation with Kennecott Copper Corp. for the development of the Ok Tedi mine as well as the successful renegotiation of the PNG government's Bougainville agreement with Conzinc Riotinto of Australia, from which the government and its foreign advisors learned a good deal. The BHP agreement was signed in March 1976, but did not become final until October 1976 when Amoco Minerals and a German consortium joined the project. BHP and Amoco will each hold 30 per cent of the equity, the German consortium 20 per cent and the PNG government 20 per cent (as it does in Bougainville Copper Ltd).

The companies can claim accelerated depreciation sufficient to give a total cash flow in each year of at least 25 per cent of the initial investment. Thus, if earnings are adequate, the project should earn its original investment back in four years. After recovery of initial capital, the normal corporate tax (36.5 per cent) plus a dividend withholding tax of 15 per cent will apply until the mine has earned a 'reasonable return', which is, in effect, defined as a 20 per cent discounted cash flow return on total investment in the project (equity plus debt capital). For profits in excess of this rate of return, the corporate tax rate rises to an effective rate of about 58 per cent. For example, with a debt-equity ratio of three to two and an average interest rate of eight per cent on debt financing, the foreign investor could earn a DCF return on equity of over 35 per cent before the excess profits tax becomes effective, assuming no reinvested profits.

In this agreement, the equity share of the PNG government will be covered in part by the work that Kennecott had already done on the project, for which $17.5 million in bonds has been offered to Kennecott by PNG, subject to the actual construction of the Ok Tedi mine. Also, any infrastructure provided by the government, even if financed by loans from agencies such as the World Bank or ADB, will be credited to the government's equity interest.

The foreign companies, which will hold 80 per cent of the equity, must bear the entire risk of the project through the feasibility study, which was expected to be completed at the end of three years at a cost of $12 million. If the foreign companies decide not to go ahead with the project after the feasibility study has been completed, they have no further obligation. However, they do bear all the risk up to this point.

According to the BHP-PNG agreement, the company must prepare proposals to be approved by the government for the progressive replacement of foreign technicians, operators, supervisors, clerical, professional, administrative and managerial staff, and for a training program designed to achieve this objective. The agreement also provides for the preparation of an environmental impact study, the scope of which is set forth in some detail, and the company is required to comply with specified environmental protection standards.

Arbitration procedures are also set forth in considerable detail. Each side nominates one arbitrator, and if they cannot agree on a third arbitrator, he shall be appointed from a panel of five arbitrators to be nominated by the president and chairman of the board of directors of the ADB.

The agreement recognizes the right of the company to retain outside PNG the foreign exchange proceeds of exports to the extent necessary to enable the company to meet its foreign exchange obligations or to pay dividends to overseas shareholders.

The Texasgulf-Panama Agreement on Cerro Colorado (1973)

The Texasgulf-Panama agreement for the development of the Cerro Colorado copper ore body illustrates the use of the management contract and other contract arrangements for the protection of a minority foreign equity holder. The agreement also illustrates the provision for future government acquisition of the foreign investor's equity under terms and conditions specified in the agreement. Finally, this is the first investment agreement with a Latin American country in recent years that provides for external arbitration of disputes.

The Texasgulf-Panama agreement was preceded by lengthy and ultimately unsuccessful negotiations by the Panamanian government with two other firms, Canadian Javelin and Noranda.

In this agreement, Texasgulf holds only 20 per cent of the equity, the remainder being held by the Panamanian government enterprise, CODEMIN. Under this agreement the Panamanian government will share in proportion to its equity interest the cost of the feasibility study and, in addition, is reportedly paying (in bonds) $20 million to Canadian Javelin for the work that it did on the project. Texasgulf's earnings from its 20 per cent equity participation will be supplemented by a management fee (initially at a rate of 1.5 per cent of gross sales, but declining to 0.75 per cent) over the 15-year period of the management agreement, plus a sales and marketing fee. The joint venture will pay a 50 per cent corporate tax to the Panamanian government, and there is a ten per cent dividend withholding tax.[3]

Despite the fact that Texasgulf will have only 20 per cent of the equity in the project, management control is guaranteed to Texasgulf for the first 15 years of commercial production. After this period, management will revert to the Panamanian government. In addition, the Panamanian government has the option of acquiring Texasgulf's 20 per cent equity at the end of 20 years at a price based on average earnings during the prior five years. It is interesting to note that during this five-year period, management will be fully in Panamanian hands so that Texasgulf would be encouraged to do a good job in training the new managerial team.

The management agreement provides that in hiring personnel, preference shall be given to Panamanians in all job classifications. The administrators are to submit to the board of directors of Cerro Colorado SA (the operating company) a program for the training and instruction of personnel, which is designed to achieve the gradual transfer to Panamanian personnel of all in employment classifications; such transfers are to be virtually complete at the expiration of the management agreement. This program, together with subsequent modifications, requires the approval of the board of directors of Cerro Colorado SA, on which Panama will have a majority vote.

Disputes arising in connection with the management agreement are to be settled by arbitration under the Rules of Procedure of the Inter-American Commercial Arbitration Commission. If the two arbitrators chosen by the parties to the dispute are unable to agree upon a third arbitrator, the Commission designates the third arbitrator and the decisions of the arbitral tribunal shall be by simple majority. The contract provides, however, that 'judgments of execution of the arbitral awards' are to be issued by 'courts of justice of the Republic of Panama'. Such arbitral awards 'shall be considered as if they had been rendered by Panamanian arbitral tribunal in accordance with provisions of laws presently enforced'. Presumably this language was used in order to preserve the principle that all matters of litigation shall be in accordance with Panamanian law.[4]

The 1977 Chilean Mining Agreements

The 1977 mining agreements negotiated between the Chilean government on the one hand and individual foreign mining companies — St Joe Minerals Corp., Noranda, Falconbridge Foote, and Metallgesellschaft — on the other, illustrate the principle of guaranteeing the foreign investor a maximum tax burden while at the same time allowing him to be taxed at the domestic corporate tax rate if lower than the guaranteed rate.

Under the 1977 Chilean agreements, the total income tax burden on the foreign companies is fixed at 49.5 per cent of net profits (including the housing tax and the dividend withholding tax) for the life of the agreement. Should the normal tax regime applicable to domestic firms in Chile be reduced during the life of the contract, however, the companies have the right to elect the normal tax, but in this case they lose the guarantee that the tax applicable to them will not be changed. The foreign companies are also guaranteed exemption from any new taxes on production or exports.

The 1977 Chilean agreements give the foreign investors the right to retain export proceeds abroad of an amount sufficient to meet debt service and certain other obligations which become due within a stated period of time. The agreements also provide that the foreign investor will have the right to retain abroad foreign exchange in an amount equal to profits that have been delayed in remittance for more than one year after the date of application for transfer, in compliance with applicable laws and regulations.

The agreement with St Joe Minerals Corp. gives the company the right to contribute up to 85 per cent of the external capital in the form of advances, thus facilitating repatriation of capital without being subject to the corporate tax.

The Indonesian-RTZ Agreement (1977)

The 1977 Indonesian agreement with Rio Tinto Zinc (RTZ) illustrates a method by which the host government's requirement for the repatriation of all export proceeds can be reconciled with the need by both the company and its creditors to retain foreign exchange from export proceeds to meet debt obligations and to transfer net profits.

The unwillingness of the Indonesian government to grant foreigners the right to retain export proceeds abroad needed to meet foreign currency obligations was a major barrier to the negotiation of any mine development agreements in Indonesia for about four years prior to the agreement with RTZ in March 1977. The issue was settled in the agreement by the adoption of an arrangement whereby export proceeds would be deposited in a foreign investment account held at a foreign bank in Indonesia in the name of the Bank of Indonesia as agent for the company. Such funds would be available for use by the company in discharging its obligations and for transferring net profits and depreciation on imported capital assets, according to regulations set forth in the mining agreement.

A similar arrangement was negotiated between Southern Peru Copper Company (SPCC) and the Central Bank of Peru for handling export proceeds of the Cuajone mine needed to meet SPCC's external debt obligations. In that case, however, the account is held in a New York bank in the name of the Central Bank of Peru.

Indonesian participation in the ownership of the operating subsidiary, PT Riotinto Indonesia, is made possible under the agreement by providing that RTZ will offer to sell shares in the company to the government or to Indonesian nationals in each year following the end of the first full calendar year after commencement of production. The offer of shares in each year is not to be less than five per cent of the total number of shares outstanding when the offer is made, and the offer of such shares shall be made on terms and conditions reasonably intended to insure that such shares are not thereafter transferred to non-Indonesians. The company must continue to offer shares each year until 51 per cent of the shares in PT Riotinto Indonesia are held by private Indonesians or the Indonesian government.

CONCLUSIONS

It is now appropriate to extract the most important features of the mine development agreements discussed above. The following provisions, each of which may be found in one or more of the agreements analyzed, illustrate approaches to the resolution of conflicts between MNCs and host governments:

(1) Delegating management control by means of a long-term management contract to a foreign investor having only a minority equity participation. In addition, the minority investor may be given an equal vote on the board of directors of the company with respect to certain important policy issues, such as the distribution of earnings and investment and financing policies.

(2) Sharing high-risk exploration outlays by the government and the foreign investor in proportion to their equity ownership in the mining enterprise, with full payment by the government for its equity share in the enterprise.

(3) Negotiating a mine development contract that covers all phases of the development of a mine, including exploration, feasibility study, mine construction and mine operation, with a maturity of the contract of at least 30 years after the beginning of commercial operations.

(4) Establishing a tax formula in the contract which assures full repatriation of initial capital before any corporate tax is levied on earnings. This can be accomplished through accelerated depreciation or by means of a tax holiday. In addition, the tax formula may provide for carry-forward provisions that assure no more than an average agreed tax rate on earnings over a period of years. Finally, the tax formula may provide that no more than the normal tax rate would be levied until the investor has earned an agreed minimum discounted cash flow on his investment, after which excess profits tax rates would apply. The excess profits tax would be eliminated in years when the accumulated earnings reflect a discounted cash flow at a rate lower than the agreed minimum.

(5) Depositing foreign exchange earnings in a special account of the host's central bank at a foreign commercial bank under an escrow or trustee arrangement whereby debt service and other agreed obligations must be paid from this account before funds become available to the government.

(6) Exempting the foreign investor from any new taxes, such as production taxes, export taxes, import duties, etc., for a period of years following the initiation of commercial operations.

(7) Providing for a review of contract provisions a certain number of years after the full repatriation of the investor's capital, together with safeguards against demands for contract revision that would significantly impair the profitability of the investment.

(8) Giving the government the option to acquire all or a portion of the equity shares after a certain period of commercial operations, say, 20 years, with the terms of payment fully specified.

(9) Giving the investor the option of financing with a high debt-equity ratio, with all or a portion of the debt constituting parent company advances, the interest and principal payments on which are not made subject to local taxation.

(10) Providing for the arbitration of disputes over the interpretation of the implementation of the contract in ways satisfactory to both the foreign investor and the government.

These features are possible building blocks to be used in future agreements which will help to establish the foundations for a new era of cooperation between MNCs and LDC governments, in which all parties will perceive that a mutually advantageous balance between benefits and risks can be achieved.

NOTES

1. In the analysis and interpretation of certain of these arguments, the author has benefitted greatly from articles written by S. Zorn, 'New Developments in Third World Mining Agreements', and T. Walde, 'Lifting the Veil from Transnational Mineral Contracts: A Review of Recent Literature', both in *Natural Resources Forum*, 1, 3 (1977), 239-250 and 277-284, respectively.

2. For a discussion of the renegotiation of the PNG-Bougainville Copper Ltd agreement (initially negotiated in 1967), see R.F. Mikesell, *Foreign Investment in Copper Mining* (Baltimore: Johns Hopkins University Press for Resources for the Future, Inc., 1975), 130-132.

3. The author was told by one of the Panamanian negotiators that the management, sales and marketing fees, together with the tax arrangements, were found to yield a 23 per cent discounted cash flow (DCF) rate of return to Texasgulf on its equity investment, and that DCF rate calculations were employed in the course of the negotiations. This was not confirmed, however, by the Texasgulf officials whom the author interviewed.

4. Whether this provision actually avoids compromising the 'Calvo doctrine' on international arbitration is something on which the author is not qualified to express an opinion. One of the Panamanian negotiators told the author, however, that if a dispute under the agreement ever goes to international arbitration, 'the agreement is dead'.

12

RECENT TRENDS IN LDC MINING AGREEMENTS

S. Zorn

Much recent writing on investment agreements between LDC governments and MNCs expresses the view that there has been a basic shift in favor of the LDCs in the content of such agreements in the past decade or two.[1] In this view, the old concession agreements typical of natural resources projects, with their lengthy terms, low fiscal returns to the host country and minimal linkages with the rest of the economy, have been replaced by new arrangements, involving governments more directly in ownership, control and management of natural resource ventures; assuring more equitable financial results, from the host government's point of view; and providing for use of natural resource development in the context of countries' overall development and industrialization planning. Depending on the political orientation of the commentator, this perceived trend in favor of LDC governments is either a problem, because it makes investment by MNCs in LDCs more risky, or is to be applauded as concrete evidence of the emergence of a New International Economic Order (NIEO).[2] But the basic belief in a long-term shift in favor of LDCs seems not to be in dispute.

When one examines actual investment patterns and the precise terms of mining agreements negotiated in recent years, however, it becomes increasingly apparent that the presumed shift in favor of LDCs may not have occurred. There has been a sharp reduction in MNC investment in LDCs' mineral projects during the 1970s; as much as 85 per cent of new mining investment since 1974 has reportedly been concentrated in the USA, Canada, Australia and South Africa,[3] while at the same time there has been a process of disinvestment by major MNCs in LDCs in Africa and Latin America. In addition, the renegotiation of certain old arrangements with MNCs or the nationalization or partial nationalization of certain foreign-owned mines has not necessarily secured for host governments a markedly increased share of the benefits from mining; in some cases, foreign companies have earned a greater cash flow from payments to them as managers or service contractors than such companies had previously earned from their direct equity investments. In particular, although many mines in LDCs have

---

The views expressed in this chapter are those of the author and do not necessarily reflect the views of the UN.

Notes to this chapter may be found on pages 227-228.

come under government ownership, this has not in most cases meant that host governments have been able to exercise more effective real control over the development of mineral resources in their countries or to secure increased returns from the sale of their mineral products on international markets.[4]

This paper first discusses some of the general factors that influence the content of mining agreements between MNCs and host governments, including the particular nature of resource projects as opposed to other kinds of investment, the objectives typically held by host governments, and the nature of world mineral industries. The paper then considers some recent trends in mining agreements, including both the new flexibility in agreements that is often remarked on,[5] and the less frequently noted counter-attack by MNCs to reduce the bargaining power of LDC governments.[6] In the most general terms, the conclusion is that many, if not most, LDCs have yet to reach the point where their governments are in effective control of the mineral sector or where the country receives a satisfactory return, taking all costs and benefits into account, from mineral production.

BASIC FEATURES OF NATURAL RESOURCE PROJECTS

The principal features differentiating natural resource projects from other forms of investment available to MNCs are the following: (i) the gains that may be realized from natural resource projects in the form of differential economic rent, (ii) the nature of the markets for natural resource projects, and (iii) the enclave nature of natural resource development. Each of these features will be taken into account both by LDC government negotiators and by representatives of the MNC in their joint determination of the project's character. In certain important respects, the existence of these features militates against the attainment by the host country of control over negotiations and of significant benefits from the project.

Among the most significant aspects of natural resource projects are the gains that may be realized from most such projects in the form of differential economic rent, i.e. from the earnings attributable to the richness of a particular deposit and the ease and cost of production. For example, while some oil fields can produce at a cost lower than the market price of oil, a 'marginal' field may have a production cost (including normal profit margin) equal to the market price of oil. To the extent that actual market prices reflect the costs (including profits at a normal rate) of this marginal producer, then all fields in which costs are lower will earn a premium in excess of the normal profit. This premium is typically referred to as a differential or resource rent; it should be distinguished from monopoly or oligopoly rent which derives from the structure of an industry and the possible lack of competition. In some natural resource industries both differential resource rents and monopoly or oligopoly rents may occur.[7]

Although differential rents are due to differences in the quality of mineral deposits, these rents do not necessarily accrue to the owner of the deposit or resource (which, in LDCs, is usually the state). Depending on the circumstances of each project or industry, the rents may be captured by one or more of the economic actors involved in the production, processing, sale or consumption of the product. For example, before the crude oil price increases of 1973-74, the largest share of differential economic rent from low-cost Middle East oil production was in fact captured by consumers in the DCs, in the form of low prices, and by the governments of these countries in the form of import duties and excise taxes. After the 1973-74 price increases, the producing countries captured a much larger share of the rent. It is, in fact, precisely the question of how any possible differential economic rent is to be divided that is at the heart of most resource project negotiations. For a very low-cost source of supply, the amount of differential resource rent that is generated may far outweigh all other potential economic benefits of the project.

Another significant feature of resource projects that will be taken into account by LDC negotiators is the nature of the markets for natural resource products. The structure of the market for any particular commodity will determine to a great extent both the amount of 'quasi-rent' (which accrues as a result of the market power or superior knowledge of the investor or seller) which can be generated and how such quasi-rent can be distributed. In most cases, LDC negotiating teams are not in a position, during the course of their negotiations, to alter the structure of the international market for the product, but the negotiators must be aware of this structure in order to devise appropriate fiscal and control provisions. There are, very broadly, four types of markets for natural resource products.[8]

At one extreme in a typology of international market structures is the product for which there is no organized world market and for which prices are basically determined by the foreign companies that invest in LDC resource projects. An example is the tropical timber industry in Indonesia, Malaysia, the Philippines and Papua New Guinea, much of which has been developed with Japanese investment. Because each project involves a somewhat different mixture of species, many of which have little or no history of being sold in international markets, it is difficult for LDC governments to refer to any market price standard or reference. Where timber, wood chips or pulp are sold within the MNC, the price is likely to be entirely arbitrary, reflecting the MNC's global interest in minimizing total taxation. In such cases host country negotiators need to establish some method for placing a value on the product at the time it is exported which fairly reflects the ultimate importance of the raw materials in final product values. While none of the major minerals exhibit as extreme a lack of standardized pricing as does the market for tropical timber, these problems are important in the case of minerals like building materials and some industrial minerals.

A second kind of market structure is one in which export prices are set by negotiation, usually between unrelated parties, and in the context of relatively long-term commitments. Examples are the markets for coal, iron ore, uranium and natural gas. In these cases, the LDC government has access to certain information concerning representative market prices, but there are likely to be differences in the grade of the product (i.e. thermal content of coal, or iron content in iron ore) or in the regulations governing its sale and use in the consuming countries (as in the case of natural gas) that make each major long-term sales contract slightly different from all others and that offer opportunities for foreign investors, consumers and other economic actors to gain a portion of the overall differential rent (in addition to any oligopoly or monopoly rent). A frequently used control mechanism in this type of market is for the host government itself to negotiate the terms of export sales contracts or, at a minimum, to require government approval before such contracts become effective. Enforcement of such a requirement, however, will depend on the knowledge, experience and commercial negotiating skill of the host government officials responsible for making or approving export sales agreements.

A third kind of market structure is that in which, although the raw material produced in the LDC is largely traded between subsidiaries of a single MNC, a product that is processed or refined from the raw material is sold internationally at a determinable market price. An outstanding example of such a market is that for bauxite. In 1974, the Jamaican government began to tax bauxite mining operations on the basis of the aluminum metal price, applying a standard technical ratio to equate the bauxite and aluminum tonnages. Such an approach eliminates the need for establishing a market price for the bauxite, thereby vastly simplifying the government's tax collection task.

The final category of raw materials markets comprises those in which a generally recognized market price, determined independently of any specific MNC or project, is available as a standard. Two examples of commodities for which this kind of price is available are copper, for which the price set on the LME is widely used as a pricing base, and crude oil, for which the OPEC 'marker crude' price has frequently been used as a reference price for tax and participation purposes by host governments. Even in negotiations relating to commodities for which such basic reference prices exist, however, LDC negotiating teams must be alert to the methods which can be used by MNCs to divert revenues from the government to the company. For example, there may be opportunities for the MNC to hide revenue from host governments through manipulation of shipping charges or through overcharging for the processing of raw materials, where processing is not carried out in the country where the mine is located. In the case of OPEC, for example, the continuing uncertainty over the legitimate extent of gravity and sulfur-content differentials demonstrates that there are almost always some opportunities for tinkering with any established price structure.

A third special feature of resource projects, as opposed to manufacturing or commercial investments, is the tendency of natural resource projects to have an enclave character. The typical large mining, petroleum or timber project is not well-integrated with the national economy of a LDC, but exists, in many respects, as a separate political and economic unit. The enclave character of resource projects increases the problems for host governments. In many LDCs, for example, major mining projects have more direct links with the outside world than they do with other sectors of the local economy. Instead of purchasing food and other supplies in local commerce, many mining communities have such supplies (for a largely expatriate workforce) flown in from abroad. Communication links may often be better and more efficient to the head office of the mining company, located thousands of miles away, than to the capital city of the host country. In many mining and petroleum projects, there is readily available transportation to other countries (for employees' 'rest and recreation'); expatriate employees rarely feel themselves a part of the country in which they work; and the isolated nature of the project community tends to impose the same feeling of being an outsider even on the host country nationals employed on the project.

A further aspect of the enclave character of resource development is the demonstration effect on the rest of the economy of the high levels of wages and facilities often provided by the project. Because wages are a relatively small proportion of the total value of mineral production, most mining MNCs are willing to pay wages far higher than the generally prevailing levels in the host country. These high wage levels tend to pull labor from other occupations, either by supporting general upward revisions in wage rates which make some labor-intensive industries uneconomic, or by attracting people to the mine area in the hope of finding jobs. This phenomenon is readily apparent in the towns of the Zambian Copperbelt or the mining areas of Bolivia, Chile and Peru, for example.

A similar demonstration effect exists with respect to public facilities and infrastructure. Compared to the hundreds of millions of dollars that may be spent to develop a large-scale mine, a few more millions for schools and medical facilities may seem unimportant to the MNC, and well worth the additional cost because of the effect of such facilities on labor-force stability and public opinion. But for the host government, which can rarely afford comparable facilities for the rest of the country, such largesse by MNCs may seem an intolerable burden. The government may feel itself driven to provide higher levels of public services than it can afford, in a kind of competition with the foreign company or, alternatively, it may alienate large segments of the population by refusing, albeit for the best economic reasons, to engage in this kind of competition.

For all these reasons, then, resource projects in general and mining projects in particular, are not quite the same as other foreign investments. The next section of this paper considers the objectives of LDC governments relating to mining projects in the light of the special nature of such projects.

GOVERNMENT OBJECTIVES

In general terms, LDC governments will usually have five types of objectives relating to mining projects. These objectives, which may be pursued through the negotiation of concession agreements and the enactment of legislation, through participation in joint ventures with foreign investors or through the operations of state mining enterprises with technical assistance from abroad, are as follows: (i) revenue and foreign exchange benefits; (ii) objectives relating to ownership and control of the mining project; (iii) objectives concerning the transfer of technology, employment and training of nationals and diminution of the country's dependence on foreign expertise; (iv) objectives concerning linkages between the mining project and the rest of the national economy, including requirements for local purchasing, local processing, and other indirect linkages; and (v) what might be called political-legal objectives, dealing with such issues as assertion of sovereignty over natural resources, paramountcy of national law and procedures for settling disputes between the government and MNCs.

Revenue and Foreign Exchange Objectives

For a significant number of LDCs the foreign exchange earnings and government revenue derived from mining represent a major factor in national economic planning and even survival. Table 12.1 shows the importance of mining in the foreign exchange receipts of a number of countries in 1973-75 and in 1975-77. It is noteworthy that even as some countries have reduced their previous extreme dependence on mining (e.g. Chile), other new mineral producers have emerged on the list of nations that rely heavily on mining earnings. The situation is particularly serious for small countries, where a single mine may account for one-third or more of the nation's total foreign currency earnings.

Two different issues are involved in negotiations relating to the economics of mining projects in LDCs: one concerns government revenue and the other foreign exchange earnings. With respect to the revenue question, numerous governments have found that mineral production produces a highly variable and unpredictable source of income. This is particularly true where government income is directly related to the profitability of mining ventures, either through government equity ownership or through a revenue system that relies heavily on income taxation of the mining company. The variability of revenues is especially marked in some new mining agreements that incorporate an excess profits tax in years of high profitability.[9] Government revenue variations result from the price fluctuations typical of some metals and minerals, notably copper, lead/zinc and phosphate rock. For example, in a copper mine with annual production of 50,000 tonnes, with production costs of $1500 per tonne and with sales contracts related to the LME price, a shift of perhaps ten per cent in the market price (e.g. from $1650 to $1815) would mean an increase of more than 100 per cent in the profitability of the mine and, most likely, in the income derived from the mine by the host government. Such an example is not unrealistic, and much greater fluctuations in government revenue from year to year have occurred. Thus, even in those mineral agreements where the government has succeeded in capturing a high proportion of the prospective differential resource rent, the government will still face planning problems associated with the unpredictability of revenues. In a few cases, governments have established mineral resource

Table 12.1. *Export Dependence of Mineral Producing Countries 1975-77*
        Individual Mineral Commodity Exports as Percentage of Total
        National Exports, 1975-77 Average

	1973-75	*1975-77*
A. *Bauxite*		
Guyana	19.6	29.7
Haiti	9.6	14.0
Jamaica	19.4	17.0
Surinam	24.2	17.6
Guinea	77.0	75.9
B. *Copper*		
Chile	66.4	55.6
Peru	20.0	18.5
Botswana	–	43.4
Namibia	67.4	65.0
Zaire	68.8	63.9
Zambia	91.9	91.6
Papua New Guinea	44.5	31.6
C. *Tin*		
Bolivia	41.3	40.9
Malaysia	12.5	11.0
D. *Lead/Zinc*		
Peru	14.4	18.1
Namibia	32.6	27.8
E. *Iron Ore*		
Liberia	68.3	70.9
Mauritania	78.1	86.5
Sierra Leone	10.6	10.5
Swaziland	–	14.3
F. *Phosphate Rock*		
Morocco	48.5	45.2
Senegal	21.7	14.8
Togo	62.0	56.3
Jordan	36.8	28.5
Kiribati	98.4	94.6

Source: World Bank, *Commodity Trade and Price Trends* 1977 ed., 21-22; 1979 ed., 25-26
(Washington).

stabilization funds, into which mining revenues are paid and from which a relatively steady and predictable flow of funds can come into the national budget.[10] The ability of such stabilization arrangements to survive national economic crises and political demands for higher budgets, at the expense of the balance in the stabilization fund, however, is not well-established. This extreme unpredictability of mining revenue, which must necessarily increase as governments take greater direct ownership positions in mining projects and impose more effective income taxation, adds much of the force to LDC concern for price stabilization efforts such as the Integrated Program for Commodities (IPC) proposed by UNCTAD.[11]

The second economic aspect of mining agreements concerns foreign exchange. Since the oil price increases of the mid-1970s, in particular, most LDCs have faced severe balance-of-payments difficulties. In such circumstances, it becomes increasingly important for governments (a) to maximize foreign exchange earnings from mining and (b) to secure effective government control over those foreign exchange earnings which are generated.

The first objective, higher foreign exchange earnings, is to a large extent independent of any single government's efforts. To a limited extent, increased government vigilance over transfer-pricing abuses of MNCs may avoid foreign exchange leakage, and increased national knowledge of mineral markets may assist in avoiding unfair sales contracts, but for many minerals, the actual price received cannot be affected by a single country's actions. Conflict will always exist, however, between MNCs and host governments with respect to the management and control of foreign exchange earnings. The form that the resolution of this conflict will take in each case will depend only in part on the agreement that is negotiated between the MNC and the government. The MNC will wish to hold all sales revenues abroad, under its control, except for that part required to meet local costs in the host country (including any fiscal obligations to the host government). The government, on the other hand, will wish to have all sales receipts brought back into the host country, or at least deposited in accounts under the control of the central bank, so that the receipts effectively become part of the country's foreign exchange reserves. Contractual devices for accommodating these conflicting interests have been negotiated in several recent contracts,[12] but have not fully resolved the issue. Even where the MNC agrees with a host government on a method for assuring national control of sales receipts, the international banks (including government export credit institutions in the DCs) are increasingly insisting on the establishment of trustee accounts into which all sales proceeds are paid and from which the banks apportion payments for debt service, costs, etc. — commonly with the host government coming last in the queue for payment. Thus, as a result of the shift to debt financing typical of recent large-scale mining projects, the international banks have assumed an ever more significant position in allocating foreign exchange earnings from mining.

As the above discussion suggests, not all the economic objectives of host governments can be met through a well-negotiated mining agreement, even one that incorporates such 'modern' features as flexible and progressive taxation and innovative foreign exchange provisions. To a great extent, the benefits that the LDC may receive from a mining project depend on forces beyond the immediate control of government negotiators or even of the entire government. International markets for minerals and the international banking system which finances mining projects play key roles, the impact of which may well outweigh any gains resulting from improved investment agreements.

Ownership and Control

LDC governments have increasingly asserted their desire for both ownership of, and control over, natural resource developments in their countries; such owner-ship and control is seen as an integral part of the NIEO, a system whose outlines at least have been sketched in numerous international forums.[13] Table 12.2 indi-cates changes in the relationships in the mining sector between MNCs and host governments which have occurred in recent years with respect to equity owner-ship.

Ownership and effective control, however, are very different things. Even 100 per cent equity ownership by the government provides no guarantee that it will be able to exercise a significant influence on key policy decisions in the mining sector, as the experience of Zaire indicates.[14] Ownership or control, however, may each be desired as ends in themselves, i.e. for reasons of prestige, national pride, a sense of political and economic independence, or in conformity with a particular ideological position. Ownership and control may also each be desired as instruments or means to assist in the achievement of other ends (e.g. as a means of increasing revenue for use in the government's development plans).

Governments may want control over mining ventures in order to ensure that MNCs involved in the ventures conform to government policy; in some cases, the desire for effective government control may grow out of dissatisfaction with previous policies of the MNC (e.g. failure to invest so as to maintain or expand production) or because the government believes that planning in major economic sectors is necessary for effective development and that control over major enter-prises is a necessary condition for effective planning.

Ownership or equity participation may be seen by the government as a means (a) of ensuring effective control, (b) of obtaining a larger share of profits or rents than could be obtained solely through taxation, or (c) of gaining experience, with the aim of increasing national capacity. As numerous recent examples indi-cate, the mere fact of ownership does not guarantee the achievement of any of these objectives; what is important is the way in which ownership is acquired and the arrangements that are made for the exercise of control and for the dis-tribution of profits from the venture in which the government owns equity. Equity participation in local subsidiaries or affiliates of large, technically ad-vanced MNCs may not be the most rewarding use of LDC governments' financial resources and personnel. Whether equity should be sought, and in what pro-portions, depends very much on the particular circumstances of each case, in-cluding the cost of equity and the attitude of the MNC toward government par-ticipation (if the MNC is strongly opposed, the government may have to look for another foreign partner or give up this objective), as well as the need for board or management committee representation to get necessary information. On the other hand, government participation may well be politically useful and may, in addition, be a good investment. One can make a strong argument for a gradually-increasing government equity share, consistent with the growth of national ability to exercise effective control. In some recent contracts, however, a 'phase-out' of the MNC's equity has been negotiated in advance, at a price which appears very high.[15] It may be preferable to postpone negotiation of the acquisition of additional equity until after some years of operation, by which time the government's bargaining power will have increased.[16]

Table 12.2. *Changes in Relationships Between MNCs and Host Governments in the Mineral Sector*

Country	MNC	Year	Result
Chile (copper)	Kennecott/ Anaconda	1967	acquisition of 25/51 per cent interests in producing companies
Chile (copper)	Kennecott/ Anaconda	1971	nationalization of remaining foreign interest
Gabon/ Mauritania (iron ore)	Miferma/ Somifer	1974	partial/complete takeover
Ghana (gold)	Lonrho	1973	55 per cent government equity interest acquired; Lonrho management contract
Ghana (diamonds)	CAST	1973	55 per cent government equity interest; CAST management contract
Guyana (bauxite)	Alcan/Reynolds	1971/ 1974	100 per cent ownership acquired by nationalization
Jamaica (bauxite)	Kaiser *et al.*	1974- 1977	acquisition of 51 per cent interest in bauxite mining operations; imposition of production levy
Senegal (phosphate)	Taiba	1974	50 per cent government participation
Sierra Leone (diamonds)	CAST	1970	51 per cent government equity interest
Venezuela (iron ore)	US Steel/ Bethlehem Steel	1974	negotiated complete takeover
Zaire (copper)	Union Minière	1967	100 per cent ownership interest acquired; management contract
Zambia (copper)	Anglo-American/ AMAX	1969	acquisition of 51 per cent equity interest
Zambia (copper)	Anglo-AMAX	1974	increase in national control over management

Source: S.K.B. Asante, 'Restructuring Transnational Mineral Agreements', *American Journal of International Law*, 73 (1979), 344-345; 'Permanent Sovereignty over Natural Resources', Report of the Secretary-General (UN Doc. E/C.7/53; 31 January 1975); UN Commission on Transnational Corporations, *Transnational Corporations in World Development: a Re-Examination* (UN Doc. E/C.10/38, 1978), 77-134.

As for the question of government control,[17] there are two broad approaches through which a host government can establish nominal control over the operations of a firm: internally, by majority control of the board of directors or joint venture management committee, or, externally, through statutes, regulations and directives imposed by government authority. To be effective, the first approach requires government directors who can acquire a thorough knowledge of the firm's operations in order to exert their authority over management on significant policy issues. The second approach requires that government officials responsible for promulgating and enforcing regulations and directives understand the industry they are regulating and are able to detect violations of the rules.

Both approaches require reasonably uncorruptible government personnel whose own objectives are consistent with those of the government. As soon as one states these requirements, the difficulties of exercising effective control are immediately apparent; even in many industrialized countries, both MECs and CPEs, such effective government control is often absent.

Control of an enterprise through majority representation on the board of directors (even where such control can theoretically be exercised and the minority, or MNC, shareholder has not enshrined its power through the creation of preferential voting rights) is extremely difficult to exercise effectively on any but the most general policy issues. The area of management discretion must necessarily be considerable, if the enterprise is to operate efficiently. It is usually impractical for part-time government directors to take a day-to-day role in the management of the enterprise. Unless proposals brought up to the board are manifestly contradictory to established government policy, it is difficult for the government directors to make an effective case against management recommendations in the absence not only of the full range of information available to management but also in the absence of background and experience in the industry. Government directors can have an impact in particular policy areas (e.g. relations with local residents, employment and training of nationals) and can sometimes ask awkward questions, but as a general rule they are unable effectively to challenge managerial decisions.

One of the most important functions of government directors is often to obtain information for the government, which can then use the information in shaping its regulatory policies. But for this purpose majority control is not necessary; a very small equity share and even a single director, provided he is supported by an adequate staff, is sufficient. The government may even secure board representation without owning any of the equity in the enterprise.

A further difficulty associated with the exercise of control is that acting as a company director, even on a part-time basis, may be time-consuming and burdensome if a few individuals are expected to take on such functions for a large number of companies, as is frequently the case. It is common for LDC governments to appoint ministers or senior civil servants, who are already extremely busy in their normal jobs, to the boards of a number of companies. Such a policy is extremely wasteful of scarce human resources and is often very inefficient. Using deputy or alternate directors may somewhat alleviate the problem, but may also be an inefficient use of human resources, especially in small countries.

An alternative to government control through board of directors representation is direct regulation and monitoring by the government's administrative apparatus. In any case, the need for some sort of regulatory and monitoring structure is not eliminated even where the government has a majority share of the equity and representation on the board.

With regard to financial issues, government control is usually exercised through regulation. For example, dividend remittances are largely a matter of exchange control policy, enforced by regulations. Transfer pricing abuses cannot easily be dealt with at the board of directors level, since control requires a close examination of detailed accounts. Access to local credit is another matter that can most effectively be dealt with as a matter of general government policy, through banking regulations. Finally, tax and royalty payments are normally enforced through the government's fiscal bureaucracy. While some financial issues such as capital budgets are often handled at the board level, it is also possible, and has in fact been attempted in countries such as Papua New Guinea and Chile, to require government review of these budgets as a matter of regulation, even if the government owns a minority share of the equity or none at all.

A number of non-financial issues can also be dealt with through direct regulation as well as through company policy set by the board of directors. Examples are training and employment policy, which can be enforced through regulations as to the disclosure of training plans and the enforcement of national employment quotas, as well as through controls on the issue of work permits to expatriates. Similarly, government policy to promote economic linkages can be enforced through regulations that require local purchase of certain inputs, or through taxation measures that encourage the local processing of minerals.[18]

An example of a mining agreement in which the government preserved substantial control powers even though it held only a minority of the equity is the Colombian Cerro Matoso nickel agreement, between the government and two US resource companies. The agreement required government approval even though the government did not have a majority on the board of directors, in respect of the following issues:

(a) the purchase or sale of goods, services, technical assistance or know-how to or from a partner or affiliate of the foreign shareholder;

(b) the appointment of a management group and the terms of any management contracts;

(c) the approval of annual exploration, development investment, production and operating plans;

(d) the approval of purchases by the operator in excess of specified limits;

(e) the geographic location of facilities;

(f) the appointment of an auditor and approval of financial statements;

(g) the contents of annual reports;

(h) the mortgaging of assets;

(i) the purchase or sale of goods, services, etc., from or to nations unfriendly to Colombia; and

(j) the use of technology that might be harmful to the environment.[19]

As this list indicates, the range of issues that can be dealt with through government approval can extend quite far. Thus, majority government ownership is not necessarily a pre-requisite for effective control, nor does majority ownership necessarily increase the likelihood of effective control. The decision as to the proportion of government ownership to seek in an individual case must depend on the particular circumstances of the case, and on national policy, but not on the belief that ownership and control are synonymous.

Technology Transfer, Employment and Training

A major objective of many governments in negotiating resource development is the acquisition both of specific kinds of technology (e.g. a new copper smelter) and of technical expertise from MNCs in the mining sector. In the past, requirements in concession agreements for the transfer of technology were often minimal; MNCs pledged to train and employ host-country nationals 'to the maximum feasible extent'[20] or 'consistent with the efficient operation of the project'. More recently, mining agreements have included detailed plans for the progressive replacement of foreigners with nationals in various skill categories. An example is the following clause from the 1977 Rio Tinto Zinc/Conzinc Riotinto of Australia agreement with the government of Indonesia:

The Company shall employ Indonesian personnel to the maximum extent practicable consistent with efficient operations, provided however that the following percentages of all positions in each employment classification shall be held by Indonesian nationals within the periods stated beginning with the commencement of the operating period:

	3 years	5 years	8 years
unskilled labor	100%	100%	100%
skilled labor	75%	75%	100%
clerical	75%	90%	100%
technical/supervisory	50%	75%	85%
management/professional	50%	75%	85%

Similarly, recent agreements have made very specific commitments for training programs, generally financed by the foreign mining company. Increasingly, the actual content of such training programs is subject to periodic government review and approval. The effect of mining industry training, it should be noted, can extend well beyond the mine itself. In Papua New Guinea, for example, employment at the Bougainville copper mine is about 4000, of whom 3200 are nationals, but several thousand additional Papua New Guineans have received training in operating heavy vehicles and earth-moving equipment and are now working elsewhere in the economy. Such spill-over benefits can be an important effect of well-planned mining projects.[21]

Many aspects of the technology used in constructing and operating mining projects are widely known, and can be purchased by LDCs from numerous sources. Thus there is not, usually, a significant problem in a country's acquiring the basic knowledge needed to run a mining venture. In negotiating agreements, however, care should be taken to ensure that the price paid to the MNC for technical services is not overly high. This issue is likely to become increasingly important as more governments take majority ownership of projects and employ MNCs under service and management contracts. In the copper industry, there are two recent examples of major projects in which service contracts have been used and which have involved substantial payments to the MNC. In the Sar Cheshmeh project in Iran (owned 100 per cent by the Iranian National Copper Co.), Anaconda of the US was hired to oversee all technical aspects of the project and to provide relevant expertise and staff. In this case, Anaconda's fee was set at a flat monthly rate during the feasibility study and construction period, and as a percentage of the value of production during the operating period. Aside from these fees, the Iranian enterprise also was to pay all Anaconda's direct expenses. Similarly, in the Cerro Colorado copper agreement in Panama, Texasgulf, which holds a 20 per cent equity share compared to the government's 80 per cent, was also appointed to manage operations under a technical service contract which provided for fees expressed as percentages of (a) the cost of construction, (b) gross sales, and (c) net profits. These fees, it was expected, would produce more income for Texasgulf than would the dividends on its 20 per cent equity share.[22]

An advantage of the service contract approach is that it permits the government to take increasing responsibility over various aspects of the project, as it gains experience and knowledge. On the other hand, a central feature of service contracts in non-fuel minerals (though not in the case of petroleum) is that governments bear an increasing share of the risk associated with the project. Only if the government has substantial financial resources (as in the case of Iran with Sar Cheshmeh) or if particularly favorable international financing arrangements can be negotiated (as appears to be the case for Cerro Colorado) can governments accept these financial risks.

Economic Linkages

By most standards, mining projects are inefficient devices for stimulating large-scale economic activity beyond the perimeter of the mine. Table 12.3 indicates (in 1977 prices) the estimated output per man-year and the cost of employment creation in mineral processing industries.

Table 12.3. *Employment in Mineral Processing*

Process	Output per man-year (tonnes)	Capital cost per job ($)
alumina refining	800	520,000
aluminum smelting	90	243,000
copper smelting/refining	140	350,000
steelmaking	200	163,600
lead smelting/refining	225	157,500
nickel processing (sulphides)	150	1,200,000
tin smelting	20	160,000
zinc smelting	200	320,000

Source: UNIDO, *Industry 2000 New Perspectives* (Vienna: UNIDO, 1979), 82.

There are more cost-efficient ways to generate employment. In addition, the value added in the processing of most minerals, except for bauxite and iron ore, is relatively low compared to the value of the mineral in its first saleable stage. If the local market for metals is limited, as it usually is in small countries, and if there is world-wide competition among mineral processors, it may be financially advantageous for a country to remain a seller of concentrates or semi-processed minerals, rather than attempt to integrate forward to full processing. On the other hand, if either a sufficiently large domestic or (more likely) regional market exists, or if the processing technology involved permits efficient development of relatively small-scale facilities (as in the case of direct-reduction processing of iron ore for 'mini' steel mills), significant benefits can be obtained from an insistence on the maximum feasible degree of local processing.

Some DCs have negotiated very detailed processing provisions in their mineral agreements. An outstanding example is Australia, where most mining agreements contain precise timetables for the submission of feasibility studies of processing and for the construction of processing facilities. In practice, however, these agreements have apparently not resulted in more mineral processing taking place within Australia than normal economic considerations would in any case produce. Where the contract requirements appear to the mining company to be undesirable, it has become normal practice to seek, and to be granted, delays in meeting those commitments. The lesson, from the point of view of LDCs, is that it is difficult to force the MNC to construct facilities against its will; a more productive strategy might well be to negotiate a requirement that, if and when a local processing facility is constructed, the mining project will make available sufficient raw material to enable the processing facility to operate efficiently.

Political-legal Objectives

Governments have become increasingly concerned with asserting clear national sovereignty over natural resources.[23] Thus there is a long-term trend toward the revision of mining codes so as to designate a government entity as the body initially responsible for mining production; the government entity may then contract with MNCs in joint ventures or service contract arrangements. Such an approach avoids the creation of legal enclaves under traditional concession agreements.[24]

Despite the general trend toward greater recognition of national sovereignty, however, two serious legal-political issues remain important in many current mining negotiations. These are (a) the extent to which arrangements made with mining companies are to be protected against subsequent changes in the national law and (b) the question of dispute settlement and arbitration.

Mining companies have typically sought to 'entrench' the provisions of agreements, by including clauses which give the agreement the force of law and which purport to prevent subsequent laws from changing the position of the company. In most legal systems, such clauses are ultimately of little or no effect; subsequent legislation can almost always be passed which overrules or repeals the earlier agreement. But psychologically and politically, entrenchment clauses are damaging, because they create the appearance that the foreign company has been granted particularly favorable status. In several recent renegotiations of agreements,[25] LDCs have taken care to eliminate the most blatant forms of entrenchment provisions from mining agreements. On the other hand, mining companies increasingly have taken steps to 'entrench' their agreements by other means, such as the involvement of international financing agencies and export credit institutions of DCs. These company strategies are discussed in greater detail in the next section of this paper.

LDCs have also secured significant gains with respect to arbitration and dispute settlement clauses in mining agreements. The traditional provisions for arbitration by bodies like the International Chamber of Commerce and for resort to such legal principles as *ex aeque et bono* or the 'general principles of law accepted by civilized nations' have to a certain extent been replaced by greater recognition that the host country's national legal system applies, even though the individual selected to resolve a dispute may still be selected from some outside source. In view of the limited number of investment disputes which actually go to arbitration, however, it may be that these provisions are more important for the psychological reassurance that they give investors and bankers than for their real-life impact.[26]

CORPORATE STRATEGIES

Mining corporations have adopted clear and identifiable strategies to deal with the growing assertion of host country nationalism. One can identify at least four broad aspects of these strategies: (i) the use of sanctions by governments of the MNCs' home countries; (ii) the shift to management and service contract arrangements to reduce corporate risk; (iii) the trend to undertake mining projects through joint ventures involving several MNCs from different countries; and (iv) the multilateralization of financing for mining projects.

Among the DCs, the USA has been the most explicit in threatening to apply sanctions against LDC governments that nationalize or otherwise adversely affect US investors' interests. Under the Hickenlooper Amendment, the US government has authority to cut off aid funds to governments that repudiate or nullify contracts with US companies. In addition, the USA has blocked loans in the World Bank and regional development banks (e.g. in the case of Chile following nationalization of Kennecott and Anaconda copper interests in 1971). While these direct coercive measures have been used relatively infrequently to date, the threat that they pose remains an important deterrent to some LDC governments.

Some mining MNCs have sharply reduced their risk exposure in mining ventures by either participating in joint ventures with host governments, in which the governments bear a proportionate share of the risk, or by signing service or management contracts. In these arrangements, a substantial part of the MNC's overall cash return is in the relatively risk-free form of payments for services, rather than in dividends which depend on the creation of profits in the mining operation and the ability to remit dividends to the head office. While such arrangements tend to give host governments a greater opportunity to exert control over mining projects, this is not an automatic feature; several recent management contracts (for example, the agreement for the Cerro Colorado

Copper Project in Panama) give the MNC very substantial management and policy control even though it has only a small minority share in the ownership of the project.

The trend toward joint ventures among mining companies from several nations has become pronounced in the 1970s. Examples of such ventures include the Ok Tedi copper project in Papua New Guinea (BHP Ltd of Australia, Amoco Minerals of the US, Metallgesellschaft, Degussa, Siemens, and Kabell und Metallwerke of West Germany); the Namosi copper project in Fiji (Conzinc Riotinto of Australia, AMAX, Anglo-American Corporation of South Africa, and Preussag); and the Boké bauxite project in Guinea (Alcan, Alcoa, Martin Marietta, Pechiney, VAW of West Germany, and Montedison of Italy). Other joint ventures, e.g. the Gabon uranium project, include both MNCs (in this case, Union Carbide of the US) and DC state corporations (the French government's energy corporation). From the MNC's point of view, joint ventures of this nature have the virtues of spreading the risk and of making it more likely that action by the host country to improve its position at the expense of the MNC will provoke a reaction from the home government of the MNC.

The desire on the part of MNCs to decrease their risks (as well as the increasing capital cost of mining projects) accounts for the trend toward internationalization of financing arrangements for major mining projects.[27] In the complex financial arrangements that are now being negotiated, both commercial banks and government export credit institutions from several different DCs are involved, which means that all loans can be called due if there is any default by the government on any one loan, or even if the government fails to honor any of the terms of its original investment agreement with the MNCs involved in the project. In addition to spreading the commercial risk from the project, these arrangements also are used by MNCs to offset the 'political risk'; by using banks from as many countries as possible, MNCs attempt to ensure international pressure against a host government that contemplates 'hostile' action against the MNC. Frequently, financing agreements require that the lead bank in a lending syndicate establishes an escrow account (usually in New York or some other location beyond the jurisdiction of the host country) into which proceeds of mineral sales will be deposited. The trustees of the account (usually a bank) then distribute the proceeds to lenders, project sponsors (the MNCs) and, finally, the host government, according to procedures set out in the financing agreements. The existence of such accounts ensures that it will be much more difficult for the government to act unilaterally than would be the case if sales proceeds were required to be brought back into the host country.[28]

CONCLUSION

This paper has indicated some of the major problem areas in mining negotiations between LDC governments and MNCs in the 1970s and, it seems likely, in the 1980s as well. Despite the advances that have been secured by LDCs in recent years, there remain significant problems for host governments in achieving effective national sovereignty over the development of natural resources. Some of these problems are associated with the nature of the mineral industry itself; except in a few cases, any one country must deal with the reality of a worldwide market, in which many factors are beyond the control of any single actor. In addition, MNCs and banks have devised effective strategies for dealing with what they perceive as the risk associated with increased LDC nationalism in respect of resources. In these circumstances, the gains that can be achieved by better negotiation of mining agreements, though they are considerable, have certain real limits. In the long run, the contribution of mineral resources to the development of LDCs will depend not only on how skilfully investment agreements with MNCs can be negotiated, but also on the ability of the LDCs themselves to evolve new arrangements for the development of mineral resources (e.g. regional cooperation and 'South-South' trade) and rely less heavily on MNCs and investment banks.

NOTES

1. See the preceding paper and D.N. Smith and L.T. Wells Jr, 'Mineral Agreements in Developing Countries: Structure and Substance', *American Journal of International Law*, 69 (1975), 560-590.

2. For the former view, see the preceding paper or statements by mining industry spokesmen, e.g. K.C.G. Heath, 'The Right to Mine', *Trans. Instn. Min. Metall.* (Sect. A: Min. Industry), 83 (1974), 19-24. For the latter view, see, e.g. H. Zakariya, 'New Directions in the Search for and Development of Petroleum Resources in the Developing Countries', *Vanderbilt Journal of Transnational Law*, 9 (1976), 545-577.

3. R. Bosson and B. Varon, *The Mining Industry and the Developing Countries* (New York: Oxford University Press – The World Bank, 1977), 31-32.

4. On the question of ownership versus control, see S.K.B. Asante, 'Restructuring Transnational Mineral Agreements', *American Journal of International Law*, 73 (1979), 335-371.

5. For example, see S. Zorn, 'New Developments in Third World Mining Agreements', *Natural Resources Forum*, 1 (1977), 239-250; Schanze *et al.*, 'Mining Agreements in Developing Countries', *Journal of World Trade Law*, 12 (1978), 135-173; and T. Wälde, 'Revision of Transnational Investment Agreements: Contractual Flexiblity in Natural Resources Development', *Lawyer of the Americas* (1978), 265-298.

6. The most comprehensive exposition of this counterattack is in T. Moran, 'Transnational Strategies of Protection and Defense by Multinational Corporations: Spreading the Risk and Raising the Cost for Nationalization in Natural Resources', *International Organization*, 27 (1973), 273-287.

7. For a more detailed discussion of the potential gains from mineral production, see H. Hughes, 'The Distribution of Gains from Foreign Direct Investment in Mineral Development', SEADAG Paper 74-10 (New York: The Asia Society SEADAG, 1974).

8. For a complementary analysis of the features of the market structures in the copper, bauxite and iron ore industries see paper 7 *supra*.

9. Examples of such agreements include the re-negotiation of the Bougainville Copper Agreement in Papua New Guinea in 1974 and the agreement between the government of Indonesia and RTZ/CRA in 1977.

10. For a description of such a stabilization fund in Papua New Guinea, see J. Kinna, 'The Development of a Resource Policy in Papua New Guinea 1967-1977', *Journal of the Royal Society of Arts* (March 1978), 221-232.

11. On the likely effectiveness of the UNCTAD program for non-fuel minerals, see paper 14 *infra* and C.D. Rogers, 'Non-Fuel Minerals and the Integrated Program for Commodities', *Natural Resources Forum*, 3 (1979), 337-348.

12. See the description of the Indonesian and Papua New Guinea arrangements in the preceding paper.

13. General Assembly Resolutions 3201 (S-VI) and 3202 (S-VI) of 1st May 1974 and 3362 (S-VII) of 16th September 1975 contain the basic summary of the goals of NIEO. For further material, see K.P. Sauvant and H. Hasenpflug (eds), *The New International Economic Order: Conflict or Co-operation between North and South?* (Boulder: Westview Press, 1977).

14. On the Zairian experience, see I. Ilunkamba, 'Copper, Technology and Dependence in Zaire: Towards the Demystification of the New White Magic', *Natural Resources Forum*, 4, 2 (1980), 147-156.

15. See, for example, the description of the Cerro Colorado (Panama) and Indonesia-RTZ/ CRA contracts in S. Zorn, 'Mining Agreements in Developing Countries: Some Recent Examples', *Metall*, 28 (May 1978), 79-83.

16. The process by which government bargaining power tends to increase over time is described in T.H. Moran, *Multinational Corporations and the Politics of Dependence* (Princeton University Press, 1974), 153-224.

17. The following section relies heavily on E. Penrose, 'Participation and Control' (prepared for the United Nations Centre on Transnational Corporations, Roundtable on Negotiations with Transnational Corporations, April 1978; (mimeo).

18. For an example of such a tax system, see the discussion of Ontario's provincial mineral taxes in R.D. Brown, 'Canadian Taxes on Mining Income' (paper presented to the 107th meeting of the American Institute of Mining, Metallurgical and Petroleum Engineers, Denver, Colo., 1978; mimeo).

19. The Colombian agreement is cited in Smith and Wells, 'Mineral Agreements in Developing Countries'.

20. Agreement (1978) between the Government of Gabon and Union Carbide/CEA/Leon Tempelsman.

21. For views on appropriate forms of training and localization agreements, see paper 19 *infra*.

22. The terms of the Cerro Colorado contract are discussed in more detail in Zorn, 'New Developments in Third World Mining Agreements', and 'Mining Agreements in Developing Countries'.

23. See Note 13 above.

24. The traditional concession agreement is described in Schanze *et al.*, 'Mining Agreements in Developing Countries'.

25. For example, in the renegotiation of the Bougainville copper agreement in PNG. See Kinna, 'The Development of a Resource Policy in Papua New Guinea'.

26. On the subject of arbitration, see T. Walde, 'Negotiations for Dispute Settlement in Transnational Mineral Contracts', *Denver Journal of International Law and Policy*, 7 (1977), 33-76.

27. For more details see paper 10 *supra*.

28. For detailed descriptions of the provisions of recent mining agreements see M. Fritsche and A. Stockmayer, 'Mining Agreements in Developing Countries: Issues of Finance and Taxation', *Natural Resources Forum*, 2 (1978), 215-228; Schanze *et al.*, 'Mining Agreements in Developing Countries'; D.N. Smith and L.T. Wells Jr, *Negotiating Third World Mineral Agreements* (Cambridge, Mass.: Ballinger, 1975); and Zorn, 'New Developments in Third World Mining Agreements'.

MINERAL PROCESSING IN LDCs

M. Radetzki

INTRODUCTION

The Third World is becoming an increasingly important source of world mineral supplies. While resource-endowed LDCs and extractive MNCs have a strong communality of interests in getting the rich minerals out of the ground, there is a growing conflict between them about the location of further mineral processing activities. The MNCs' desire to maintain the *status quo*, i.e. to have a major share of the processing undertaken in the industrialized West, contrasts with the energetic efforts of LDCs to expand the degree of local processing. The purpose of this paper is to study the causes of this conflict of interests between the two parties.

The objectives underlying the MNCs' wish to continue to process the minerals in their home countries are relatively simple and easy to explain in rational terms. The firms are also used to employing sophisticated spokesmen to present their case. The national objectives of mineral-exporting countries are far more complex, and hence more difficult to comprehend. The policies towards these objectives are sometimes made to appear irrational when they do not coincide with the interests of the firms. A subsidiary purpose of the present paper is therefore to assess the rationality of the strategies pursued by the mineral-endowed LDCs in this field.

The following argument is developed with reference to metal minerals only. Its essence and most of the conclusions seem to be equally valid for non-metal minerals as well as for agricultural commodities whose production is tied by physical conditions to limited geographical areas.

The issues to be dealt with are in essence a variation of the common economic problem of conflicts of private vs social benefits and costs. Normally, such conflicts are considered at the national level, and the difference of views arises from the fact that the social assessment is more comprehensive than the private one. In the case to be treated, the context is international, and at least four parties, each with its own distinct delineation of benefits and costs, can be

This is a revised version of 'Where Should Developing Countries' Minerals Be Processed?', published in *World Development*, Vol. 5, No. 4 (1977), and published here with the permission of Pergamon Press.

Notes to this chapter may be found on pages 242-243.

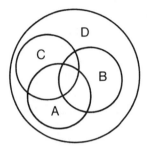

discerned. Thus, the problem will look different when regarded by (A) the MNC involved in mineral extraction, (B) the mineral-exporting LDC, (C) the mineral-importing DC, and (D) the overall world community respectively. The outlook of the four parties can be illustrated by each of the four circles A, B, C and D. Some of the issues considered as costs or benefits by the firm (A), will be of relevance to the host and/or home country (B and/or C) as well. Others will be specific to one of the parties only, but not to the others. The global view (D) is the broadest in that it takes into consideration all factors relevant to the other three parties. In what follows, our attention will be limited to the benefits and costs of relevance to the MNC and the exporting LDC with only marginal attention given to the considerations of the importing DC or of the world community as a whole.

We start with a brief sketch which puts the current situation into its historical context. In the two sections which follow we identify the objectives and study the policies pursued by the firms and national governments respectively. The concluding section summarizes the discussion and categorizes the various arguments for and against location of mineral processing in the exporting countries, so as to clarify the communality and conflicts of interest between the two parties.

THE BACKGROUND

The DCs (excepting such nations as Australia, Canada and the USSR), have been explored in detail with regard to metal mineral resources. Exploitation of the deposits found has also been going on for a long time. Thus, the metal mineral potential has been gradually depleted. The mineral deposits now taken into use are frequently on the margin of what is economical.

The situation is quite different in the Third World. Most LDCs constitute a virtual virgin territory to the mineral prospector. Even in traditional mineral-exporting LDCs such as Peru or Indonesia, only a small proportion of the total territory has hitherto been covered by exploration. Hence, there is no likelihood of depletion within the coming decades. As exploration is intensified, new deposits are uncovered. The size and richness of these usually exceeds the global average in the respective mining industries. Hence, even though infrastructural costs may be high in new areas of mineral development, the deposits, once under exploitation, frequently give rise to considerable rents. For those reasons, the role of the Third World as a metal mineral supplier is likely to grow in future years.

Foreign capital has played a completely dominant role in the mineral sectors of the Third World. The normal colonial pattern was for an extractive MNC to develop a mine in a colonial territory, to treat the ore insofar as this was essential due to transport cost considerations, and to export it to the industrialized world for further processing, fabricating and manufacturing. The pattern was not much different in those LDCs which never served as colonies or which, like the Latin American nations, became independent long ago.

Since about 1960, however, the complete dominance of the firms has been substantially circumscribed. In the past 15 years the governments of most LDCs have increased their economic emancipation. One expression of this is their gradual takeover of control over mining and metal processing within their territories. With the help of increased taxation, or outright nationalization, the national administrations of Third World countries have succeeded to extract a major share of the 'excess' profits emerging from the exploitation of their rich mineral deposits.

In more recent years, efforts to break the colonial heritage have been extended into new areas. Anxious to expand the national benefit from mineral exploitation, a majority of LDCs currently pursue energetic policies to increase the degree of local processing of the minerals exported. The success of these efforts can be measured by the figures of Table 13.1. The policies aiming to expand mineral processing have frequently come into conflict with the interests of the extractive MNCs, which commonly have a strong preference for maintaining the existing pattern in this respect.

Table 13.1. *Mineral Processed as a Percentage of Total Mineral Mined in LDCs**

	1960	1970
Bauxite	3	10
Copper	75	78
Iron ore	23	25
Lead	57	69
Tin	66	79
Zinc	29	42

* Computed at the value produced by mining and processing operations as a percentage of total value produced, had all ore mined been processed to metal ingots (or pelletized in the case of iron ore).

Source: World Bank.

MNC VIEWS ON LOCATION OF MINERAL PROCESSING

The objective of the mineral-extracting MNC is long-run profit maximization, subject to a number of economic and para-economic side-constraints. The latter pertain to such issues as desire to assure survival and maintain market shares, avoidance of excessive risks, a sense of common cultural heritage with home country government, etc.

The tradition of locating mineral processing in mineral-importing DCs is well-entrenched. A marginal economic advantage would ordinarily not be sufficient to bring forth a relocation decision. A mining MNC would need substantial inducements to overcome the thresholds of reluctance, and to reconsider its habits in this respect. The rationale for this behavior, as seen by the company's eyes, is the subject matter of the rest of this section.

The argument proceeds as follows. We start out by discussing the most common case, where the extractive MNC is integrated forward into mineral processing. Consideration is first given to a few circumstances under which important cost advantages could be derived from location of mineral processing in the mineral-exporting LDC. We then elaborate on the reasons why the MNCs may nevertheless be unwilling to relocate. Brief attention is finally given to the attitudes towards local processing in the exporting LDC likely to be taken by the unintegrated mining MNC.

Circumstances Enhancing the Competitiveness of Mineral Processing in LDCs

Reduction in the cost of transport is the first major economic advantage from location of processing in the country of mineral extraction. The distance between exporting and importing nation is frequently substantial, and the metal content of the ores mined may be low. Precious metal ores, but also ores for some base metals like copper or tin, commonly have a metal content below one per cent. Transport costs would become quite prohibitive in such cases, if the material were to be shipped in its unprocessed form. For each ton of metal contained in the ore, one hundred tons of useless rock would have to be shipped. The transport savings from concentrating the material close to the mine site are crucial to the overall economy of extraction, and concentration is regularly undertaken in the mineral-exporting country.

International trade over large distances is quite common, on the other hand, for such materials as bauxite with 15-20 per cent metal content, copper concentrates containing 25-35 per cent copper, and iron ore where the iron metal constitutes about one-half of total weight.

A rough idea of the savings in transport costs in the case of bauxite and copper can be obtained from the following indicative figures, relating to the early 1970s. Taking ocean shipping costs at $5 per ton, and the processing costs to convert five tons of bauxite into two tons of alumina at $50, the savings in transport from conversion of the ore into alumina, amounting to $15, will equal 30 per cent of the processing cost involved. Conversion of three tons of copper concentrate into one ton of blister copper (99 per cent metal content), costs about $220. With the same ocean shipping costs, the saving would be $10, or 4.5 per cent of the processing cost. These figures provide a rough indication of the importance of feasible savings in transport a few years ago. It is true that attainable savings may be reduced by the bias in international freight rates in favor of unprocessed materials and by the cost-reducing modern facilities for bulk handling of ores and concentrates, established in many ports. On the other hand, it should be noted that transport is highly oil-intensive, and in view of the increased oil prices in 1973-74, the relative importance of the savings involved would probably have risen in recent years.

A second circumstance, likely to reduce the cost of processing in the mineral-endowed LDC, is of relatively recent origin. It has to do with the availability and cost of environment. Many mineral-processing activities are highly polluting. The densely populated industrial centers of the world have become increasingly environment-sensitive in recent years. Costly regulations and restrictions have consequently been imposed on mineral processing.

The situation is quite different in most LDCs. The relative laxity in environmental restrictions considerably improves the competitiveness of polluting metal processing located in the Third World. As in the case of transport, location to the country of mineral extraction can be instrumental in obviating an important cost item.

There is, of course, a risk that industrialized nations may impose a 'sweated environment' tariff, to reap part of the advantage arising from the competitive superiority of LDCs in this respect. This would be in line with the common 'sweated labor' tariffs which reduce the benefit to LDCs from their low-cost supply of labor willing to undertake exercising tasks. Pressures to establish 'sweated environment' tariffs have been noticeable for some time.

A third circumstance which works in favor of locating mineral processing and metal fabricating in some of the mineral-exporting LDCs has to do with the energy-intensive nature of many such activities. More than half of the aluminum smelting costs, and about a quarter of copper smelting and refining costs consist of energy. High energy proportions in total processing costs can also be found in other metals, e.g. nickel or zinc. It is obvious that the availability of immobile low-cost energy in the country of mineral extraction can make the metal processing exceedingly competitive when energy is important in the total cost structure.

Abundant and cheap energy resources occasionally become available in mineral-exporting LDCs. This is true for instance in Ghana, and will soon be true in Zaire. Hydro-electric projects have been or are being developed in the two countries, with supplies far in excess of current local needs, and without economically feasible export outlets. The large amounts of electric power available at rates substantially below current energy prices in industrialized nations constitute a strong attraction to local processing of bauxite, copper and other ores mined in the two countries. The natural gas emerging as a by-product of oil production in the Caribbean is another relevant case. Primarily because of transport costs, it is uneconomical to export this gas. Rather than wasting it, plans are now in progress to use this resource as a cheap energy base for aluminum smelting activities in the region. (It is significant that these plans have been initiated by the governments of the region and not by the mining MNCs operating in the area.)

Low labor costs in LDCs are sometimes brought out as a fourth circumstance, in favor of location of mineral processing in the developing exporting nations. This factor is probably much less important than the preceding ones, in view of the high capital-intensity and low share of labor costs in mineral processing.

The circumstances discussed above have certainly contributed towards company decisions to relocate mineral processing in some cases. Greater awareness of the economic importance of these factors probably explains some of the ongoing change reflected in Table 13.1 above. In a majority of cases, however, the cost advantages involved have apparently not been sufficient to make the companies reconsider their location policies. Thus, large amounts of bauxite and copper concentrates continue to be shipped over great distances. Costly technological development programs have been initiated to make mineral processing environmentally acceptable in industrialized countries. And the cheap stationary energy resources in some mineral-exporting nations tend to remain under-utilized for want of large-scale energy consumers. The international mining industry's decisions to relocate processing are apparently inhibited. We shall now consider the nature of these inhibitions.

Company Reasons against Relocation of Processing Facilities

Even where pure cost considerations point in favor of location in LDCs, the existence of processing installations at home will deter the companies from building up new capacity in the mineral-endowed exporting countries, at least in the short run. The short run may be quite extended, however, in view of the longevity of processing plants. Furthermore, because of the very far-reaching scale economies, it is only seldom that new investments in complete processing installations are undertaken. Expansion and/or gradual, partial replacement of existing facilities is much more common. The short-run disadvantages to the company of relocating its processing activities thus develop into semi-permanence.

Another short-run deterrent to relocation could be the ready availability of infrastructural facilities required by the processing industry in the importing DCs. In the mineral-exporting nations, in contrast, such installations may be non-existent. Even if the long-run economy of processing in the developing exporting country, including the costs for required infrastructure, would be favorable, the company may decide against it, for instance due to constrained availability of finance.

The tariff structure in importing DCs is frequently biased against mineral processing in exporting LDCs. Thus, effective tariffs on the processing value added may be quite high. The importing nation's motivation for creating such a bias has various grounds. These probably include the colonial desire to maintain the economic dependence of the exporting country by creating hindrances to its economic diversification. Another ground to the bias would be a wish to protect the processing installations at home along with the employment they create. In both objectives there is likely to be a communality of interests between the home country and the extractive MNC. The firm would therefore be unwilling to influence its home government to remove the bias even if it had the opportunity to do so and the removal would be to its own long-run advantage. Maintenance of the skewed tariff structure provides the companies with a strong argument for their reluctance to relocate.

The companies' feeling of exposure to 'political risks' when investing in LDCs is probably a major factor inhibiting decisions to relocate mineral processing. The fear that the host country government might increase taxation, nationalize without adequate compensation, or otherwise fail to honor the agreement it has signed with the multinational company, creates a desire to minimize the resources at stake. The mine location is geologically given, and necessitates the company's presence in the developing country. In mineral processing, on the other hand, where a choice of alternative locations is available, the company's desire to avoid the 'political risk', whether warranted by reality or not, would usually be expressed by a higher rate of return requirement from the project located in the mineral-endowed LDC.

A related factor at a more general level is the MNC's unfamiliarity with the social and economic environment of the developing country. The cost of obtaining, and the mental barrier to absorbing, the relevant information is a factor which inhibits the company's relocation decisions. Thus, in a wish to reduce its involvements in economically and socially unfamiliar surroundings, the company may take location decisions in favor of the industrialized importing country, even though more and better information would have warranted the opposite choice.

The company decisions about location of mineral processing in LDCs, emerging from all the above arguments, are likely to be more negative than the expected results from a location policy aiming at optimal resource allocation from a global point of view. Needless to say, the decisions fall far short of the desires and ambitions of the governments of mineral-exporting LDCs.

The Views of the Unintegrated Mining MNC

No lengthy discussion is required to clarify the attitude of the non-integrated mining MNC towards the establishment of local mineral processing plants. In the absence of such plants, the company has the liberty of selling its produce in the international market to the customer of its choice. Once local processing is established, the government is bound to circumscribe the company's freedom by demanding that the mineral be sold to the local processing industry. Economies of scale would restrict the number of processing ventures in each mineral-exporting country. Apart from being exposed to a greater degree of government direction, therefore, the reduction in the number of potential customers would weaken the company's bargaining position. For these reasons, the unintegrated mining company can be expected to oppose efforts to establish local mineral processing in the mineral-endowed LDC.

THE ADVANTAGES OF FORWARD INTEGRATION FROM MINING INTO MINERAL PROCESSING: THE VIEW OF PRODUCING COUNTRIES

We shall now proceed to discuss the factors which underlie the strong wish of exporting LDCs to process their minerals at home. Say that expansion of GNP, creation of employment and increased government revenue are long-run objectives in the economic policies of an LDC richly endowed with metal minerals. Assume further that investment funds constitute a constraint to economic progress, and that part of the overall domestic investment expenditure is covered by capital imports. How does forward integration from mining into mineral processing help in achieving the policy objectives pursued? Would the objectives be better satisfied if the investment resources required for mineral processing were instead spent on opening additional mines or on the non-mineral sectors in the economy?

In order to design an optimal investment pattern, one would need to study and compare all possible investment projects in terms of their contribution to the development goals of the government.[1] Such an approach is not practicable in our case. We will instead provide some general observations on the desirability of mineral processing in the development efforts of a mineral-exporting country.

It may be instructive to ask at the outset why the mineral-endowed country should invest in its minerals at all. Modern mining projects are highly capital-intensive ventures, and their employment effects are limited. The answer is that if the mineral deposits are rich and cheap to operate, their profitability and hence their contribution towards GNP and government revenue will be so high as to compensate for their small employment creation. Despite their capital-intensity, therefore, investments in mining will be socially attractive.

The capital-intensity of mineral processing ventures is commonly even higher than that in mining.

There is a substantial and at times confusing literature on the measurement of relative capital-intensities of industries.[2] For whatever they are worth, some of Leontief's figures on total direct and indirect capital and labor requirements in selected industries in the USA in 1947 are reproduced in Table 13.2.

Two observations emerge from a scrutiny of Leontief's figures. First, the capital/labor ratios in mining and processing of metals are considerably higher than in a variety of other industries, such as textiles, lumber and wood, paper, rubber, leather, or in most lines of electric and non-electric machinery. Table 13.2 also indicates a relative increase in the total capital/labor ratios as one moves from mining to processing of the respective metals, and a decrease of the ratios when forward integration is extended into metal fabricating activities.

Both observations are reconfirmed by data provided by Lary.[3] Lary's study relates to manufacturing industries in the US in 1965, and measures the capital-

Table 13.2. *Direct and Indirect Requirements per Million Dollars of Final Output*

	Capital, mill. dollars	Labor, man-years	Capital/labor ratio
Mining			
Iron ore	3.2	212	0.015
Copper	3.2	198	0.016
Lead and zinc	2.6	230	0.011
Bauxite	2.7	221	0.012
Metal mining processing			
Steel works and rolling mills	2.8	180	0.016
Copper and lead smelting and refining	2.4	121	0.020
Zinc smelting and refining	2.4	166	0.014
Aluminum smelting and refining	3.3	144	0.023
Metal fabricating			
Iron and steel forgings	2.0	180	0.011
Copper rolling and drawing	2.4	155	0.015
Aluminum rolling and drawing	2.2	178	0.012
Structural metal products	1.7	184	0.099
Fabricated wire products	2.0	165	0.012
Tubes and foils	2.0	207	0.010
Fabricated pipe	1.7	176	0.010

Source: J. Bhagwati (ed.), *International Trade* (Harmondsworth: Penguin, 1969), 102-121.

intensity in each industry by its value added per employee. In Lary's compilations, US metal processing industries have a value added per employee 15 per cent above the manufacturing average, while the corresponding figure for metal fabricating is seven per cent below the average.

Furthermore, since the costs of metal smelting and refining are unrelated to the mineral-exporting country's rich natural endowments, there are now obvious reasons to presume that these processing activities would render high levels of profit. Unlike the mining ventures, mineral processing activities are not self-evidently attractive in terms of the national goals pursued by the country. The reasons for the government's desire to promote investments in mineral processing, therefore, remain to be identified.

The Validity or Otherwise of MNC Views
in the Context of National Development Objectives

The companies' assessment of alternative locations for processing installations has only a partial validity to the national government of a mineral-exporting country, and we propose to start by eliminating some of the obviously irrelevant arguments. The MNCs' doubts and hesitations about location of mineral processing in the exporting LDC have no validity to the national government insofar as they are based on the firms' ownership of processing facilities abroad, on their assessment of political risk exposure, or on their unfamiliarity with socio-economic conditions in the host country. The difficulty posed by importing countries' biased tariff barriers would appear as more of a transient and nego- tiable problem, when looked upon by the national government of the exporting country.

On other issues, the MNC's and government's outlooks appear to converge. In scrutinizing the company view above, we have brought out four circumstances in favor of locating the processing ventures in the mineral-exporting LDCs. The validity of these remains when the problem is regarded from the national govern- ment's point of view. To the extent that savings in transport, absence of environ- mental restrictions or availability of cheap energy and labor reduce the costs of metal smelting and refining, the competitiveness and profitability of such ven- tures will improve. Their contribution to GNP and tax revenue, and hence their attractiveness to the government, will consequently be enhanced.

The social benefit of non-existent or low levels of environmental levies could, of course, be questioned. One might argue that the social advantage arising from increased profits in polluting industries is nullified by the welfare loss from en- vironmental deterioration. But then there are strong reasons to believe that the welfare loss involved would be small. Numerous mines and mineral processing plants in the Third World are located in uninhabited areas like jungles or empty deserts, where the harm of pollution is insignificant. More generally, where there is a trade-off between environmental quality and output, one would expect the willingness to accept a deterioration in the former for a given rise in the latter to be higher in countries at low levels of income. The social attractiveness of pollut- ing industries would then be greater in poor than in rich countries. This could explain the relative laxity in environmental restrictions imposed upon industry in LDCs.

Bargaining Advantage for Capital Imports into Mineral Processing

For a mineral-exporting LDC which supplements its national investment re- sources with capital imports, there may be an advantage in emphasizing mineral processing because foreign funds for such activities are easier to obtain. The background to this is the fact that certain industrialized nations heavily depen- dent on minerals imports, are prepared to provide public support to programs which would assure their long-run mineral supplies. France, Germany and Japan, for instance, subsidize their mining and metal processing corporations' foreign ventures with that objective in view.[4]

The foreign investors in mining, keen to obtain the right to exploit and ex- port the mineral may be amenable to accepting the condition that their engage- ment also include local processing of the crude material, especially in cases where they can expect subsidies from their home governments for the entire investment package. The policies adopted by DCs in pursuance of their own supply security objectives, happen to be transformed in this case into an ad- ditional benefit from mining and mineral processing, accruing to the LDCs which possess comparative advantages as mineral suppliers.

The LDC government ordinarily has no similar leverage when trying to obtain foreign capital for other sectors. When comparing investments in mineral processing on the one hand, and in such activities as agriculture and manufacturing on the other, account must therefore be taken of the superior ability of the former to attract foreign resources.

Less Scope for Harmful Transfer Pricing Practices

In cases where mining and mineral processing are under the same ownership, location of the latter in the exporting LDC would benefit the government by reducing the MNC's opportunities to manipulate profits and tax payments through transfer pricing. This is because control of the company's overall operations would be facilitated if both mining and mineral processing are located in the same country. Furthermore, when exports consist of refined metal, the export prices could easily be compared with available international quotations. Such comparisons would not be feasible in the case of unprocessed mineral products, since there are fewer uniform international price quotations for the latter.

The Implications of Market Structure at Different Levels of Processing

The structure of the market among the importing buyers becomes a relevant consideration when exports of the mineral product take place at arm's length. The market where unprocessed metal minerals are bought is highly concentrated. Non-ferrous metal smelters and refineries as well as steelworks have very important advantages of scale. Their huge capacities frequently require supplies from many mines. Their limited number can reasonably be expected to give rise to monopsony gains. In contrast, refined metals and metal components are bought by a variety of industries, and the concentration among the buyers of each metal is lower. The cases presented in Ch. 7 *supra* illustrate the differences between the two markets.

The discussion of those cases provides a further argument in favor of the government's efforts to build up a mineral processing industry at home. It is not claimed that refined metal prices could be increased with the help of forward integration. Such increases would indeed be problematic. The manufacturers who buy refined metal have considerable scope for substitution of one metal for another, and their price elasticity of demand for each is likely to be high. What we claim is that forward integration could be instrumental in transferring to the mineral exporting country some of the monopsony profits now earned by the buyers in unprocessed product markets. An assessment of the size of the possible gains involved, raises formidable problems, and will not be attempted. The literature on market structure suggests that such gains may not be very large.[5] If they were, one would have expected to see more efforts among the unintegrated miners to acquire their own processing facilities.

A further point related to the market structure requires clarification. It is frequently stated that forward integration from the crude mineral into refined metal or fabricated product would carry the additional benefit of reducing the instability in prices and export revenues now plaguing the mineral exporting LDCs. In reality there appears to be little foundation for such a belief.

The predominant cause of price instability in minerals markets is the business-cycle-induced variation in demand. This has its origin in the fluctuations in demand for mineral-containing finished consumer and capital products. The producers, both of the raw materials, components, and finished products, can react in different ways to the regularly occurring temporary shortfalls in demand. They can either continue to produce at full capacity and accept the ensuing price fall, or they can make an effort to keep prices stable by contracting their capacity utilization. Finally, their reaction may be a combination of the two. The choice of reaction pattern is related to the price elasticity of demand in each case, and more generally to the degree of market power held by the sellers. But it should be clear that whichever method is chosen, the variation in demand is bound to destabilize the producers' revenues. And there is nothing to suggest that the social cost of adjusting supply by varying capacity utilization would be smaller than the cost of having to operate in markets with unstable prices.

Economic Diversification Through Forward Integration

The issue now to be treated is subtler than the preceding ones. Apart from the other development goals, specified at the outset of this section, the governments of mineral-exporting LDCs are also likely to pursue the objective of economic diversification. The desire to diversify the economy is motivated by the fear that the feasible growth of minerals exports in the very long run may be inadequate to sustain the desired expansion of GNP, employment and public revenues. This could be either a consequence of resource limitations on the supply side, or follow from curtailed demand for the mineral due to changes in fashion or technology. In effect, then, economic diversification is not an independent development objective, but one derived from the other goals pursued.

Empirical evidence suggests that economic diversification may be quite difficult to achieve in many LDCs. The mineral-exporting countries listed in Table 13.3 have long pursued policies aimed at reducing their dependence on the minerals sector. Their endeavors have not achieved much success. It seems as if the rich opportunities offered by mineral exploitation attract a higher than desired proportion, not only of capital, but also of qualified human resources and of the time and preoccupation of the government administration. Opportunities in other activities are consequently left fallow, and the high dependence on minerals develops into a permanent feature.

The desire to diversify the economy coupled with the difficulty to do so creates a dilemma. It is possible that the dilemma would be easier to resolve by basing the diversification process on the mineral sector itself. Instead of trying to reduce the dominance of mineral extraction by efforts to expand agriculture, forestry or the textile industry, diversification could be promoted by far-

Table 13.3. *Exports of Ten Major Minerals as a Share of Total Exports (%)*

	1960	*1972-74*
Bolivia	83	80
Chile	77	78
Peru	49	57
Zaire	23	74
Zambia	98	96

Source: World Bank, *Commodity Trade and Price Trends* (1973 and 1976 editions).

reaching forward integration from mining into smelting, refining and fabricating, as well as manufacturing of metal-containing finished products.

The initial advantage of such a policy is that it could rely on the technology, infrastructure and production capital employed by the mining enterprises, and make use of the talents and experiences developed in mining. By fitting into an already existing economic structure, diversification through forward integration will require less initiative and reorientation of resources, and may consequently be easier to carry out.

It is true that the suggested policy has its contradictions and problems. As already noted, the capital-intensive nature of mineral processing does not fit well into the factor availabilities of LDCs. One can also argue that forward integration, at least insofar as mineral processing and metal fabricating are concerned, is a doubtful method of diversification since it would not substantially reduce the economy's dependence on its mineral base.

The objections just stated would be overcome provided that forward integration was carried far enough. As suggested above, the capital intensity of metal industries is reduced as one proceeds upward in the production process beyond the smelting and refining stage. Forward integration into manufactured metal-using products which also require substantial non-metal inputs could constitute the definitive breakaway from the one-sided reliance on the mineral base. The reduction of mineral dependence could take various and not always easily measurable forms, e.g. through a broadened development of manpower, through widening industrial and export market experience, or through backward integration into production of non-metal inputs for the predominantly metal-based manufacturing industries.

CONCLUSIONS

Our analysis has not resulted in any hard and fast conclusions on the benefits and costs of location of mineral processing in the country of mineral extraction, as seen by the two involved parties. But the arguments brought out certainly help in clarifying why the MNCs are hesitant and the governments eager to promote such location.

We have earlier tested the rationale of the various government arguments in favor of forward integration, against the development goals pursued in such countries. The validity of some of the arguments was put in question. For instance, we found little reason to believe that one or two steps of forward integration would contribute towards economic stability in the exporting country. In other cases, though the validity of the arguments was not refuted, we found their importance to be small. This was the case of the prospective reduction of buyers' monopsony gains, consequent upon forward integration.

On balance, however, the discussion clearly suggests that the mineral exporting countries could derive substantial benefits from the establishment of mineral processing within their territories, even when such location is against the economic interests of the MNCs. Government efforts to promote forward integration in the minerals sector seem to be well in line with the general development goals pursued. This observation obviously does not preclude the need to scrutinize each proposed processing venture on its individual merits.

Our analysis should also have clarified that the divergent views held by the governments and MNCs respectively, are mainly a reflection of the differences in outlook and objectives pursued by each. In terms of the graphical illustration in the introductory section, the reason for the divergence is simply that the area of concern to the LDC contains more positive and fewer negative factors than the area of concern to the MNC. Both parties would benefit by certain consequences emerging from location of mineral processing in the developing exporting countries. This is true, for instance, of the cost reduction that might emerge from such location. Other consequences are relevant to only one of the parties. Thus, the governments are not concerned with the capital loss to which the MNCs may be exposed when relocation of processing necessitates contraction of existing capacity in the industrialized world. Similarly, the governments would be alone in appreciating the advantage of economic diversification resulting from forward integration.

Still other consequences of relocation involve a clash of interests between the parties. The greater scope for government control of the company, following from the location of processing in the exporting country, and the simultaneous reduction in the firm's opportunities to manipulate transfer prices, is an illustrative example.

Given the differences in outlook and objectives, some of the divergent views on location of mineral processing will necessarily remain. But the conflicts between the two parties could be reduced if each made an effort to understand the background to the other's motivations, and tried to yield and adjust to the other's interests, where this could be done without much loss to the yielding party.

NOTES

1. How this could be done is described in I. Little and J. Mirrlees, *Manual of Industrial Projects Analysis in Developing Countries* (Paris: OECD, 1969).
2. For a summary see, for instance, A.S. Bhalla (ed.), *Technology and Employment in Industry* (Geneva: ILO, 1975), Ch. 1.

3. H. Lary, *Imports of Manufactures from Less Developed Countries* (Columbia University Press, 1968).

4. For a description of these subsidies, see Z. Mikdashi, *The International Politics of Natural Resources* (London: Cornell University Press, 1976), Ch. 1.

5. G.J. Stigler, *The Organization of Industry* (Homewood, Ill.: Irvin, 1968), Ch. 13; also, Ch. 7 *supra*.

14

IMPACT OF THE INTEGRATED PROGRAM
FOR COMMODITIES ON SELECTED MINING ECONOMIES

J.D.A. Cuddy

After several years' preparatory work, the international community in May 1976 launched the Integrated Program for Commodities (IPC) at UNCTAD IV in Nairobi. This IPC would contain activities which for analytical purposes may be categorized into price and non-price activities. In the former category would fall all attempts to stabilize or alter commodity prices, as defined by the program's objectives spelled-out in UNCTAD Resolution 93 (IV), chapter 1, operative paragraphs 1 and 2.

(i) To achieve stable conditions in commodity trade, including avoidance of excessive price fluctuations, at levels which would:
 (a) be remunerative and just to producers and equitable to consumers;
 (b) take account of world inflation and changes in the world economic and monetary situations;
 (c) promote equilibrium between supply and demand within expanding world commodity trade.
(ii) To improve and sustain the real income of individual LDCs through increased export earnings, and to protect them from fluctuations in export earnings, especially from commodities.

It will be noted that the resolution establishing the IPC does not call for *increases* in commodity prices; rather, its focus is on *stabilizing* such prices and on promoting equilibrium between supply and demand. Moreover, as international commodity agreements (ICAs) would be administered jointly by producing and consuming countries, price levels and ranges would similarly be jointly determined, so that the very structure of agreements reinforces the focus on stabilization, rather than alteration, in regard to the IPC's activities in price matters.

The second category of IPC activities deals with non-price considerations. The IPC is required:

2. ... to protect [individual LDCs] from fluctuations in export earnings, especially from commodities;
3. to seek to improve market access and reliability of supply for primary products and the processed products thereof ... [and]

Notes to this chapter may be found on pages 254-255.

4. to diversify production ... and to expand processing of primary products in developing countries.[1]

Among those measures listed in the resolution which are relevant to these additional non-price objectives of the IPC are: expansion of processing and diversification; establishment and extension of multilateral long-term supply and purchase commitments; and improvement and enlargement of compensatory financing facilities.

Although a great deal has been written about the economic benefits of price stabilization, such as would be undertaken under the IPC, most investigations, both theoretical and empirical, have worked with simple linear or log-linear models. Recent work, however, has shown these models to be of limited applicability;[2] indeed, evidence is mounting from empirical work with less crude models that one frequently-cited conclusion from the simpler analytical studies,[3] namely, that price stabilization may well destabilize producers' revenue and/or export earnings, does not hold up in actual practice.[4] For this and other reasons, therefore, it seems appropriate to look more deeply into what the impact on mineral economies would be of a major international program like the IPC.

SOURCES OF BENEFITS FROM THE IPC

Consider first the benefits arising from the IPC in respect of its price activities. Two classes of interests may be considered: those of the producers and those of the consumers of the commodities falling under the IPC's purview. It has been argued elsewhere[5] that these two groups, so generally considered to have antagonistic objectives and thus largely incompatible interests in price stabilization,[6] in fact have a joint interest in promoting the conclusion of ICAs whose main objectives coincide with those of resolution 93(IV). The two groups are considered briefly in turn; for a fuller discussion see the article noted in note 5.

The major advantages to producers from price stabilization accrue at the micro level, from the reduction in risk which accompanies the more certain knowledge (even if within a band) of future prices which a price stabilization scheme (like IPC) provides. A further effect is that of increasing the competitiveness of primary commodities for which synthetic substitutes are available. Price stabilization also reduces the occurrence of structural disequilibria attributable to the cobweb response of producers to price changes. It could well also alter the margin which intermediaries are able to obtain under the cover of the informational noise generated by rapid price fluctuations.

So far as consumers are concerned, price stabilization would reduce the risk-averse manufacturer's need to hedge by reducing both the instability of supplies consequent upon an (otherwise) unstable production environment and the instability of input prices. Price stabilization would also reduce the impact of the ratchet effect in prices of final goods in which the value of the primary input is significant.[7]

Turning now to non-price activities of the IPC, three seem to stand out as important: expansion of processing and diversification; establishment of multilateral long-term supply and purchase commitments; and improvement and enlargement of compensatory financing facilities. These are considered below.

Processing and Diversification

The effect of an increase in the processing of primary commodities brought about by the IPC would be manifested in the producing country in two areas: the added value from increased processing prior to export, and the savings obtained from replacement of imports by domestically-processed products. In the consuming country, the equivalent effects would be measured in the reduction in local processing and the loss of exports to producer-country markets. In a strict comparative statics model, these effects would be expected to cancel each other out. There would, however, be a net benefit to the global economy as a whole if the resource cost of producing the processed product were lower in the (now) producing countries than in the (now) consuming countries, and/or if the consumption multiplier were larger in the producing than in the consuming countries.

The effect of diversification upon countries attempting it would be felt in the added value of domestic production of new commodities (less the loss of added value from the reduction of production in the old commodities); and in the net added value of domestic production now displacing imports. The commodities for which such diversification, and import displacement, is most likely to be of any significance, however, are of necessity mainly agricultural, since mineral products depend much more heavily on natural endowments; both effects are therefore not considered further.

Long-term Contracts

The effect of long-term contracts would be to eliminate completely the volume and price fluctuations associated with trade in the products so covered. That part of this effect relating to price can be taken as subsumed in the analysis of the preceding section, so that what is of importance here is the effect on volume. It seems reasonable to suppose that this effect can be expressed as leading to two results: (1) savings from superior planning in a stable investment climate, in the form of a reduction or even elimination of investments which would otherwise have been undertaken on account of faulty signals sent by fluctuating output prices; and (2) an increase in the (risk-compensated) rate of return to the producer arising from a reduction in the risk premium, consequent upon (relative) price stability.

Compensatory Financing Arrangements

As viewed within the IPC, compensatory financing arrangements would be complementary to the stocking and other measures undertaken, and would be used to smooth out any residual fluctuations in export earnings which might remain following the application of the remainder of the basic instruments of the IPC. Since it may be presumed that such arrangements would be based on the insurance principle, with perhaps some net transfer of resources to the poorest countries under certain conditions, and since the effect of stabilized export earnings on income growth is a controversial one,[8] this effect will be ignored here so as to avoid entering the debate without the benefit of a major study on the subject. But it should be noted that this approach will certainly understate the net positive impact of the IPC on the global economy.

This completes the qualitative analysis of the sources of benefits from the IPC. In the next section the attempt is made to quantify these benefits, but the reader should be forewarned that doing so satisfactorily is difficult, if not impossible, given the paucity of empirical information on many of the parameters involved. It is necessary to make the attempt, however, in order to obtain orders of magnitude for the benefits to be gained, and thus to determine which are the effects on which attention should most usefully be concentrated.

QUANTIFYING THE BENEFITS FROM THE IPC

Quantification of the benefits identified in the preceding section requires an appropriate methodology. Existing treatments of this issue are unsatisfactory, however, particularly because of their extreme sensitivity to assumptions made about the form of the models underlying the analysis. For these reasons, this study has relied on a simple common-sense and rule-of-thumb approach, which attempts to relate the specific benefits identified in the previous section to the basic variables from which the benefits arise, and scales these benefits for each country and commodity by that country's (and commodity's) share in global production or consumption of the commodity in question.

The implicit assumption in this procedure is, of course, that market structures with regard to a given commodity are sufficiently similar for the producers and consumers of that commodity that each producer and each consumer would share *pro rata* in the benefits to be expected by the producer or consumer group as a whole. Put in another way, the assumption is that a country's power to arrogate benefits from price stabilization is proportional to the country's market share. This may understate the importance of dominance on either side of the market, but there seems little choice but to adopt such an assumption as a first-order approximation, given that a complete model combining countries and commodities and their interactions (and paying special attention to market structures) is not yet available.

Twenty-two effects have been identified and quantified for the purposes of this study, and Table 14.1 provides a summary of the results of this analysis. Rather than using production values as scale factors, however, this table shows results based on exports as a scale factor. There are two reasons for so doing.

Table 14.1. *Summary of Estimated Benefits from IPC, By Commodity (1970-74 US $ million, per annum)*

A. Micro Benefits by Commodity

	Copper	Tin	Bauxite	Manganese	Iron Ore	Phosphate
RPE	18.12	2.94	0.99	0.69	9.40	2.21
IME	0.77	0.11	0.05	0.04	0.26	0.07
SCE	0.0	0.0	0.0	0.0	0.0	0.0
OCE	49.25	7.99	2.69	1.87	51.94	4.21
UIE	74.25	7.14	0.85	2.27	38.14	6.88
RRE	19.41	1.87	0.22	0.59	4.90	2.56
CUE	18.12	2.94	0.99	0.69	9.40	2.21
LIE	226.34	3.30	25.56	20.18	126.64	31.49
IEE	45.70	7.41	2.49	1.74	9.61	6.49
RHE	0.27	0.04	0.02	0.01	0.18	0.04
IMF*	0.17	0.02	0.01	0.01	0.08	0.02
OCE*	52.00	8.13	3.15	2.50	70.21	5.74
UIE	10.97	4.34	0.76	0.62	17.63	1.99
RRE*	2.87	1.14	0.20	0.16	2.27	0.74
CUE*	38.25	5.98	2.32	1.84	25.40	6.02
IPE	133.92	33.83	6.84	10.87	138.26	35.56
CSE	31.88	4.99	1.93	1.53	21.17	5.02
SUM	722.30	92.15	49.07	45.62	525.49	111.25

* relative to countries which consume a given commodity.

B. Macro Benefits by Commodity

	Copper	Tin	Bauxite	Manganese	Iron Ore	Phosphate
SFO	184.70	18.33	3.33	8.41	71.34	22.90
NAD	26.30	0.94	0.0	0.0	0.0	0.0
TBE	5.94	0.02	1.04	0.15	0.45	0.17
LTC	14.05	1.35	0.16	0.43	6.46	1.42
AIC	0.0	0.0	0.0	0.0	0.0	0.0
SUM	230.99	20.64	4.54	8.99	78.25	24.49

Glossary

RPE	risk premium effect	CSE	capacity strain effect
IME	intermediary margin effect	PGNP	price deflator of gross national product (GNP)
SCE	synthetic competitiveness effect	CPI	consumer price index
OCE	overhead cost effect	SFO	saving of foregone output
UIE	unwarranted investment effect	NAD	net additional demand
RRE	return – raising effect	AIC	additional income created
LIE	longer-term income effect	TBE	tax base effect
IEE	increased employment effect	LTC	long-term contracts effect
RHE	reduced hedging effect	CUE	capacity utilization effect
IPE	input price effect		

Firstly, the use of the production/consumption share would entail the further assumption that the IPC would affect the totality of production/consumption of a product, thus providing an upper bound to the estimate of the beneficial effect; whereas, since at a minimum the IPC would affect the world price for the commodity, the export scale factor provides a lower bound to the estimates of benefits derived. Secondly, as Table 14.2 shows, production and exports differ significantly for the mineral products included in the IPC. While it is beyond the scope of the present study to examine in detail domestic policies with regard to these commodities, it appears not unreasonable to argue that much of the difference may be accounted for by the processing of raw materials within vertically-integrated mining companies. If this be even approximately true, then the well-known practice in these companies of applying arbitrary transfer prices to such transactions means that these prices are also likely to move largely independently of world market prices, since factors such as local and parent-country tax policies and earnings from other portions of the MNCs play determining roles in the setting of such transfer prices.[9]

It will be clear from Table 14.1 that two effects dominate the results: that in the micro section labelled LIE and that in the macro section labelled SFO, respectively producers' long-term income effect and saving of foregone output. Since these two effects bulk so large in the results (they account for 39 per cent of the total), it is worth examining them in detail.

Producers' Long-Term Income Effect (LIE)

As argued above, a likely effect of the IPC and commodity price stabilization is that the average (risk-compensated) prices 'perceived' by consumers of at least some of the minerals included in the program would ultimately be lower than they would otherwise have been had the IPC not been in existence, because of the reduction in risk implied by lower price variability. Since most commodity models relate supply to the level of (relative) prices, and not to the stability of these prices, such models do not capture this effect, nor do existing models take account of the behavior of consumers in the face of risky price expectations, behavior which will also influence commodity markets from the demand side.[10]

Whatever be the initial effect of such benefits to consumers, the ultimate effect is not likely to be that of a zero-sum game, in which producers lose what consumers gain. For the lower average prices (relative to levels otherwise attained) will call forth an increase in the volume of consumption which will offset to some extent the (relative) decline in producer income which might occur.[11] Moreover, this lower price effect is not likely to come about for several years, since there is a substantial lead-time in mineral investment. Thus, the lower prices would appear after a much more solid base had been formed in the producer economies, from which inefficiencies (which in the absence of the IPC would have continued during the period of otherwise higher relative prices), would have been eliminated. Finally, the increased disposable income of consumers resulting from the lower input prices would call forth, at the macro level, increased imports from the producer economies, relative to those which would otherwise have occurred.

As to the increase in the volume of consumption of the stabilized commodities, this would result from the reduction in the total cost of consumption of a unit of the commodity (as perceived by the consumer) which would be brought about by his factoring into overall costs the benefits (negative costs) of the IPC to be discussed below. This increased volume would depend upon the responsiveness of market demand to the perceived price change, and the scale of that change.

In order to estimate the quantitative extent of this effect, it was necessary to consider first the formation of consumer demand for a commodity, and its response to price. In so doing, explicit account was taken of consumer behavior under risk. In the approach adopted, the first step was to view demand for a primary commodity as related to price expectations; and the second step to link price expectations to risk. The results obtained (on the basis of an econometric model developed elsewhere)[12] led to the conclusion that a one per cent decline in risk (as measured by the coefficient of variation) would, for example, result in a .033 per cent increase in the expected demand for copper, and a .002 per cent rise in that for tin. The overall results of these calculations are presented in Table 14.1.

Table 14.2. *Production and Exports of Minerals Included in IPC*
        (1970-74 $ million)

Commodity	Average global production 1970-74	Average global exports 1970-74
Bauxite	821.7	336.1
Copper	9786.6	6122.5
Iron Ore	6359.4	3102.7
Manganese	441.0	231.4
Phosphate rock	1776.0	823.4
Tin	902.2	970.4
Mineral total	20086.9	11586.5

Source: UNCTAD secretariat estimates based on UN, FAO and national sources.

Savings of Foregone Output (SFO)

The other major effect of the IPC is that on inflation in countries consuming primary commodities. Clearly, the IPC, by reducing the fluctuations historically observed in the prices of primary raw materials, would have some effect on price movements in the domestic economies of these consuming countries. In order to estimate this effect, it is first necessary to identify the impact of changes in commodity prices on indices of inflation in those countries.[13] The best method for such analysis would clearly be to work the prices of imported and domestically produced primary commodities through a sufficiently detailed input-output model, incorporating the appropriate timelags and margin adjustments which occur during the cyclical course of the economy. Unfortunately, no such models exist at the necessary level of disaggregation, so that this approach is not presently possible.[14]

A second-best model, pioneered by Popkin,[15] is the use of a 'stage-of-process' model,

...in which raw commodity prices...are related to prices of intermediate materials and components which in turn are related to manufacturers' prices of both consumers' and producers' finished goods ...[and] the prices of [these] goods...then used to explain the behavior of appropriate components of the consumer price index.[16]

Popkin has constructed such a model for the US economy, but no similar models exist at present for other countries. If the view is taken that the economies of other major consuming countries are sufficiently dissimilar to that of the USA, then it becomes inappropriate to apply Popkin's conclusions[17] that 'the CPI has an elasticity of 0.069 with respect to crude materials prices (excluding fuels and forest products)' to these other countries, and some alternative approach must be adopted.

One possible way to treat this issue might be to relate changes in the prices of primary commodities to changes in import prices in consuming countries, and thence to changes in PGNP or CPI. For those commodities which are not produced in consuming countries, this method would provide a reasonable approximation to the measure of impact desired. For those commodities which are both produced and consumed in the same country, further analysis would be required. If the share of imports in total consumption of the commodity is known, then a weighted measure of impact could be obtained from combining the effect of import price changes on PGNP or CPI and the effect of changes in the domestic price of the commodity in question on the same indicators.[18]

The effect of import price changes on PGNP, which is the price indicator to be used in the remainder of this paper (since it is more closely related than CPI to aggregate output and employment), can be estimated from the share of imports in GNP.[19] Estimation of the effect of changes in domestic commodity prices on PGNP would require the detailed input-output tables mentioned above. Since these are not available, rough approximations of the impact can be estimated from the breakdown in expenditure categories contained in the national accounts, if total consumption of the commodities is known and if commodities are 'assigned' to the various expenditure categories. These effects can be aggregated to obtain the overall impact on PGNP of changes in the prices of a number of commodities simultaneously. This aggregated effect in turn can be used to calculate the impact on GNP of commodity price stabilization.[20]

It is possible to trace this impact of price stabilization further throughout the economy, in particular examining its effect on potential output, using estimates of the parameters of the Phillips curve to calculate the decline in unemployment associated with the reduction in PGNP (from the level it would otherwise have attained), which would then be related to the corresponding increase in output (from the level it would otherwise have reached) via a relation of the form of Okun's law. This method has in fact been used by Behrman to calculate the impact of the IPC on the US economy.[21] Another approach would be to allow explicitly for price shifts in calculating (potential) production functions, thus obtaining direct estimates of the impact of price changes on output. Artus has carried out such an analysis but his conclusions relate only to the 1973-1975 period and confound the effect of all commodity price changes together.[22]

For this reason, a third approach to the problem, suggested in a quite different context by Lundberg,[23] has been adopted in this study. This method consists in relating directly changes in PGNP to the gap between potential and actual GNP, leading to conclusions of the sort: a one per cent decline in a country's PGNP effected through domestic policy intervention leads to a β per cent increase in the gap between actual and potential GNP for that country. This implies that if a global policy of commodity price stabilization were pursued which obviated the necessity of domestic policy intervention, then this would 'save' the country under consideration a loss of β per cent of potential GNP. When these values for β are scaled by the values obtained for the reduction in PGNP resulting from commodity price stabilization, the impact of stabilizing the prices of various commodities, expressed in terms of saving of foregone output (SFO, measured, it should be noted, in real terms) can be determined.

Calculations carried out in my study mentioned in note 12 led to the results indicated in Table 14.1 for savings on foregone output generated by the IPC. Since the effect of the IPC on the variance of commodity prices is intended to be symmetrical, the savings arise only because of the asymmetrical response of the domestic economy, both through oligopoly and via government policy decisions, to upward movements in commodity prices, as discussed above. Since this asymmetrical response, while plausible, rests at present on somewhat limited statistical and theoretical support, however, the results for SFO should be treated as orders of magnitude. It should also be noted that, owing on the one hand to the severe data limitations for the LDCs, and on the other hand to the existence of rather considerable unemployment or underemployment of resources in LDCs, the results for these countries should be treated with special caution.

CONCLUSIONS

The preceding sections of this work have presented a method of calculating the benefits for mineral economies of the IPC, and have attempted some initial estimates of the magnitude of the lower bound of those benefits. As seen in Table 14.1, this lower bound is of the order of 1.9 billion[24] 1970-74 dollars (equal to roughly 4.6 billion 1980 dollars) per annum. Against this, of course, must be set the costs of the program, costs which it is not the purpose of this study even to begin to estimate. Nevertheless, it seems most unlikely that, if the estimates made here of the benefits to be derived from implementation of the

IPC are within even an order of magnitude of the true lower bound of such benefits, the costs would exceed the benefits of the program. Of course, other proposals might have even higher benefit-cost ratios, and the whole issue of distribution of benefits has been ignored here; but the results do seem to suggest that the application of the IPC to mineral commodities would provide a positive economic payoff to the international community.

NOTES

1. Resolution 93(IV), Ch. 1, paras. 2-4, page 3.
2. See, for example, J.D.A. Cuddy, 'The Case for an Integrated Program for Commodities', *Resources Policy* (March 1979).
3. For example, E.M. Brook, E.R. Grilli and J. Waelbroeck, 'Commodity Price Stabilization and the Developing Countries', World Bank Staff Working Paper No. 262 (Washington: World Bank, 1977).
4. E.C. Hwa and N. Kulatilaka, 'Stabilizing World Commodity Markets through Buffer Stocks' (Washington: IMF, 1979; mimeo).
5. See J.D.A. Cuddy, 'Commodity price stabilization: its effects on producers and consumers', *Resources Policy* (March 1978). The model and mathematical calculations upon which the arguments made in this paper are based, are drawn from Cuddy, 'An Analysis of the Impact of the IPC' (mimeo).
6. This is clear enough from the very title of studies such as those of Turnovsky ('The Distribution of Welfare Gains from Price Stabilization'), and Waugh ('Does the Consumer Benefit from Price Instability?'). A more simple-minded view finds its expression in the notion that if prices rise, the producer gains and the consumer loses, whereas if prices fall, producers lose and consumers gain.
7. On this important point, see R.N. Cooper and R.Z. Lawrence, 'The 1972-75 Commodity Boom', *Brookings Papers on Economic Activity*, No. 3 (1975) and N. Kaldor, 'Inflation and Recession in the World Economy', *Economic Journal*, Vol. 86, No. 344 (December 1976).
8. For a recent contribution to the extensive literature on this subject see C. Rangarajan and V. Sundararajan, 'Impact of Export Fluctuations on Income: A Cross Country Analysis', *Review of Economics and Statistics* (August 1976).
9. In this connection, see for example, S. Lall, 'Transfer-pricing by multinational manufacturing firms', *Oxford Bulletin of Economics and Statistics*, Vol. 35, No. 3 (August 1975), 160-190 and G.K. Helleiner, 'Freedom and Management in Primary Commodity Markets: US Imports from Developing Countries', *World Development*, Vol. 6, No. 1 (1978), 23-30.
10. Recently, Just has developed a model of commodity supply which incorporates risk through the inclusion of a 'subjective risk' variable identified in practice with the historical variance of price, i.e. with price instability. See, *inter alia*, R.E. Just, 'An Investigation of the Importance of Risk in Farmers' Decisions', *American Journal of Agricultural Economics*, Vol. 56 (1977) and 'Estimation of a risk response model with some degree of flexibility', *Southern Economic Journal*, Vol. 42, No. 4 (April 1976). The incorporation of risk into demand functions has not progressed to the same extent, however.
11. It bears repeating that given the margins between prices actually received by producers, and those paid by consumers, actual producer unit returns might not decline at all, if the intermediary margins absorb the entire reduction in actual consumer prices. Furthermore, what is important here is *perception* of price by consumers: given risk aversion on their part, actual prices would remain constant in the face of a reduction in perceived prices (through the risk premium effect) and a consequent increase in consumption volume. The combination of these two effects could well be sufficient to lead to stable producer prices, yet rising consumption volume, in appropriate circumstances.
12. J.D.A. Cuddy, 'An Analysis of the Impact of the IPC' (mimeo; n.d.).
13. The two most commonly-used such indices are the GNP price deflator (PGNP) and the consumer price index (CPI).
14. An attempt at specifying such a model for Australia has been made in another context;

see B.D. Haig and M.P. Ward, 'A Dynamic model for Analysing Price Changes', in K. Polenske and J. Skolba (eds), *Advances in Input-Output Analysis* (Cambridge, Mass: Ballinger Pub. Co., 1976), 73-91.

15. See J. Popkin, 'Commodity Prices and the US Price Level', *Brookings Papers on Economic Activity*, No. 1 (1974), 249-259.

16. *Ibidem*, 253.

17. *Ibidem*, 354.

18. F.G. Adams of the Wharton School at the University of Pennsylvania has recently constructed the COMLINK system, which combines 23 commodity models (for 30 separate commodities) with the 15 country-group models of project LINK. This system enables him to calculate the impact of commodity price changes on PGNP of the countries included, in a manner similar to, but more sophisticated than, that described here. Unfortunately, this system is new and relatively untested, and not yet fully debugged.

19. Since GNP consists of unduplicated output (added value) this approach implies a one-to-one pass-through of commodity price changes. Some (e.g. Popkin, *loc.cit.*) would argue that this exaggerates the impact; presumably they would prefer a measure relating imports to final demand (i.e. GNP less imports), as can be obtained from input-output tables using the $B(I-A)^{-1}$ matrix. (An interesting approach to the use of such information is contained in R.S. Preston, 'The Input-Output Sector of the Wharton Annual and Industry Forecasting Model', in G. Fromm and L.R. Klein (eds), *The Brookings Model: Perspective and Recent Developments* [Amsterdam: North-Holland Pub. Co., 1975], 607-629). Others, however, (e.g. Cooper and Lawrence, *loc.cit.* and Kalder, *loc.cit.*) would argue the reverse, that this understates the impact. Perhaps, therefore, the approach taken here represents a reasonable compromise position.

20. See Cuddy, 'An Analysis of the Impact of the IPC'.

21. J.R. Behrman, *International Commodity Agreements: An Evaluation of the UNCTAD Integrated Commodity Program* (Washington: Overseas Development Council, 1977).

22. J. Artus, 'Measures of Potential Output for Eight Industrial Countries, 1955-78', *IMF Staff Papers*, Vol. XXIV, No. 1 (March 1977), 1-35.

23. E. Lundberg, *Instability and Economic Growth* (New Haven: Yale University Press, 1960), 96-123.

24. This figure is obtained by adding together the elements in the final row (labelled SUM) of Parts A and B of the table, across commodities. The elements of the SUM rows themselves are the sums of the respective columns.

15

NO OPEC FOR MINERALS?

E. Penrose

The modern history of the petroleum industry is the history of an industry characterized by the prevalence of a strong controlling hand, be it public or private. At some times, and in some areas, some parts of the industry have been conducted in what could reasonably be called a 'free competitive market'. But much more important have been the activities of powerful private groups or governments, which provided the framework and established the rules with respect to which the operations of the industry have been organized on both a national and an international scale. Whether one looks at the dominance of the great private trusts in the early history of the industry in the USA or at the multifarious interventions of the government in more recent periods, or at the operations of the large companies in Europe, the Far East and the Middle East, the story is much the same: regulation and control, particularly affecting the production of crude oil, was as important, and often more important, than 'market forces' in determining both the level and location of output (and therefore of prices). This does not mean, of course, that the market has been of little significance; it is a very great mistake to underestimate the strength of market forces to which even the tightest cartel must pay due homage. But for a variety of reasons the oil industry has tended to provide especially strong incentives and often favorable conditions for private firms to establish monopolies, as well as strong inducements for governments to intervene, sometimes to assist companies, sometimes to establish controls over them.

The very large concession areas granted to a very few companies by governments in the Middle East and elsewhere, giving exclusive rights for exploration and production, inevitably created monopolistic conditions even though considerable rivalry among the companies existed downstream in refining and product markets. In addition, the large and experienced companies had substantial competitive advantages over smaller companies and, further assisted by privileged access to oil, they obtained an almost unassailable position in world markets.

Economies of scale in refining, and in transportation both by pipeline and later by tanker, together with long-established brand names and in some cases collusively monopolistic positions in distribution, gave them further advantages.

Notes to this chapter may be found on page 265.

Of especial importance from the point of view of the subsequent position of the governments of the oil-producing countries was the high degree of vertical integration in the industry. Integration, plus strong market positions was sufficient to enable the companies, which were among the first MNCs, to provide secure outlets for their crude-oil producing affiliates, even when these passed to other hands.

The uncertain results of exploration meant that there was frequently a considerable disparity between the amount of oil supplied and demanded in the neighborhood of ruling prices with the result that in free markets prices could fluctuate widely as 'gluts' and 'scarcities' reflected the success (or lack of it) of exploration. The urge to 'adjust supply to demand' through some form of explicit or implicit regulation and control was obviously not only strong in such circumstances, but could plausibly be presented as desirable in the interest of both producers and consumers. For example, the very large discoveries in the Middle East which took place between the two world wars, if produced under fully competitive conditions, would have resulted in a very rapid and steep fall in prices, which would have had very serious consequences for the existing higher cost producers in Venezuela, Indonesia and elsewhere.

The major companies attempted to regulate the rate at which this oil came on to world markets and for a while they were successful. For this they were attacked as monopolistic imperialists by many in the oil-exporting countries, and as a sinister cartel by many in the consuming countries. Nevertheless, during the 1950s both the companies and the producing countries prospered as the increasing supplies of oil flowed to the consuming countries. But the majors were unable adequately to control output for very long. At the end of the 1950s prices began to fall, and it is an irony of history that the very failure of the attempt to resist competitive and market forces should lay the foundations for the successful establishment of OPEC — the fall in market prices induced the companies to cut tax prices and thus called forth OPEC.

OPEC AS A 'CARTEL'

OPEC has been widely regarded as a remarkably successful 'cartel', especially after 1973 when, observing the increases in the price of oil, other raw-material producing countries dreamed of taking similar action for their own products. Certainly OPEC is a collusive association of producers, but the description of it as a 'cartel' immediately evoked in the minds of observers the classical textbook image of an organization which almost inevitably breaks up under the strain of attempts to compose the divergent interests of its members and to police their efforts to evade the agreed rules. The imminent collapse of OPEC was widely predicted, especially by university professors of economics. As often happens, in other connections, a general 'model' was applied rather indiscriminately to the particular case, with inadequate attention being given to an examination of the extent to which the various elements of the model were present in the special circumstances.

In fact, OPEC had few of the salient characteristics of the classical cartel. It did not administer output or agree on market shares (the primary issue over which cartels have tended to break down). It had no control at all over aggregate supply, nor did it attempt to exercise any, each country being free to produce as much as it liked. Nor did it attempt any detailed price administration; only one reference price for crude oil was agreed but the 'differentials' permitted around this price for oil with different qualities and characteristics and from different sources were only loosely specified. With such a simple mechanism, and with so few of the major characteristics of cartels, it is not surprising that OPEC experienced few of the classical problems.

To be sure, some of the characteristics traditionally held to be essential for the success of cartels existed. Demand was very inelastic with respect to price, especially in the short run, while the long run was rather too long to be seriously worried about. The proportion of actual output (and even medium-term potential output) controlled by OPEC countries was very high and in general the elasticity of supply from the outside was also low in the short run. The gains from raising prices were therefore considerable, but no arrangement for the distribution of market shares was necessary and the issue never became a serious problem for OPEC. At times there was some price-cutting which many members believed bordered on cheating, but at no time did it become significant.

It is not, therefore, because of its cartel characteristics that OPEC has been successful. The explanation lies rather in the historical circumstances associated with its origin and development, circumstances not shared by any other group of mineral producers in as large a measure. To understand this we must briefly look at its history.

The history of OPEC is clearly divisible into three major periods (with perhaps a new one beginning in December 1979): the first from 1960 to 1970; the second from 1970 to 1974; and the third from 1974 to 1979.

1960-70: Market Surplus and Bargaining Power

As indicated above, the formation of OPEC was a response to the reduction of crude oil prices by the companies, which, in turn, was a response to a crude-oil surplus creating a 'downward' pressure on prices in product markets. In principle, such conditions should not be favorable for a producers' cartel created to raise prices, a fact which was repeatedly pointed out by the oil companies. Moreover, OPEC was not in a position to regulate supply, which was entirely under the control of the majors. Nevertheless, even in these circumstances OPEC had some success: although it was unable to raise prices to previous levels, it did prevent any further reduction. This limited success, in the face of continuing weak markets and falling prices, was a considerable achievement. It was made possible more by certain special and peculiar weaknesses in the position of the companies than by any inherent strength of OPEC.

The governments of the producing countries controlled the terms of the concessions and could, with some degree of plausibility, threaten to 'legislate' to obtain their demands — on the grounds of changed circumstances. The companies were in a weak 'moral' position with respect to some of the specific demands of governments: the existing arrangements governing the payment of royalties were manifestly inequitable and, moreover differed from royalty arrangements in other major producing areas of the world. The maintenance of exclusive rights over large areas which could not even be explored adequately by the concessionaires, let alone brought into production, was also manifestly unreasonable. On the crucial issue of the prices to be used for calculating taxes, which were the prices that OPEC was attempting to raise but only succeeded in freezing, the companies were in a much weaker position than might have been expected in view of the evident market pressures and their concentration of control over the industry.

This weakness arose from the fact that the major companies feared outsiders and each other as much as, or perhaps even more than, they feared the governments of the producing countries. Among the most important factors giving rise to the crude-oil 'surplus' and the pressure on prices in the late 1950s and 1960s was the competition for market shares among the major companies themselves as well as competition in product markets from outsiders, who often obtained their crude from the majors. Hence, even though the subsidiaries actually producing the crude oil in the Middle East were consortia owned by some combination of the major MNCs, the divergent interests of the individual majors, and the fact that the company composition of the consortia differed from country to country, left each consortium and each company vulnerable to the pressure of the relevant governments.

In other words, the bargaining power of the MNCs, who were not linked in any formal cartel but who acted merely as a collection of oligopolies behaving in 'parallel fashion' (with perhaps some informal contacts among themselves), was nevertheless weakened in much the same way as that of a cartel might have been expected to be weakened in bargaining with the producing countries. OPEC, though in some ways closer to a cartel, did not suffer from similar weaknesses. In addition, each MNC could afford to accept the diminution of its profits, which followed an unchanging tax per unit of output in the face of falling prices, easier than it could accept the risk of loss of its crude oil position as a result of a serious conflict with its host country. (Iraq had already provided an example of the cost of such a conflict.)

1970-73: Market Conditions Favor OPEC

The weakness of the companies was not fully appreciated by their host governments, who still lacked confidence in their collective strength. Had market conditions continued to weaken, as had been widely predicted by some eminent observers of the industry, it is quite possible that the still limited cohesion of the OPEC countries could not have sustained the risks of taking direct action against the companies to force the reduction in supply necessary to strengthen prices. In the event the problem did not arise.

As the OPEC countries began to consider more serious action to support their demands, market conditions became increasingly tighter, partly as the long-term decline in the oil reserves of the United States became reflected in declining output. At the same time, demand strengthened under the impact of a more-or-less simultaneous boom in the major manufacturing countries, the effects of both being aggravated from time to time by interruptions of supply due partly to political unrest in the Middle East as well as to a variety of accidental factors.

Libya, with a new revolutionary government which was not averse to taking risks and was in a peculiarly strategic position for the supply of oil to Europe because of the closure of the Suez Canal, could, and did, take advantage of the situation to force a large increase in both tax rates and tax prices on the companies operating there. She shattered the bases of the agreements that the MNCs had vigorously defended for 20 years. Libya's action was quickly followed by the other OPEC countries and in 1971 and 1972 agreements were made with the companies on prices, tax rates, adjustments for monetary fluctuations, relinquishment of concession territory, participation by the governments in the ownership of the crude-oil producing affiliates, and other matters. These substantially improved the position of the oil-producing countries and gave their governments a decisive voice in most important decisions.

Very few, if any, of these gains, however, could be attributed to the *cartel* power of OPEC. Different individual countries took the lead in demanding and negotiating changes; certainly they were backed by OPEC as a group, but market conditions were so favorable and the position of the individual countries with large reserves was so strong that, had those countries in the strongest positions chosen to act independently with the same demands, the result would probably have been very much the same in the absence of the OPEC.

OPEC was not responsible for the market supply problem, for it had no policy on restriction of output; nor was it responsible for the industrial boom, the monetary inflation, the continued weakness of the companies in the individual countries, nor the Arab/Israeli conflict. The embargo on supplies to the United States and the Netherlands was a decision of the Ministerial Committee of the Arab Gulf States, not OPEC; the subsequent fourfold price increase was an OPEC decision, but was taken largely under the pressure of the Shah of Iran who pointed to the very much higher market prices then being paid as an indication of the 'true value' of this 'noble resource'. Such a price increase could have come about by Saudi and Iranian action alone, since all others would certainly have followed.

The continuing rise in market prices for crude oil and products in response to strong demand and aggravated by increasing world-wide inflation, soon made the price agreements of 1971 out of date in that the position of the oil-producing countries deteriorated steadily relative to that of the companies, in a manner not anticipated by either party when the agreements were made. In consequence, OPEC demanded renegotiation of the agreements early in 1973. The Arab-Israeli war broke out in the midst of these negotiations, but even after the outbreak of war the companies refused to accept as reasonable the OPEC demands for an increase in price of not much more than $3.00. The result is wellknown.

1974-79: Recession and Surplus

The drastic and sudden increase in the price of oil in January 1974 coincided with an intensification of world recession; the market was no longer sustained by strong demand pressing on supply. The recession was accompanied by continued inflation, the real price of oil steadily declined and in consequence, also the terms of trade of the OPEC countries. There was still no concerted attempt by OPEC to control supply, although some individual countries imposed or increased ceilings on output, partly to reduce the rate of depletion of their most important (or only) resource, which was being sold on increasingly disadvantageous terms.

The emergence of surpluses and of falling prices provides the real test of a cartel's cohesion; and every dispute that arose among OPEC members provided the occasion for a spate of predictions of its imminent collapse. It survived the test primarily because there was no serious dispute over the issue of market shares, and consequently no country in a position to do so was willing to go very far in cutting prices to increase its own share. To be sure, there was bickering and some apparent cheating, but neither went far enough to endanger OPEC. There was considerable discussion of the problem of 'differentials' (the relative prices of different crudes from different sources) and new formulae were developed to deal with this technically difficult question. No doubt, some of the announced differentials were designed to offset the adverse impact of sluggish demand on the output of some of the countries which were particularly in need of revenues. But the spread of prices of the different crudes around the price of the reference or 'marker' crude was chiefly determined by market forces reflecting the value to refiners of the different crudes. At no time did the problem of differential prices seriously threaten the unity of OPEC.

The continuing decline in the real price of oil due to the continued rise in the prices of other things, including OPEC imports of industrial goods, as a result of the continuing high levels of inflation, gave rise to strong pressures from OPEC members to increase the nominal price of oil at least enough to offset the effect of inflation on the value of their revenues. In 1978, the price of crude oil in real terms was below the level of 1974. Saudi Arabia, supported by the United Arab Emirates, which on most OPEC matters took its cue from the Saudis, was strongly opposed to OPEC further raising the price of oil and the Saudis refused in successive OPEC conferences to accede to the demands of the other members. The Saudis even went so far as to increase their own output in an effort to bring prices down towards the levels they considered appropriate. In this they were only partly successful since Saudi Arabia did not have spare productive capacity sufficient fully to attain their objective. One effect was to increase the profits of the American companies which obtained the cheaper oil.

Some economists, still clinging to traditional cartel analysis, have interpreted

Saudi attitudes on the question as the result of a desire to increase their own sales.[1] There is no evidence for this at all. To be sure the Saudis raised the ceilings they had set on production in order to help keep prices down, but there seems little reason to think they did this in order to increase their revenues by increasing their own sales. Increased prices would have had the same effect on revenues without depleting oil reserves since the OPEC price was probably still below the 'monopoly price' which in principle sets the ceiling above which further price increases would reduce total revenues. Moreover, Saudi Arabia was not concerned about its market share. It seems more likely that the Saudi government was concerned to retain its special relationship with the USA and that it really believed higher prices would damage the world economy, weaken the currencies of the industrial countries, especially the dollar, and thus affect adversely not only oil revenues (which were paid in dollars) but also the value of the foreign assets held by the producing countries. Saudi Arabia, together with a few other countries has been unable to spend all of the oil revenues received and has had, therefore, to hold assets abroad. Moreover, many officials increasingly suspected that even the current rate of expenditure was giving rise to unacceptable overheating of the economy, bringing inflation, shortages and other unfortunate economic and social consequences. These worries were intensified after the overthrow of the Shah in an Iranian revolution. Those countries who pressed most strongly for an increase in prices were the countries most desirous of greater revenues but whose rates of output were limited by the state of their oil reserves. In other words, those most likely to want to increase output to obtain higher revenues or a greater share of the market could not in any case increase production enough to endanger OPEC policies, even if they had tried it.

Thus, in spite of surpluses and weak markets, the OPEC countries wanted to raise prices and for some time were prevented from doing so effectively by the reluctance of the largest producer who, at the same time, was willing to absorb a great deal of the slack in demand by accepting a decreased offtake of its own oil. As long as there were surpluses that Saudi Arabia was willing to absorb, it could effectively prevent increases in prices unacceptable to it. But as soon as the market became tight and demand again pressed on total supply, the power of the Saudis to influence prices weakened and disappeared as the limits to their own productive capacity were approached.

After the Iranian revolution the market precipitately turned around once again as the reduction of supply from Iran and the expectation of further reductions and shortages set in train a scramble for oil on the part of consumers. The rise in the market price of oil accelerated and Saudi efforts to moderate it came to nought. By the beginning of 1980 OPEC as a 'price cartel', or 'price administrator' – to use Mabro's terminology[2] – had broken up for all practical purposes. The market had taken over and each OPEC country went its own separate way. The Saudis may continue to sell at lower prices but almost the only result will be to augment the profits of those companies which succeed in obtaining the cheaper oil and in selling it, or its products, at market prices.

The disarray of OPEC following its meeting in Caracas in December 1979 may presage a new stage in the history of the organization. It is too early to say. Undoubtedly, in the longer run, the very high prices together with uncertainty and the desire of consuming countries to reduce their dependence on imports, will encourage the development of new sources of oil and of new sources of energy, and will stimulate 'conservation' in consumption. In time the demand for oil will slacken as a result, but speculation about the position of the individual OPEC producers, their relations with the new non-OPEC producers who may have grown in importance as the older ones decline, or indeed supply conditions generally, cannot now usefully be indulged in. But by then, the immediate job of OPEC will have been finished; the OPEC countries should have further developed and diversified their economies and their international trade if even minimally sensible use has been made of their revenues. Even 20 years from 1980 is too far away to reward attempts to discern the outlines of the international order which by then will have emerged, if any such order is to exist. Suffice it to say that, for the moment at least, one set of raw-material producers has, for better or for worse, brought into being for itself a new international economic order.

OPEC: A SPECIAL CASE?

It should be clear that there are a number of special circumstances surrounding the success of OPEC which are closely related to the particular characteristics of the oil industry, to the geographic distribution of oil reserves in relation to the revenues needs of the different producing countries, to the characteristics of the monopolistic positions obtained by the MNCs and of the oligopolistic rivalry among them, and to the developments in the world economy and in Middle East politics during the first 20 years of OPEC's existence. The fact that the oil industry also displayed characteristics traditionally considered favorable to the formation of a successful cartel — low elasticity of demand, high concentration of control over total production, low medium-term elasticity of outside supply, etc. — was in some respects a necessary condition for OPEC's successful action but is by no means sufficient to explain the course of events.

One may ask why the oil-producing countries did not act in concert much earlier than they did. United action had long been talked about. In fact, they did act with considerable speed considering that it was only after the end of the Second World War that the great oil fields of Saudi Arabia and Kuwait were developed and the oil brought on to the market in large quantities, and that only in the 1960s did the oil of Algeria, Libya and Nigeria come on the scene. The 50/50 agreements to share revenues were made only in 1950-51 and the decade had hardly passed before OPEC was born. In the late 1940s some of the largest producers were very little developed politically and it is not surprising that they took some time to obtain the confidence required to move against the notoriously powerful oil MNCs, which were believed to be firmly linked with, and backed by their own governments, among the strongest in the world. (Whether or not such reputations and beliefs were justified is, of course, beside the point.) In addition, all of the countries had been receiving very large revenues and, in most of them, the sources of discontent were few. Indeed, left to themselves it is unlikely that either Saudi Arabia or Kuwait would have joined in the cry against the oil companies when they did; their willingness to undertake concerted action with other oil producers was in the beginning motivated as much as anything by political expediency.

To imitate OPEC would clearly be extremely difficult for other producers, given all these particular aspects of OPEC's history. Apart from a fuller appreciation of the importance of such conditions as concentration of production, likemindedness of producers, conditions of substitution and other factors affecting elasticities of demand and supply, favorable market conditions, etc., is there anything else to be gained for others in a study of the OPEC experience? Not much, I am afraid, that is not already well enough understood.

Initially, part of OPEC's success was due to the willingness of at least one radical producer, Libya, to be extremely bold and to take risks. But the time was right; Iraq had acted even more drastically against its concessionnaire in the early 1960s and fully nationalized the Iraq Petroleum Company somewhat later, but Iraq's actions did not spark off any serious move on the part of others. The time was not right then and Iraq suffered the losses alone for nearly a decade. Nevertheless, without great confidence and risky action, OPEC's successes of the early 1970s would have had to wait longer to be achieved.

Of more importance perhaps was the tacit cooperation of the companies. Such cooperation was not deliberate, nor was it due to any desire on the part of the oil MNCs to encourage OPEC countries. Rather it was the result of their fear that open confrontation with or challenge to the governments was a greater risk and might result in greater losses than cautious appeasement in the form of firm but conciliatory bargaining. Some observers of the industry hold that Libya's successes in the early 1970s were attributable to the weakness of the new companies who had established themselves there and who, having a lesser degree of integration and fewer sources of oil than the established majors, had more to lose from a struggle with the Libyan Government. They therefore were more ready to concede the government's demands. There is a good deal of truth in this, but of more importance, in my view, was the rivalry among the majors themselves, and between the majors and the newcomers, which prevented the formation of a common front by the companies.

In any case confrontation risking a breakdown of talks was avoided in spite of periods of brinkmanship. This was a great advantage to OPEC since the MNCs were still needed to produce much of their oil and to provide technology and training. The companies also dominated downstream markets, and their cooperation helped the governments in the transition from dependence on the MNCs to the direct management of their own sales. OPEC's experience suggests that in circumstances where MNCs will continue to be important for either their inputs in production or in marketing, producers on the road to establishing their own control may find it useful to try various combinations of sticks and carrots to obtain at least the acquiescence of the MNCs to their preliminary moves.

This, of course, implies that the MNCs become convinced that more is to be gained by acquiescence than by outright resistance. Hence, they must be offered something; it may also be possible when several companies are involved to play them off against each other (and against potentially dangerous outsiders), exploiting their individual weaknesses. There is, of course, some danger in this for a developing country which runs the risk of being out-manoeuvred by the MNCs. Nevertheless, a government might be wise to be wary of the advice of some 'Southern separatists' (sometimes called 'delinkers') who would cut off an LDC nose to spite a capitalist face.

But the chief problems are, as always, likely to arise over the distribution of market shares once a cartel is formed and in operation. Here the experience of OPEC is so tied-up with the special distribution of oil reserves among its members, the distribution of oil revenues, and the distribution of 'absorptive capacity' or 'need' for revenues, that it provides no model. Few other industries can easily produce a 'Saudi Arabia' — a 'swing' producer willing to maintain a reference price by itself, absorbing the swings of the market in variations of its own output and revenues.

NOTES

1. Cf. Albert Fishlow, 'Saudi Arabia, with less need for immediate revenues, has shown itself unwilling to raise the price of petroleum in order to maximize the development potential of Iran and Venezuela *at the continuing expense of its own potentially larger sales*' (Italics added); A. Fishlow, C.F. Diaz-Alejandro, R.R. Fagen (eds), *Rich and Poor Nations in the World Economy* (New York: McGraw Hill, 1978), 34.
2. See Robert Mabro, 'The Dilemma Between Short-and-Long-Term Oil Prices' (Paper delivered at the Fourth International Symposium on Petroleum Economics, Groupe de Recherche en Economie de l'Energie, Université Laval, Quebec, Canada, October 1979).

16

RECYCLING AND SUBSTITUTION

N. Iwase

Recycling and substitution have been an integral part of the supply and consumption patterns of mineral resources for some time, but in the past have not received much attention, except in emergencies.

The situation has been changing in recent years and it is becoming increasingly clear that recycling and substitution will play essential roles in any efforts to conserve energy and resources and to protect the environment. Producers of primary metals, however, sometimes regard recycling and substitution as potential threats, on the grounds that increased secondary production may result in a reduction in their exports and in lower prices for primary metals.

RECYCLING

To recycle is to return waste to economic usefulness. Waste — either as by-product of various production processes or as residue of products which have ended their economic service lives — is material that is useless in its current state. Metals are recyclable to the extent that they can be recovered from waste, and for this reason their recovery is often referred to as 'mining above ground'.

The Structure of Secondary Industries

There is a fairly well-established classification of scrap metals based on their sources: 'home' scrap; 'prompt industrial', or 'new' scrap; and 'old', or 'obsolete' scrap. Home scrap is generated in the smelting, casting and manufacturing processes and re-used within the same corporate entity; thus, producers and users of home scrap are the same. Prompt industrial scrap also originates in a production process but passes through commercial transactions. Old scrap is metal recovered from products whose economic service life has terminated. The term

---

A more extensive discussion of this topic is to be found in the *Report of the Secretary-General* (UN, Committee on Natural Resources, E/C.7/101, 11 April 1979); much of this paper is derived from this source. The views expressed here are those of the author and do not necessarily reflect those of the organization by which she is employed.

Notes to this chapter may be found on page 279.

Fig. 16. 1. *The flow of scrap in the system of mineral production and consumption*

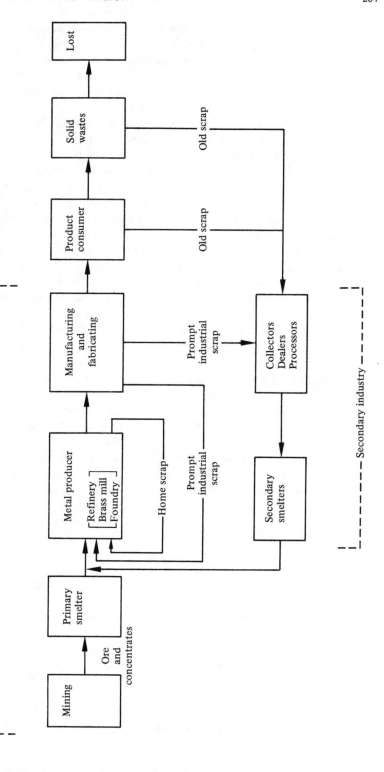

'purchased' scrap refers to both prompt industrial and old scrap, traded within a country or internationally (see Fig. 16.1).

It is obvious that both home and prompt industrial scrap are recycled first. Actually, they cannot be regarded as net additions to supply, because they have not been used in final form; the metal merely takes longer to reach the stage of final consumption. Conceptually, the distinction between home scrap and prompt industrial scrap is useful. Yet in most cases, with the exception of ferrous scrap, home scrap is not separately reported. Therefore, the main focus of this paper will be on purchased scrap, i.e. prompt industrial scrap and old scrap, whose recovery is a function of economic, social and institutional factors. Because the availability of data varies from metal to metal and also from country to country, however, statistics here presented are fragmentary, not always fully comparable, and limited mostly to countries with developed market economies.

Secondary industries collect economically recoverable wastes, and process and sell them to consumers of secondary materials; they thus form an institutional framework for returning wastes to economic usefulness.[1] The suppliers of scrap include manufacturing plants, public and private utilities, dismantlers, governmental agencies and households. Household scrap is the most troublesome, because it requires a great deal of cleaning and sorting.

Proper and accurate identification and sorting of scrap are the key stages in recycling, an activity that to a large extent still requires human judgment and remains labor-intensive. After being identified, materials may go through cleaning, cutting, bailing and bundling procedures before being sold, either through brokers or intermediary merchants or directly to scrap consumers.

Non-ferrous scrap is consumed by primary and secondary smelters, refiners, ingot makers, brass mills and foundries. Both primary and secondary smelters have facilities for upgrading all grades of prompt industrial and old scrap. Secondary smelters are important in the sense that generally they rely solely on scrap as input. Secondary smelters and refiners operate on a larger scale than wholesale scrap merchants, although for a manufacturing industry the scale is relatively small.[2] Ingot makers, brass makers and foundries, on the other hand, basically have only re-melting facilities. Understandably, this group tends to prefer high-grade and clean scrap, particularly prompt industrial scrap, whose chemical composition is wellknown. There are two forms of secondary product: refined metal and alloy ingot, depending on the nature of the scrap.

Ferrous scrap is also classified into home, prompt industrial and old scrap. The amount of home scrap in the total consumption of ferrous scrap varies from country to country, depending on the type and efficiency of the production process. Generally, between 40 and 60 per cent is home scrap, and the remainder is purchased ferrous scrap, i.e. prompt industrial and old scrap. The principal use of ferrous scrap is as a metal-bearing raw material in electric, open-hearth and basic oxygen furnaces, to produce raw steel. The demand for ferrous scrap, consequently, is determined by the level of crude-steel production and the technology of each production process. Although there is some flexibility in the relative amount of scrap used, each process has a different typical scrap-use ratio: the electric furnace can use virtually 100 per cent scrap, whereas the basic-oxygen furnace generally uses about 20-30 per cent.

The Pricing System and International Trade

The market for much non-ferrous scrap is complex and involves the negotiation of prices between scrap dealers and consumers. Secondary smelters and custom smelters seeking additional feed will offer prices based on operating costs and profit objectives. Dealers will set prices according to what the market will bear, although some indication of price may be taken from published quotations.[3] The value of the scrap also depends on the metal content, preparation costs, and expectation of future primary metal prices.

Prices of scrap are generally more volatile than those of primary metals. A study in the United States showed that secondary materials have roughly 1.5 to two times as high a degree of price variability as the primary metal.[4] Since it takes a long time to expand smelter facilities or develop new mines, producers tend to increase their intake of scrap to substitute for primary metals when the market is tight, which pushes up scrap prices. On the other hand, when demand slackens, scrap purchases are the first to be curtailed because they are usually not on long-term contracts as often as are primary metals.

In international markets, trade in scrap, like that in any other commodity, depends on the balance between domestic supply and demand at the prevailing price. In fact, a considerable amount of ferrous and non-ferrous scrap is traded internationally. In 1975, 1.6 billion dollar's worth of ferrous scrap was exported within MECs, as compared with 5.1 billion dollar's worth of iron ore. Exports of non-ferrous metal scrap — about one-third of which was copper scrap — amounted to 1.3 billion dollar's worth in the same year. Exports and imports of scrap are more volatile than those of primary ores.

The world-wide recession in 1975 and 1976 reduced exports of scrap sharply. In contrast, the total value of exports of iron ore increased steadily even after the world economy turned sluggish.

Most scrap is traded between DCs. In 1976, 95 per cent and 87 per cent of ferrous and non-ferrous scrap exports. respectively, originated in those countries (see Table 16.1). Unfortunately, data on the trade, broken down by prompt industrial and old scrap or by grade, are not available.[5] Although ferrous scrap is still imported largely by DCs, it is noteworthy that the share of LDCs in total imports of ferrous scrap has been gradually increasing, from nine per cent in 1967 to 16 per cent in 1976.[6] Since a number of LDCs are starting or increasing domestic steel production and the level of scrap collection is low, exports of ferrous scrap to those countries is expected to increase.

The Importance of Secondary Supplies

It is useful now to consider the factors which determine the supply of scrap and, in turn, the level of scrap recovery and secondary production.

Table 16.1. *World exports and imports of scrap, DCs and LDCs, 1976*
           (Percentage)

Kind of scrap	Exports	Imports
Iron and steel scrap		
DCs	95.3	84.1
LDCs	4.7	15.9
Non-ferrous metal scrap		
DCs	84.3	94.1
LDCs	15.7	5.9
Copper scrap		
DCs	89.3	89.1
LDCs	10.7	10.9

Source: Yearbook of International Trade Statistics, 1977, Vol. II, *Trade by Commodity* (New York: UN, E.78.XVII.14).

Because prompt industrial scrap is generated in fabricating and manufacturing processes, its availability depends largely on the current demand for refined metals and on the production of fabricated products, the level of which, in turn, depends on general economic activity. The other important factor is the technology employed in the fabricating and manufacturing processes, which determines the percentage of prompt industrial scrap generated. The supply of prompt industrial scrap will be curtailed if technological developments improve efficiency. Although a high price of scrap encourages the supply of prompt industrial scrap, the price elasticity appears to be low.

Various other factors influence the collection and recovery of old scrap. First of all, the quantities of metal which are accumulated in end-use products determine the overall size of potentially available metals. This potential reserve of old scrap becomes available for recycling only when these products terminate their useful lives. The length of the service life of end products varies; consequently, the age distribution of end-use products, combined with their varied compositions, makes it difficult to estimate the size of potential old scrap at a given time.

Potential scrap reserves will be recycled only if recycling is economical. The price of scrap influences the supply of old scrap, which appears to have a higher price elasticity than that of prompt industrial scrap. Higher prices make it profitable to recover metals from low-quality scrap, from miscellaneous scrap in small lot sizes, or from scrap located at greater distance.

A reduction in the cost of recycling has the same effect on the supply of old scrap as an increase in the price. The cost of recycling changes in accordance with the quality and composition of scrap, labor costs, transportation costs, the cost of energy and of environmental protection and, of course, as a result of technological development.

In addition to the direct cost of recycling, the cost of waste disposal also affects the level of recycling of old scrap or low-grade industrial wastes. If the cost of disposal is lower than that of recovering wastes, waste utilization may be hindered. Usually, the disposal of wastes is undertaken and regulated by local governmental bodies. Therefore, changes in public policies related to waste management and environmental protection will greatly affect the level of recycling.

Among recycled non-ferrous metals, copper is first in terms of the largest amount of recovered metal and the highest proportion of recycled to total consumption — about 50 per cent. Aluminum is second in terms of the absolute amount recovered from scrap; however, the proportion of recycled to total consumption is low — a little over 20 per cent, similar to that of zinc and tin. Lead has achieved almost as high a level of recovery as copper — about 50 per cent of total consumption. The ratios of recovered metal to total consumption show a slight and gradual decline for copper and tin over the past decade. Aluminum and zinc show more or less stable trends of recovery, and only lead shows higher recovery ratios in recent years (see Table 16.2).

Table 16.2. *Recovery ratios[a] of selected metals, 1967-1977[b]*

Metal	1967	1972	1977	Recovered from scrap (thousands of metric tons)
		%		
Copper	58.7	52.2	47.0	3,210.4
Aluminium	22.0	20.9	22.8	3,260.8
Lead	46.1	44.6	49.7	1,590.8
Zinc	24.0	21.7	21.1	869.8
Tin	35.0	25.1	23.7	41.3

Source: *Metal Statistics, 1967-1977* (Frankfurt am Main: Metallgesellschaft, 1978).

a   Total recovery divided by total consumption.
b   Excluding centrally planned economies.

Current levels of consumption and scrap recovery have a fairly close correlation. High levels of secondary production are concentrated in DCs such as the US, Japan and Western European countries. Whereas data on scrap recovery in most of the LDCs are not available, it may be assumed that such recovery is minimal, since the level of consumption of metals and manufactured products by the LDCs in the past has been low. Considering the commonly long life cycle of products using metal, secondary metals will play a minor role in their metal consumption for many years to come. This does not mean, however, that the LDCs can neglect recycling activities. Secondary industries which require more labor and less capital than primary industries can be advantageous. If the appropriate system of recycling is designed from the beginning, it will help recover metals from scrap efficiently in the long run. It may, however, be necessary to develop technologies which can make a small-scale operation feasible, because the reserve of scrap in the LDCs may be too small to benefit from economies of scale by mechanization, at least in the short run.

The Potential Supply of Scrap

It is interesting to examine the relative importance of metals recovered from prompt industrial scrap and from old scrap. Unfortunately, most countries which report secondary production do not differentiate their sources. The only data available are for the US in 1976 (see Table 16.3). For copper, aluminum and zinc, a large portion, ranging from 60 to 75 per cent, is recovered from prompt industrial scrap. In contrast, about 85 per cent of secondary lead and 60 per cent of the tin recovered from old scrap is obtained from old copper alloy scrap.

Table 16.3. *US: recovery from prompt industrial and old scrap, 1976*

Metal	Total recovery (thousands of short tons)	Recovery from prompt industrial scrap (%)	Recovery from old scrap (%)
Copper	1,145	63	37
Aluminum	1,155	70	30
Lead	727	14	86
Zinc	373	75	25
Tin	181	39	61

Source: Preprint of *Mineral Yearbook, 1976* (US Bureau of Mines, Washington, D.C.: Government Printing Office, 1976).

Virtually all home and prompt industrial scrap is already being recovered, due to its high quality and known composition. Table 16.4 illustrates this fact for the United Kingdom. Among total identified losses of metals, old scrap accounts for 95 per cent for copper, 99 per cent for aluminum and 93 per cent for tin. The remaining five, one and seven per cent, respectively, represent losses generated during pyrometallurgical processes and electrolytic refining. The shares of old scrap in the total losses for zinc and lead are relatively low, because considerable amounts of those metals are lost as pyrometallurgical residues which are not considered as old scrap.

Table 16.4 also shows the ratios of losses of non-industrial scrap, mainly domestic wastes and uncollected old scrap. Non-industrial scrap constitutes a significantly large portion of the total losses of copper, aluminum and tin — 82 per cent, 91 per cent and 65 per cent, respectively. On the other hand, for zinc and lead, the losses of non-industrial scrap account for less than half of the total losses.

Since most prompt industrial scrap is already being recovered, the potential for increasing secondary production is greatest in old scrap. To provide a rough indication of the level of magnitude, recycling rates of old scrap in the US in 1970 are shown in Table 16.5. The percentage of recoverable scrap actually recycled is derived from the amount of recycled old scrap divided by the total amount of recoverable old scrap (i.e. old scrap discarded minus old scrap lost). As the table shows, substantial percentages of lead and copper — 68 per cent

Table 16.4. *UK: Losses of Non-Ferrous Metals*[a]*(Metric tons per annum)*

	Copper	Aluminium	Zinc	Lead	Tin
Total identified losses	78,900	131,300	91,800	17,400	10,800
Losses of old scrap	75,000 (95)	130,000 (99)	40,000 (44)	11,000 (63)	10,000 (93)
Losses of non-industrial scrap	65,000 (82)	120,000 (91)	43,000 (47)	8,000 (46)	7,000 (65)

Source: L. Whalley and V.E. Broadie, 'UK metal reclamation: prospects for improvement', *Resources Policy*, 3, 4 (December 1977), 243-260.

a   Figures in parentheses are percentages.

Table 16.5. *US: Old Scrap Recycling Rates, 1970 (Thousands of short tons)*

Metal	Discarded	Lost[a]	Old scrap Available	Recycled	Recoverable scrap recycled (%)
Copper	1,611	97	1,514	644	42.5
Aluminium	1,334	183	1,151	175	15.2
Lead	1,416	541	875	595	68.0
Zinc	1,065	900	165	43	25.8
Iron and steel	57,053	8,558	48,495	14,263	29.4

Source: *Barriers to the Use of Secondary Metals* (Prepared for the US Bureau of Mines, Washington, D.C.: US Government Printing Office, 1977).

a   Old scrap is never available for recycling due to consumptive uses or corrosion losses.

and 43 per cent, respectively — are already recovered from recoverable old scrap. On the other hand, recovery rates from old scrap are notably low for ferrous scrap, zinc, and particularly aluminium (29 per cent, 26 per cent and 15 per cent, respectively). The data for the United Kingdom similarly show that the recovery rate of old scrap from potentially available old scrap is estimated to be relatively high for copper (60 per cent) but low for aluminium (35 per cent).[7]

   The difference in recovery rates of these metals may be partly attributed to the nature of the end-use products. Naturally, the recovery of metals which are found in pure form and in sizeable amounts in old scrap is easier and less costly than the recovery of small quantities of impure metals. Another important factor is the technology of secondary production. Some metals, for example, aluminum, face certain technological difficulties to remove metallic impurities or alloy constituents from the scrap. The length of the service life of goods using metal is also likely to affect recovery rates from old scrap. Because of certain time lags between the periods of consumption and those of scrap recovery, it is shown that the higher the demand for a metal, the smaller the share of secondary supply in the total demand.[8] Thus, rapid growth of demand, together with long service lives of the end products, may explain the lower recovery rate of scrap for some metals.

The factors described above are by no means invariable. Recovery from old scrap is ultimately influenced by economic factors. Even technological constraints may possibly be overcome by strong economic incentives. Estimates of the ratio of actually recovered metal from old scrap to potentially available old scrap are scarce for most countries, and one cannot draw general conclusions from data in one or two countries. Since among countries various differences exist in the structure of secondary industries, governmental policies, and the overall situation with regard to raw materials, the analysis attempted here may not be fully representative.

SUBSTITUTION

The substitution of one metal for another dates back to the very beginning of history. In fact, the ages of human history are labelled in terms of materials substitution − from the stone to the bronze, from the bronze to the iron. Today, substitution has become extremely complicated in DCs, due to advanced technology and widely varied applications.

Types of Substitution

Basically, there are three types of substitution: material; process; and functional. Material substitution is the replacement of one material for another, such as aluminium for copper. This type of substitution, which is of primary concern for the present chapter, is the most commonly discussed. Process substitution results from cost-minimizing efforts and technological development. Functional substitution refers to the substitution of one technique for another which performs the same function. The impact of functional substitution can be so great that an entirely new industry may be created.

It is obvious that these three types of substitution are closely related, but the main emphasis in this paper is on material substitution among major metals, since it is the most important if different materials are compared.

Three types of material substitution can be distinguished: physical; quantitative; and invisible. The physical type is simply the replacement of one material by another; the quantitative type is the reduction of material used per unit of output. Invisible material substitution takes place when a new product entering the market uses materials other than those which would have been used at an earlier time. This type of substitution is often difficult to trace statistically, although it can be clearly shown in some instances − for example, in the automobile industry, when a new model is introduced.

Possible Substitutes for Major Metals

Any one material can have various applications, depending on what is required of it. Substitution of one material for another occurs only if the substitute has properties comparable to those of the original and provides them at lower cost, or when the preferred material becomes scarce or temporarily unavailable because of disruption in the supply.

The metals discussed have both superior and inferior substitutes. Inferior substitutes can only partially satisfy technical requirements. Except in emergency situations, such as war, embargos or physical depletion, substitution by inferior metals is unlikely to occur. On the other hand, there is no doubt that technically superior substitutes will eventually replace materials used at present, although cost factors are still important in deciding actual replacement.

Copper

Copper is vulnerable to substitution by other materials because many of its properties can be matched to a large extent by rival materials. Roughly 50 per cent of the total amount of copper consumed is used in products that carry or generate electricity, namely, power transmission lines, cables, general electrical wires, generators and motors. For these purposes, aluminium is the major potential substitute. Aluminium has two-thirds the conductivity but only one-third the density of copper, and is therefore favored when weight is a factor. Optical fibres are a substitute for copper in the field of telecommunications.

The remaining 50 per cent of all copper consumed goes to various non-electrical sectors, in such items as construction, industrial and transportation equipment, and domestic appliances. Copper pipes can be replaced by stainless steel, protected steel, aluminium and plastics.[9]

Zinc

Of the total amount of zinc consumed, 39 per cent is used for protective coatings on steel, by the common process of galvanizing.[10] Substitutes for galvanized steel are aluminium, plastic-coated steel, stainless steel, aluminium alloys, concrete and plastics. The second largest use of zinc — 27 per cent of total consumption — is in die-casting. Zinc die-cast alloys are suitable for making components that require complexity of shape, close dimensional accuracy and good mechanical properties. The threat of substitution for zinc comes from aluminium, plastics and magnesium. Many types of zinc alloys — mainly brass — are also vulnerable to substitution by aluminium, cast iron and plastics.

Tin

Tin also has characteristics which make it indispensable. Tin-plated steel, however — the 'tin can', which accounts for 45 per cent of total consumption — is facing competition in the packaging industry from aluminium, plastics, glass, paper and tin-free steel, which is steel-coated with a thin chromium/chromium-oxide layer.[11] Solder (21 per cent of total consumption), made of 70 per cent tin and 30 per cent lead — although the actual composition may vary — maintains a fairly safe position because few acceptable substitutes or equally effective processes of joining are available.

Antimony

Substitutes are already technically available for most of the antimony used, although they may be more expensive. Antimony is largely used in storage batteries (47 per cent of total consumption) to harden lead.[12] For this purpose, calcium and tin can replace antimony, while indirect substitution may be possible by the manufacture of batteries not based on the lead-acid technology. For chemicals and pigments (18 per cent), many acceptable substitutes such as titanium, zinc, chromium and zirconium are available.

Lead

Lead-acid batteries use more lead (36 per cent of total consumption) than any other product.[13] Batteries have been developed which operate on nickel-cadmium, zinc-cadmium or other alternative materials, but at present these are more expensive than lead-acid ones. The high recycling rate of lead-acid batteries is also likely to continue to favor the use of lead for batteries. Lead sheet and pipe (16 per cent) have been losing ground to plastics, stainless steel, and fiber-glass. Lead is also used in anti-knock compounds (12 per cent of total consumption). Although there are no practical alternatives to lead anti-knock compounds, the use of lead for this purpose is expected to decline because of increasingly stringent air pollution controls. Until recently, lead was an important material (11 per cent) in cable sheathing, keeping moisture away from the insulated core of cables. But plastics and aluminium, which are cheaper and stronger, are strong rival materials, particularly in telecommunication cables and low-voltage power cables.

Cobalt

Two major intermediate uses for cobalt are in magnets and alloys (28 per cent of total consumption in each).[14] In permanent magnets, which also contain iron, aluminium and nickel, cobalt is an essential component (5-50 per cent) and cannot be replaced without a loss of magnetic properties. The cobalt in high-temperature alloys could be replaced by molybdenum, vanadium and tungsten, and cobalt-containing alloys by nickel-based alloys and ceramics. As a paint drier (13 per cent), cobalt compounds may be replaced by manganese, chromium and copper. In binding tungsten and other carbides used in machine tools, however, no acceptable substitute for cobalt has been developed.

Tungsten

Tungsten has unique properties such as hardness, toughness, and resistance to corrosion and wear. A little over 50 per cent of all tungsten[15] is used in the form of tungsten carbides for lathes, milling cutters, drills and other tools which require hardness at high temperatures, strength and resistance to wear. For these purposes, titanium carbide, tantalum carbide and niobium carbide may be possible substitutes in some cases. The next largest application of tungsten is in steels alloy (23 per cent). In the category of tool steels, tungsten may be replaced by molybdenum, but in the superalloys used for gas turbine parts and the cast alloys used for hard-facing, no satisfactory substitute for tungsten is currently available.

Manganese

A great deal of manganese is used as a desulphurizer and deoxidizer in the manufacture of steel. It is also used as agent in alloys, to increase hardness and toughness. Titanium, zirconium and molybdenum are some of the possible substitutes but they cannot individually provide the wide variety of properties of manganese, are not produced in sufficient quantity, and are much more expensive.[16]

Nickel

Nickel is mainly used as an agent in alloys to impart strength, toughness, and resistance to heat and corrosion. In the most important of the nickel alloys, stainless steel, the nickel content ranges from six to 22 per cent and represents 41 per cent of the total amount consumed. The other major application for nickel is electroplating (16 per cent). Direct substitution by chromium, manganese, molybdenum, cobalt or titanium for nickel in alloys seems unlikely to take place because of the technical superiority of nickel.[17] Nickel may be replaced indirectly, however, as in the case of stainless steel, being replaced by plastics and aluminium.

Factors Determining the Use of Substitutes

The mere existence of technically acceptable substitutes — although a prerequisite for substitution — obviously does not guarantee that substitution will actually take place.

In the MECs, the foremost factors, which are closely related and should, in most cases, be considered together, have been physical performance and economics. Without doubt, a manufacturer will be willing to use a substitute material if the resultant product has the same performance record and costs less, or is better and costs no more than the original product.

Among economic factors one of the significant considerations is the relative price of substitutes. It should be noted here that the price per unit of property is the important factor, not the nominal relative prices per unit weight.

It is very rare for direct substitution of one material for another not to involve changes in production processes and product designs. Therefore, what has to be carefully examined is not only the relative price of alternative materials but also the total cost of making the substitution, including necessary capital investment for retooling, the introduction of new manufacturing processes, and the lead time required for various changes, usually at least several years. In other words, long-term relative price is an important consideration, and unless an industry expects the price of a given material, currently in use, to remain high relative to its substitute for a long time in the future, substitution will not pay off.

Although physical performance and the reduction of costs are the major factors in the decision to use or not to use substitutes, there are many other relevant considerations, among them governmental regulations relating to environmental quality, energy conservation, health and safety.

Temporary supply shortages and the fear of physical depletion are other factors which may lead to substitution. Supply shortages can be created by sudden increases in demand, disruption in production caused by strikes, wars and other kinds of economic and political strife. Cobalt and chromium exemplify minerals that may be vulnerable to economic and political disturbances, because their major producers are limited to a small number of countries.

The necessary new technology is not always available to cope with material shortages, particularly if the materials have certain critical and specific properties, not easily or readily provided by substitutes. To develop new technology or to redesign manufacturing processes requires a long lead time as well as costly investment in research. Therefore, if an industry expects or foresees supply shortages or physical depletion, research and development efforts must be initiated well in advance, and actual substitution may take place even after the causal factors have disappeared. Naturally, the expectation of a supply shortage tends to be formed during periods of high prices.

Finally, the desire to substitute domestically available materials for imported ones arises for various reasons: balance-of-payments constraints; fears of disruption in supply and international trade by embargoes or price-gouging. Some governments may wish to decrease their dependence on imports of critical materials for strategic reasons, or in order to have a freer hand in formulating their own foreign policy.

CONCLUSIONS

Recycling and substitution are closely related in a complex way. Since secondary metals are close substitutes for primary metals, even short-term changes in their relative prices may easily induce the substitution of one for the other.

The prices of primary metals appear to have considerable influence on both substitution and the production of secondary metals. If the price of a certain metal is kept high, relative to that of rival materials, substitution may take place. High prices of primary metal make it profitable to recycle low-grade scrap, and this will lead to higher secondary production. In both cases, the primary metal in question may lose some of its market to substitutes and secondary metal.

Appropriate technology for secondary production and the processing of scrap is essential if a higher recovery of metals from scrap is to be attained. If, for technical reasons, secondary metals fail to meet required specifications, they will lose their market to primary products. In the case of substitution, technological development is even more essential. Usually substitution, involving the promotion of new uses and applications in order to expand markets, requires extensive and continuous research. Efforts to develop recycling technology and technical possibilities for substitution should continue to be made, at international and national levels.

NOTES

1. *Operation in the Nonferrous Scrap Metal Industry Today* (New York: National Association of Recycling Industries, 1973), 4-5.

2. Richard Gordon *et al.*, *Effective Systems of Scrap Utilization: Copper, Aluminium and Nickel* (University Park, Pennsylvania State University, 1972), 60.

3. For example, *American Metal Market* (New York, daily) and *Iron Age* (Radnor, Pa., weekly) quote ferrous and non-ferrous scrap prices.

4. Roger Dower and Robert Anderson, 'Future markets: an alternative for stabilizing secondary materials market?', *Resources Policy*, 3, 4 (December 1977), 230-236. The coefficient of variation, which is used as a measure of the relative variation in a data series, is calculated by dividing the standard deviation by the mean.

5. In the case of copper, 'industry sources believe that old scrap constitutes the larger share of exports'. Elizabeth Bonczar and John Tilton, *An Economic Analysis of the Determinants of Metal Recycling in the United States: A Case Study of Secondary Copper* (University Park, Pennsylvania State University, 1975), 44.

6. *Yearbook of International Trade Statistics, 1976*, Vol. II, *Trade by Commodity* (New York: UN, Sales No. E.77.XVII.14).

7. L. Whalley and V.E. Broadie, 'UK metal reclamation: prospects for improvements', *Resources Policy*, 3, 4 (December 1977), 240.

8. Marian Radetzki and Lars Svensson, 'Can scrap save us from depletion?', *Natural Resources Forum*, 3, 4 (1979), 365-378.

9. *Rational Use of Potentially Scarce Metals* (Report of a NATO Science Committee Study Group. Brussels: NATO Scientific Affairs Division, 1976), 52.

10. *Ibidem*. The percentages are averages of seven major Western countries in 1972-1973.

11. *Ibidem*. The percentages are for DCs in 1968.

12. *Ibidem*. The percentages are for the USA in 1970-1974.

13. *Ibidem*. The percentages are for DCs in 1969.

14. *Ibidem*. The percentages are for the USA in 1970-1974.

15. *Ibidem*. The percentages are for the world in 1974, excluding CPEs.

16. David Brooks, *Low-Grade and Non-Conventional Sources of Manganese* (Washington, D.C.: Resources for the Future, 1966), 51-52.

17. John Camaron, *Investment in the Nickel Industry, 1950-1975* (Washington, D.C.: National Science Foundation, 1976), 9, 16. The percentages are estimates for world nickel consumption excluding CPEs.

PART III

TOWARDS BETTER MINING POLICIES FOR DEVELOPMENT

17

LDC POLICIES TOWARDS FOREIGN MINERAL INVESTORS

M. Radetzki

This chapter deals with those LDCs which are heavily dependent on the non-fuel mineral industry. Its purpose is to discuss the policy options of the governments of such countries towards the foreign parties involved in the development and exploitation of their mineral resources. Minerals play a very important role in numerous LDCs (see Table 1.4). In countries such as these, economic and social progress may stand or fall depending on the appropriateness of policies towards the minerals sector designed and executed by the government.

Only a general overview of the feasible policy choices can be provided in the present paper. While such an overview should be instructive for a general policy delineation, the reader has to be warned that in concrete situations the merit of specific policies to be introduced must always be judged on the basis of prevailing circumstances in the particular context and time.

The following discussion assumes that all national involvements in the minerals sector in LDCs are also public involvements. This does not greatly distort reality. Although private national mineral interests exist in some LDCs, they are dwarfed in most cases by the public national interest in this field.

Profound foreign involvement is a typical feature in the mineral endeavors of LDCs. In consequence, most of our analysis concentrates on the policy aspects relating to the foreign parties which participate in the mineral development work.

The mineral sector policies of LDCs must be seen in the broader framework of overall national development policies and goals. Broadly speaking, national development goals can be said to consist of (a) growth as such, but also of the establishment of capacities needed to permit the country to initiate and pursue independent national growth policies; (b) distribution of the benefits of growth among major population strata; and (c) economic diversification, to help the country avoid the disadvantages and risks of one-sided dependence. These major goals can be dissolved into a number of sub-goals of special relevance in the formulation of policies for the minerals sector. Such sub-goals may include increases in earnings of foreign exchange, in government revenue and in the

Financial support from the Bank of Sweden Tercentenary Fund for the present work is gratefully acknowledged.

Notes to this chapter may be found on pages 295-296.

volume of investments; creation of employment; training of local talent and institution building; expansion of domestic mineral processing; more diversity in terms of the foreign companies involved in mineral exploitation activities; and a greater variety of export markets.

NATIONAL BASES FOR AN INDEPENDENT MINERAL POLICY

Four major factors are needed to make a mineral exploitation venture a viable economic proposition. Firstly, there is a need for the mineral resource itself. Secondly, ample access to expertise and technology is required, both during the investment stage and later in running the venture. Thirdly, capital is needed to finance the investment. And fourthly, it is necessary to ensure a market for the output.

Mineral-endowed LDCs, while holding sovereign control over the national resource, commonly lack, to a larger or smaller degree, the other factors required for profitable exploitation. Hence, such countries regularly have to seek a collaborative working arrangement with a foreign mining firm which can provide the required technology, capital and marketing competence. Additional arrangements have to be worked out, commonly by active intermediation of mining MNCs, with international financial institutions which supplement the MNCs' capital contribution, and with the governments of mineral-importing countries, to assure undisturbed market access for the output produced.

The foreign parties involve themselves in mineral projects of developing countries in the pursuit of their own objectives. Thus, mining and financial MNCs pursue global after-tax profit maximization in the long run, subject to the side conditions that complicated management problems and excessive risks are persistently avoided, while mineral-importing DCs aim at ensuring themselves a steady mineral supply at favorable prices to satisfy their national needs.

Clearly, these objectives differ from, and may conflict with, the development goals of the mineral-endowed countries. The more dependent an LDC is on foreign factors, the more it will have to subordinate itself to foreign wishes and the less freedom it will be able to exercise in choosing and executing policies to satisfy national objectives. In a situation where appropriate national inputs are not available, the only feasible way for the government to shape events is by inducing its foreign partners, through pecuniary or other offers, to follow its desires. The major theme in the following discussion is how LDCs can go about acquiring greater freedom for national policy formulation in the mineral field.

There are, by and large, two avenues open towards a lessening of dependence and increasing freedom of action for governments in mineral exporting LDCs. One is through efforts to create institutions and competences within the nation, which can supply the required inputs. The other is to seek or create conditions where the government can coerce foreign parties to comply with its wishes, with little or no damage to itself. Each avenue implies strengthening the government's bargaining position vis-à-vis its foreign partners. Combinations of the two avenues will of course be common.

Conscious efforts to increase national technological competence are time-consuming but necessary in order to reduce a country's dependence on the MNCs. Varied degrees of such competence are required to accomplish different purposes.

A somewhat limited technological competence level is needed if a country wants to make efficient use of an alternative source of technology which competes with that supplied by mining MNCs. This alternative is provided by a variety of consultants and equipment manufacturers, in disembodied forms such as turnkey projects, management contracts, etc., without foreign equity participation. Basic technological competence that enables government institutions to judge the quality of alternative suppliers, to control the execution of their commitments, and to tag on and take over where foreign obligations end, is preconditional to enable the government to benefit from such alternative technology suppliers. In countries like Guinea, Liberia or Papua New Guinea which have not yet developed much of a national technological base in the minerals field, attempts to use technology separate from a total foreign direct investment package could easily end in economic disaster. Countries like Peru and Malaysia, on the other hand, appear to have reached the level of national technological advancement required to make successful use of such 'unbundled' technology transfers.

The degree of independence vis-à-vis foreign technology suppliers can become still greater with further progress in national technological capacities. In such countries as Brazil, Chile or the Philippines, mineral ventures can be established and run under national management, with very little foreign personnel involvement, and with physical foreign technology inputs required only on a piecemeal basis to supplement nationally available supplies.

As mineral-exporting LDCs progress economically, they may also become less dependent on foreign finance in the execution of mineral investments. A greater degree of financial independence can result from the establishment of national financial institutions which, in addition to encouraging national savings, have the capacity of diversifying the sources of foreign capital inflow, and of seeking out the ones whose lending conditions best satisfy national needs.[1] Brazil and Mexico have reached such levels of financial sophistication, with ensuing reductions of one-sided financial dependence.

Dependence on a single market can also create constraints on national policy. In the years after independence, Zaire and Zambia were extremely dependent on Belgium and the UK as buyers of their mineral output. Hence, careful consideration had to be given to the marketing repercussions before taking any important decision on mineral activity. Such concerns become less grave where national marketing institutions have succeeded in spreading the mineral exports more evenly among many markets. Further policy independence in this field is reached where a mineral nation develops an internal consumption market for a sizeable part of total output. Brazil, Iran and Mexico have gone some way in that direction.

The second avenue towards an increase in the freedom of action of a mineral-exporting nation is by creating conditions where foreign parties can be coerced to comply with the exporting government's wishes. In some cases, such conditions come naturally, without any effort on the part of the government. In others, conscious and elaborate measures are needed to create the required circumstances.

A limited and short-run ability to coerce arises where the MNC has become tied to the exporting country by commitments of investment funds. By threatening to nationalize the MNC's assets, the government can force through concessions from the company up to a value equal to the return on the investments.[2] The squeezed company, however, may react by an unwillingness to maintain its investment position in the country. By not reinvesting, the amount of net return and the maximum concessions that the MNC is willing to provide will be reduced over time. This issue will be discussed again later.

Some degree of national technological, financial and marketing competence is required for the successful exercise of a threat of nationalization. If the threatening nation has no such competence at all, the MNC will have little fear of nationalization, knowing that its services are indispensable in any case. The need for Zaire to reinvite the former Belgian owner, Union Minière, on a very profitable management contract soon after nationalization of the copper mines, is a relevant case in point.

A similarly limited but long-run case for coercion arises where the foreign-owned mining venture secures higher than normal profits on account of the economic superiority of the mineral deposit. In this case, the company can be forced to use its excess profits as the government desires. Such an arrangement may be made permanent, since the firm can be assumed to undertake necessary reinvestments so long as it is allowed to make a normal return on the overall capital which it has invested.

Wider-ranging coercion usually requires a degree of resource monopoly power on the part of the mineral exporting country. This monopoly power will be greater, the higher the country's share of world supply and the lower the price elasticities of demand and of other supplies.[3] If used excessively to benefit the supplier, the monopoly power would tend to be reduced over time. Long-run price elasticities are regularly higher than the short-run ones. Consumers turn to substitutes and alternative producers emerge if the supply conditions imposed by the monopolist become too tough.

While individual mineral exporting countries typically account for too small a share of global supply to wield much monopoly power in the world market, there is always the possibility for several such countries to band together for the purpose of achieving this end. OPEC, whose thirteen members account for 84 per cent of world petroleum exports, provides a clear-cut illustration of successful collaboration of this kind. More recently, nine copper producing countries (53 per cent of world exports), have initiated collaboration within CIPEC, eleven bauxite producers (92 per cent of world exports) have formed IBA, and ten iron ore exporters (44 per cent of world exports) collaborate within AIEC.[4]

A dominant market position is a necessary but not sufficient condition for wielding monopoly power beyond the short run. Other prerequisites include a degree of homogeneity among the partners of the group and, as in the dominant single exporter case, low price elasticities of demand and of outsiders' supply in the medium and longer run. In the case of the OPEC group, all these conditions are reasonably fulfilled. For the other groups of mineral producers, the situation is less clear on some counts.[5] It is indubitable, however, that the bargaining position of each individual member country vis-à-vis the foreign parties can be strengthened considerably when negotiations take place collectively rather than on an individual national basis. This is due both to the increased market power of the group, and to the fact that the producer-country collaboration affords technical and other exchanges between the group's members, thus reducing the need to rely on mining MNCs and other outside institutions.

The discussion in this section suggests a regular sequence of mineral sector policies which commonly emerge as the LDC becomes increasingly emancipated and able to assert its own desires over events. This sequence is illustrated in Fig. 17.1.

Figure 17.1. *Alternative Routes for Establishing National Control over the Mineral Sector*

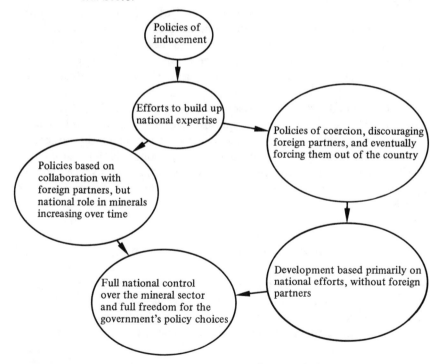

At the time of political independence, LDCs have regularly been highly dependent on foreign partners for the management of their mineral sectors. In such circumstances, government's hands have been relatively tied, and the only policies which could be implemented with reasonable success have been those of inducement.

In its attempt to obtain a better grip over the national economy, the government is likely to undertake efforts at building up national expertise and institutions, in order to widen the feasible policy options in the mineral field.

With a gradual buildup of the national resources required in running mineral activities, the government can choose between one of two options for its continued mineral policies. The first one (left-hand loop of Fig. 17.1) is to maintain close collaboration with the foreign partners, but to assure a gradual increase in its involvement and control as the national competence build-up is continued.

This sequence ends by the government having acquired all the control it desires over the sector. This may imply either that the foreign partners have been phased-out completely or that they are relied upon only for limited and well-defined tasks. It may also mean that the MNCs continue to play a more important role but that over time they have developed stronger loyalties to the host country. The possibility of a transfer of loyalties by extractive MNCs should not surprise us, given the overriding dependence of such firms on access to rich natural resource assets. A process of this kind appears to be taking place in the petroleum field.

The second government option, once a base of national expertise has been established is to adopt policies of coercion, making life difficult for the foreign parties, and eventually forcing them to leave (right-hand loop of Fig. 17.1).

The next step for countries which choose this option is to continue their mineral development without foreign involvement. The eventual outcome of this policy option will also be full government control.

The following discussion is structured along the lines of Fig. 17.1, starting with the policies of inducement and distinguishing between economic and political inducements. Further analysis is made of the approaches to, and implications of, various policies of coercion. In conclusion, attention is given to the problems likely to be experienced by mineral exporting LDCs which choose to develop their minerals activities without or with only limited involvement of foreign partners.

HOW AND WHEN TO PROVIDE ECONOMIC INDUCEMENTS

A variety of policies can be pursued by a LDC government to induce foreign partners such as mining or financial MNCs into desirable behavior. In the choice between inducements those measures should be adopted which provide the maximum incentive effect with a minimum of social cost to the country.

First there is the policy tool of taxation. Taxes can be used in innumerable ways to induce desirable behavior. A temporary income tax holiday could, for instance, be an efficient measure to attract mining MNCs to undertake investments in mining in the country. In many cases, tax holidays have been extended over the entire period during which the project repays its loans, with the purpose of making lenders more willing to provide required credits.[6] Other temporary fiscal incentives could have the form of provisions for fast depreciation of capital assets, or exemptions from import duties for the capital equipment required to carry out the investment program.

More permanent tax incentives may be needed, for instance, to alleviate the MNC's feeling of political uncertainty. Government guarantees that the level of taxation will not arbitrarily be changed could be another helpful measure for the same purpose.

Important advantages can sometimes be derived by determining tax incentives in close consultation with the foreign firms. Given the different tax structures in the countries where the firms maintain operations, such consultations may reveal possibilities to design the provisions so that the MNC obtains a saving in its global tax burden, with a minimum loss in tax revenue to the host country. Where the MNC's head office is permitted to offset the taxes of its foreign subsidiaries against the tax paid at home, most of the tax incentives outlined above would be ineffective in reducing the fiscal burden to the firm, and merely shift the tax income to the DCs. Subsidies would be a more purposeful tool than tax reductions in these circumstances.

There is a special advantage in providing government subsidies to such activities of the foreign mining firms which have positive external effects. Training of personnel and establishment of infrastructural facilities are two cases in point. Subsidies for such purposes constitute a special encouragement to the firm to expand training and infrastructural installations. When trained personnel leave the firm to take up other jobs, there is a benefit to society, which is external to the firm. As other industries use the power or transport facilities established by the minerals venture, a similar positive external effect ensues. Hence, subsidies of the kind considered here are likely to carry smaller net social costs than subsidies in general.

As an alternative to the above subsidies, the government could lower the operating costs of the firms by establishing training activities and infrastructural installations of its own and then providing the foreign-managed minerals industry with the trained personnel without charging for the training, and with infrastructural services at rates below full cost coverage.

The permissive environmental legislation in many LDCs can be seen as a subsidy to polluting industries in the sense that local environment is provided for the use of the industry at less than the social cost to society, much in the same way as, for instance, subsidized infrastructural services. In principle, permissive environmental legislation should be treated by the government on a par with other subsidies to industry, and used to the extent that its incentive benefits exceed its social costs more than by alternative forms of inducements. It has been noted elsewhere that the social cost of pollution from mineral exploitation could be relatively low in low-income countries, especially when the installations have been located in sparsely populated areas.[7] This could make 'environmental subsidies' a relatively advantageous form of incentive from the government's point of view.

The government can also provide inducements by procuring finance for mineral ventures. As borrowing capacities of mining MNCs become increasingly strained, host country efforts to obtain part of the funds required would be greatly welcomed by the firms. Inducements in the field of loan finance would become stronger if they also involved a subsidy in the rate of interest. Governments of LDCs, as distinct from MNCs, have access to some sources of concessional finance, like public aid agencies or international development banks. In procuring such finance for investments in the minerals sector, the government could pass on the capital to the MNC, along with the subsidy contained in the low interest rate.

THE FEASIBILITY OF POLITICAL INDUCEMENTS

Mining firms and financial institutions claim that they experience risks of political exposure when investing in mineral ventures in many LDCs. They therefore avoid investments altogether in such countries, or else require higher than 'normal' after-tax return prospects in order to commit their funds. Reducing the causes for the firms' political fears, therefore, is an important task for governments which are keen to secure broader foreign participation in their mineral sectors.

The concept of 'political risk' is both complex and subjective. Assessment of the political risk element in an LDC may render very varied results from one MNC to another, because different factors are taken into account, and because outlook and experiences of the company executives who undertake the assessment, may vary.[8] This means that it is difficult to design general policies which would appease all MNCs.

A few general points about the perception of 'political risk' can be noted. Firstly, the insecurity felt by the firm is heavily influenced by their past experience in a particular country. The task of re-building a reputation of 'fair treatment' of MNCs, once such a reputation has been tarnished, may take a long time. Secondly, it appears that the MNCs are prepared to accept even relatively tough conditions in terms of taxation and government control, if only these conditions are known from the outset. In building up a climate of confidence vis-à-vis the firms, the government should therefore avoid frequent changes in the rules applying to the MNCs. Thirdly, it is evident that ignorance on the part of company executives may be a strong contributory factor to the feeling of 'political risk'. Hence, close relations between the government administration and the companies, and efficient dissemination of information about the government's plans and intentions in the field of economic policy should reduce the feeling of uncertainty.

A clear-cut foreign investment code, specifying the scope of government intervention in foreign activities can do much to alleviate the political risk felt by MNCs.[9] These firms naturally prefer a situation where they decide on their own in such matters as capacity expansion, imports of technology, pricing, remittance of profits and direction of exports, but in any case, they want to know beforehand the limits to their freedom of action, and be assured that this freedom will not be infringed.

The policies ought also to clarify the taxation applicable to the foreign interests. To raise its confidence with the foreign entities, the government should endeavor to avoid frequent changes in the system of taxation. Another confidence-building measure could be to issue guarantees against nationalization or, alternatively, to publish unequivocal rules for compensation if nationalization were to occur in the future. A declaration by the government that it is willing to submit arising conflicts with foreign investors to international arbitration could constitute a further complementary measure to a policy package aimed at encouraging foreign investment in the minerals field.

An efficient way to reassure foreign firms politically is by inviting international development banks to participate in projects, either simply by supplying some of the capital needed, or in some more complex oversight capacity. The banks' presence is often regarded as a guarantee that both the government and the company obtain a reasonable deal. The MNCs' fears of harsh political treatment are reduced when they know that, while the government might be willing to take the consequences of a head-on conflict with a single firm, it would be more hesitant to face the international repercussions, financial and other, of a struggle involving the World Bank or a regional development bank.

Collaboration in varied fields with the mining firm's home country would probably provide further political reassurance. Such collaboration could pertain to general commercial policy and consist of agreements on bilateral trade, on reciprocal rules for investment, on movement of labor, or on double taxation. It could also relate more specifically to the minerals sector. If the home country depends on mineral imports, an agreement could be reached to assure its mineral needs in the long run in exchange for an assured market on preferential terms, or for access to the technology needed by the mineral industry. Alternatively, the home government could itself become involved in one way or another in the mineral ventures, for instance through financial contributions.

Involvement of third parties like international development banks or importing country governments would probably constitute a stronger political inducement to the MNCs than the unilateral policies of the mineral-exporting LDCs, as spelled out earlier in this section. Simultaneously, such third party involvement would restrict the LDCs' freedom, by reducing their possibilities to back out from earlier commitments. Hence, these policies would be appropriate only for countries which desire to maintain a constructive and wholehearted collaboration with foreign parties in the long run.

It is worth noting that the political inducements discussed here, namely, publicity, stability, the issuance of various guarantees, and involvement of third parties, do not entangle the government of the mineral-endowed country in any direct cost at all. In this way they differ from the economic inducements treated in the preceding section.

HOW AND WHEN FORCE COULD BE APPLIED

The policies of inducement discussed so far could ordinarily only have positive results on the goals pursued by government. In exchange for a clear-cut inducement, the foreign partner is likely to go at least part of the way along with the government's desire in respect to such issues as a decision to commit investment funds for a proposed mineral project, forward integration through local processing, expansion of employee training programs, or a greater role for nationals in the management of mineral ventures. With policies of coercion, a new and possibly counter-productive element comes into play. When the government tries to force MNCs towards a particular behavior, the companies, instead of complying, can react by sudden or gradual withdrawal. If, for instance, the government commands that all management functions be transferred into national hands in a situation where, in the corporate opinion, appropriate national personnel is not available, the firm may not find it worthwhile to continue its activities in the country.

The feasibility for withdrawal differs sharply between firms which are only in the process of planning their entry into the country, and those which have already established ongoing operations. In the former case, the scope for coercive action on the part of government will usually be limited. So long as the firm has little that ties it to the country, it cannot be forced into behavior which it judges to be against its own interest. In contrast, where the company has made heavy financial and other commitments to an ongoing operation, the government's coercive power will be greater. Even then, there is a limit to what can be enforced. For if the government asks for too much, the company may simply relinquish its operations altogether and leave. In the absence of national managerial and technical resources to run the enterprise independent of the foreign firm, such action is bound to hurt national development. In a less drastic case, the company may decide to stay on, but to gradually reduce the scope of its operations by abstaining from replacement of worn-out capital. While coercion in this case may result in an immediate contribution towards national goals, its longer-term effects on development could well be damaging.

When designing and exercising policies of coercion, the government should be aware of the possibility of counter-productive repercussions as just spelled out, and take care not to push coercion beyond the point where the overall effect will be detrimental to national development.

The above discussion suggests that an all-or-nothing type of coercion policy may not be the most productive in achieving the ends pursued by the government. Even a flexible foreign investor, prepared to go a long way to meet the government's wishes, could decide to pull out or go bankrupt, when confronted by a sudden and non-negotiable requirement to double employment, to build infrastructural facilities that he does not need, to add a processing unit to ongoing installations, or to pull out from established export markets. A somewhat softer and more gradual type of coercion could well prove to be more efficient in achieving the government's ends in each case.

As demonstrated by the OPEC experience, the ability to use force both against foreign-owned corporate interests and foreign importing governments, in order to achieve national aims will be greatly enhanced when the policy executors command monopoly power in the market. Success is much more likely once a close collaboration between several mineral producing and exporting countries has been established and permits a coordination of their coercive policies in the mineral field.

THE IMPLICATIONS OF GOING IT ALONE

All the policies discussed have assumed that foreign corporations, in addition to their management control, have major ownership positions in the mineral activities of LDCs. In the present section we consider the case where MNCs have been forced into a marginal position where they hold only a minor share of the equity or none at all.

A variety of inputs have to be available to the government which desires to carry on mineral exploitation entirely on its own, or with only limited MNC involvement. Quite frequently, the government of such an LDC will have to reach special arrangements with foreign suppliers of inputs, to supplement a deficient national availability. The type of arrangement and extent of foreign input requirements will vary and depend on the national deficiency in each case. In the following discussion of possible arrangements in this field, we distinguish between the establishment of new ventures on the one hand, and the running of existing ventures on the other. The requirement for complex technological and organizational inputs as well as for capital is commonly much greater in the first case.

Where a mineral project is to be built up from scratch, and the level of national managerial and technological competence is relatively low, it would commonly be necessary to involve foreign suppliers of capital equipment in a comprehensive way, by commissioning the plant in the form of a turnkey project. Where there is a greater availability of national managerial and technical resources, the foreign supplies for carrying-out the investment could be more limited and provided on a piecemeal basis. With their great experience in carrying out this kind of investment, the MNCs would quite commonly figure among the suppliers to the investment venture. Other contributors would include manufacturers of capital equipment and specialized consulting firms. Some CPEs, notably the USSR and Romania, have shown competence and willingness to become engaged in mineral investment ventures in LDCs, and thus constitute an alternative to suppliers of technology and management from the DCs.

Another key input, usually in scarce supply for the LDC government, is investment capital. There are many potential sources of finance that the government can approach if it is not in a position to cover the capital requirements from its internal revenue or through the national banking system. These include credits from equipment suppliers, advances from future purchasers of the

mineral output, international development banks and project finance arrangements in the Eurodollar market.[10] Although a government with a good international credit rating can obtain a major proportion of the investment funds
needed to finance an economically-promising processing venture from the
sources just enumerated, it should be underlined that high indebtedness can
cause subsequent strains both to the venture itself and to the government budget
if the profitability turns out to be less than expected.

National competence to run the mineral ventures has proved much easier to
create than the building-up of skills required for independent handling of investments to establish such ventures. Nevertheless, the management of an ongoing
minerals project also requires considerable inputs of technology, administrative
and marketing expertise and here, too, foreign support has to be called in whenever national resources are inadequate. In several nationally-owned minerals
industries it has proved necessary to reach comprehensive management contracts
with mining MNCs in order to assure efficient operation. In other cases, where
nationally available manpower resources may be sufficient for day-to-day
technical and commercial management, foreign support has to be relied upon for
varied special tasks, like supervision of the technical installations, or seeking out
the best sales opportunities in the international market. The choice of sources of
foreign expertise to assist in running the venture would probably be narrower
than during the investment phase; it would be hard to avoid involvement with
large mining firms altogether.

Management services on contract obviously cost money. When they are required on a comprehensive scale, the suppliers are in a strong position to dictate
their own terms, and the outlay often becomes so heavy as to make an otherwise
promising venture economically less attractive to the national owner. Another
problem is that where the service suppliers are remunerated through a fixed fee,
they may lack sufficient incentive to deliver to their best ability, and the project
will suffer as a result. A way out is to pay the foreigners on the basis of the project's performance, or simpler still, to let them become part-owners in the venture. At this stage in the argument it becomes apparent that majority ownership
by itself has little to offer the government of the exporting LDC.

CONCLUSIONS

Most mineral-endowed LDCs are heavily dependent on foreign inputs and
foreign institutions in the running and development of their mineral sector. This
dependence severely limits their freedom of action in the minerals field. The
major approaches that the governments of such countries might adopt in their
policies towards the foreign agents involved in mineral activities in their territories have been surveyed. The discussion suggests that countries with limited
national managerial and technological competences have little choice but to
adhere to policies of inducement towards foreign institutions in seeking to
achieve their national development goals. With growing national emancipation

such governments have the choice *either* of continued heavy reliance on mining MNCs, but with an increasing ability for the government administration to assert its own will against the foreign interest, *or* of attempting, in the main, to go it alone, with only marginal foreign contributions. In the preceding section an attempt has been made to disentangle the implications of the respective options.

In several contexts the analysis has pointed to the bargaining strength which can be derived by monopoly power on the part of the mineral-endowed countries. The discussion suggests that the policy options open to each country will be considerably widened by the establishment of international collaboration between several mineral-producing countries, permitting the group as a whole to reap the benefits of a stronger position in the market.

The major conclusion that emerges from the preceding analysis, however, is that the key precondition to freedom and independence in mineral policies, be they of the inducement, coercion or go it alone type, is the development of national competence in the minerals field. It has been shown that the advantages of national ownership become hollow if the nation does not have knowledgeable individuals and appropriate institutions with a wide experience of minerals. The national ability to control even 100 per cent-owned installations becomes illusory when foreign management, technology and capital are required on a wholesale basis to establish and to run projects. In contrast, execution of national control can be efficient even with very limited equity participation, once the relevant national skills and competences have been created.

A number of measures can be taken to speed-up technical and economic emancipation in LDCs with little prior experience in the minerals field.[11] Thus, one important step would be to establish a minerals office within the government administration with the function of monitoring national and international mineral issues, and providing a training ground for government personnel. Another measure could consist in building-up a national bank with special interest in developing and financing the mineral sector. A third step would be the setting up of formal training institutions like a college of management or a college of mining and metallurgy, where national expertise for the minerals sector could be developed. A fourth could consist in sending personnel abroad for training, or for practice by attachment to the head offices of mining MNCs, or to the secretariats of international producers' bodies like AIEC, CIPEC or IBA.

NOTES

1. For a detailed discussion of national financial institutions, which help to finance mineral ventures in LDCs, see Ch. 10, *supra*.
2. For an elaboration, see Ch. 7, *supra*.
3. See M. Radetzki, 'The Potential for Monopolistic Commodity Pricing by Developing Countries', in G.K. Helleiner (ed.), *A World Divided* (Cambridge: Cambridge University Press, 1975).
4. UN, 'Transnational Corporations in World Development, A Reexamination' (New York, 1978).
5. M. Radetzki, 'The Potential for Monopolistic Commodity Pricing by Developing Countries'.

6. See M. Radetzki, 'Changing Structures in the Financing of the Minerals Industry in LDCs', *Development and Change*, Vol. 11, No. 1 (January 1980), 1-15.

7. See Ch. 7, *supra*.

8. See for instance R.J. Rummel and D.A. Heenan, 'How Multinationals Analyze Political Risk', *Harvard Business Review* (January-February 1978).

9. See Ch. 18, *infra*.

10. These sources are discussed in considerable detail in Ch. 10, *supra*.

11. For a more complete elaboration of measures to increase national independence in the minerals sector, See R. Bosson and B. Varon, *The Mining Industry and the Developing Countries* (London: Oxford University Press, 1977), Ch. 6.

18

THE ROLE OF FOREIGN PRIVATE INVESTMENT IN FUTURE LDC MINING PROJECTS

R.F. Mikesell

On the basis of calculations made by the author,[1] taking into account various estimates of growth in demand for the remainder of the century, it is estimated that the additional capacity to supply the needed amounts of the major minerals for all MECs over the period 1977-2000 would require a financial outlay of nearly $280 billion, of which $96 billion would be for expansion of capacity in LDCs (see Table 18.1). The addition of other important minerals such as lead, zinc, phosphate and manganese would perhaps increase the total by ten or 15 per cent.

Table 18.1. *World Capital Expenditures for Estimated Additional Capacity Requirements for Selected Minerals, 1977-2000*[a] *($ billion)*

	Total	LDCs
Bauxite	6.9	5.2
Alumina	24.4	6.1
Aluminum	76.6	17.6
Copper	58.0	29.0
Nickel	12.5	5.0
Iron Ore	98.2	31.4
Tin	1.7	1.4
Total	278.3	95.7

a   Excludes capital outlays for pollution abatement and exploration.

If capital requirements for all non-fuel minerals are included, plus outlays for pollution abatement and exploration, as well as outlays for infrastructure in the form of highways, railroads, communities, which are not included in the estimates of capital requirements for productive capacity, annual capital requirements for the LDCs are obtained of some $5.5 billion[2] a year in 1977 dollars, or over $1.3 trillion for the 24-year period.

Although this is a staggering sum, it is at the low end of the scale of projections. For example, the World Bank suggests that gross investments required by the non-fuel minerals sector in LDCs for the period 1976-1985 may run as high as $9.5 million per year, and that as much as two-thirds of this amount may have to come from foreign private sources.[3]

If financing is not found for increased mineral producing capacity in the LDCs, a larger share of the capacity expansion is likely to take place in the DCs, especially for such commodities as copper, iron ore, nickel, lead and zinc for which there are substantial reserves in the DCs. The outlook for financing differs considerably from commodity to commodity.

SOURCES OF FINANCING

Of the projected $5.5 billion per year of financing required by the LDCs to finance warranted increases in their non-fuel mineral producing capacity, between $4 and $4.5 billion per year will need to come from external sources. Although data do not seem to be available on the annual volume of aggregate investment in the primary metals industries of the LDCs over the past few years, external capital flow to these industries during the 1970s has been only a fraction of projected annual requirements to the year 2000. In the past, the principal external sources of financing for mining and smelting industries of the LDCs have been foreign direct investment, private international bank loans, suppliers' credits, and loans from public international development agencies, e.g. the World Bank.

Over the period 1973-1976 net US direct investment capital flow to the mining and smelting industries in LDCs averaged less than $200 million per year. In 1976 the US, UK, and Japan, the principal foreign investors, invested an estimated $400 million of equity capital in all the extractive industries of the LDCs. Over the five-year period ended June 1976, World Bank and IDA loans to the non-fuel minerals sector averaged only $50 million per year. In recent years, most of the external capital for the mining industries of LDCs has taken the form of intermediate commercial bank loans and credits from mining equipment companies supplied or guaranteed in part by government credit institutions. Much of these credits has been associated with equity investment by international mining companies. On the basis of a very cursory review of the financing of known projects, it may be concluded that external financing of mining projects in the LDCs has averaged no more than $1 billion per year over the past five years. What will be the source of external financing for four times this amount over the next couple of decades?

This question has been of considerable concern to officials of the UN and World Bank as well as to governments of DCs, such as the USA. Various proposals have been put forward, some of which will be discussed below.

Countries with growing economies and good export earning prospects may have little difficulty in financing the development of their mineral resources. Brazil, Venezuela and the oil surplus economies of the Middle East obviously fall into this category. There are undoubtedly others, but not everyone would make up the same list. For other LDCs, external capital for mineral development will depend heavily upon the willingness of mining MNCs to undertake exploration and equity investment without which external financing is unlikely to be forthcoming in sufficient quantities. Some governments will be able to borrow directly in the international financial markets on their own guarantee, but several important mineral economies, including Peru, Zaire and Zambia, are in such dire financial circumstances that large net borrowing by their governments in the international markets appears unlikely for the foreseeable future.

Over the past couple of years, the World Bank has been reviewing its policies with respect to the financing of projects in both non-fuel minerals and petroleum sectors of LDCs. It has concluded that in the light of the financing requirements that have been discussed, the World Bank Group, including IDA and IFC, should expand substantially its activities in the minerals industries. The *Annual Report* of the World Bank in 1978 stated that the organization's share might eventually average about 15 per cent of total project costs of non-fuel minerals in LDCs.[4] This suggests that the World Bank might step-up its financing of this sector to about $800 million per year. The World Bank report states, however, that it views its role as an 'active catalyst' for attracting both direct investment capital from mining MNCs and loan capital from private international financial institutions such as banks.

In recent years mining projects have become so costly that mining MNCs have been financing only 25 or 30 per cent of the total project outlay with equity capital, and have relied on external financial institutions for the remainder. The financing of the Cuajone copper mine in Southern Peru provides a good example. As of June 1977, the sources of financing for Cuajone were as follows:

International bank consortium loans from some 50 banks	$253 million
Equipment financing	140
International Finance Corp. (World Bank affiliate)	15
Loans from future purchasers of copper	54
Total debt	$462 million
Equity from SPCC and Billiton	264 million
Total financing	$726 million

Other recent mines heavily financed by external debt are the Bougainville copper mine in Papua New Guinea (PNG), the Ertsberg copper mine in Indonesia, and the Botswana-RST nickel-copper mine in Botswana. It is expected that the Cerro Colorado mine in Panama, which will cost over $1.3 billion, will be financed to the extent of a billion dollars or more by external loans. The La Caridad mine in Mexico, in which the Mexican government has a minority interest, was financed very largely by loans from the Mexican government, which in turn borrowed the capital from abroad. Iran's Sar Cheshmeh mine, which is 100 per cent government-owned, was financed mainly by government oil revenues.

In the case of the Bougainville mine, a portion of the capital for infrastructure such as roads, communications, power and transmission lines, was provided by the PNG government and financed in part by loans from the Australian government. In some cases, governments have financed infrastructure with the aid of loans from the World Bank or the Inter-American Development Bank (IADB). Such financing reduces the capital costs of the mine and increases the revenue for the government, since in most cases the government taxes 50 per cent or more of the net profits. Sometimes the mining agreement provides for the acquisition by the government of a portion of the equity in the mining company, either at book value or without cost, in recognition of the government's financing of the infrastructure.

Although mining MNCs provide only a portion, perhaps less than one-third, of the financing of mining enterprises in LDCs with their own equity, they play an important role in mobilizing the external financial capital. First of all, they are responsible for the feasibility study which is the basis for the creditworthiness of the project. Second, although the foreign investor usually does not guarantee the loan, it normally guarantees on its own responsibility that the mine will be completed within a given period and be producing up to a certain percentage of capacity by a certain date. The reputation and financial strength of the mining MNC making the investment determines the validity of this guarantee. Third, the foreign investor must negotiate with dozens of suppliers of loans and credits and negotiate with them a creditor agreement which sets forth a number of conditions, including: (a) the negotiation by the mining company of supply contracts covering the planned output of the mine through the period of debt repayment; (b) a limitation on total indebtedness, priority on the use of cash flow for debt repayment (including in some cases the prohibition of any dividends until the loans are paid off); and (c) a guarantee that a portion of the export proceeds from the mine will go directly into a fund for discharging debt obligations.

It should be kept in mind that the contribution of a mining MNC to the financing of a mining project need not involve 100 per cent foreign ownership. In recent years, more and more mines are joint ventures with the government. It should be recognized, however, that the presence of an experienced mining MNC which is responsible for the completion of the mine and its operation is an important factor in the mobilization of private international capital. It may also be an important factor in a World Bank loan unless the government mining enterprise is one that has had considerable experience and has shown competence in putting together mining projects.

In the case of wholly-owned government mines, much of the financing may come through direct government borrowings from the private international financial markets. This has the disadvantage of reducing the capacity of the government to borrow for other purposes, since creditors look primarily to the government for repayment and not to the mining enterprise. The World Bank has made some loans to government mining enterprises, but most of these have been for expansion of existing mine complexes rather than for new large mines.

One type of capital expenditure that cannot ordinarily be supplied from external loan sources is exploration. Exploration in non-fuel minerals in LDCs declined substantially during the 1970s, largely because mining MNCs have been unwilling to accept the political risks. In addition, exploration has been discouraged by the high cost of holding mining claims, and in many cases by the inability of a mining firm that has explored a deposit to hold that deposit without constructing a mine within a relatively short period of time. Governments, of course, undertake geological surveys and some exploration, but exploration costs have soared and the risks are very high. Large mining MNCs not only have the experience and technical personnel for exploration, but by diversifying their investigations over a number of regions with a large exploration budget, they are able to reduce risk. Although there are proposals for the expansion of the UN Revolving Fund for Natural Resource Exploration, it does not appear that it will have sufficient funds to undertake more than a small percentage of total exploration required in the LDCs. At the present time, it is difficult to see any alternative to the operations of mining MNCs for undertaking the bulk of the exploration in LDCs. This applies to petroleum and uranium as well as to non-fuel minerals.

ENCOURAGING FOREIGN PRIVATE INVESTMENT

Because of the importance of foreign private investment in exploration, in mine development, and in the mobilization of external financing for mining projects in LDCs, there are various programs and proposals by which to promote it. Programs to promote foreign investment in mining in LDCs include (a) insurance for equity and loan financing against expropriation, damage from war or revolution, and currency inconvertibility; (b) the negotiation of investment treaties with the governments of LDCs; and (c) loans and equity investment by public development agencies such as the World Bank and IFC to serve as a catalyst for foreign and domestic private investment and to provide confidence, especially to the foreign investor.

Bilateral Investment Insurance

The US, Japan and several Western European countries have programs for insuring foreign investments by their nationals against various types of political or other non-commercial risk. The US Overseas Private Investment Corporation (OPIC) has perhaps received the greatest attention because of the large volume of mineral investments that it has insured. Although in recent years the number of new policies covering mineral investments has been relatively small, OPIC hopes to expand its coverage of new mineral investments under the authority provided in the Overseas Private Investment Corporation Amendment Act of 1978.

Because of the widespread expropriation of foreign mineral investments in the past two decades, it is widely believed that expropriation insurance removes an important deterrent to foreign investment in minerals. Many mining firms, however, regard the violation of contract terms, short of outright expropriation, as constituting an even greater risk than expropriation. Until recently, so-called 'creeping expropriation'', arising from host government actions that restrict the profitability or limit the control of an investment, was not specifically covered by OPIC. Under a new program adopted in 1978, however, insurance coverage may be designed for host government breaches of contract that prevent or impair profitability of operations, such as new taxes or government control over marketing. OPIC will cover losses arising from a breach of contract for a two-year period, following which the investor would have the option of closing down the operation and recovering the insured book value as of the date of the breach, less the amount of any compensation paid by OPIC during the two-year period.

Some critics of government insurance of foreign investment have regarded such programs as an improper intrusion by the foreign investor's government into conflicts between the foreign investor and the host country government. It is argued that political and commercial relations between countries will be influenced by investment disputes in a manner harmful to the mutual interests of the countries involved. Other critics argue that government-sponsored investment insurance constitutes a subsidy to MNCs that cannot be justified in terms of the national welfare.

In answer to the first criticism, it is argued that the home government of a foreign investor inevitably becomes involved in an expropriation or breach of contract. (In a sense, the US government is financially involved in a loss by a US corporation as a consequence of expropriation since the loss is written off against the corporation's US tax obligations.) OPIC has argued that the existence of expropriation insurance fosters the settlement of disputes between a foreign investor and a host government. The host government is more willing to reach an agreement with the investor on compensation, since OPIC (i.e. the US government) assumes the claim of the foreign investor against the host government if OPIC compensates the investor.

The argument that government investment insurance is a form of subsidy is more complicated. OPIC correctly asserts that the insurance premiums it has collected have exceeded its claim settlements and administrative expenses over the life of the program, and that OPIC has built up a large reserve.[5] Its potential liabilities arising from insurance contracts, however, are far in excess of its reserves accumulated from net earnings — as is normally the case for any private insurance company. Life and property insurance contracts are based on actuarial principles, but there is no generally accepted actuarial basis for political risk investment insurance. OPIC does reinsure a portion of its portfolio with private insurers, such as Lloyds of London, but OPIC's entire risk exposure could not be transferred to the private market except at substantially increased premiums — probably too high for prospective foreign investors. Therefore, investment insurance may be regarded as a subsidy, just as the absorption of political risk on loans by the Export-Import Bank or the World Bank may be regarded as a subsidy. It seems, however, that subsidies that increase the flow of capital for the development of minerals required by the world economy can be justified in terms of social welfare.

As of 30th September 1978, OPIC estimated its maximum potential exposure on claims arising out of political risk investment insurance to be $3.2 billion (excluding obligations under guarantees issued in settlement of claims). On that same date, OPIC's insurance and guaranty reserves totaled $383 million.[6]

OPIC's insurance program for mineral projects is limited in several ways, including a limitation of $150 million on combined equity and loan guarantees for any one project. This is much too small to cover large mine projects with total required investment running up to a billion dollars or more. In addition, OPIC insurance is not available for investment in certain countries and for certain commodities.

Multinational Investment Insurance

Multinational investment insurance has been discussed in the World Bank and in the United Nations. It has also been considered by the EEC.[7] Recently IADB put forward a proposal for insuring foreign equity investment in the resource industries of its members against expropriation and other risks, and for guaranteeing foreign loans to foreign investors in these industries. Multilateral insurance would have the advantage of spreading the risks among a number of countries. In the past a serious barrier to an agreement on a multilateral insurance plan has been the unwillingness of many LDCs to agree to international arbitration. Such countries hold to the principle that a sovereign nation has an absolute right to take any action against foreign-owned property that it believes to be in its national interest and to determine what compensation, if any, is due under its national laws and judicial procedures. The IADB multilateral insurance proposal provides for international arbitration of disputes between the IADB as administrator of the program and the government of a country in which an investment has been insured. Since governments have generally been willing to agree to international arbitration of disputes with international development organizations of which they are a member, Latin American governments may join the IADB insurance program if it is established.

The World Bank has established an International Center for Settlement of Investment Disputes (ICSID) which provides for international arbitration. No Latin American country is a member of ICSID, however, nor are the governments of several other important LDCs, including Algeria, India, Iran, the Philippines and Thailand. It may be noted that a number of new investment agreements in the non-fuel minerals industry have provided for international arbitration of disputes employing arrangements other than ICSID.

Bilateral Investment Treaties

Several European countries, including France, Germany, the Netherlands and the UK, have negotiated specialized bilateral investment treaties with a number of

LDCs covering such important issues as non-discriminatory or national treatment, expropriation and arbitration of investment disputes. The US has also negotiated investment treaties with LDCs, but this program, which was rather active during the earlier post-war period, has tended to lag, in part because of the failure of Congress to ratify treaties entered into by the Executive. The last such US treaty with an LDC to be ratified was that with Thailand in June 1968.

Investment treaties tend to be drawn up in rather broad terms, and while they do provide an important framework for negotiations relating to investment disputes, they offer little in the way of legal protection to foreign investors. An important component of any investment treaty should be an agreement to submit disputes arising out of foreign investments to international arbitration — either through the ICSID, the International Chamber of Commerce Court of Arbitration, or some other international tribunal. Host countries, however, usually reserve the right to determine which investments shall be subject to arbitration or which provisions of investment agreements shall be subject to international arbitration.

Intergovernmental Actions to Promote Non-fuel Mineral Investments

Government spokesmen for a number of DCs and the secretariats of several intergovernmental agencies have emphasized the need to promote an adequate level of investment in the mineral industries of the LDCs through international action. This issue was dramatized by former Secretary of State Kissinger's proposal for an International Resources Bank (IRB) at UNCTAD IV in Nairobi, Kenya, in 1976. The IRB proposal was largely rejected by the LDCs, principally because of its emphasis on promoting foreign investment in their resource industries. Although the Carter administration has not supported the proposal for an IRB, it has advocated increased loans for mineral development by the World Bank and by the regional development banks of which the US is a member.

The staff of the World Bank has prepared several studies on the technical, financial and managerial requirements for expanding mineral-producing capacity in the LDCs and on the possible roles of the World Bank in facilitating the transfer of resources for these purposes. These studies led to the statement of policy on non-fuel mineral development in the World Bank's 1978 annual report to which reference has been made above.[8] A further indication of the interest in this problem is found in a proposal for an International Minerals Investment Trust (IMIT) which was presented by the UN Secretary-General in May 1977 to the UN Committee on Natural Resources.

Although it is unlikely that public international development institutions can be counted on to provide a large share of the financing required to expand non-fuel mineral capacities in the LDCs, even their modest participation in both loan and equity financing could be a powerful instrument for mobilizing private international loan financing and for giving greater confidence to potential private international lenders. Two reasons account for this. First, private financial institutions often rely on the project investigation and evaluation undertaken by a public international agency, such as the World Bank; second, there is a general belief that governments are less likely to default on loans in which public international agencies have participated. This confidence might be further increased by the use of cross-default obligations which provide that a default to one creditor constitutes a default to all creditors. Public international agency participation in project formulation and equity financing could give private foreign equity investors considerable security against expropriation or other contract violations which would affect the earnings of the enterprise. In such cases, the initial amount of international agency participation would not need to be a large share of the total project cost.

Both loan and equity investments by IFC has been a factor in attracting private investment in LDCs, but equity investment has rarely been used by IFC in support of foreign investment in mining. A notable exception was an IFC loan of $26 million plus an equity subscription of $4 million to CODEMIN, a Brazilian nickel mining and refining project sponsored by the Hochschild Group, a South American international mining and metal trading organization. The IFC also recently made three small loans of $15 million each in support of mining operations, one of which represented IFC's participation in a $400 million loan package for Cuajone copper mine in Peru; another represented a share in the loan financing of a $200 million nickel mining and processing plant in Guatemala sponsored by INCO Ltd; and the third was made to a Brazilian company, Mineracao Rio do Norte SA, a joint venture involving Brazilian and foreign equity organized to mine and process bauxite.

The degree to which public international development agencies should be involved in the actual negotiation of mine development agreements has been a matter of some concern to the executives of mining MNCs. For example, the head of a large US mining firm has expressed the view that a three-way negotiation would be cumbersome and that in any differences between the foreign investor and host government, the international agency might well side with the host country. On the other hand, it might be argued that the international agency would be able to view objectively the conditions necessary to attract foreign direct investment, and that its participation in the negotiations would provide a measure of support to host government officials who accepted politically unpopular provisions of a mining agreement.

International Investment Codes

Several international organizations have been negotiating codes of conduct for MNCs and for their treatment by the governments of host countries. In June 1976, 23 members of the OECD adopted a 'Declaration on International Investment and Multinational Enterprises' which included voluntary guidelines for MNCs, a commitment by the OECD governments to accord national or non-discriminatory treatment to MNCs vis-à-vis domestic firms, and a commitment by host countries to respect contracts negotiated with MNCs and to treat them in accordance with international law.

Negotiations on an investment code for MNCs involving both DCs and LDCs have been underway in the UN Commission on Transnational Corporations, the ILO, the OAS, and other international and regional organizations. Progress in reaching agreement on a code of conduct has been exceedingly difficult because of the wide differences between the DCs and the majority of LDCs. The latter want a set of legally-binding principles which it would be the duty of the home country governments to enforce, while the DCs insist that any code be voluntary in nature. LDCs emphasize the sovereignty of host governments with respect to MNCs, while the DCs have argued for a commitment by the host countries not to discriminate against MNCs as opposed to domestic firms, and to maintain contract provisions.

The outlook for an international investment code that would provide any significant encouragement to foreign investors in LDCs is not promising. In fact, the kind of code advocated by the majority of LDCs appears likely to place additional obligations on foreign investors without according them protection for their investments.

Although bilateral investment treaties have considerable advantages since they may provide specific commitments between governments enforceable under international law, multilateral agreements involving both DCs and LDCs would also offer certain advantages. Even though such agreements might be voluntary in nature and involve commitments only to certain principles, the violation of these commitments by one MNC or one host government would be regarded as a default on an obligation undertaken by all parties. Since it may be impossible, however, to reach an agreement involving a large number of LDCs that would be effective in stimulating the flow of foreign investment, it might be possible for a more limited group encompassing those DCs and LDCs that are particularly interested in reducing barriers to the flow of investment to adopt their own multilateral investment code. The fact that such a code might encourage MNCs to invest in those countries that were signatories to it, in contrast to countries that were not, might serve to encourage additional countries to become parties to the code.

CONCLUSION

If the LDCs are to expand their non-fuel minerals capacity in line with world demand and their reserve potential over the next two decades, they will require external capital of the order of $4 billion to $5 billion annually. Much of this capital must be provided directly or mobilized by foreign direct investors. This will require a favorable investment climate and actions by governments and international agencies to reduce risks to suppliers of both equity and loan capital. The IADB proposal for multilateral insurance could be important for assuring private investors, especially if it were followed by a similar initiative on the part of the World Bank. Perhaps the most important contribution to the flow of foreign direct investment in mining would be an expansion of the activities of the public international development agencies such as the World Bank Group in making loans and equity investments to projects in which foreign private investors were involved.

NOTES

1. For the source and methodology of these calculations, see R.F. Mikesell, *New Patterns of World Mineral Development* (Washington: British-North American Committee, 1979); and *The World Copper Industry* (Baltimore: Johns Hopkins University Press for Resources for the Future Inc., 1979).

2. See Chapter 10, *supra*, where a smaller figure is assumed.

3. *Annual Report, 1978* (Washington: World Bank, 1978), 21.

4. *Ibidem*.

5. OPIC's basic premium rates for insured equity investments in mining projects are 0.9 per cent per year for expropriation; 0.6 per cent for war, revolution and insurrection; and 0.3 per cent for inconvertibility. However, higher rates may be charged according to the risk for specific projects. *Investment Insurance Handbook* (Washington: Overseas Private Investment Corporation, 1977), 11.

6. *Annual Report, 1978* (Washington: Overseas Private Investment Corporation, 1979), 17, 62.

7. The recently signed Lomé II Convention between the EEC and 58 LDCs – the ACP countries – encourages further development of mining in these countries by a series of provisions designed to attract increased external flows of technology and capital to this sector. Furthermore, the Convention establishes an insurance scheme, similar to Stabex, covering the main minerals exported by the ACP countries, namely copper and cobalt, phosphates, manganese, bauxite and alumina, tin and iron ore. The scheme is backed by financing amounting to 280 million ecus (European units of account), equivalent to $372 million.

8. See note 3 above.

19

TRAINING AND LOCALIZATION
AS STRATEGIES FOR DEVELOPMENT

W. Armstrong

Policy options can remain in an intellectual vacuum unless nationals both gain training and experience in their jobs and work in organizations which link authority and accountability.

Establishing processes which enable nationals to take on full responsibility and which utilize local sources of supply and service are considered in this chapter, with examples of efforts that have worked.

TRAINING

Where mining is new to a region or culture, training often starts with the man with the first shovel. How to set up a system where that man can develop his abilities and increase his tasks (and remuneration and status, etc.), and select, train, and build on that experience is a daunting exercise, for which there is, however, much relevant experience.

Selection

Basic mining aptitude tests for people with little formal education or experience were developed and used successfully in Ghana, Namibia, Zambia (and the US). More advanced aptitude/evaluation tests for secondary school leavers have been developed with mining companies' participation and utilized successfully in Liberia and Zambia. When a new manning structure was proposed in Zambia in the 1970s which would reorganize jobs with consequent changes in training, the two mining companies, with the cooperation of the Zambian mineworkers union, developed a testing and assessment of employees which provided a basis for determining which employees would be best suited for which training opportunities. Clear selection procedures are only a beginning, but they can help reduce on-the-job failure and wastage.

What Requisite Education?

Assumptions that a certain level of education is prerequisite to perform a job have often blocked able people from advancement. (Assumptions that attaining a certain level of education automatically enabled one to perform a job have been equally hazardous.) But conscientious employees have often risen through training and hard work to a plateau they could not go beyond without a more formal scientific, technical or general education. Mining companies in Africa and elsewhere have gained on-the-job experience both in: (1) utilizing employees with less formal education than desired by adapting training content and method accordingly, and (2) providing (often in cooperation with government or other educational bodies) on or off-duty education courses ranging from basic literacy to secondary school and technical theory and skills. Raising the level of employees' formal education thus becomes part and parcel of job training, with successful results for people and productivity. Experience also suggests, however, that there are upper limits to the success of combining part-time formal education with on-the-job experience and that senior mine jobs require integrated scientific, technical and administrative skills for which formal educational background is virtually a prerequisite. Mining companies everywhere have long provided scholarships to local and foreign universities and supported technical and vocational institutes as well as mining schools, often also helping to devise curricula and provide faculty. Sometimes this is insufficient to assure a flow of candidates with the requisite background for mining. In one African country, shortage of mathematics and science teachers resulted in poor performance in these subjects by secondary school leavers. Yet past experience showed university students in mining subjects had done well only if they had a strong mathematics and science background. So with the cooperation of the Education Ministry, the mining companies organized a two-year post-secondary course in maths and the sciences. Students who passed successfully were eligible for mining company scholarships to universities.

To analyze cause and effect, and take appropriate remedial steps in cooperation with other local organizations sounds easy as described above, but it often takes more innovation and follow-through than many mining or ministry officials expect of themselves.

Choices in Job Organization

The people who organize mining companies (or anything else) tend to create structures comparable to those in which they have worked before. If the training, experience, and therefore current capabilities of the employees in the new situation are not comparable, recreating an old structure in a new environment does not make sense. Far too few mining (and other) organizations have innovated accordingly. Some have.

Determining employees' capabilities and reorganizing existing job functions *and* training opportunities to build on existing capabilities are difficult of conception and execution. It is an ongoing, not a once-and-for-all, process. Where it has been well done the results have been excellent — in rising productivity and advancement, reduced costs (after the initial investment), speedier replacement of expatriates by locals, reduced turnover, etc.

It was a major feat in Zambia where the companies, starting in the mid-1950s, undertook the restructuring of hundreds of jobs in the mining, concentrator, smelting, refining, engineering, medical, personnel and administrative departments, and set up literally hundreds of training programs for technical and general education, to the extent that in some subsequent years up to 75 per cent of the more than 40,000 employees were engaged in one or more training courses in any given year.

Certainly not all mining companies need to go through such a total overhaul. Probably all need to be more open to the possibilities of some job restructuring to take advantage of, and move forward with, local capabilities more effectively.

LOCALIZATION AS PART OF MANAGEMENT AGREEMENTS

That LDC nationals should have both authority and capability to run the enterprises in their countries has become almost platitude. They expect to take decision-making and operating responsibility in the financing, choice of technology, management, sales, costing, pricing, research and development, and processing carried out by enterprises in their countries. But few LDCs yet have made specific provisions in their agreements with outside investors or contractors to set in motion *a process* by which nationals will take on increasing responsibility for all the functions of the enterprise. Yet some foreign companies, recognizing the inevitability of pressures for localization, have become reluctant to participate in projects *unless* specific agreement is reached on the steps of the process.

Two examples can be cited of such initiatives to set up a localization process. One European company with long overseas experience proposed to join, as managing minority partner, with a LDC government holding company (as majority shareholder) in a small metal manufacturing plant. The European company insisted, as part of the negotiation of the management arrangement, that (1) a plan be drawn up jointly by representatives of the government and the European company of what the manpower needs would be for skilled, technical and professional personnel over the next several years; (2) a rough assessment be made of the availability of employees wholly or partly qualified, of those in training, and of competitive openings; and (3) a step-by-step plan be devised for assisting local people to obtain appropriate education and training in school, and on the job, such that over a set period — with a per cent for fall-out and failure — nationals would take on or participate in all of the technical and policy functions as originally stipulated.

Another approach to planned, graduated management take-over was tried in Zambia, where a government entity became a principal shareholder in the two major mining companies. The mine holding company set up its small staff in parallel structure to the companies in which it was a partner. Thus, both the government shareholding organization and the local companies had staff with responsibilities for purchasing, training, exploration, and other specific functions, who consulted with each other as professionals on all decisions in their respective fields. The companies continued to have responsibility for their own management, but it was understood that those in the parastatal corporation would take an increasing role over the ten years during which the management contract would be phased out. As the holding company included local people with a growing knowledge of specific operations and policies, the suspicions that often arise when local people know little of how decisions are made in large companies were allayed, and political and bureaucratic interference was reduced.

Expatriate managers are often sought for short or medium-term service, yet few foreign companies have good managers to spare. Companies are unlikely to release their able managers unless there is incentive for both company and manager. In negotiating management contracts with outside organizations, an ongoing commitment that the foreign company may share in the benefits of good management may therefore be important in securing effective managers. Has the outside group got at least a modest investment in the project on which they can externalize a return? And/or are they tied into benefits from increased sales, developing new markets, promoting successful research, undertaking further processing? If so, the manager will have an incentive, both professional and economic, to build. If not, he is a glorified maintenance man; no good manager wants to take a job where there are no rewards of recognition or remuneration and the only place to go is out.

Localization Is Useless Without Accountability Within the Organization

Virtually no enterprise succeeds without a management staff whose first responsibility is making the enterprise succeed. People whose primary links are to a political party, a ministry, or an overseas organization are understandably less likely to risk making the often tough, fast, sometimes unpopular decisions required in any operating enterprise. A good manager, whether from a LDC or a DC, must feel his/her remuneration, recognition and authority depend on performance within the enterprise; if he/she reports to a master whose future is not principally engaged in the success of the operation, commitment will be compromised.

Many countries complain of too few experienced managers. The great problem in recent years is the propensity of LDC companies to shift people in and out of jobs before they develop the expertise and relationships which underlie efficacy in a particular job. Shifts of managerial personnel are often rationalized on grounds of shortages or politics, but the staffs who spend too little time on a job to have the satisfaction of doing it well lose commitment, and the consequently less efficient and less profitable enterprises which they manage make a 'Hobson's choice' of alternatives.

CATALYST TO LOCAL ENTERPRISE

Mining companies can significantly spur local enterprise by increasing their purchases of local goods and services. Three examples can be mentioned:

(1) One Zambian mining company analyzed the 120,000 different stock items it purchased annually to determine if more could be manufactured by or purchased from Zambian entrepreneurs;

(2) Shell (Nigeria) worked with a local businessman who knew some chemistry to develop local clays to replace its imported ones. The ensuing successful enterprise became a supplier not only to Shell but also to local cosmetic and other companies;

(3) Lamco (Liberia) helped several employees spin-off a building construction/ maintenance business which started with contracts from the mine, and then expanded to take on others in the community.

Small is significant, and margins can make a difference, as the following cases suggest:

(1) An American mining company executive and a local amateur Latin American geologist found a way to sift and utilize residual sands from a declining mine. A loss of $.005 per pound was turned around to a profit of $.005 per pound which, although modest, kept the mine alive.

(2) In an African country government insistence and persistence was required to persuade five foreign mining companies (two with major existing investments) to build a small, marginal plant to produce copper wire for local consumption. Output expanded to meet slowly growing local needs, plus exports to neighbouring countries. Staff was trained, modest foreign exchange saved, local availability assured, with a net contribution to employment, wages and taxes.

It is precisely such a contribution, together with the expanding linkages connecting mining to local enterprises in other sectors, that is significant for development. Because these effects tend to be modest individually, they are too often ignored by mining companies which could and should be catalysts for this expansion of indigeneous enterprise. Taken together with training and localization programs, these activities of mining enterprises can make a substantive contribution to development.

20

A MINING POLICY FOR DEVELOPMENT:
THE CASE OF NAMIBIA

W.H. Thomas

The distinctive situation of Namibia makes it possible to focus on the centrality of the relationship between mining and development in a mineral-rich LDC that is characterized by a dualistic export-oriented enclave economy.

Namibia is still a colonial state, closely linked to, and largely dependent upon, South Africa. Its 'illegal' colonial status has been highlighted by the formal termination of South Africa's mandate by the UN General Assembly in 1966, endorsed by Security Council Resolutions 264/1969 and 276/1970.[1] Namibia has been administered by South Africa since 1919, and the economic, financial, cultural and political linkages virtually transformed the region into a 'fifth province' of South Africa. This applies to the mining sector, to labor legislation, taxation and other relevant issues, especially since deliberate steps were taken in 1969 to integrate the Namibian economy into that of South Africa.[2]

Since the mid-1970s, when it became clear that increasing internal and international pressure would be exerted upon South Africa to release Namibia to full independence, this trend has been gradually reversed. From the political point of view, the recent years have been characterized by an increase in the military struggle between South Africa and the guerillas of the country's externally-based liberation movement, the South West African People's Organization (SWAPO-N); the creation of new internal political groups — the Democratic Turnhalle Alliance (DTA), the Namibia National Front (NNF), the SWAPO-Democrats (SWAPO-D), and the right-wing Aktur — competing with SWAPO-N; and, since early 1977, the attempt by five Western powers (the US, UK, Germany, France and Canada) to mediate in the deadlock between South Africa, the UN, SWAPO-N, and the more conservative internal leaders. It is still not clear how and when Namibia will become independent, i.e. whether it will evolve out of internationally recognized elections or through an 'internal' process determined by South Africa or by an ultimately successful guerilla struggle. Notwithstanding this uncertainty, competing political groups are already in the process of shaping development strategies and socio-economic policies for the future government. This also relates to many of the issues relevant to uranium mining.

Apart from its transitional political status, Namibia's economy and society

Notes to this chapter may be found on pages 323-324.

also display contradictory characteristics. The modern sector of this vast and sparsely populated country has a well-developed infrastructure, an efficient administration, and profitable mining, ranching and commercial enterprises, but the more remote rural areas are characterized by subsistence peasant farming, low income, and a deficient social and physical infrastructure. The distribution of personal income and wealth between regions and racial groups is extremely unequal (about 100,000 whites and some coloureds on the one hand, and the heterogenous black groups totalling about one million on the other hand).

Namibia has a typical export-led economy: mineral exports constitute more than 60 per cent of total exports, and the mining sector contributes about 40 per cent of government revenue and 30 per cent of the GDP. The ownership structure of Namibia's mines closely resembles the colonial capitalist model: little state ownership and negligible local shareholding and control, with the bulk of investment controlled by South Africa and by Western interests. In addition, the two main minerals — diamonds and uranium — are both of a special nature as far as marketing and final uses are concerned.

Our focus here is on uranium mining, which will be analyzed in the context of Namibia's present economic structure with a view to possible (and probable) future developments. The writer does not explicitly side with any of the competing political groups nor does he believe that any one particular strategy would be optimal for the country's future development.

NAMIBIA'S ECONOMY ON THE THRESHOLD OF INDEPENDENCE[3]

Namibia covers an area of 824,300 sq.km. and has a population currently estimated at about 1.1-1.25 million, expected to increase to about 1.6 million by the end of this century. The populated is concentrated in a few towns (Windhoek, Walvis Bay-Swakopmund-Arandis, Oranjemund, Keetmanshoop, and Tsumeb) and in the relatively densely-populated peasant farming areas in the north (Ovambo, Kavango, Caprivi). Over three-quarters of the total area is of a semi-desert or arid nature, while the remainder has a delicate ecological balance. For its small size the population is extremely heterogenous, comprising various black, coloured and white groups with widely differing cultures.

The country's GDP for 1977 has been estimated at $1,365 million, i.e. about $960-1,300 per capita. Due to the racial and regional inequality in the distribution of income, these figures have little significance. The estimated sectoral breakdown of the 1977 GDP is as follows: agriculture, forestry, and fishing 17 per cent; mining 27 per cent; secondary industry and construction 15 per cent; tertiary and informal sectors 41 per cent. During the 1960s the economy achieved impressively high rates of growth but this levelled-off during the 1970s and the economy has stagnated in recent years. This is the result of structural and cyclical economic factors as well as of the political uncertainty caused by the transitional process. Economic factors have included low world market prices for copper and some other base metals, the long gestation period before the Rössing uranium mine was brought into production, a drastic decrease in the annual off-shore fish catch, a decline in construction activities, and a noticeable exodus of capital and of white-skilled labor. The heavy inflow of South African funds for defense and the public sector (administration and infrastructure) has not offset the negative impact of these trends.

Namibia's agricultural sector is characterized by a sharp dichotomy between the monetary (ranching) sector, i.e. the export of cattle/beef, wool and karakul hides, and the subsistence farming (cattle, maize and mahango) in the densely-populated black 'homelands'. The ailing fishing industry, including the canning factories, located mostly in the South African-controlled enclave of Walvis Bay, is dominated by less than a dozen large companies.

Namibia's industrial base is as yet extremely narrow due to its small population, the low purchasing power in the more populous northern areas, and the dominance of South African suppliers of manufactured goods. Little processing of agricultural and mining products takes place in the country, reflecting the nature of the products and their international markets (e.g. karakul hides and diamonds), the close proximity of South Africa, and technical as well as business considerations of the mining companies.

As in most African countries, the creation of sufficient employment opportunities for the rapidly increasing population constitutes a central issue. Hitherto, the absorptive capacity of the capital-intensive ranching, mining and commercial sectors has been limited, while industrial employment has fallen mainly due to the decline in fishing. More dynamic development in the peasant farming areas may require further movement of the population out of those regions in which the rural-urban push-pull effect has operated for many years. New pressures exerted during recent years on modern-sector enterprises to improve black wages and employment conditions have led in many cases to the introduction of labor-saving techniques and rationalizations, thus further aggravating the employment problem.

Contrasted with other African economies Namibia's long-run prospects for development are promising. Assuming that a successful transition to internationally recognized independence can be achieved and that a large exodus of the (white) technical and entrepreneurial elite can be prevented, the combination of exportable mining resources (diamonds, uranium, copper, and a number of other minerals) and agricultural products (mainly cattle and karakul) on the one hand, and a relatively fertile agricultural area in the very north of the country on the other hand, might make a phased process of gradually widening development possible. The well-developed infrastructure, a potentially very healthy balance of payments (due to mineral exports), rapidly rising government revenue (initially also due to the mining sector), and the existence of a dynamic entrepreneurial and administrative establishment could facilitate such a development.

Against such a longer run perspective the more immediate future looks far less promising. Until an acceptable political solution is found the low-profile war at the northern border and inside the northern areas will continue (possibly even expand); foreign investors interested in prospecting for minerals and in other ventures will probably remain outside; integrated rural development strategies needed for the northern region will not get off the ground; the outflow of capital and skilled (white) labor may continue, and overall economic stagnation will further aggravate the unemployment problem, which could even become politically explosive in the larger urban areas.

URANIUM MINING IN NAMIBIA – THE BASIC FACTS[4]

Radioactive minerals have long been known to exist in the Rössing area of the Namib desert, inland from Swakopmund. Systematic aerial surveys undertaken in the 1960s by the Geological Survey Section of the South African Department of Mines revealed the full extent of these findings. The orebody at Rössing is estimated to contain more than 500 million tons of the porphyry type in alaskite and granite intrusions. The ore grade is a mere 0.8 pound per ton (0.03 per cent uranium), but the nature of the mineralization allows upgrading.

Rio Tinto Zinc Corporation (RTZ) already had mining interests in South Africa and Zimbabwe. It acquired the mining rights in the Rössing area in 1966 and in 1969 announced that it would open a large open-pit mine with an initial target output of 60,000 tonnes of ore/waste per day (i.e. the equivalent of 2,500 tons of uranium oxide per annum), later to be doubled to reach an annual 5,000 tons of oxide. The project was started in 1973 with capital costs initially estimated at £100 million, but by 1979 these had escalated to about £150 million. Construction of the metallurgical plant and the uranium ore treatment plant, together with ancillary facilities (road and rail links as well as water and power supplies), were completed during 1976. The oxide plant was commissioned in October 1976 and by the end of that year the first 771 short tons of uranium oxide had been produced. In 1974 it was decided also to build an underground mine. Underground and open-pit prospects were reassessed during 1977, and as a result, full capacity was scheduled for 1979.

The major shareholders of Rössing Uranium Ltd are as follows: RTZ 36.5 per cent; Rio Algom of Canada, a subsidiary of RTZ, 10 per cent; the Industrial Development Corporation of South Africa (IDC) 13.2 per cent; General Mining/ Federale Mynbou (GM) 6.8 per cent; and Minatome 10 per cent; with RTZ managing the mine and IDC/GM holding control over voting rights. About two-thirds of the capital has been financed through loans. For this reason, and due to generous provisions for the write-off of capital investment against initial profits, it is not expected that Rössing Uranium will generate any substantial government revenue before 1980-81.

Rössing's major customers on a long-term (re-negotiable) contract basis are British Nuclear Fuels Ltd (initially the contract was with the UK Atomic Energy Authority), France, Japan and Germany. Little is known about actual prices and other terms negotiated with the contractors, except that the contract price negotiated with the UK (about $15 per pound) was substantially below 1977-78 spotmarket prices of up to $45 per pound.

Two other uranium deposits are being developed in addition to Rössing, i.e. Langer Heinrich (near Tinkas, in the Namib Desert Park) by GM, and Trekkopje (north-east of Rössing) by the Goldfields group. The former deposit is substantial and work started on a pilot plant in 1976. In addition, Anglo-American is prospecting jointly with Minatome of France and Union Corporation – all partners of Swakop Exploration (Pty) Ltd – for low-grade, secondary uranium deposits near Swakopmund. Some other companies, like Aquitane, Falconbridge and Johannesburg Consolidated Investments, include uranium in their exploration programs. These programs are encouraged and financially assisted by the South African Government, which has also indicated that (through IDC) it would want to be a partner in any future mine.

Little detailed information is as yet available with which to assess the economic dimension of the Rössing mine or of uranium mining *per se*. At an average price of $20 per pound for uranium oxide, the 5,000 ton annual capacity should earn the country $200 million, or about R160 million. This is about half the total 1978 non-uranium mineral exports. A higher renegotiated price could increase the relative significance of uranium even further, some longer-run estimates going as high as R300 million in annual export value. This figure may not be unrealistic once the additional mines at Langer Heinrich and Trekkopje become operational. At such a rate, annual government revenue from uranium could reach R100 million (although there would be some delay due to capital write-off), a sum which is about 50 per cent of the total government revenue in 1977-78. Eventually, uranium could surpass diamonds as the major export product and source of tax revenue.

In the short run there is need for caution concerning the expected expansion of uranium production and of export earnings. Recent years have shown that annual production volumes can fluctuate considerably due to technical and operational factors. World demand is also somewhat erratic due to doubts about uranium as a source of energy and to the opening of new mines in other countries.[5]

The impact on employment of Rössing Uranium is very limited. Its total present labor force is less than 2,500 (about 700 whites) and this may decline once the construction and consolidation phases are completed. Substantial labor needs may arise in the construction phase as new mines are developed, but in the longer run the employment component will be small, particularly when compared with the annual 8,000-10,000 increase in the Namibian labor force. In line with this trend Rössing already functions as a high pay, modern sector enclave in the Namib desert area, comparable to the diamond mines in Oranjemund and the modern mining complexes in other African countries. It is characterized also by integrated 'non-racial' wage scales, comprehensive in-company training schemes, company housing (in the black township of Arandis and in Swakopmund) and reasonable social services and amenities.[6] At the same time, the mine suffers a relatively high labor turnover, partly due to the unstable political climate of the country and to the remoteness of the mining area. Relations between company management and black trade unions (cooperating with SWAPO) have also been strained in recent times.

The close link between Namibia and South Africa is to be seen in the uranium mining sector. Before exploring in Namibia RTZ had already been active in South Africa, particularly in copper mining at Phalaborwa. Technical assistance and supervision by the government was exercised by the South African Department of Mines which, under South-West Africa Affairs Act No. 25 of 1969, had taken over all 'mining and matters related to minerals' from the Mines Division of the South-West Africa Administration. The state's shareholding in the Rössing venture is channelled through the South African government-financed IDC. The other major non-foreign partner is GM, a leading mining finance house in South Africa. The strict rules about non-disclosure of information which, under the South African Atomic Energy Act of 1967, apply to all atomic energy matters in South Africa, also apply to Namibia. According to some sources, much of the technical knowhow developed in South Africa's uranium industry has been applied in Namibia. Most of Rössing's skilled labor has been recruited from South Africa, Zimbabwe and Zambia, and the bulk of the construction and engineering input coming from the region has been of South African origin.

As part of the Rand zone and the South African customs area, foreign exchange earned through the export of Namibian uranium benefits the region's balance of payments. The same could apply to any eventual tax revenue generated by Rössing.

Finally, the close links between Namibian and South African uranium mining industries strengthen the latter's bargaining position on the international uranium market. Taken as an entity, South Africa and Namibia constitute one of the major producers of uranium ranking after the USA and the USSR. It has been argued at length that in planning its own uranium-enrichment industry, South Africa is counting upon the future supply of Namibia's uranium oxide to justify minimum capacities. Some critics go as far as to link Namibia's uranium to the suspected nuclear armament of South Africa.[7]

It is difficult, if not impossible, to verify these linkages and their significance because Rössing, the first Namibian uranium mine, has only been in operation since 1976 and has not yet achieved planned capacity nor contributed any tax revenue. Much of the reasoning about Namibia's dependence on South Africa is based on conjecture and will have to be tested in the light of the policies of the government of an independent Namibia.

DEVELOPMENT STRATEGIES FOR INDEPENDENT NAMIBIA

In speculating about Namibia's development strategies and their impact upon the uranium industry, it is necessary to distinguish between party political programs (or ideals) on the one hand, and the dictates of a progressive yet realistic development strategy, as would seem logical and feasible in the light of national characteristics and experiences in other LDCs, on the other hand. The programs of the various political parties, i.e. SWAPO-N, DTA, NNF/SWAPO-D, Aktur, are not yet very specific, particularly with regard to the treatment of foreign investors, mining activities, trade and other business links with South Africa, the tax structure and other relevant aspects. Aktur and DTA place strong emphasis on maintenance of the 'private enterprise system' with only minimal interference by the state, while SWAPO-N almost goes to the other extreme of propagating the nationalization of all larger enterprises and all natural resources (including the mines).[8] SWAPO-D and NNF politicians have been more cautious in their policy statements although many of their members undoubtedly favor far-reaching steps towards state control and some form of socialism. In fact, the active debate about Namibia's future socio-economic system has only just started and is bound to intensify once formal independence has been achieved and political parties compete for leadership. SWAPO-N leaders, while playing down internal dissent about alternative development strategies, have urged that 'at the present moment there is not much work done in the field of development strategy by SWAPO-N due to the fact that much energy and effort are spent in the execution of the liberation struggle'.[9] Similarly, DTA politicians have been far too busy with the establishment of their party and the consolidation of its political and leadership positions to elaborate upon alternative development strategies.

In view of these problems, we shall suffice here with a summary of the main aspects of a 'middle-of-the-road' development strategy which, in the opinion of the author, is relevant to Namibia's potentials and development problems.[10]

The long-term goal of a realistic development strategy is taken to be efficient utilization of the country's substantial but precarious resources, in such a way that the basic needs of the whole population are satisfied within the shortest possible time, that reasonable employment opportunities are created, and that the long-run growth potential of the country is realized. The achievement of these ends requires that particular attention be paid to the following problem areas.

Safeguarding the Country's Export Potential
This implies proper handling of the modern agricultural sector (cattle and karakul farming) and maintenance of a steady level of output of the mining sector, the country's major foreign exchange earner. Given rising world market prices for diamonds, uranium, copper and other exportable minerals, and given substantial though not inexhaustible reserves of exportable minerals, Namibia would be prudent if it expanded its mineral exports only to the level necessary to meet balance of payments and taxation needs. Thus, while in the modern agriculture sector there might be some conflict between the increase of exports, the maintenance of the ecological balance and the satisfaction of basic needs (including employment), in the mining sector the potential conflict might be between higher output (and exports) and long-run stabilization of mineral exports.

Creation of Employment Opportunities
Both the modern mines and the big ranches are relatively insignificant as employers. If employment opportunities are to be provided for the rapidly growing labor force, the peasant farming sector in the north (and wherever else there is some potential), the informal services sector in the towns and villages and a consumer goods-oriented industrial sector will have to be developed. An expanding social and administrative infrastructure will also absorb some labor. Yet all of these policies require public funds, entrepreneurship and expertise, government leadership, etc., and would need to be linked to a strategy of capital-saving investment and labor-intensive technologies *wherever feasible* (which is not often the case).

Satisfaction of the Basic Needs of the Whole Population
This nucleus of a progressive development strategy relates to expansion of the social infrastructure (basic education, health care, and housing) and to redistribution of income in order that all households may afford at least basic food and clothing requirements. It implies that money wages must be increased to minimum levels and that peasant agriculture be improved to enable peasants to meet minimum food requirements.

Although Namibia's relatively small overall production (about 250,000 households) reduces the dimension of this task, it still constitutes a major challenge which the government will hardly be able to meet within the first few years after independence.

Maintenance of Overall Economic and Administrative Efficiency
Namibia lacks indigenous skilled manpower, efficient administrators and managers, technical and innovative knowhow, and investment capital, all shortages that could be aggravated if radical steps towards solving the problems discussed above were taken. Given the importance of sophisticated technical knowhow for the efficient functioning of the diamond, uranium, copper (and other) mines and of the modern ranching sector, and taking into account the risk of ecological imbalances, evolutionary rather than drastic changes are called for in the recruitment of foreign capital and skills.

Namibia therefore should aim at a mixed-economy strategy, utilizing foreign investment and skills to develop its mining, ranching, tourism, fishing and commercial/financial sectors, though with sufficient local and state participation to be able to guide the pattern of development and to control the repatriation of profits. State revenue derived from these activities should be utilized for high priority programs of peasant agricultural development and for expansion of the physical and social infrastructure, while also aiming at a more balanced regional pattern of development and a gradual reduction of income inequalities.

Namibia's future relations with South Africa and other countries should be judged on the basis of these goals. Economic links which further stable export returns, high local employment, the meeting of basic needs and overall economic efficiency, should be maintained although possibly adjusted to strengthen Namibia's national economic interests and to reduce the potential leverage of foreign powers. Thus it may well be in Namibia's interest for the time being to remain in the Rand zone and the South African customs area and even to market some of its exports through South Africa. At the same time, the country might benefit by steadily improving its economic cooperation with Angola, particularly between northern Namibia and southern Angola.

THE ROLE OF URANIUM MINING IN NAMIBIA'S FUTURE DEVELOPMENT

It is now possible to make some preliminary and tentative suggestions about the future role of the uranium industry. Much will depend, of course, on the nature of the transition to independence and the composition of the new government.

(i) The uranium mining sector (i.e. Rössing and any additional mines) will undoubtedly be regarded as a *vital part of Namibia's economy* and of great instrumental significance in the future process of development. In fact, this sector will have a crucial effect on exports, potential government revenue, employment and, indirectly, the transition of the peasant agricultural sector.

(ii) To assert its independence and enhance its international standing, it can be expected that any future Namibian government will *loosen the present close ties between the uranium mining industry of Namibia and South Africa*, even though pragmatism may call for close cooperation in various spheres. Namibia should have a Ministry of Mining, its own legislation covering mining and exploration activities (including special provisions for uranium), and possibly an inspector of mines and a state mining corporation.

(iii) No matter which socio-economic system is chosen by any future government, it will probably want to *have a direct stake in all the larger mines*, and in particular in all uranium mines. In the case of Rössing Uranium this might be done by transferring IDC's shares to a Namibian state mining corporation or some other appropriate body. In addition, some local (private sector) shareholding might be required and/or other foreign shareholders might be sought in order to diversify ownership. Thus, the degree of state ownership and control of such a strategic enterprise could be adapted with flexibility. A SWAPO-N government, however, might want to nationalize Rössing altogether, justifying its action on the basis of the 'illegality' of the present mine as specified in the UN Council for Namibia's Decree No. 1 for the Protection of the Natural Resources of Namibia, of 27th September 1974. Presumably a future government would also want to become the controlling shareholder in any new ventures in this mining subsector.

(iv) With proper controlling bodies set up for the Namibian mining industry and with the state as a substantial shareholder in all the major mines, it seems possible and highly probable that exploration and actual mining will be *planned and programmed on a longer-term basis* (taking into account balance-of-payments and taxation needs). This would be particularly important for uranium mining in that short-term trends on the world market sometimes differ significantly from long-term trends, and Namibia's substantial reserves could increase in value during the coming decades.

(v) The Namibian government can also be expected to play a direct role in the *marketing of the uranium oxide*. Similar to those of other independent black African countries, the government may want to insist on the peaceful use of exported uranium, i.e. put a total ban on its sale to countries which do not subscribe to the Nuclear Non-Proliferation Treaty, or may limit its exports in some other way. Secondly, in the case of Rössing Uranium, the government may insist on renegotiation of all supply contracts in the hope of increasing the price and/or of improving other terms of the contracts. Thirdly, it seems conceivable that Namibia might try to cooperate with other major uranium exporting countries in order to stabilize long-term prices. Under present world market conditions, however, the scope for such a cartel seems to be limited.

(vi) The *taxation* of uranium mining, particularly of Rössing Uranium, will no doubt be reconsidered by the new government at an early stage. Critics of the present system argue that conditions for the writing-off of capital expenses are far too generous, that income tax rates are too low, and that additional export duties or other taxes (e.g. a loan levy or development tax) should be added. These issues will have to be investigated in detail, taking into account the need to attract foreign capital for new mines. Once the state becomes a major shareholder, present suspicion about unreasonable profits may quickly fade. Given the need for government revenue to stimulate development in the agricultural sector and to improve the social infrastructure, however, taxes will most likely be raised until they absorb an increasing share of the profits.

(vii) Critics of Rössing Uranium have condemned the alleged lack of *safety precautions*. In theory at least, more direct state participation would enable more effective control of these aspects, as well as other ecological and environmental considerations (which may be of special importance in the case of uranium mining). In practice, however, much will depend on the overall efficiency of the controlling institutions.

(viii) It could also be argued (and probably is implied by critics of the present system) that *employment conditions* for workers in the mines would improve after independence, given more direct state control, especially if the new government encouraged trade unions and instituted better supervision of employment conditions (including minimum wages). Recent censure of Rössing Uranium's treatment of its black employees would seem to lead to such expectations. Yet much will depend on the future quality and style of mine management and on the government's overall labor policies. The rest of Africa shows little evidence that a greater degree of state ownership or control necessarily implies better conditions of employment (or more scope for trade unions). In fact, Rössing's 2,500 employees even now constitute a 'labor elite'. Independence or a change in government is hardly likely to affect this situation, except perhaps that greater emphasis will be given to employing permanent rather than temporary, i.e. migrant, labor.

(ix) The urgent need to create additional employment opportunities for Namibia's rapidly increasing labor force would seem to imply that a future government should exert pressure on the mines to increase their labor intensity. Yet for technical reasons there is little scope for change, other than in the administrative and social services. A strict approach can be expected, however, regarding the employment of foreigners other than those who possess special skills.

(x) Like many other LDC governments, that of Namibia may want to have its minerals (and mining inputs) processed locally inasfar as this is technically and practically feasible. Such possibilities are quite limited, however, for uranium oxide.

(xi) South Africa presumably will be interested in using Namibia's uranium in its enrichment plant, should current plans materialize, and might even offer a relatively higher price than foreign competitors. Namibia's government may be reluctant to cooperate, however, unless certain conditions are met, such as South Africa's adherence to the Nuclear Non-Proliferation Treaty.

(xii) Finally, as a catalyst in the development process, Rössing and other uranium mines may be expected to play a significant role in the technical and managerial training process as well as in the development of the social infrastructure. In fact, Rössing Uranium already performs this function at the mine and through the Rössing Foundation, but its scope may have to be expanded substantially.

If action in all these spheres is taken, the accusation that the mining sector merely 'robs the country of its resources to the benefit of outside investors', i.e. the accusation of neo-colonial exploitation, can hardly be justified. It seems significant that in each of these spheres action might be taken either by a DTA-type of government or by a SWAPO-N/SWAPO-D government. Furthermore, foreign mining companies are unlikely categorically to oppose such developments.[11] The differences are rather of degree. A DTA-type of government would probably tend towards evolutionary policy adjustments, while a SWAPO-N government would want more drastic changes.

NOTES

1. On Namibia's recent history see J.H. Serfontein, *Namibia?* (Randburg, 1977); and G.K.H. Tötemeyer, *South West Africa/Namibia: Facts, Attitudes, Assessment and Prospects* (Randburg, 1977).
2. On these aspects and other issues of Namibia's economic development see the author's book, *Economic Development in Namibia: Towards Acceptable Development Strategies for Independent Namibia* (München/Mainz: Kaiser/Grünwald, 1978).
3. In addition to the book cited in (2) see the following two studies on Namibia's economy by the German Development Institute: W. Schneider-Barthold, *Namibia's Economic*

Potential and Existing Economic Ties with the Republic of South Africa (Berlin, 1977); and P. Waller (ed.), *Multisektorstudie – Namibia* (Berlin, 1979). Another recent study of relevance is R.H. Green's work, published by the UN Institute for Namibia: *Manpower Estimates and Development Implications for Namibia* (Lusaka, 1979).

4. This section is largely based on Roger Murray's recent report for the Commonwealth Fund for Technical Co-operation, *The Mineral Industry of Namibia: Perspectives for Independence* (London: Commonwealth Secretariat, 1979), esp. 11-13. Also see W. Ulbricht, *Bergbauliche Ressourcen im südlichen Afrika* (Hamburg: Institut für Afrika-Kunde, 1976); W. Gocht, 'Sektorstudie über den Bergbau in Südwestafrika/Namibia' (unpublished report for the German Development Institute, Berlin, September 1978); and the literature quoted by Murray and Thomas.

5. Cf. 'Looking for Uranium', *West Africa*, 3246 (1 October 1979), 1802/03.

6. Cf. *Rössing Uranium 1979* and other *Information Fact Sheets* issued by the company. For a critical view see B. Rogers, 'Namibian Uranium' (New York, 1976; mimeo).

7. The case has been argued at length by Barbara Rogers, Roger Murray, representatives of the Anti-Apartheid Movement, and other radical critics of South Africa. For an example see B. Rogers and Z. Cervenka, *The Nuclear Axis* (London, 1978).

8. This could be deduced from the 1976 'Political Program' of SWAPO released in Lusaka, though a different line is taken in the 1975 'Draft Constitution, Discussion Paper'.

9. See M.J. Kaulinge, 'Synopsis of the Strategy for the Mining Industry in Namibia', a paper presented to the Policy Workshop on 'The State Sector and the International Economy' (The Hague: The Institute of Social Studies, 1979; mimeo), 1. A similar line was taken in discussions during this Workshop and in consultations between this writer and staff of the UN Institute for Namibia in Lusaka (August 1979).

10. For more details see the author's book, *Economic Development in Namibia*, especially chapters 3 and 4.

11. See in this respect the critical article by D. Mezger, 'How the Mining Companies Undermine Liberation', *Review of African Political Economy*, 12 (May-August 1978), 53-66.

21

PLANNING FOR DEVELOPMENT IN A MINERAL-BASED LDC

A. Seidman

A deeply structured dualism typically characterizes the economies of mining LDCs.[1] A relatively small percentage of the national labor force, working in an isolated enclave, employs modern, highly complex, capital-intensive machines and equipment to dig out rich minerals which are then freighted in high-powered trains of trucks to ports for shipment to foreign factories. Almost all inputs are imported: machinery and materials used for construction of the mines, the workers' houses, the roads — even some of the foodstuffs the workers eat.

Outside the mining enclaves, the great majority of the populations, mostly peasants, commonly live in grinding poverty. Few can afford to buy any of the consumer goods ultimately fabricated from their nation's mineral wealth in far-away lands. Their main hope for escape is to migrate to overcrowded urban slums, joining the growing ranks of unemployed looking for paid jobs.

For those mining countries whose minerals contribute an unusually large share of export and tax revenue, the national economy becomes particularly sensitive to the fluctuations of an uncertain world market. When prices for exported ores rise, those sectors associated with the mines boom. The government spends augmented revenues to build schools, hospitals and roads. Construction industries hire workers who buy food and clothing, stimulating local factories or, more often, expanding imports. But when mineral prices fall, the entire economy stagnates. The government must borrow money to pay ongoing expenses, incurring heavy international debts. Frequently, it must request IMF assistance — and accept the 'austerity' measures prescribed:[2] slash government expenditures and employment, devalue currencies (thus raising the cost of imported goods on which the economy has come to depend) and raise taxes, especially on middle and lower income families.

This study aims to pinpoint the causes of this pattern of externally dependent dualism which condemns the majority of the population of mining economies to poverty. It will then outline the kinds of policies which the experience of the independent countries of Africa suggest may be most likely to help overcome them.

Notes to this chapter may be found on pages 333-335.

DEPENDENT DUALISM AND ITS CAUSES

The MNCs which establish most mining enclaves in LDCs primarily seek raw materials which are usually then processed in their home countries. They introduce machinery and equipment embodying the most advanced technologies developed in the DCs, ensuring both their control over the mining projects and their competitiveness in the world market. They generally control the international marketing networks through which they sell the ores and frequently own factories which fabricate the final products. They keep their eyes on the bottom line: the maximization of their global profits. Of course, very substantial portions of the potentially investable surplus generated by mining projects are often taken out of the country in the form of dividends, interest, high salaries and/or management and licensing fees for the technologies they introduce. Attempts by LDC governments to obtain a greater share of profits through taxes or direct equity participation may encourage the MNCs to siphon profits out indirectly by raising the cost of imported machinery and equipment and, in the case of highly vertically integrated MNCs, by lowering the prices paid by their marketing subsidiaries for the exported crude or semi-refined ores.

Furthermore, attempts by LDC governments to augment national returns from their mines have tended to falter because the same governments are unable to take adequate measures to create a new pattern of self-sustained growth by initiating a transformation to a balanced, integrated economy capable of providing increasingly productive employment opportunities and raising living standards in every sector. In fact, they tend to spend their augmented revenues on expansion of the civil service to provide roads, schools, hospitals, energy projects — the infrastructure which western orthodoxy traditionally recommends to stimulate private investments in productive activities. The governments have been structured to pursue this advice: their ministries know how to build schools, roads, hospitals and energy projects. Their personnel have generally been schooled to believe that the civil service should not become directly involved in production activities; if a government should undertake the latter, it should do so through parastatals, autonomous state corporations, which should behave as much as possible like private enterprises.

Private investors — whether domestic or foreign — invest in those areas of the already distorted economy where short-term profits will be highest: speculative trade and real estate and a limited range of import-substitution industries primarily catering to the needs of the small high-income elite. Those industries are mainly located in the export enclave, use imported machines and materials, and provide relatively few jobs. Parastatals, seeking to stimulate industrial growth — often with no other criterion than to maximize profits — not infrequently follow suit.[3]

Meanwhile, the government has created new high-paying posts for growing numbers of civil servants staffing the growing number of new infrastructural posts. If it establishes parastatals, their managers, operating autonomously, may increasingly act like officials of a state within a state. They also often rely on the advice of foreign 'partners' eager to sell them new technologies and semi-processed materials.

Nobody planned it that way, but a 'bureaucratic bourgeoisie' and associated 'managerial bourgeoisie' tends to emerge.[4] Not infrequently, these individuals take advantage of their new posts: they discover that they can obtain ten per cent on contracts with foreign partners; they borrow money from banks to finance their entry into speculative real estate and trade, taking advantage of inside knowledge; and they channel government funds into their own undertakings. The growth of the bureaucractic/managerial bourgeoisie is not caused by corruption; rather, corruption is a by-product of the emergence of a bureaucratic/managerial bourgeoisie.

When the world price for its specific mineral export declines, the LDC government finds itself saddled with expensive infrastructural and parastatal projects[5] which, nevertheless, still require the continued import of parts and materials. Simultaneously, government revenues fall off and foreign exchange reserves vanish. As a result, the government must borrow funds, at home, stimulating inflation, and/or abroad, incurring mounting foreign debts which it cannot repay as long as its minerals sell at low prices. Eventually, it must turn to the IMF and submit to its 'discipline'. To implement the IMF proposals, the government devises policies whose costs are almost invariably disproportionately borne by the peasantry and wage earners.

The experience of LDC mining economies suggests that any solutions for the problems identified above require the restructuring of the national political economy to meet the needs of the majority of the population. This seems to have been the goal of the leaders of many African states when they attained independence in the 1960s.[6] Yet their efforts to attain development along conventional lines within the framework of inherited institutions almost invariably spawned a bureaucratic/managerial bourgeoisie which, in the end, sought only to perpetuate the *status quo* which gave it power and privilege. More recently, the leaders of newly independent Mozambique, Guinea-Bissau and Angola, who came to power through a decade of guerilla struggle, have expressed renewed determination to make key institutional changes in order to restructure their inherited political economies.

Any leadership committed to the restructuring of their dualistic economy to meet the needs of the people must first formulate a long-term industrial strategy — say for a 20-year period — and carry out major changes in key institutions to insure its implementation.[7] The government, working in close contact with the masses of the population in the rural areas, as well as in the cities, should formulate a long-term strategy to increase productive employment opportunities in every sector. Within the framework of a long-term strategy, the nation's planners would need to formulate specific five-year plans, which would encompass physical and financial plans for each project. Specific projects would be identified for each period and their backward and forward linkages with the rest of the economy would be detailed. For mineral-exporting LDCs this requires capturing the surpluses produced in the mining sector and reinvesting them in specific projects carefully designed to augment productivity and living standards. Wherever possible, inputs for the mines and associated roads and railroads, as well as housing and consumer goods for the workers, should be produced locally, rather than imported. The resulting increased market should facilitate formulation of physical plans to expand output in other sectors of the economy. Peasants could be encouraged to purchase new locally-produced inputs and expand their output of crops to provide raw materials for new factories and foodstuffs for the growing industrial labor force. Their increased incomes would broaden domestic markets for national products. Small-scale industries could be established to process tools embodying appropriate levels of technology both for agriculture and new small-scale industries.

Eventually, basic industries could be constructed. A plant to produce explosives might be linked with one producing fertilizers or a factory might be built to produce standardized trucks and buses, first by assembling imported parts, and then later by producing them in the country. Planners would need to assess the nation's resource potentials, and develop education and training programs to create the cadres required to provide the necessary technical and managerial skills. In view of the smallness of many mining economies, coordinated planning with neighboring countries will almost inevitably be required to establish more basic industries.

Implementation of the long-term strategy proposed above calls for fundamental institutional changes. Unfulfilled and discarded plans abound in LDCs. Inherited institutions and structures were simply inappropriate for implementing them. Two interrelated sets of institutional changes are necessary: those relating to structures of the state machinery designed to assume responsibility for formulating and carrying out plans; and those facilitating participation of the majority of working people in that process.

The state should exert direct control over basic industries, in particular, the mines which shape the economy and its relations to the world commercial system. The form of control may, of course, vary depending on the foreign 'partner' and the particular circumstances prevailing in the country. That there will be a foreign 'partner' for a prolonged period is almost inevitable. At independence, the typical African mining economy, inherited from prolonged colonial rule, has few technically qualified persons to manage the mines. What engineering skills or commercial expertise its nationals possessed usually had been acquired within the world commercial network through which the nation sold its mineral output.

A potential mining economy may choose among a variety of 'partners'.[8] It may bargain with various mining MNCs based in DCs or it may negotiate with one of the CPEs. The latter are increasingly able to provide the necessary technologies, markets and capital. It might also arrange with a wealthier LDC with surplus capital to finance the mine, the output of which will be shipped to a processing plant in the capital-providing LDC. Several oil-producing nations, for example, plan to utilize their natural gas, formerly simply burned-off, to process aluminum, and hence may be willing to finance a mining project to provide the necessary bauxite ore, or semi-processed alumina. Obviously, the LDC will need to bargain hard to get the best possible deal, no matter with which potential partner it negotiates.

The mining economy that 'inherits' a MNC which had for years been exploiting both its mineral wealth and its labor force has less choice.[9] It cannot easily shift to another 'partner' because the MNC has already installed its own technology and marketing system, geared to the particular way the ore is mined. Getting spare parts for the mine's machinery may be difficult, and it may not be easy to find markets for the particular form in which the ores are exported. On the other hand, the company, too, is to a certain extent trapped. It may be willing to renegotiate its relationship with a resolute government in order not to lose its existing investment.

For any LDC government the best possible arrangement, whether it is entering on a new project or renegotiating its role in relation to an old one, depends crucially on its ability to identify the specific role which the mines can play in helping to realize a carefully formulated long-term development strategy. The issue distinctly is *not* simply whether the governnment owns 51 per cent or more of the shares of ownership. Country after country has learned to its sorrow that ownership does not necessarily imply adequate control.[10]

The government must focus its attention on at least five aspects of the relationship it seeks to establish with its foreign 'partner' to ensure that the mine plays its intended role in the country's overall economic transformation.

(i) *The government's share of profits and foreign exchange earnings.* The government should seek, not only to maximize its returns, but also to reduce the negative impact of world price fluctuations for its mineral exports, in order to plan effectively to restructure the economy. Whether by sharing profits, taxing income, or taking royalties, the government will need to ensure that it obtains as regular and steady returns as possible so as to implement smoothly its plans to reduce the country's excessive dependence on mining, foreign partners, and/or uncertain world markets.

(ii) *Arrangements to train nationals.*[11] The agreement reached with the foreign partner must specify categories of required skills and fix timetables for the recruitment and training of nationals for each. While nationals are acquiring appropriate skills, the government must introduce safeguards to ensure that they remain committed to the central role of mining in the implementation of the nation's long-term development strategy. This should help to prevent future managers and technicians from placing self-advancement ahead of national welfare. Of course, such a commitment is insufficient unless the necessary institutional changes are simultaneously undertaken.

(iii) *Construction of dual purpose infrastructure.* The government should ensure that, wherever possible, infrastructure built for mining — ports, roads, railroads, power projects, training institutions, health facilities — also contributes to increased productivity and/or higher living standards throughout the country. In the construction of infrastructure, planners should attempt to identify technologies and materials most appropriate for the stimulation of productivity. It may, for example, be preferable to construct a road using local materials and truck haulage, rather than building a rail line direct from the mine to the port, utilizing imported materials. Over time, construction of roads feeding into the main road may facilitate the spread of agricultural and small industrial projects. Training of workers to make repairs on standardized models of trucks might further spread development. Eventually a standardized truck may be assembled in the country itself, and finally the parts, the body and even, after some years, the engine may be produced locally. Planners must weigh such possibilities, along with the relative costs of construction and maintenance, against the greater efficiency and heavier loads that trains may carry.

(iv) *Local production of inputs.* Mining projects use a wide range of inputs, from the basic equipment and machines required to blast out the ores, to the food, clothing and other consumer goods needed by the miners. Foreign 'part-ners' often conclude it is more efficient to import everything from their home countries, often augmenting their own profits by purchasing goods from associ-ated enterprises.

Planners must, however, study which inputs might be produced immediately in the country, stimulating productive employment opportunities in other sec-tors of the economy, and which might be produced over a 20-year period to facilitate the transformation of the entire economy. Obviously, foodstuffs should be produced locally from the outset. To increase output, institutions must be created to provide farmers with the necessary credit, marketing and pro-cessing facilities, as well as fertilizers and tools. Within a few years, some tools and parts for simpler mining machines, and even more complex inputs like ex-plosives, might be produced locally. Later on, it may be possible to produce all the inputs for which local raw materials are available or can cheaply be im-ported, contributing to the growth of domestic industrial capacity.

(v) *Utilization of outputs.* The typical small mining economy will be unable, in the early years of industrialization, to mobilize the capital to construct profit-able large-scale processing facilities. It might be able to undertake more advanced stages of processing if it could secure markets abroad for a major share of its more finished, and hence more valuable output. Or it might be able to cooperate with neighboring countries in a planned regional development program in which each will build a specific large-scale project, based on its own resources, as a pole of growth around which other planned industrial developments could take place.[12] In each agreement with any foreign partner, the government of an LDC mining country should ensure that its terms will most effectively stimulate an overall balanced, integrated industrial and agricultural growth.

To restructure the inherited economy in accord with its long-term strategy, the government will need to achieve adequate control of the other 'commanding heights': foreign and internal trade, and banks and financial institutions. Typical-ly, the exports of an LDC are almost entirely handled by MNCs. The ores that constitute the predominant share of the country's exports are marketed by the very mining MNC that operates the country's mines. Increased state control over the marketing of minerals abroad could facilitate expansion of sales to new and diversified markets. A state trading agency could be established to obtain higher prices and longer-term contracts which might facilitate planned investment in other sectors of the economy. Furthermore, as part of a program to upgrade local processing, the government could directly negotiate the sale of newly processed minerals, something which the foreign partner might refuse to initiate on its own.[13] The state could also cooperate with other producers of the same mineral to regulate output and raise prices.[14]

Trading MNCs handle most of the imports of consumer goods, concentrating on the more profitable items purchased by the small high-income group, as well as machinery, equipment and semi-processed materials utilized in other sectors of the economy. Often they buy these from other subsidiaries of their parent companies, which sell them at the highest possible prices to maximize the MNCs' global profits. Government control of trading institutions will facilitate reduction of imported consumer goods, machinery and equipment to the bare minimum required to complement and supplement the expanding domestic output of industrial and agricultural projects established in accord with the long-term plan. State control will also help to ensure that the prices of goods imported do not include unwarranted profit margins for foreign firms.

If several neighboring countries plan together for regional development to make possible the construction of complementary basic industries, each country will need to exert direct control over both exports and imports to fulfill its part of the regional plan. Each country will have to purchase the amounts of the other's products at the prices stipulated by long-term contracts regionally negotiated. Consequently, the import of competing items by private traders seeking to reap higher profits would not be permitted.

A state trading agency could halt the expenditure of scarce foreign exchange on the import of luxury items for the wealthy. It could negotiate directly for the purchase of mining machinery, thereby avoiding the high prices which often result when mining MNCs buy from their own subsidiaries. It could also purchase machines and equipment to implement its long-term industrial and agricultural development plans. In all these activities, it could shop around for the best sources of supply, perhaps bargaining for an exchange of a part of the country's mineral exports to obtain needed imports. Simultaneously, through control of internal wholesale networks, it could ensure better distribution of necessities, tools and equipment throughout the economy, replacing imported items, wherever possible, with locally produced goods.

Experience also suggests that any LDC seeking to implement a long-term development strategy must intervene directly to control banks and financial institutions. These institutions provide crucial channels for the mobilization and direction of investable surpluses produced in the economy. Acting in concert with the managements of the mining[15] and trading MNCs, banks and financial MNCs too often siphon surpluses out of the country — a major but concealed explanation for the persistent capital shortage which plagues most mining economies despite decades of production and export of minerals.

State control and reorganization of these institutions can contribute in several important ways to implementation of a long-term development strategy. First, it can ensure that they mobilize and direct available surpluses within the framework of a carefully designed financial plan to the specific industrial and agricultural projects for which physical plans have been drawn up. Secondly, it can provide a means of checking up on the way the managers of those projects fulfill initial investment plans, and their ongoing expenditure of working capital. Over time, the surpluses of these projects will be returned to the banking system for reinvestment in the projects designed for the next stage of the overall development plan. Eventually, the banks and financial institutions will control and direct the major flow of funds created within the economy for investment; taxation will become less and less important, since the state, through these channels, will directly supervise the accumulation and reinvestment of capital in planned projects.

Increased state control over the 'commanding heights' of the economy requires two major kinds of institutional changes. The first involves creating appropriate new institutions to enable the state to maximize national welfare.[16] Clearly, the old ministries and parastatals, forms inherited from the colonial past, cannot perform these new tasks; they were designed to leave key decisions to private firms and so perpetuated the external dependency relations of the past. Nor is it possible simply to import models from elsewhere. Leading cadres must design appropriate institutional forms in light of the particular problems of their own country.

Yet a real danger exists in such a situation as two somewhat contradictory aims must be achieved at the same time. The national leadership must drastically alter the institutional machinery while, simultaneously, it must keep the economy in running order. In more than one country, maintaining the machinery has taken precedence; old rules and corruption have rapidly reasserted themselves in the very institutions to be changed. The result has been the re-emergence of an expanding bureaucratic/managerial bourgeoisie wielding state power to advance its own interests.

Various devices may be attempted to thwart this trend. A sharply defined incomes policy could be instituted to limit the high salaries of civil service and managerial personnel. In mining LDCs where MNC personnel are likely to play a major role for a number of years, government officials argue that it would be discriminatory to reduce salaries of newly promoted indigenous managers below those of expatriates.[17] The high salaries of the latter, they insist, are essential to induce them to work in the country. Yet these high salaries constitute a significant drain on national funds. Those funds might otherwise be used either to raise the wages of those in the lower income brackets or to help finance projects in rural areas which will expand productive employment opportunities and raise living standards for large numbers of peasants. The fact that expatriate personnel may remain for some time cannot be allowed to justify policies entrenching permanent inequalities, and thus prolonging the drain of potential investable surpluses. Some countries have therefore reduced all supervisory and managerial salaries to levels more commensurate with the nation's ability to pay, and set aside specific inducement allotments, if necessary, to ensure an adequate supply of expatriate personnel until local cadre can be trained to replace them.

Any national incomes policy should be accompanied by some form of leadership code prohibiting civil servants, managers and political leaders from engaging in speculative real estate, trade, or other private business. The governments of Tanzania, Mozambique and Angola[18] have sought to further reduce such possibilities by taking over rental housing as well as major trading companies. Such measures may help to prevent individuals from utilizing their state jobs to advance their private interest.

Not only may these kinds of policies increase funds available for further development; they may also help to persuade the public at large that the leadership is serious about restructuring the nation's political economy to fulfill basic needs. This may be especially important in a mining economy where the mines themselves produce a major share of the investable surpluses. Unless the mine workers are convinced that the mine's managerial and supervisory personnel, along with the rest of government, is dedicated to spreading productive employment opportunities to the rest of the population (including members of their own families, and even themselves, if the mines are forced to cut back employment due to world market conditions), they are likely to press for higher wages. In country after country, mine workers whose wages constitute a relatively small share of total mining costs (typically less than 25 per cent) have pressed for and won wages well above those of workers in other sectors of the economy. This tends to create a privileged aristocracy of labor and spurs other workers to demand wage increases which reduce funds for further investment. No government or political leaders can expect to retain legitimacy when they ask workers to restrain their wage demands while they themselves are seen to be living at levels far above the rest of the people.

Above all, it is imperative to discover ways to enable an increasing number of men and women to participate in decision making[19] and to exert ongoing constructive pressures on those in charge of running the state to ensure the implementation of essential changes at all levels. Clearly this process of reshaping and, in some cases, completely replacing existing institutions and working rules will be far from easy.[20] But it must be tackled, otherwise the majority of the population of mining LDCs will remain condemned to lives of poverty.

NOTES

1. This structured dualism is analyzed in A. Seidman (ed.), *Natural Resources and National Welfare: The Case of Copper* (New York: Praeger, 1976). It should be emphasized that to describe the economies of mining countries as dualistic is not to explain why they are that way. This author completely rejects explanations of dualism, such as that of Boeke, which blame the attitudes, values and institutions of the people of LDCs.
2. This has often occurred in Africa, most recently in Zambia. See *Financial Statistics* (Washington, D.C.: IMF, 1979) for the size of IMF loans and the extent of devaluation. For

a more general analysis, see C. Payer, *The Debt Trap* (New York: Monthly Review Press, 1974).

3. See A. Seidman, 'The Distorted Import-Substitution Industry: The Zambian Case', *Journal of Modern African Studies*, 12, 4 (1974), 601-31.

4. Sklar, referring to the managers of Zambia's rapidly expanding parastatal sector, characterized them as a 'managerial bourgeoisie'. R. Sklar, *Corporate Power in an African State: The Political Impact of Multinational Mining Companies in Zambia* (Berkeley: University of California Press, 1975). For extensive discussion of the reasons for the emergence of this group, see R.B. Seidman, *The State, Law and Development* (New York: St Martin's Press, 1978), chapter 20.

5. This was the case in Zaire and Zambia as copper prices plummeted in real terms to record lows in the 1970s.

6. Otherwise, one would have to claim that Nkrumah, Kenyatta, Kaunda, Obote and Azikiwe – to name a few – were all hypocrites. That seems unlikely.

7. The ingredients of such a long-term strategy and the kinds of institutional changes required are detailed in A. Seidman, *Planning for Development in SubSaharan Africa* (New York: Praeger, and Dar es Salam: Tanzania Publishing House, 1974). How laws might be formulated and implemented to achieve these goals is discussed in R.B. Seidman, *The State, Law and Development*.

8. It has been suggested that Guinea-Bissau, when considering the possibilities of producing bauxite and/or alumina for export, should evaluate the alternative advantages and disadvantages of choosing among one or more of the six major aluminum MNCs which dominate MEC production, the oil countries which seek to process alumina as a means of utilizing their otherwise wasted natural gas, and the CPEs. See Economic Development Bureau, *Report to the Government of Guinea-Bissau* (New Haven: Economic Development Bureau, 1979).

9. See A. Seidman, *Natural Resources and National Welfare*, where the problems confronting the copper-exporting countries and their efforts to adopt different strategies are discussed.

10. Long ago, A.A. Berle and G.C. Means exposed the fact that in the USA ownership of shares in a large corporation does not mean control; *the managers* of the corporation make the key decisions. See A.A. Berle and G.C. Means, *The Modern Corporation and Private Property* (rev. ed. New York: Harcourt, Brace and World, 1968). In an LDC, government ownership of shares in a MNC's local subsidiary may merely mean that it has paid – often handsomely – for the right to share the risks, but it has not obtained adequate control over the management supplied by the parent firm.

11. Promised affirmative action to train and upgrade nationals in mining economies, as in the case of women and minorities in the US, has turned out to be a cruel joke unless goals and timetables are established and enforced. See C. Simwinga, 'Africanization on Zambia's Mines after Government Acquired 51 Per Cent of the Shares' (unpublished doctoral dissertation, University of Pittsburgh, 1975). See also Chapter 19, *supra*.

12. These possibilities are being considered by the front line states in Southern Africa through the medium of the mechanisms created at the Arusha Southern African Coordinating Conference, July 1979.

13. MNCs typically do not invest in processing facilities in LDC mining economies, except to reduce initial bulk or transport costs; they prefer to send their ores to their home factories which ensures their ability to retain control over the ultimate marketing networks.

14. See Chapter 15, *supra*.

15. Barclays Bank DCO and Standard and Chartered Bank both tend to dominate the banking sectors of most of the former British colonies. On their boards of directors sit a number of directors of major mining companies. For example, Anglo-American Corporation (of South Africa) is represented on the Barclays' board by its chairman. Both Barclays and Standard do a major share of their banking business in South Africa as well, where together they own about two-thirds of the assets of the largest banks. A third bank with important holdings in Central and East Africa is National Grindlays Bank, affiliated to the British parent bank of that name, in which the second largest US bank, Citicorp, owns 49 per cent of the shares. A number of US mining company representatives sit on Citicorp's board as well. Citicorp also owns 49 per cent of one of the two French banks which dominate the commercial banking sectors of the former French colonies in Africa; see N. Makgetla and A.

Seidman, *The Activities of Transnational Corporations in South Africa* (United Nations Committee Against Apartheid. New York: United Nations, 1978).

16. For the potentialities and difficulties involved in the establishment of those institutions, see the analysis in R.B. Seidman, *The State, Law and Development*.

17. This argument was advanced before the incomes commissions appointed by the Zambian government in 1973 of which this author was a member.

18. The policies of these countries are summarized in C.G. Rosberg and T.M. Callaghy, *Socialism in SubSaharan Africa: A New Assessment* (Berkeley: Institute of International Studies, University of California, 1979).

19. In Mozambique, Angola and Guinea-Bissau, the political leaderships realized early in the decade of guerilla warfare that women, who produced most of the food and played a crucial role in the families, must be involved in the struggle directly and be assured participation in decision making at all levels. Stephanie Urdang has reported on the status of women in Guinea-Bissau in her recent book, *Fighting Two Colonialisms: Women in Guinea-Bissau* (New York: Monthly Review Press, 1979). The head of the Guinea-Bissau Women's Commission, in a conversation with the author, emphasized the need to continue to press for women's participation in managerial and supervisory posts, including those in any proposed mining project.

20. The problems and possibilities of achieving participatory institutions in Africa are discussed in detail in R.B. Seidman, *The State, Law and Development*, especially chapter 21.

22

CHANGING ROLES OF MNCs
IN THE EVOLVING WORLD MINERAL ECONOMY

C. Fortin

This chapter is not so much a report of research results as an attempt at present-
ing a hypothesis regarding current trends in the international political economy
of mineral exploitation, together with some preliminary evidence and some
suggestions as to the determinants and implications of the processes involved. Its
purpose, therefore, is to identify an area for further research. Briefly stated, it
argues that there are signs that MNCs are starting again to invest in LDC mining
in a major way, and that this might amount to a reversal in the 1980s of the
trend towards a withdrawal that was apparent in the late 1960s and early 1970s.
It further argues that there are both structural and conjunctural factors that explain this new trend. In order to put the discussion into perspective, however, it
starts by examining the situation in the 1960s and 1970s and the alternative
explanations that have been suggested from various theoretical viewpoints.

BACKGROUND: THE WITHDRAWAL OF THE MNCs FROM LDC MINING
IN THE 1960s AND 1970s

As recently as the mid-1960s the bulk of the mineral resources under exploitation in Africa, Asia and Latin America were in foreign hands. Legal and economic arrangements governing the relations between the foreign capitalists and
the host countries varied greatly; the range went from situations resembling
straightforward ownership of the deposits to more or less qualified concessions
for their exploitation. In most cases, however, it was clear that the foreign
capitalist enjoyed the same rights and privileges as would a private owner, i.e.
full control over the operations and a claim to the whole of the returns generated by it. In many cases, furthermore, these rights and privileges were not
accompanied by any significant obligations on the part of the foreign company,
whether in the areas of taxation, import duties, profit remittance, the building
of infrastructure, the purchase of local inputs, the training of local manpower
or the re-investment of profits. The explanation of — and justification for —
this odd state of affairs was the purported inability of LDCs to put together

Notes to this chapter may be found on pages 345-346.

the package of financial resources, technological knowhow and access to markets required to develop and exploit successfully their own natural wealth: MNCs had to be offered very attractive terms for investment because without their presence the resources would simply be left in the ground.[1]

By the second half of the decade, this situation began to show noticeable signs of change. On the one hand, trends towards increasing the participation of the host country in the returns of the foreign-controlled mining ventures — which, in fact, had been apparent for some time — were intensified;[2] on the other hand, the host governments increasingly began to feel that they should retain the ownership of the operations in order to increase their level of control: total or partial nationalizations took place — sometimes by agreement, at other times in conflict, with the foreign companies — and new ventures tended to include provisions for local ownership of the whole or part of the equity. The MNCs responded to these trends by developing various forms of relationship with host governments, which satisfied the demand for local ownership while in many cases preserving the substance of foreign control. Three such formats became particularly popular:

1. *Joint ventures* with either the host state or local private capitalists, with varying proportions of equity distribution. These were agreed upon for the purposes of exploring and/or developing and exploiting mineral deposits, or for introducing local participation in an existing operation. The incentive to the foreign investor was often in the form of a regime of taxation, tariffs and repatriation of profits that was more favorable than that accorded to foreign capital in the country concerned and which was normally guaranteed not to change for a period of years. Often, also, such joint ventures incorporated the feature that the foreign partner be in charge of the management of the operation as well as of the marketing of the product; in those cases, the foreign company was normally paid a fee for such services in addition to its normal equity share of the profits. The joint venture, while by no means unique to natural resources operations,[3] became a characteristic format of foreign investment in minerals in the second half of the 1960s, beginning with the partial nationalization of American copper companies in Chile in the period 1967-69 and the very similar arrangements introduced in the Zambian copper industry in 1969.

As can easily be seen, the joint ventures format, in its extreme form, may mean for the foreign capitalist a degree of access to revenue and control equivalent to that derived from 100 per cent ownership. In effect, the distribution of profits on the basis of shared equity can be more than offset by the privileged tax regime accorded the joint venture, and through management and marketing contracts control may remain almost entirely in the hands of the foreign capitalist.

2. *Service contracts* with foreign companies without equity participation. These might refer to the management of the operation, or the procuring of inputs from abroad, or the international sales of the product, or the provision of technology,

engineering and knowhow, or combinations of these, for all of which fees are paid. Through these arrangements the MNCs can retain control over the industry and secure for themselves a flow of surplus which is not necessarily less than what their profits would have been had they owned the exploitation. Some cases of nationalization of natural resources industries, beginning with that of copper in Congo (Kinshasa) in 1967, incorporate arrangements of this kind. In fact, it was argued that these became the preferred formats for the operation of MNCs in the field of natural resources in the Third World in the early 1970s.[4]

3. *Agreements* for the privileged supply of unprocessed raw materials to mining MNCs. They would include packages of finance and technology provided by a single MNC or a group of MNCs in order to open up a natural resource exploitation in the LDCs, with an agreement for the long-term sale of the products of the new operation to the same companies providing finance and technology, on somewhat better terms than those prevailing in the market. The actual exploitation might be done by a joint venture or by a national company with service contracts with the foreign companies. The arrangement, pioneered by the Japanese, appeared to offer advantages to both parties: to the host government, it offered the capital and the technology to start a new natural resource exploitation, in some cases wholly owned by the State, and an assured outlet for its products; to the foreign investor it offered an assured source of supplies of raw materials, plus possibly revenue from equity partnership or management fees, plus a guarantee of repayment of the loans, whose installments are deducted from the proceeds of the sale of the products to the same companies providing the money in the first place. In practice, these arrangements – whereby copper, iron and nickel mines were opened in Australia, Canada and Chile in the late 1960s – ran into serious difficulties during the recession of 1975-76, and Japan had to renege on some of its commitments to purchase minerals.[5]

The extent to which these features could in all three cases effectively eliminate the advantages for the host country and essentially preserve the situation of multinational control is a matter of controversy. It would appear that by the early seventies many arrangements of the sort described did entail an increased degree of local control. Together with cases of straightforward nationalization in which control and revenue were taken over fully by the host government – like the nationalization of copper in Chile in 1971[6] – the new situation led analysts to suggest that what was happening was a withdrawal of MNCs from direct presence in LDC mining. Figures on foreign investment in mining in LDCs appeared to lend additional credence to the analysis: on the whole, MNCs seemed to reduce their level of direct investment in LDC mining in the 1960s and early 1970s as compared to the 1950s.

THE ALTERNATIVE INTERPRETATIONS

Why would mining MNCs withdraw from direct investment in LDCs in the 1960s and 1970s? Three main explanations have been offered.

1. The simplest one is put forward by the mining MNCs themselves, and adopted in various degrees by some academic analysts in the advanced capitalist centres. It suggests that the withdrawal was due to the nationalistic tendencies which began to predominate in LDC governments. A study put out in 1976 by the British-North American Committee, whose co-Chairmen were the Director and Senior Vice-President of Exxon Corporation and the President of British American Tobacco Co., states:

During the decade of the 1960s there emerged an increasing atmosphere of antagonism to private foreign investment. Conditions for assembling the huge amounts of private capital needed for modern mineral development became still more unfavorable. The 15-year record of nationalization of existing projects in Zaire, Zambia, Peru and Chile in the case of copper, in Guyana in the case of bauxite/alumina and in some other minerals, as well as in petroleum, plus the attitude of 'sovereign-take-all' on the part of many countries, had entirely predictable results..., Recent years have seen a sharpening of these trends and an increasing disillusionment of private investors with the prospects for existing investments, coupled with greatly increased caution in making new investments.[7]

While undoubtedly containing an element of truth, this interpretation presents at least two difficulties. Firstly, it is not clear that investment by MNCs in LDC mining went down at the end of the 1960s relative to investment in other sectors. Figure 1 shows that the trend in the percentage of US mining investment abroad — measured in terms of net capital outflows and total undistributed subsidiary earnings — over total US investment abroad went down sharply between 1952 and 1956, and again between 1957 and 1962, and that it actually *went up* between 1962 and 1969; in the first five years of the 1970s it dropped again. Only the last decrease seems to be explainable through nationalism in LDCs. By contrast, in the 'nationalist' period of the late 1960s, the emergence of some of the MNCs' responses discussed above (notably the joint ventures) carried with it an actual increase in the relative importance of mining investment within the general pattern of US investment in LDCs.

A second problem has to do with the need to carry the explanation further. One is left with the question, What determines nationalism in LDCs? Is it solely a function of political factors — e.g. decolonization? How does it interact with trends in the advanced capitalist economies? The answer to these questions is, of course, particularly important when it comes to trying to predict the behavior of investment in the future; by itself, this explanation is therefore not a useful guide as to what is likely to happen.

2. A second explanation puts the emphasis not so much on nationalistic trends in LDCs as on the changing bargaining context in which the relations between MNCs and LDC governments proceed. This approach, associated with the names

Fig. 22.1. *US Investment Abroad: Percentage of Total Net Capital Outflows and of Total Undistributed Subsidiary Earnings Corresponding to Mining and Smelting in DCs 1950–1974 (5-year moving averages).*

Original data: *Survey of Current Business.*

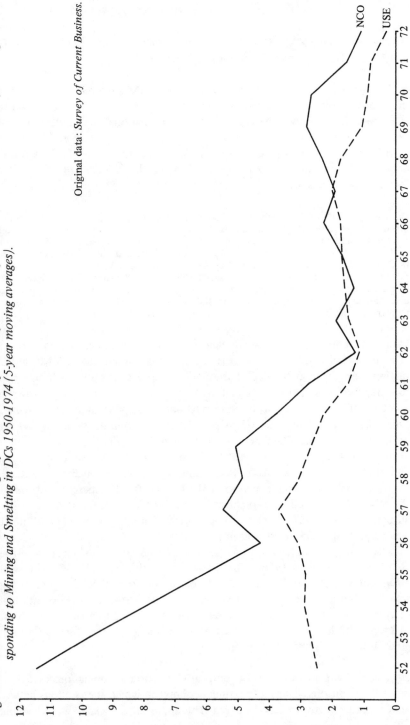

of Vernon and Mikesell,[8] identifies as its basic variables the bargaining power of the foreign investor and the host government; their perspectives on goals and possibilities of achieving them; their knowledge of both the substantive elements of the relationship − i.e. the operation of the industry − and of the bargaining process itself; and the way in which all three − power, perspectives and knowledge − change through time in a more or less predictable manner.

Whether applied to the operation through time of a single concession, or to the various relationships between a given host government and foreign investors, or to general trends in the terms of new concessions, the model suggests that at the beginning of the relationship it is the foreign investor who is in a position of strength through his control over capital, technology and markets; he is also keen to use his advantage to get maximum privileges in view of the risks involved in committing substantial capital − of the kind required by mass mining − to a venture that he perceives as uncertain both in terms of its economic profitability and of its political life expectancy. On the other hand, the host government's eagerness to put the country's natural riches to good use − in whatever definition − is only matched by its acute awareness of its inability to do so without the foreign investor. Hence the 75-year concessions without any serious obligations for the investors. As soon as actual operations start, however − as soon as the prospective deposit is confirmed as economically valuable, oil starts to flow or minerals to surface, and profits begin to show − then the bargaining strength position is reversed and the perspectives change. It is now the investor, who has sunk his capital, who is more or less at the mercy of the host government: he can be taxed, subjected to regulations of various kinds and in the last resort expropriated. Furthermore, the risk has either disappeared or been considerably reduced, and the government begins to find the original terms of the concession excessive. It is at this point that the government will request and, if necessary, impose a revision of the terms. When next time round the same or another investor is called upon to expand the operation, or to extend it downstream into more processing, or to introduce new technology, the relative power positions and the corresponding perspectives are reversed again, only to be re-reversed when the investment is sunk and profitable.

The process, however, is not simply cyclical. For one thing, the advantages of the MNCs generally have a tendency to be eroded through time, as technology becomes standardized and disseminated, patents expire, capital markets develop and become more competitive − including 'aid' markets − and production and marketing knowhow becomes available on a for-hire basis. For another, a cumulative learning process is undergone by each individual host government on the basis of its own experience in successive negotiations, on diffusion of relevant knowledge generally and, perhaps less commonly, on sharing bargaining experience with other host governments. The government becomes increasingly capable of handling the foreign investor and indeed the industry itself, and its bargaining strength is commensurately higher. Finally, there are also cumulative trends that affect the perspectives of the host government towards emphasizing the need to change to its advantage the terms of the relationship with the foreign investor: the inevitable growth of contacts between the foreign enclave and the economy and the legal system of the country makes for difficulties and tensions which require adjustment; fiscal budgetary needs associated with development call for an ever-growing claim on the proceeds of the foreign operation; and the sense of dependency that the latter creates fosters feelings of nationalism.

The model therefore predicts that the cyclical and reciprocal pattern of strength and weakness for the foreign investor and the host government will be reflected in the changing terms of their relationship through time, but within an overall cumulative trend for the host government to increase its share of benefit from the relationship.

This explanation goes some way towards addressing the issue of the relations between the MNCs and the host countries. It does not, on the other hand, place them within the context of the changing relations between the centre and the periphery of the capitalist system as a whole — which further have an 'internal' expression in the latter. Thus the objectives and interests of the foreign investor appear unrelated to those of the larger system of which they are part, as well as to the particular national objectives and interests of their individual home economies and governments.[9]

3. A third explanation — this time from a Marxist viewpoint — purports to deal precisely with this question of the trends in advanced capitalism which determine the pattern of MNC presence in LDC mining. This approach is well presented by Girvan, who is worth quoting at some length:

Imperialism is interested in the periphery principally as a source of primary products — food and industrial raw materials which can yield substantial profits at the same time as their supply helps to sustain the process of accumulation in the industrial-center countries.... But since 1945 the pattern has radically changed. The bulk of incremental international investment since then has been in manufacturing industry and among the industrial center countries themselves. This reflects the emergence of technology-intensive consumers' and producers' goods industries as the main bases of incremental capital accumulation in the contemporary period, and the growth of direct foreign investment by the large manufacturing corporations in the center countries (for the purpose of mutual interpenetration of each other's markets) as the principal form of international capital flows. This, of course, is not to suggest that primary production and the periphery are in any way expendable to contemporary international capitalism — far from it. Raw materials from the periphery are just as essential as before — perhaps more so — in order to permit the process of accumulation in the industrial center countries to continue. Nevertheless, the point is that the principal loci of incremental accumulation are technology-intensive manufacturing and service activities (such as information processing and transmission), and in the industrial center countries, and it is on these activities that the rapidly growing power of transnationalized capitalism chiefly rests.

The implications of this should be carefully considered. It means that international capitalism's interest in peripheral raw materials is more and more in a reliable and adequate supply of such materials, which permits the generation of more and more surplus-value *outside* of these industries; while its interest in these industries as sources of *direct* generation of surplus-value is relatively diminishing. This in turn creates possibilities for a new alliance with national state capitalism in the periphery for the provision of vital raw materials in return for a much increased share of the surpluses, and perspectives for national industrialization using technology from transnationalized capital.[10]

The explanation is elegant and seems to square, *prima facie*, with the evidence. On the other hand, it contains a number of tricky theoretical problems; more importantly, it seems to suggest that the trend is cumulative and irreversible, rooted in basic trends in the development of modern capitalism. It is precisely this assumption of progression and irreversibility which seems to be challenged by trends that began to emerge in the latter part of the 1970s and which might well be intensified during the 1980s.

THE SECOND COMING OF THE MNCs:
SOME EVIDENCE AND INTERPRETATION

We would like to suggest that this withdrawal of the MNCs from direct presence in LDC mining is now being reversed; that MNCs are beginning to come back in force employing the original format of direct investment with complete, or at least majority, ownership; and that this development is due to a combination of structural features of contemporary world capitalism and to conjunctural factors associated with the oil crisis that began in 1973-74.

We have already indicated that we shall not be offering systematic evidence for this proposition; however, some empirical data that support the plausibility of the hypothesis can be presented, stemming from our work on the world copper industry.[11] During the late 1960s and early 1970s copper mining was singled out by analysts as the prime example of the withdrawal of MNCs from the LDCs. Complete or partial nationalizations in Zaire in 1967; in Chile in 1967-69 and then in 1971; in Zambia in 1970; and in Peru in 1973, led to a situation in which by the middle of the decade nearly 60 per cent of the copper mine production of LDCs was − at least formally − accounted for by state companies.

This situation is beginning to change visibly. In Zaire projects for expansion involving foreign capital add up to 200,000 tons of mining capacity, while expansion plans in the state sector aim at no more than 120,000 tons.[12] In Peru, major investment plans by the state company to develop the deposits of Michiquillay and Quellaveco have been abandoned because of problems in arranging finance, and negotiations with a German firm for a turnkey plant in Cerro Verde II have broken down; at the same time, negotiations for the development of the Tantaya deposit by a consortium of Canadian, French and Japanese interests are well advanced.[13] In Papua New Guinea, the agreements between the government and the Australian group BHP for the development of the OK Tedi deposit are near finalization.[14] The clearest example, however, is Chile, where the state company is being held back in its investment by the government while major concessions are being handed out to foreign capital for exploration and exploitation of new deposits or expansion of existing ones. The most important single events are: (a) the purchase by Exxon of a medium-size copper mine near Santiago, previously owned by the state. The mine produced about 40,000 tonnes in 1977 and has reserves of 100m tonnes. Exxon plans to invest up to US$1 billion to expand production to 200,000 tonnes per year, thus making it the third largest copper mining operation in the country;[15] (b) the acquisition by Anaconda of the mining rights to the Los Pelambres deposit in the north of Chile. The price paid was a very low US$20m. Reserves are estimated at 430m tonnes, and an investment of US$1.5 billion is contemplated, leading to a maximum potential output of about 300,000 tonnes within the next 5-6 years;[16] (c) an agreement in principle with Noranda of Canada to form a joint venture (Noranda to hold 51 per cent of the equity) to exploit the Andacollo deposit in the north of Chile. Reserves are estimated at 310m tonnes and the projected output is 70,000 tonnes per year.[17] All these projects are still in their preliminary stages; if they materialize, however, they will mean that within the next decade international capital will regain control over a substantial portion of the Chilean copper output, roughly equivalent to 70 per cent of the state share.

How to account for this hypothesized reversal? Some elements from the preceding explanations for the withdrawal are useful for an understanding of the new trend. Through a combination of ideological preferences and objective constraints – mostly financial – many LDC governments are paying less attention to the nationalist rhetoric that dominated LDC positions in the field of mineral resources in the early 1970s, and which found legal expression in the doctrine of permanent sovereignty over natural resources.[18] Chile is, again, the clearest example, with its economic model of full integration into the world capitalist economy. Moreover, a significant factor has intervened which results from the changes in the international political economy of oil, i.e. the decision of the oil MNCs to move into mineral exploitation, and more specifically into investment in LDC mining. This they can do because of the large surpluses they hold resulting from the increases in oil prices which began in 1973-74. Their motivations are diversification, taking advantage of a lack of supply of capital for mining ventures, and the technological possibilities of metal-related sources of energy, such as solar, which requires copper. A leader in this move was Atlantic Richfield, which purchased Anaconda in 1977. Exxon, for its part, started negotiations in 1978 with RTZ for joint ventures in minerals. Commenting on this development, the Chairman of RTZ probably expressed the feeling of most mining MNCs when he wrote: 'large oil companies, with their substantial cash flows and engineering experience, and their interests in diversifying into minerals seem to us just the sort of partners we should be seeking in this capital cost escalating business in which we are engaged.'[19] As the discussion on Chile indicated, both Anaconda and Exxon are very actively considering major investments in Chilean copper.

All this explains the renewed interest shown by MNCs in involvement in LDC mining, but it does not explain their hypothesized preference for direct investment. To answer this question we have to resort to more structural factors which relate to the crisis of the world capitalist system in the 1970s. Analysis of that crisis is still in a very embryonic state, and therefore we are in no position to offer a theoretically coherent and at the same time empirically validated explanation of the relationship between crisis and direct MNC investment in LDC mining. Let us, however, conclude with some suggestions as to possible interpretations. One straightforward line of reasoning that has been advanced — again from a Marxist viewpoint — suggests that the crisis is one of profitability, resulting from increasing labour and other — e.g. environmental — costs in the advanced capitalist industries. Recapturing direct control over sources of minerals would allow central capitalism to reduce the cost of its raw materials, thereby increasing the rate of profit. This explanation merits further investigation, although preliminary analyses seem to indicate that the characterization of the crisis as one of profitability is doubtful. Alternatively, one can suggest that the basic element is control: central capitalism in crisis wants to maximize its ability to manipulate its environment, thus preserving maximum flexibility to face the crisis. Direct investment in LDC minerals would allow maximum control over the sources of basic raw materials for the process of accumulation in the center to continue.[20]

NOTES

1. R. Vernon, *Sovereignty at Bay. The Multinational Spread of US Enterprises* (Harmondsworth, England: Penguin Books, 1973), 35.

2. *Ibidem*, 60-61.

3. There is abundant literature on joint ventures in LDCs. See W.G. Friedmann and G. Kalmanoff, *Joint International Business Ventures* (New York: Columbia University Press, 1961); W.G. Friedmann *et. al., Joint International Business Ventures in Developing Countries: Case Studies and Analysis of Recent Trends* (New York: Columbia University Press, 1971); L.G. Franko, *Joint Venture Survival in Multinational Corporations* (New York: Praeger Publishers, 1971).

4. 'Mining the Resources of the Third World: From Concession Agreements to Service Contracts', *Proceedings of the American Society for International Law* (November 1973), 227-245. See also N.D. Smith and L.T. Wells Jr, *Negotiating Third World Mineral Agreements: Promises as Prologue* (Cambridge, Mass.: Ballinger Press, 1975); and S. Zorn, 'New Developments in Third World Mining Agreements', *Natural Resources Forum* (April 1977).

5. R. Bosson and B. Varon, *The Mining Industry and the Developing Countries* (Oxford University Press for the World Bank, 1977), 142-43.

6. For a discussion see C. Fortin, 'Nationalization of Copper in Chile and its International Repercussions', in S. Sideri (ed.), *Chile 1970-73: Economic Development and Its International Setting* (The Hague: Martinus Nijhoff for the Institute of Social Studies, 1979), 183-220.

7. British-North American Committee, *Mineral Development in the Eighties: Prospects and Problems* (Washington, D.C., 1976), 12.

8. R. Mikesell *et. al., Foreign Investment in the Petroleum and Mineral Industries. Case Studies of Investor-Host Country Relations* (Baltimore: The Johns Hopkins Press for Resources for the Future, Inc., 1971), 35 ff.; R. Vernon, 'Long-Run Trends in Concession Contracts', *Proceedings of the American Society for International Law* (April 1967); R. Vernon, *Sovereignty at Bay*, 53 ff. A treatment based on this approach is Smith and Wells, *Negotiating Third World Mineral Agreements*.

9. This description and critique is taken from C. Fortin, 'The State, Multinational Corporations and Natural Resources in Latin America', in J.J. Villamil (ed.), *Transnational Capitalism and National Development. New Perspectives on Dependence* (Hassocks, Sussex: Harvester Press for the Institute of Development Studies, 1979), 205-222.

10. N. Girvan, 'Economic Nationalists v. Multinational Corporations: Revolutionary or Evolutionary Change?', in C. Widstrand (ed.), *Multinational Firms in Africa* (Uppsala: Scandinavian Institute of African Studies, 1975), 40-41.

11. C. Fortin, 'The Political Economy of the World Copper Industry', in C. Fortin and G. Gunatilleke (eds), *Commodity Trade and Third World Development* (forthcoming).

12. *Ibidem*, section III, 4. 'Copper and Development of Third World Producers'.

13. Economist Intelligence Unit, *Peru. Annual Supplement 1979* (London, 1980).

14. Economist Intelligence Unit, *Australia and Papua New Guinea. Annual Supplement 1979* (London, 1980).

15. *Copper Studies* (28 February 1979), 4.

16. *Latin American Commodities Report* (6 July 1979), 102.

17. *Copper Studies* (16 February 1979), 3.

18. See note, 'UNCTAD: Permanent Sovereignty over Natural Resources', *Journal of World Trade Law*, Vol. 7, No. 3 (May-June 1973), 376-384.

19. RTZ, *Annual General Meeting* (24 May 1978). Statement by the Chairman Sir Mark Turner (London, 1978), 4-5.

20. This was suggested to me by Sandro Sideri.

INDEX

References to tables and figures are given in brackets after the relevant page number(s), T indicating a table and F a figure.

EDITORS AND CONTRIBUTORS

EDITORS

Sandro Sideri
> Professor in International Economics, Institute of Social Studies, The Hague, The Netherlands

Sheridan Johns
> Associate Professor of Political Science, Duke University, Durham, North Carolina, USA.

CONTRIBUTORS

Winifred Armstrong
> President, International Management Development Institute, New York, USA.

John Cuddy
> Senior Economist, UNCTAD.
> Professor, Graduate Institute of International Studies, Geneva, Switzerland.

Carlton E. Davis
> Executive Director, Jamaica Bauxite Institute, Kingston, Jamaica.

Carlos Fortin
> Fellow and Deputy Director, Institute of Development Studies, University of Sussex, UK.

David J. Fox
> Senior Lecturer in Geography, Manchester University, UK.

Wolfgang Gluschke
> Economic Affairs Officer, Center for Natural Resources, Energy and Transport, Department of Technical Co-operation for Development, UN Secretariat, New York, USA.

Noriko Iwase
> Associate Economic Affairs Officer, Ocean Economics and Technology Branch, Department of International Economic and Social Affairs, UN Secretariat, New York, USA.

Olle Jarleborg
> Vice-President (Europe), AMAX Nickel GmbH, Düsseldorf, Federal Republic of Germany.

Raymond Mikesell
> W.E. Miner Professor of Economics, University of Oregon, Eugene, Oregon, USA.

Edith Penrose
> Professor of Economics, Institut Européen d'Administration des Affaires (INSEAD), Fontainebleau, France.

Marian Radetzki
> Senior Research Fellow, Institute for International Economic Studies, Stockholm University, Sweden.

Christopher D. Rogers
> Lecturer in Economics, University of Dundee, UK.

Ann Seidman
> Professor of International Development & Social Change, Clark University, Worcester, Massachusetts, USA.

Wolfgang Thomas
> Professor of Economics, Transkei University, Umtata, South Africa.

Stephen Zorn
> Technical Adviser, Center on Transnational Corporations, UN Secretariat, New York, USA.